Adobe®

InDesign® CS4
① ② ③ ④ ⑤ ⑥ ⑦ **on Demand**

Steve Johnson

Perspection, Inc.

QUE® Que Publishing, 800 East 96th Street, Indianapolis, IN 46240 USA

Adobe® InDesign® CS4 On Demand

Library of Congress Cataloging-in-Publication data is on file

ISBN-13 978-0-7897-3839-4
ISBN-10 0-7897-3839-2

Printed and bound in the United States of America
First Printing: December 2008
11 10 09 08   4 3 2 1

Que Publishing offers excellent discounts on this book when ordered in quantity for bulk purchases or special sales.

For information, please contact: U.S. Corporate and Government Sales

1-800-382-3419 or corpsales@pearsontechgroup.com

For sales outside the U.S., please contact: International Sales

1-317-428-3341 or International@pearsontechgroup.com

Trademarks

Warning and Disclaimer

Publisher
Paul Boger

Associate Publisher
Greg Wiegand

Acquisitions Editor
Laura Norman

Managing Editor
Steve Johnson

Author
Steve Johnson

Technical Editor
Toni Bennett

Page Layout
Beth Teyler

Interior Designers
Steve Johnson
Marian Hartsough

Photographs
Tracy Teyler
Toni Bennett

Indexer
Katherine Stimson

Proofreader
Toni Bennett
Beth Teyler

Team Coordinator
Cindy Teeters

Acknowledgements

Perspection, Inc.

Adobe InDesign CS4 On Demand has been created by the professional trainers and writers at Perspection, Inc. to the standards you've come to expect from Que publishing. Together, we are pleased to present this training book.

Perspection, Inc. is a software training company committed to providing information and training to help people use software more effectively in order to communicate, make decisions, and solve problems. Perspection writes and produces software training books, and develops multimedia and Web-based training. Since 1991, we have written more than 80 computer books, with several bestsellers to our credit, and sold over 5 million books.

This book incorporates Perspection's training expertise to ensure that you'll receive the maximum return on your time. You'll focus on the tasks and skills that increase productivity while working at your own pace and convenience.

We invite you to visit the Perspection Web site at:

www.perspection.com

Acknowledgements

The task of creating any book requires the talents of many hard-working people pulling together to meet impossible deadlines and untold stresses. We'd like to thank the outstanding team responsible for making this book possible: the writer, Steve Johnson; the editor, Toni Bennett; the production editors, Beth Teyler; proofreader, Toni Bennett and Beth Teyler; and the indexer, Katherine Stimson.

At Que publishing, we'd like to thank Greg Wiegand and Laura Norman for the opportunity to undertake this project, Cindy Teeters for administrative support, and Sandra Schroeder for your production expertise and support.

Perspection

About The Authors

Steve Johnson has written more than 50 books on a variety of computer software, including Adobe Photoshop CS4 and CS3, Adobe Flash CS4 and CS3, Dreamweaver CS4 and CS3, Microsoft Office 2007 and 2003, Microsoft Windows Vista and XP, Microsoft Office 2008 for the Macintosh, and Apple Mac OS X Leopard. In 1991, after working for Apple Computer and Microsoft, Steve founded Perspection, Inc., which writes and produces software training. When he is not staying up late writing, he enjoys playing golf, gardening, and spending time with his wife, Holly, and three children, JP, Brett, and Hannah. Steve and his family live in Pleasanton, California, but can also be found visiting family all over the western United States.

We Want To Hear From You!

As the reader of this book, *you* are our most important critic and commentator. We value your opinion and want to know what we're doing right, what we could do better, what areas you'd like to see us publish in, and any other words of wisdom you're willing to pass our way.

As an associate publisher for Que, I welcome your comments. You can email or write me directly to let me know what you did or didn't like about this book—as well as what we can do to make our books better.

Please note that I cannot help you with technical problems related to the topic of this book. We do have a User Services group, however, where I will forward specific technical questions related to the book.

When you write, please be sure to include this book's title and author as well as your name, email address, and phone number. I will carefully review your comments and share them with the author and editors who worked on the book.

Email: feedback@quepublishing.com

Mail: Greg Wiegand
         Que Publishing
         800 East 96th Street
         Indianapolis, IN 46240 USA

For more information about this book or another Que title, visit our Web site at *informit.com/register*. Type the ISBN (excluding hyphens) or the title of a book in the Search field to find the page you're looking for.

Contents

Introduction

Welcome to *Adobe InDesign CS4 On Demand*, a visual quick reference book that shows you how to work efficiently with InDesign. This book provides complete coverage of basic to advanced InDesign skills.

How This Book Works

You don't have to read this book in any particular order. We've designed the book so that you can jump in, get the information you need, and jump out. However, the book does follow a logical progression from simple tasks to more complex ones. Each task is presented on no more than two facing pages, which lets you focus on a single task without having to turn the page. To find the information that you need, just look up the task in the table of contents or index, and turn to the page listed. Read the task introduction, follow the step-by-step instructions in the left column along with screen illustrations in the right column, and you're done.

What's New

If you're searching for what's new in InDesign CS4, just look for the icon: **New!**. The new icon appears in the table of contents and throughout this book so you can quickly and easily identify a new or improved feature in InDesign. A complete description of each new feature appears in the New Features guide in the back of this book.

Keyboard Shortcuts

Most menu commands have a keyboard equivalent, such as Ctrl+P (Win) or ⌘+P (Mac), as a quicker alternative to using the mouse. A complete list of keyboard shortcuts is available on the Web at *www.perspection.com*.

How You'll Learn

How This Book Works

What's New

Keyboard Shortcuts

Step-by-Step Instructions

Real World Examples

Workshops

Adobe Certified Expert

Get More on the Web

Step-by-Step Instructions

This book provides concise step-by-step instructions that show you "how" to accomplish a task. Each set of instructions includes illustrations that directly correspond to the easy-to-read steps. Also included in the text are time-savers, tables, and sidebars to help you work more efficiently or to teach you more in-depth information. A "Did You Know?" provides tips and techniques to help you work smarter, while a "See Also" leads you to other parts of the book containing related information about the task.

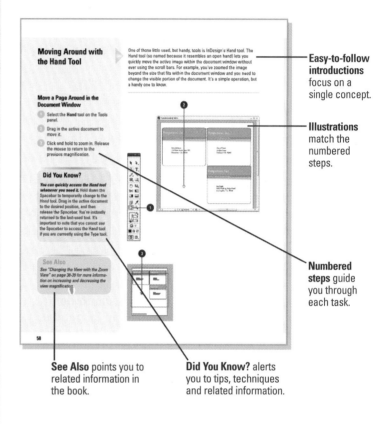

Easy-to-follow introductions focus on a single concept.

Illustrations match the numbered steps.

Numbered steps guide you through each task.

See Also points you to related information in the book.

Did You Know? alerts you to tips, techniques and related information.

Real World Examples

This book uses real world example files to give you a context in which to use the task. By using the example files, you won't waste time looking for or creating sample files. You get a start file and a result file, so you can compare your work. Not every topic needs an example file, such as changing options, so we provide a complete list of the example files used throughout the book. The example files that you need for project tasks along with a complete file list are available on the Web at *www.perspection.com*.

Real world examples help you apply what you've learned to other tasks.

Workshops

This book shows you how to put together the individual step-by-step tasks into in-depth projects with the Workshop. You start each project with a sample file, work through the steps, and then compare your results with a project results file at the end. The Workshop projects and associated files are available on the Web at *www.perspection.com*.

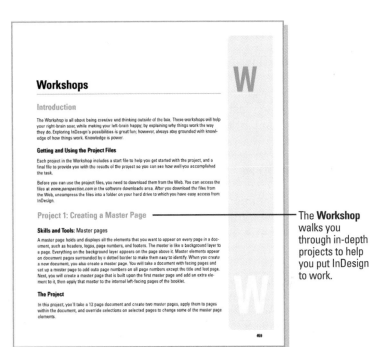

The **Workshop** walks you through in-depth projects to help you put InDesign to work.

Adobe Certified Expert

This book prepares you fully for the Adobe Certified Expert (ACE) exam for Adobe InDesign CS4. Each Adobe Certified Expert certification level has a set of objectives, which are organized into broader skill sets. To prepare for the certification exam, you should review and perform each task identified with a Adobe Certified Expert objective to confirm that you can meet the requirements for the exam. The Adobe Certified Expert objectives are available on the Web at *www.perspection.com*.

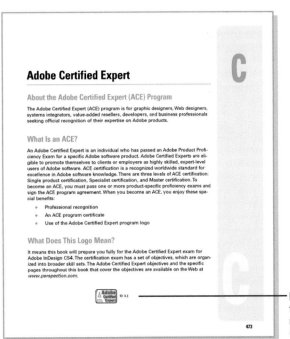

Logo indicates a task fulfills one or more Adobe Certified Expert objectives.

Get More on the Web

In addition to the information in this book, you can also get more information on the Web to help you get up-to-speed faster with InDesign CS4. Some of the information includes:

Transition Helpers

- **Only New Features.**
  Download and print the new feature tasks as a quick and easy guide.

Productivity Tools

- **Keyboard Shortcuts.**
  Download a list of keyboard shortcuts to learn faster ways to get the job done.

More Content

- **Photographs.** Download photographs and other graphics to use in your InDesign documents.

- **More Content.** Download new content developed after publication.

You can access these additional resources on the Web at *www.perspection.com.*

Keyboard Shortcuts

Adobe InDesign CS4

If a command on a menu includes a keyboard reference, known as a keyboard shortcut, to the right of the command name, you can perform the action by pressing and holding the first key, and then pressing the second key to perform the command quickly. In some cases, a keyboard shortcut uses three keys. Simply press and hold the first two keys, and then press the third key. Keyboard shortcuts provide an alternative to using the mouse and make it easy to perform repetitive commands.

If you're searching for new keyboard shortcuts in InDesign CS4, just look for the letter: N. The N appears in the Keyboard Shortcuts table so you can quickly and easily identify new or changed shortcuts.

Keyboard Shortcuts		
Command	Windows	Macintosh
Menu Commands		
Tools		
Selection tool	V, Esc	V, Esc
Direct Selection tool	A	A
Position tool	Shift+A	Shift+A
Toggle Selection and Direct Selection tool	Ctrl+Tab	Command+Control+Tab
Pen tool	P	P
Add Anchor Point tool	=	=
Delete Anchor Point tool	-	-
Convert Direction Point tool	Shift+C	Shift+C
Type tool	T	T
Type On A Path tool	Shift+T	Shift+T
Pencil tool (Note tool)	N	N
Line tool	\	\

Additional content is available on the Web.

Getting Started with InDesign CS4

Introduction

Adobe InDesign CS4 is a desktop publishing and page layout program that runs seamlessly on both Windows and Macintosh platforms. Adobe InDesign CS4 is a stand-alone program, but it's also part of Adobe's Creative Suite of professional programs that work together to help you create designs in print, on the Web, or on mobile devices. All Creative Suite 4 programs also include additional Adobe programs—Bridge, Version Cue, Device Central, and Extension Manager—to help you manage and work with files.

With InDesign, you can create books, brochures, catalogs, manuals, CD-DVD labels, certificates, newsletters, flyers, forms, label sheets, and even interactive presentations. As a page layout program, you can create a one page flyer, a 500 or more page book, or something in between. InDesign provides all the tools you need to create a page layout design, import or enter text, insert images, add drawings, create tables, and finalize the document. When you're done, you can print the document to a local desktop or commercial printer, create a template, so you can reuse the document again later for a new project, or export the document as an Adobe PDF (Portable Document Format) or Digital Edition for use online or over a network, or for use in other programs, such as Adobe Flash (XFL or SWF) or Adobe Dreamweaver.

What You'll Do

Install and Start InDesign

View the InDesign Window

Show and Hide Panels

Work with Panels

Use the Tools and Control Panel

Open a Document

Open a Document with Adobe Bridge

Insert Images or Text in a Document

Work with Document Windows

Use the Status Bar

Check for Updates Online

Get Help While You Work

Save a Document

Finish Up

Installing InDesign

To perform a standard program install, insert the InDesign CS4 DVD into the DVD player on your computer or download the software online and start the setup program, following the onscreen instructions. Make sure to have your serial number handy because you'll be asked to enter it during the installation process. If you're updating from a previous version of InDesign, you'll be required to verify the older version by instructing InDesign where to find the previous version on your hard drive, or by inserting the previous version's install disk. Adobe, in an attempt to thwart software piracy, now requires online or phone activation of the program. The process can be postponed for 30 days. However, at the end of 30 days, the InDesign program will shut down if it has not been properly activated. You can't blame Adobe for attempting to protect their products, since some surveys suggest there are more pirated than purchased versions of InDesign in use.

Install InDesign CS4 in Windows

1. Insert the InDesign CS4 DVD into your DVD ROM drive, or download the software online to your hard disk.

2. If necessary, double-click the DVD icon or open the folder with the downloaded software, and then double-click the setup icon.

3. Follow the onscreen instructions.

   IMPORTANT *During the installation process, InDesign requires you to activate the program. Activation (using the Internet or by phone), must be accomplished within 30 days of installation, or InDesign will cease to function.*

Did You Know?

The DVD comes with bonus content. The Resources and Extras DVD included with Adobe CS4 products includes bonus content and files in the Goodies folder. Check it out! For more free online resources, go to *www.adobe.com* and visit Adobe Exchange.

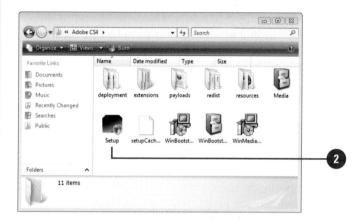

Install InDesign CS4 in Macintosh

1 Insert the InDesign CS4 DVD into your DVD ROM drive, or download the software online to your hard disk.

2 If necessary, double-click the DVD icon or open the folder with the downloaded software, and then double-click the setup icon.

3 Follow the onscreen instructions.

Did You Know?

You can create a shortcut on the Macintosh. Drag and drop the InDesign program to the bottom of the monitor screen, and then add it to the shortcuts panel.

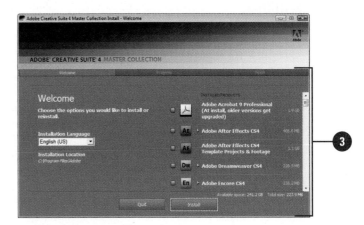

InDesign CS4 System Requirements

Hardware/Software	Minimum (Recommended)
WINDOWS	
Computer Processor	1.5 GHz or faster processor
Operating System	Microsoft Windows XP SP2 (3) or Vista SP1
Hard Drive	1.8 GB of available space
Available RAM	512 MB (1 GB recommended)
Video Card	16-bit (GPU-equipped video card for OpenGL features)
Monitor Resolution	1024 x 768 (1280 x 800 or dual monitors)
DVD-ROM drive	Any type
MACINTOSH	
Computer Processor	Power PC G5 or multi-core Intel-based Macs
Operating System	Macintosh OS X 10.4.11 or higher
Hard Drive	1.6 GB of available space
Available RAM	512 MB (1 GB recommended)
Video Card	16-bit (GPU-equipped video card for OpenGL features)
Monitor Resolution	1024 x 768 (1280 x 800 or dual monitors)
DVD-ROM drive	Any type (SuperDrive for DVD burning)
Additional	
QuickTime 7.2	Required for multimedia features

Getting Started

You can start InDesign in several ways, depending on the platform you are using. When you start InDesign, the software displays a Welcome screen and then the InDesign window. When you start a new InDesign session or close all documents, a Welcome screen appears in the InDesign window, providing easy access links to open a file, open a recent file, create a new file, and create a new file from a template. You can also use links to access help information, such as Getting Started, New Features, and online Community resources, such as the InDesign Exchange web site, where you can download additional applications and information, the Adobe Bridge Home web site, and Adobe TV, where you can view video tutorials.

Start InDesign CS4 in Windows

1. Click **Start** on the taskbar.

2. Point to **All Programs** (which changes to Back).

3. Point to an Adobe Collection CS4 menu, if needed.

4. Click **Adobe InDesign CS4**.

5. If you're starting InDesign CS4 for the first time, perform the following:

   ◆ Enter your serial number, and then click **OK** to continue.

   ◆ Click **OK** to complete the activation process.

   ◆ Fill in the registration form, click **Register Now**.

   The InDesign window appears, displaying the Welcome screen.

Did You Know?

You can create and use a shortcut icon on your desktop to start InDesign (Win). Click Start on the taskbar, point to All Programs, right-click Adobe InDesign CS4, point to Send To, and then click Desktop (Create Shortcut). Double-click the shortcut icon on your desktop to start InDesign.

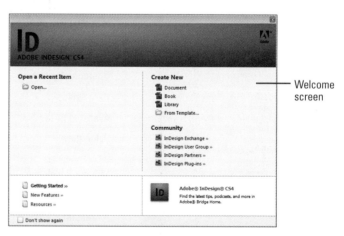

Welcome screen

Start InDesign CS4 in Macintosh

1. Open the **Applications** folder (located on the main hard drive).

2. Double-click the **Adobe InDesign CS4** folder.

3. Double-click the **Adobe InDesign CS4** program icon.

4. If you're starting InDesign CS4 for the first time, perform the following:

   ◆ Enter your serial number, and then click **OK** to continue.

   ◆ Click **OK** to complete the activation process.

   ◆ Fill in the registration form, click **Register Now**.

   The InDesign window appears, displaying the Welcome screen.

Did You Know?

You can create a shortcut on the Macintosh. Drag and drop the InDesign application to the bottom of the monitor screen, and then add it to the dock.

You can create and use a keyboard shortcut to start InDesign (Win). Click Start on the taskbar, point to All Programs, right-click Adobe InDesign CS4, and then click Properties. In the Shortcut Key box, type or press any letter, number, or function key, such as P, to which Windows adds Ctrl+Alt. Click OK to create the keyboard shortcut. From anywhere in Windows, press the keyboard shortcut you defined (Ctrl+Alt+P) to start InDesign.

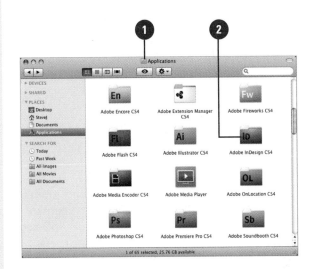

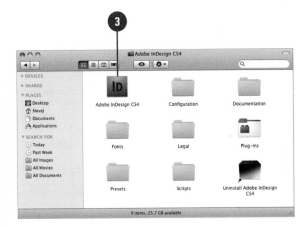

Shortcut for InDesign CS4

Viewing the InDesign Window

When you start InDesign, the program window displays several windows of varying types you can use to work with documents. In InDesign, windows appear in the workspace in panels. A **panel** is a window you can collapse, expand, and group with other panels, known as a **panel group**, to improve accessibility and workflow. A panel group consists of either individual panels stacked one on top of the other or related panels organized together with tabs to navigate from one panel to another.

The **Tools panel** contains a set of tools you can use to create shapes, such as lines, rectangles, and ellipses. You can fill and stroke shapes and text with different colors and stroke widths. When you select a tool, additional options appear on the **Control panel**.

A **menu** is a list of commands that you use to accomplish specific tasks. A **command** is a directive that accesses a feature of a program. InDesign has its own set of menus. The **Application bar** (**New!**) provides easy access to commonly used features, such as choosing zoom levels, view options, screen mode, document arrangement, workspaces, and InDesign's community online Help.

The **Document window** displays open InDesign documents. InDesign includes tabs to make it easier to switch back and forth between documents and a close button to quickly close a document (**New!**).

Application bar
Displays buttons and menus to change the document layout.

Document window
Displays open InDesign documents.

Control panel
Displays options for the currently selected tool.

Tools panel
Contains drawing and other related tools to create and manipulate documents.

Panels
Give you tools to modify and check your documents, such as Pages, Links, Color, and Layers.

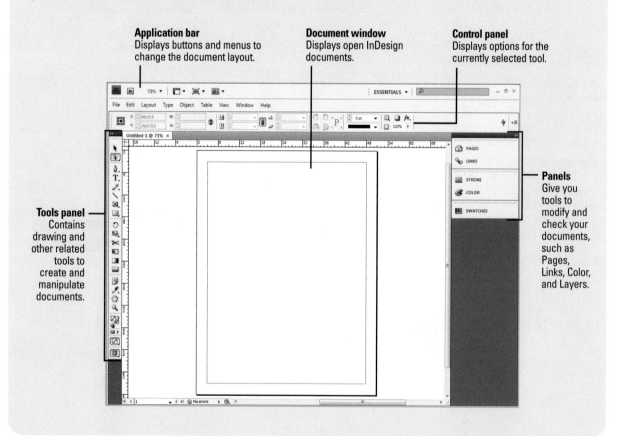

Showing and Hiding Panels

Panels give you easy access to many task-specific commands and operations from color control to vector path information. By default, the main panel display is located along the right side of your window. You can use the Window menu or click a panel tab within a group to display it, and then select options on the panel or choose panel-specific commands from the Panel Options menu to perform actions. Instead of continually moving, resizing, or opening and closing windows, you can use the header bar with the panel tabs to collapse or expand individual panels within a window to save space.

Open and Close a Panel

1 Click the **Window** menu.

2 Point to a submenu (if needed), such as Automation, Extensions, Object & Layout, or Type & Tables.

3 Click a panel name, such as Color, Layers, or Swatches.

TIMESAVER *To close a panel, or a single tab, right-click (Win) or control-click (Mac) a panel tab, and then click Close Tab Group or Close (for a single tab). On the Mac, you can also click the Close button on the panel.*

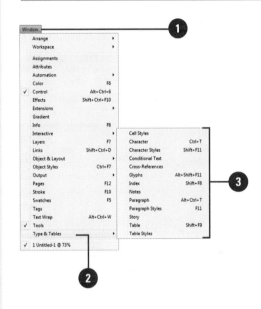

Collapse or Expand a Panel

1 To collapse or expand an open panel, click the dark gray area or double-click a title tab on the header bar of the panel.

If the panel is in icon mode, click on the icon to expand or collapse it. To reduce the panel back to icon mode, click on the double right-facing arrows in the dark gray area. To expand from icons to panels, click on the double left facing arrows.

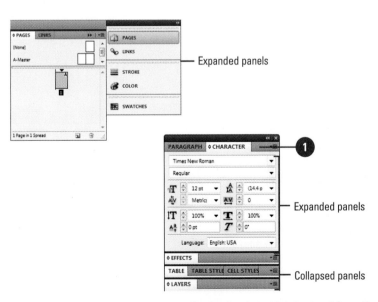

Expanded panels

Expanded panels

Collapsed panels

Working with Panels

The movable panels are organized into groups, such as Stroke/Color and Pages/Links, to save screen space and help with workflow. You can also dock (add) or undock (subtract) specific panels within a group to customize your workspace. A panel appears with a header, which includes the tab titles and three options: the Collapse to Icons or Expand Panels button, the Close button, and an Options menu. The Options menu provides you with panel commands. The entire set of panels includes a double arrow at the top you can use to collapse and expand the entire panel back and forth between icons and full panels.

Dock a Panel

1. Select a panel; click on a named panel, or click the **Window** menu, and then click a panel name.

2. Drag the panel away from the group to another panel.

   ◆ **Add to Panel Group.** Drag to a panel group until a blue rectangle appears around the panel.

   ◆ **Append to Panel.** Drag to a panel until a blue line appears along the side of the panel.

Undock a Panel

1. Select a panel; click on a named panel, or click the **Window** menu, and then click a panel name.

2. Drag the panel out of the group.

3. Drop it onto the InDesign window.

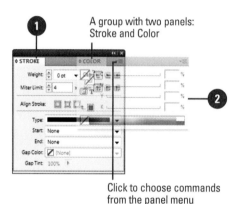

A group with two panels: Stroke and Color

Click to choose commands from the panel menu

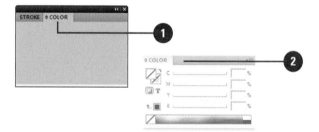

Did You Know?

You can dock and undock panels to a docking channel. You can dock and undock, panels or panel groups in docking channels. A docking channel is a region located on the left and right side of the InDesign window to which you can attach and detach panels. When you drag a panel over a dockable area, a blue line appears.

For Your Information

Hiding Panels While You Work

If InDesign's panels get in the way, just press the Tab key to temporarily hide all the panels. Or, you can hold down the Shift key, and then press the Tab key to hide the panels, but leave the Toolbox and Control panel. Press the Tab key again to restore all the panels to their most recent positions.

Collapse and Expand the Panel Set Between Icons and Panels

◆ To collapse the panel set to icons with text, click the double arrow pointing right (Collapse to Icons) at the top of the panels.

◆ To expand the panel set from icons with text to full panels, click the double arrow pointing left (Expand Panels) at the top of the panels.

◆ To have an expanded panel icon automatically collapse or hide when you click away, right-click (Win) or Control-click (Mac) a panel, and then click **Auto-Collapse Iconic Panels** or **Auto-Show Hidden Panels (New!)**.

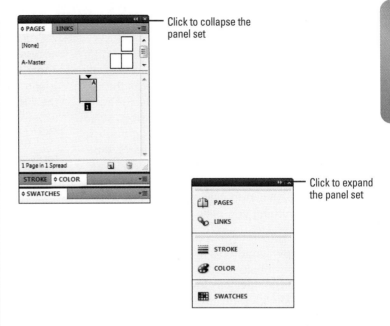

Click to collapse the panel set

Click to expand the panel set

Use the Panel Options Menu

1. Open or expand a panel.

2. Click the **Options** button on the right side of the panel header bar.

3. Click a command from the list (commands vary).

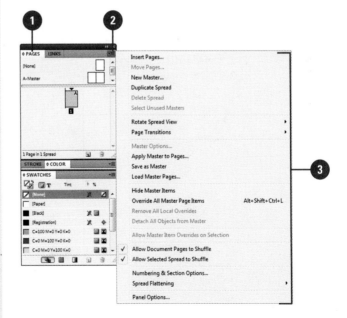

Using the Tools and Control Panel

InDesign has an abundance of tools that give an InDesign designer tremendous control over any creative designing problems that may crop up. For example, the InDesign tool-box contains a variety of different tools: selection tools (you can never have enough selection tools), drawing or shape tools, type tools, and other tools dedicated to creating documents, transforming objects, and working with pages. Add viewing tools and you have everything you need to do any job.

When you work on a document, it's important to know what tools are available, and how they can help in achieving your design goals. InDesign likes to save space, so it consolidates similar tools under one button. To access multiple tools, click and hold on any Tools panel button that contains a small black triangle, located in the lower right corner of the tool button. Take a moment to explore the InDesign toolbox and get to know the tools.

The InDesign Tools panel contains the tools needed to work through any InDesign job, but it's not necessary to click on a tool to access it. Simply using a letter of the alphabet can access all of InDesign's tools. For example, pressing the P key switches to the Pen tool, and pressing the T key switches to the Type tool. You can refer to Adobe InDesign CS4 Keyboard Shortcuts (available for download on the Web at *www.perspection.com*) for more information on all the letter assign-

Tools panel

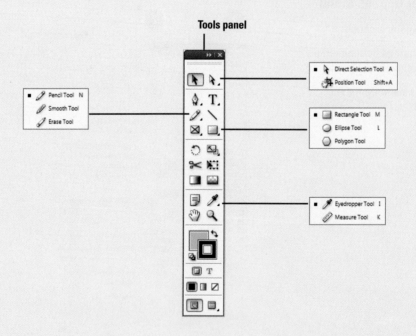

ments for the various tools. To really get efficient in InDesign, you need to learn to use both hands. Use one hand for your mouse or drawing tablet, and the other on the keyboard to make quick changes of tools and options. Think of using InDesign like playing a piano—you need to use both hands.

Using the Control Panel

The Control panel displays the options for the currently selected tool. For most tools, your options include X and Y Location, W and H dimensions, Scale X and Y, Rotation and Shear Angle, Rotate and Flip, Apply Effect, Opacity, Drop Shadow, Align and Distribute, Quick Apply, and the Options menu. When working with the Type tool, additional options include Font Family, Font Type, Font Size, Alignment, Tracking and Indents. The important thing to remember is that the Control panel is customized based on the tool you have selected.

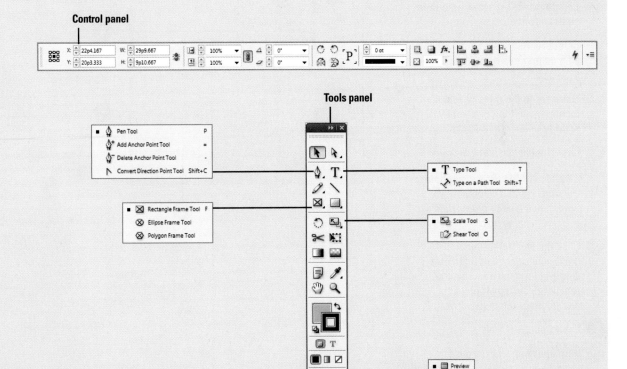

Opening a Document

InDesign lets you open document files created in different formats, such as InDesign (INDD), InDesign CS3 Interchange (INX), InDesign Markup (IDML), PageMaker (6.0-7.0), and QuarkXPress (3.3-4.1x). If you want to simply open an InDesign document, the Welcome Screen or Open dialog box are the most efficient ways. However, if you need to manage, organize, or process files, Adobe Bridge is the way to go. You open an existing InDesign document file the same way you open documents in other programs. In Windows Explorer (Win) or Finder (Mac), you can double-click an InDesign document to open the InDesign program and the document. When you open a document, a tab appears across the top of the Document window, with the document title. You can click the tab at any time to display that particular document.

Open an Existing Document

1. Click the **File** menu, and then click **Open** to display all file types in the file list of the Open dialog box.

2. Click the **Files of Type** (Win) or **Enable** (Mac) list arrow, and then select a format.

   Select All Readable Files to display all files that can be opened in InDesign.

3. Navigate to the drive or folder location with the document you want to open.

4. Click the file you want to open.

   TIMESAVER *Press and hold the Shift key to select multiple contiguous files to open while in the Open dialog box.*

5. Click the **Normal** (original document or copy of a template), **Original** (original document or template), or **Copy** (copy of a document or template) option.

6. Click **Open**.

7. If an alert appears for missing fonts or links, select an option, and then click **OK** or another button.

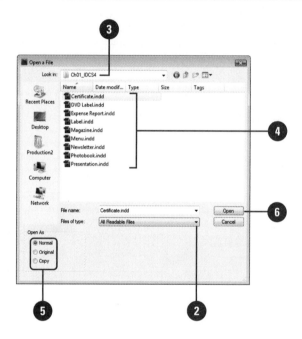

Open a Recently Opened Document

1. Click the **File** menu, and then point to **Open Recent**.

2. Click the document you want to open.

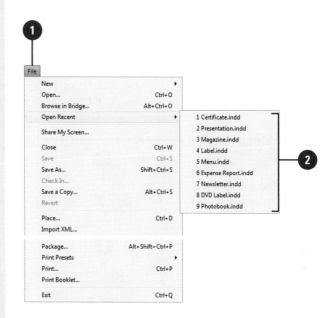

Open a Document from the Welcome Screen

1. Start Adobe InDesign or click the **Help** menu, and then click **Welcome Screen**.

2. Click a document from the Open a Recent Item list.

3. To open a document not in the list, click **Open**, select a document, and then click **Open**.

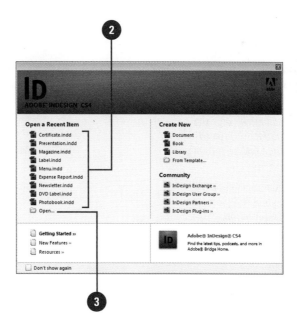

Opening a Document with Adobe Bridge

With Adobe Bridge, you can drag assets into your layouts as needed, preview them, and add metadata to them. Bridge allows you to search, sort, filter, manage, and process files one at a time or in batches. You can also use Bridge to create new folders; rename, move, delete and group files (known as stacking); edit metadata; rotate images; and run batch commands. You can also view information about files and data imported from your digital camera.

Browse and Open Documents with Adobe Bridge

1 Click the **Go to Bridge** button on the Application bar or click the **File** menu, and then click **Browse in Bridge**.

2 In Bridge, select a specific workspace to view your files the way you want.

3 Navigate to the drive or folder where the file is located.

4 To open an image in InDesign, use any of the following:

◆ Double-click on a thumbnail to open it in the default program.

◆ Drag the thumbnail from the Bridge into an open Adobe application.

◆ Select a thumbnail, click the **File** menu, point to **Open With**, and then click **Adobe InDesign CS4**.

◆ Select a thumbnail, click the **File** menu, point to **Place**, and then click **In InDesign**.

5 To return to InDesign, click the **File** menu, and then click **Return to Adobe InDesign**.

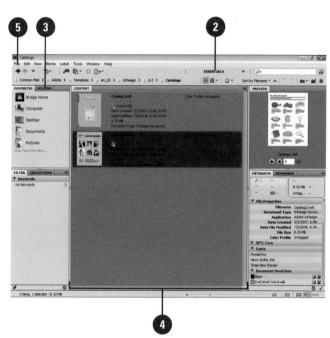

Work with Files Using Bridge

1. Click the **Go to Bridge** button on the Application bar or click the **File** menu, and then click **Browse in Bridge**.

2. Click the **Folders** tab and choose a folder from the scrolling list.

3. Click the **Favorites** tab to choose from a listing of user-defined items, such as Pictures.

4. To narrow down the list of images using a filter, click the criteria you want to use in the Filter panel.

5. Click an image within the preview window to select it.

6. Click the **Preview** tab to view a larger thumbnail of the selected image. Multiple images appear when you select them.

7. Drag the **Zoom** slider to increase or decrease the thumbnail views.

8. Use the file management buttons to rotate or delete images, or create a new folder.

9. Double-click on a thumbnail to open it in the default program, or drag the thumbnail from the Bridge into an open Adobe application.

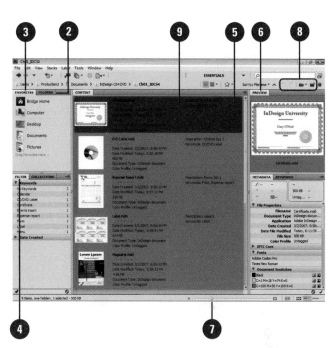

Did You Know?

You can reveal a document in Adobe Bridge from InDesign. Open a document in InDesign, click the Open icon (looks like a piece of paper with edge folded over) on the Status Bar, and then click Reveal in Bridge.

Inserting Images or Text in a Document

You can use InDesign's Place command to insert artwork into an open document. To increase your control of the new image information, InDesign places the new image into a separate layer. InDesign lets you place files saved in InDesign, Media Files, Images, Adobe PDF, EPS, Excel XLS, Word DOC, and TXT or RTF formats to name a few. When you place a vector-based image into InDesign, you have the ability to modify the width, height, and rotation while retaining the vector format of the file.

Insert an Image or Text in a Document

1. Open an InDesign document.

2. Click the **File** menu, and then click **Place**.

3. Navigate to the drive or folder location with the image, and then select the image you want to place into the active document.

4. Select any of the following options:

   ◆ **Show Import Options.** Select to specify import options for the imported item.

   ◆ **Replace Selected Item.** Select to replace the currently selected item on the page.

5. Click **Open**.

6. If you selected the Show Import Options check box, specify the Import options that you want, and then click **OK**.

   InDesign places the image in the active layer, and then encloses it within a frame.

7. Adjust the Scale X and Scale Y values on the Control panel to resize the placed image.

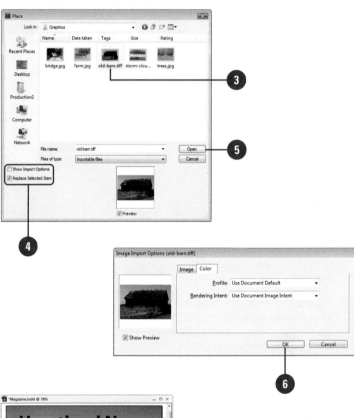

Using the Status Bar

To work efficiently in InDesign you need information about the active document. Details about the document's preflight profile can help in the design and preparation of the final document. You can quickly enable the current or all open documents as preflight documents. In addition, you can open the Preflight panel or Preflight Profile dialog box to view and set preflight options. From the Status Bar, you can also switch between pages.

Use the Status Bar

1 Click the **triangle** (Preflight menu) near the Status bar info box, and then select from the following options:

- **Preflight Panel.** Opens the Preflight panel.

- **Define Profiles.** Opens the Preflight Profiles dialog box.

- **Preflight Document.** Enables or disables the current document as a preflight document.

- **Enable Preflight for All Documents.** Enables or disables all open documents as preflight documents.

2 To locate the current document in Explorer, Finder, or Bridge, click the **Open** menu, and then click **Reveal in Explorer** (Win) or **Reveal in Finder** (Mac), or **Reveal in Bridge**.

3 To switch between pages, use any of the following:

- **First or Last.** Displays the first or last page.

- **Previous or Next.** Displays the previous or next page.

- **Page Navigation.** Displays the specified page.

Working with Document Windows

ID 1.11

When you open multiple documents, you can use the Arrange Documents (**New!**) or Window menu or tabs at the top of the Document window to switch between them. You can click a tab name to switch to and activate the document. By default, tabs are displayed in the order in which you open or create documents. When you want to move or copy information between documents, it's easier to display several document windows on the screen at the same time and move them around. However, you must make the window active to work in it. Each tab also includes a Close button (**New!**) to quickly close a document. If the document view is too small or large, you can change it to suit your needs.

Work with Multiple Documents

1 Open more than one document.

2 Click a tab name to switch to the document.

TIMESAVER *Press Ctrl+Tab or Ctrl+Shift+Tab to cycle to the tab you want.*

◆ You can also click the **Window** menu, and then click a document name at the bottom of the menu.

3 To move a document window around, do any of the following:

◆ To rearrange the order of tabbed documents (**New!**), drag a window's tab to a new location.

◆ To switch to another document when dragging a selection (**New!**), drag the selection over the document's tab.

◆ To remove a document from the tabbed documents group, drag a window's tab away from the tabbed group.

2

3 Undocked floating document window

Arrange Multiple Documents

① Open more than one document.

② Click the **Arrange Documents** menu (**New!**) on the Application bar.

③ On the menu, select an arrangement button icon:

- ◆ **Consolidate All.** Displays all active documents as tabs.

- ◆ **Tile All In Grid.** Displays all open documents in a grid pattern on the screen.

- ◆ **Tile All Vertically.** Displays all open documents vertically on the screen.

- ◆ **Tile All Horizontally.** Displays all open documents horizontally on the screen.

- ◆ **2-Up, 3-Up, 4-Up, 5-Up, or 6-Up.** Displays the number of documents in the selected pattern (in the menu icon) on the screen.

- ◆ **Float All in Windows.** Displays all open windows in separate undocked floating windows.

- ◆ **New Window.** Creates a new window with the contents of the active window.

④ To dock or undock a document window (**New!**), drag the window's tab out of the group or into the group.

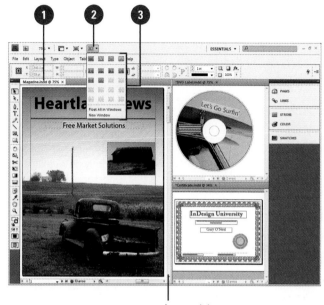

Arranged documents

Checking for Updates Online

As time passes, InDesign—like any other program—will change. There are two types of changes to a program: updates and patches. Updates are improvements to a program such as a new feature, option, or command. Patches are software fixes for problems discovered after the public release of the program. The good news is that both updates and patches are free, and once downloaded, are self-installing. Adobe gives you two ways to check for changes. You can check manually by going to the Adobe web site, or automatically through the Adobe Updater. The Adobe Updater Preferences dialog box allows you to set update options for InDesign and other installed Adobe products, such as Bridge. You can set the update preferences to check for updates monthly or weekly and automatically download them, or have Adobe Updater ask before performing the download.

Check for Updates Directly from the Internet

1. Open your Internet browser.

2. Go to the following Web address: *www.adobe.com/downloads/updates/*

3. Click the list arrow, and then click **InDesign - Macintosh** or **InDesign - Windows**.

4. Click **Go**.

   Any updates or patches appear in a list.

5. Based on your operating system, follow the onscreen instructions to download and install the software.

   IMPORTANT *Checking on your own requires a computer with a connection to the Internet. Since some of the updates can be rather large, it's recommended you have high-speed access; 56k is good, but DSL or cable modem is better.*

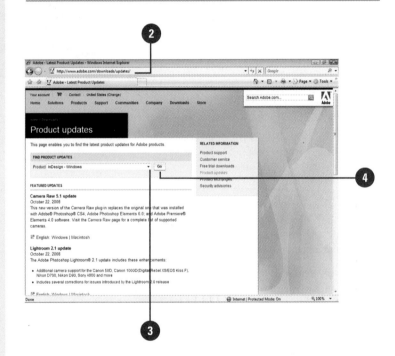

Check for Updates from the InDesign Help Menu

1 Start Adobe InDesign, if necessary.

2 Click the **Help** menu, and then click **Updates**.

InDesign automatically connects you to the Internet, and checks for updates.

3 If there are any updates available, click **Download and Install Updates**.

IMPORTANT *Remember, these files can be quite large. So, if your Internet connection speed is slow, you might want to perform downloading files at a low traffic time. Also, by making sure you don't have other programs running, you can maximize your system's resources for the downloading of files.*

When the check or download is complete, the Adobe Updater dialog box opens.

4 To change Adobe Updater preferences, click **Preferences**, select the **Automatically Check For Adobe Updates** check box, select the update and program options you want, and then click **OK**.

5 Click **Quit**.

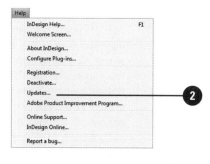

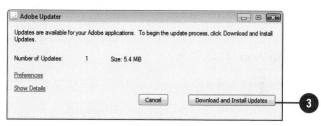

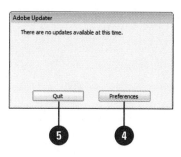

Select to update an application.

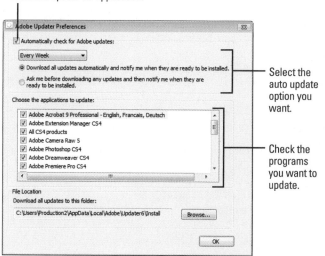

Select the auto update option you want.

Check the programs you want to update.

Getting Help While You Work

At some time, everyone has a question or two about the program they are using. InDesign Help uses a Community Help site (**New!**) on the web at *adobe.com* (which is updated regularly) to help you find the information you need. When you start InDesign Help, your browser opens, displaying a web site with InDesign help categories and topics. You can search the InDesign Help site by using keywords or phrases or browsing through a list of categories and topics to locate specific information. When you perform a search using keywords or phrases, a list of possible answers is shown to you from *adobe.com*, with the most likely answer to your question at the top of the list. Along with help text, some help topics include links to text and video tutorials. In addition, comments and ratings from users are available to help guide you to an answer.

Get Help Information

1 Click the **Help** menu, and then click **InDesign Help**.

TIMESAVER *Press F1.*

Your browser opens, displaying InDesign Help from the Web. An Internet connection is required.

2 Click the **InDesign Help (web)** link to access online help.

3 Click Help categories (plus sign icons) until the topic you want is displayed.

4 Click the topic you want.

5 Read the topic, and if necessary, click any hyperlinks to get information on related topics or definitions.

6 When you're done, close your browser.

Did You Know?

You can get resource help with InDesign on the Web. Click the Help menu, click Welcome Screen, and then click Resources or InDesign Exchange to display InDesign help resources from all over the Web.

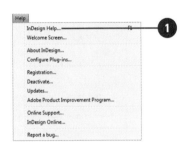

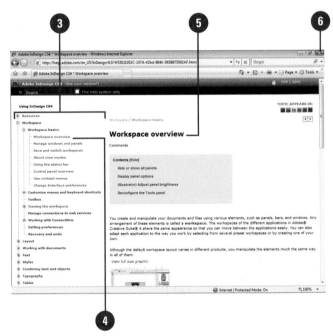

Search for Help Information

1. In InDesign, on the Application bar, type one or more keywords in the Search box, and then press Enter (Win) or Return (Mac).

   ◆ You can also click the **Help** menu, and then click **InDesign Help** to open Help and use the Search box.

   Your browser displays an Adobe web site with a list of topics that match the keywords you entered in the Search box.

2. Click the link to the topic you want from the search list of results.

3. Read the topic, and then if you want, click any hyperlinks to get information on related topics or definitions.

4. When you're done, close your browser.

Keyword to search

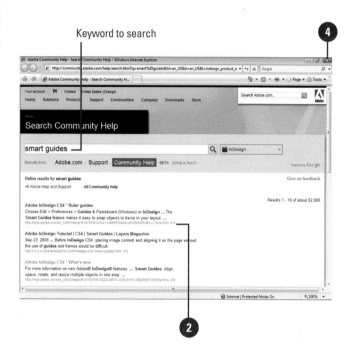

Did You Know?

You can find out what's new in InDesign. Click the Help menu, click InDesign Help, click the plus sign (+) next to Resources, and then click What's New.

You can print out the selected Help topic. Open the Help screen in your browser, select the Help topic you want to print, select the Print command, specify print options, and then click Print (Win) or OK (Mac).

You can move backward and forward between help topics. Click the Previous or Next button on the right side of the Help web page.

For Your Information

Participating in Adobe Product Improvement

You can participate in the Adobe Product Improvement Program. (**New!**) Click the Help menu, click Adobe Product Improvement Program, and then follow the onscreen instructions. This is an opt-in program that allows you to test Adobe products and make suggestions for future products. This program enables Adobe to collect product usage data from customers while maintaining their privacy.

Saving a Document

When you finish working on your InDesign document, you need to save it before you close the document or exit InDesign. While this may seem like a simple task, there are questions that must be asked before saving a file, like *What is the intended final output of the image?* Each output device, whether monitor or paper-based, requires a specific format, and it's best to know this information at the beginning of the creation process. Knowing the eventual destination of an image helps you create the design with the output in mind. A file type specifies the document format (for example, a template) as well as the program in which the file was created (for example, InDesign). You might want to change the type if you're creating a custom template or sharing files with someone who doesn't have the Adobe InDesign program.

Save an InDesign Document

1. Click the **File** menu, and then click **Save**.

2. Enter a name for the file.

3. Click the **Save as Type** list arrow (Win) or **Format** popup (Mac), and then click **InDesign CS4 document**.

4. Navigate to the drive or folder location where you want to save the document.

5. Select the **Always Save Preview Images with Documents** check box to save a preview image with the document for use in dialog boxes and other thumbnails as a preview.

6. Click **Save**.

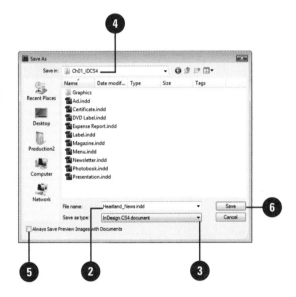

Did You Know?

You can revert to the last saved version. Click the File menu, and then click Revert.

You can save all open documents. Press Ctrl+Alt+Shift+S (Win) or ⌘+Option+Shift+S (Mac) to save all open documents to their existing locations and filenames.

Save a Copy of an InDesign Document

1 Click the **File** menu, and then click **Save As**.

2 Enter a name for the file or use the default original name with the word "copy" at the end.

3 Click the **Save as Type** list arrow (Win) or **Format** popup (Mac), and then click **InDesign CS4 document**.

4 Navigate to the drive or folder location where you want to save the document.

5 Select the **Always Save Preview Images with Documents** check box to save a preview image with the document for use in dialog boxes and other thumbnails as a preview.

6 Click **Save**.

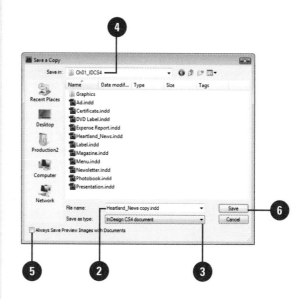

Did You Know?

You can save a document as a template. Click the File menu, click Save As, click the Save As Type (Win) or Format (Mac) popup, click InDesign CS4 template, enter a name, specify a location, and then click Save.

Finishing Up

After you work on a document, you can finish up by closing the document or by exiting InDesign. You should save the document before closing it. Exiting InDesign closes the current document and the InDesign program and returns you to the desktop. You can use the Exit command on the File menu (Win) or Quit InDesign command on the InDesign menu (Mac) to close a document and exit InDesign, or you can use the Close button on the InDesign Document tab (**New!**). If you try to close a document without saving your final changes, a dialog box opens, asking if you want to do so.

Close a Document

1 Click the **Close** button on the Document tab, or click the **File** menu, and then click **Close**.

TIMESAVER *Press Ctrl+W (Win) or ⌘+W (Mac) to close a document.*

2 If necessary, click **Yes** to save any changes you made to your open documents before the program quits.

Document tab Close button

Exit InDesign

1 Choose one of the following:

◆ Click the **Close** button, or click the **File** menu, and then click **Exit** (Win).

◆ Click the **InDesign** menu, and then click **Quit InDesign** (Mac).

TIMESAVER *Press Ctrl+Q (Win) or ⌘+Q (Mac) to exit InDesign.*

2 If necessary, click **Yes** to save any changes you made to your open documents before the program quits.

Exit (Win)

Click to exit (Win)

Creating and Viewing a Document

Introduction

You can either open an existing document or create a new one to work on in InDesign. When you create a new document, you can create one from scratch or use one of the built-in types, such as document, book or library. The built-in document presets make it easy to create documents for specific purposes without the hassle of specifying individual settings. However, if you know the individual settings you want, you can create a new document from scratch.

InDesign uses two main Screen Modes: Normal and Preview. Normal mode displays the area inside document pages, guides, pasteboard, bleed, and slug areas, while Preview mode simply displays the area inside document pages. There are two additional Screen Modes: Bleed and Slug. The bleed is an area outside the trim of the page where objects still print, while slug is an area outside the page trim that may or may not print.

Having problems squinting at the small details of a document? Using the Zoom tool is a great way to get you focused where you need to be. Zooming into a specific section of a document makes touching up the fine details just that much easier.

InDesign's navigation and measurement systems—rulers, grid, guides, smart guides—are more than just information; they represent control of the document and control of the creative process. In addition, the Info panel gives you up-to-date information on the exact position of the cursor inside the document, as well as detailed color space and profile information that can be indispensable in preparing your designs.

What You'll Do

Create a New Document

Create a New Document from a Template

Create a New Document Using Document Presets

Set Up a Document

Change the Display View

Change the View with the Zoom Tool

View and Use Rulers

Use Guides

Change Guides & Pasteboard Options

Use Smart Guides

Use the Grid

Move Around with the Hand Tool

Work with the Info Panel

Create and Display Workspaces

Use Undo and Redo

Creating a New Document

Creating a new InDesign document requires more thought than creating a new word processing document. For example, there are the number of pages, page size, columns, and margins considerations to keep in mind. The page size option also includes compact disc and monitor (**New!**) sizes for interactive documents. You can also set advanced options for the bleed and slug. The **bleed** is an area outside the trim of the page where objects still print, while **slug** is an area outside the page trim that may or may not print. The slug is typically used to add non-printing information to a document. As you specify new document settings, you can save your settings as a preset for use in the future. You can create as many new documents as you need. Once a new document is created, you have access to all of InDesign's design, text, and manipulation tools to create anything you can imagine.

Create a New Document

1. Click the **File** menu, point to **New**, and then click **Document**.

2. Click the **Document Preset** list arrow, and then select a preset, or choose your own options to create a custom document.

3. Select from the following options:

   ◆ **Number of Pages.** Specify the number of pages you want in the document.

   ◆ **Facing Pages.** Select to use facing pages (left and right), like a book. Deselect to use single pages in order.

   ◆ **Master Text Frame.** Select to use a common text frame from a master.

4. Select from the following Page Size options:

   ◆ **Page Size.** Select a preset page, compact disc(**New!**), or monitor (**New!**) size from the list.

   ◆ **Width and Height.** Specify a custom width and height for a custom document size.

   ◆ **Orientation.** Select the Portrait or Landscape button.

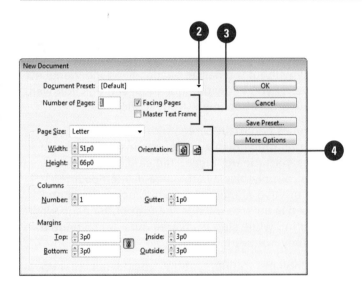

5. Select from the following Columns options:

- ◆ **Number.** Specify the number of columns you want for the pages.
- ◆ **Gutter.** Specify the space between the columns.

6. Select from the following Margins options:

- ◆ **Top and Bottom.** Specify the top and bottom margin size at the top and bottom edges of the document.
- ◆ **Inside and Outside.** If Facing Pages is selected, specify Inside margins for the space between the pages (to make room for the binding) and Outside margins for the edges of each page.
- ◆ **Make All Settings the Same.** Click the chain icon to make all settings the same or allow selection of different settings.

7. Click the **More Options** button (if you want), and then select the advanced options you want:

- ◆ **Bleed.** Specify the bleed values for top, bottom, inside and outside.
- ◆ **Slug.** Specify the slug values for top, bottom, inside and outside.
- ◆ **Make All Settings the Same.** Click the chain icon to make all settings the same or allow selection of different settings.

8. To save custom settings as a preset, click **Save Preset**, type a name, and then click **OK**.

9. Click **OK**.

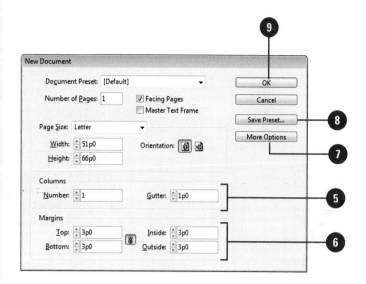

Document Page Sizes

Page Type	Page Size
Letter	8.5 by 11 inches
Legal	8.5 by 14 inches
Tabloid	11 by 17 inches
Letter-Half	8.5 by 5.5 inches
Legal-Half	8.5 by 7 inches
A4	21 by 29.7 centimeters
A3	29.7 by 42 centimeters
A5	14.8 by 21 centimeters
Compact Disc (**New!**)	4.7222 by 4.75 inches
Monitor (**New!**)	600 x 300, 640 x 480, 760 x 420, 800 x 600, 984 x 588, 1024 x 768, 1240 x 620, 1280 x 800
Custom	User-defined values

Creating a New Document from a Template

A template is a special document that makes it easier to create a new document. If you frequently use an existing document, such as Books or Brochures, to start a new document, then you should create a template, which uses the InDesign Template (INDT) file format. You can create your own template or use one provided by InDesign. InDesign comes with a variety of templates, such as Newsletters, Menus, Manuals, Labels and Stickers, Forms, Datamerge, Certificates, Catalogs, CD-DVD labels, Brochures, and Books. When you create a new document from a template, the document appears with the template extension (INDT), which you can then save as a normal InDesign document with the INDD extension. Instead of using an Open dialog box from within the program, InDesign uses Adobe Bridge to access and select templates for use back in InDesign.

Create a New Document from a Template

1. Click the **File** menu, and then click **New From Template**.

   ◆ You can also click **From Templates** in the Welcome Screen dialog box.

   Adobe Bridge opens, displaying the Templates folder for InDesign, which contains individual folders with different types of templates.

2. Navigate to the folder location where the template you want to use is stored.

3. Double-click the template file you want to use.

   The template file opens back in InDesign.

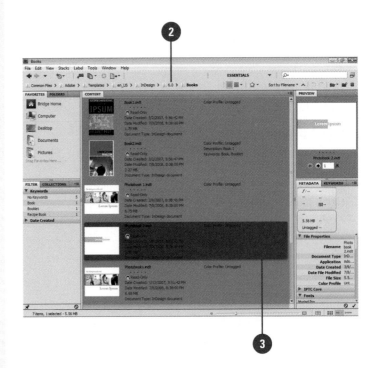

Create a Template Document

1. Open a new or existing document.

2. Create a custom document.

3. Click the **File** menu, and then click **Save As**.

4. Type a name for the new template.

5. Click the **Save as Type** (Win) or **Format** (Mac) list arrow, and then click **InDesign CS4 template**.

6. Navigate to the location where you want to store the template.

   ◆ If you want to store your template along with the pre-built InDesign templates, then save your template in the following location:

   For Windows: Program Files/Common Files/ Adobe/Templates/en_US/ InDesign/6.0

   For the Macintosh: Computer Macintosh HD/Users/*name*/ Application Support/Adobe/ Templates/en_US/InDesign/6.0

7. Select the **Always Save Preview Images with Documents** check box to save a preview image with the document for use in dialog boxes and other thumbnails as a preview.

8. Click **Save**.

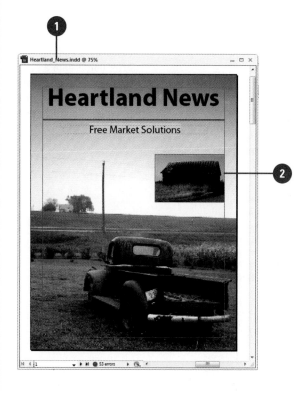

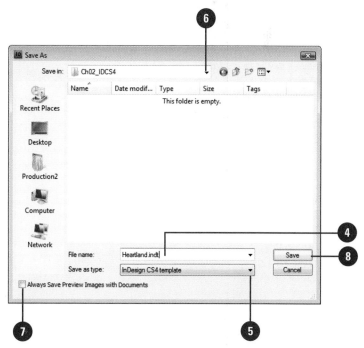

Creating a New Document Using Presets

If you frequently use custom settings to create an InDesign document, you can save time by creating a preset. You can create a preset when you create a new document in the New Document dialog box or you can create and manage presets in the Document Presets dialog box. After you create a preset, you can export and share it with others, which they can import with the Load button in the Document Presets dialog box. When you no longer need a preset, you can delete it. However, you can't delete the [Default] preset.

Create a New Document Using Presets

1. Click the **File** menu, point to **Document Presets**, and then select a preset.

   ◆ You can also click the File menu, point to New, click Document, and then select a preset.

   The New Document dialog box appears, displaying the selected preset.

2. Click **OK**.

Did You Know?

You can save a preset in the New Document dialog box. Click the File menu, point to New, click Document, specify the settings you want, click Save Preset, type a name, and then click OK twice.

See Also

See "Creating a New Document" on page 28 for more information on saving a preset in the New Document dialog box.

Work with Presets for New Documents

1. Click the **Edit** menu, point to **Document Presets**, and then click **Define**.

2. Perform any of the following:

   ◆ New. Click **New**, specify the options that you want, and then click **OK**.

   ◆ Edit. Select a custom preset (not a predefined one), click **Edit**, change the options, and then click **OK**.

   ◆ Delete. Select a custom preset (not a predefined one), and then click **Delete**.

   ◆ Import. Click **Load**, navigate to the preset file, select it, and then click **Open**.

   ◆ Export. Select a preset, click **Save**, specify a location and name, and then click **Save**.

3. Click **OK**.

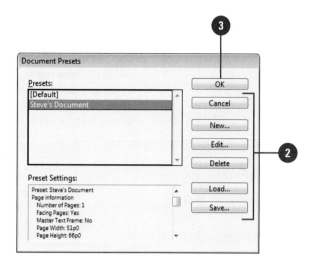

New preset

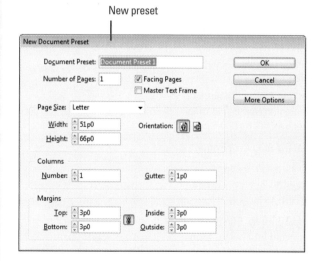

Setting Up a Document

After you create a document, you can use the Document Setup command on the File menu and the Margins and Columns command on the Layout menu to change document settings. In the Document Setup dialog box, you can specify the number of pages, page size, orientation, and advanced settings for bleed and slug. In the Margins and Columns dialog box, you can specify margin, column, and gutter settings. The changes you make in the Margins and Columns dialog box are only applied to the current page or two page spread and not the entire document. If you want to change the entire document, you need to change the master page.

Change Document Options

1. Click the **File** menu, and then click **Document Setup**.

2. Select from the following options:

   ◆ **Number of Pages.** Specify the number of pages you want in the document.

   ◆ **Facing Pages.** Select to use facing pages (left and right), like a book. Deselect to use single pages in order.

   ◆ **Master Text Frame.** Select to use a common text frame from a master.

3. Select from the following Page Size options:

   ◆ **Page Size.** Select a preset page size from the list.

   ◆ **Width and Height.** Specify a custom width and height for a custom document size.

   ◆ **Orientation.** Select the Portrait or Landscape button.

4. Click the **More Options** button (if you want), and then select the advanced options you want:

   ◆ **Bleed and Slug.** Specify the bleed and slug values for top, bottom, inside and outside.

5. Click **OK**.

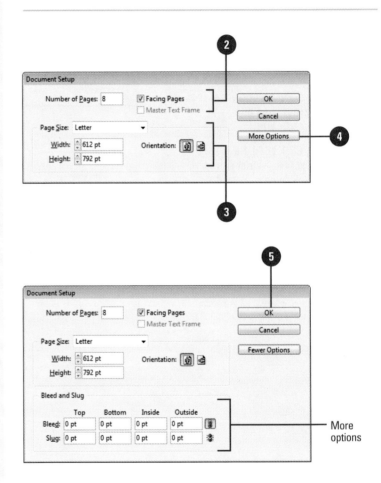

More options

Change Margins and Column Options

1. Click the **Layout** menu, and then click **Margins and Columns**.

2. Select from the following Columns options:

   - **Number.** Specify the number of columns you want for the pages.

   - **Gutter.** Specify the space between the columns.

3. Select from the following Margins options:

   - **Top and Bottom.** If Facing Pages is selected, specify Inside margins for the space between the pages (to make room for the binding) and Outside margins for the edges of each page.

   - **Inside and Outside.** Specify the inside and outside margin size at the left and right edges of the document.

   - **All Settings the Same.** Click the chain icon to make all settings the same or click again (the icon will now be a broken chain) to allow selection of different settings.

4. Click **OK**.

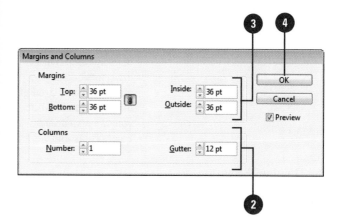

Changing the Display View

InDesign uses two main modes: Normal and Preview. Normal mode displays document pages, guides, pasteboard, bleed, and slug areas, while Preview mode displays the area inside the page boundaries. There are two additional modes: Bleed and Slug. The bleed is an area outside the trim of the page where objects still print, while slug is an area outside the page trim that may or may not print. Bleed mode displays the bleed area and document pages, while Slug mode displays the slug area and document pages. In addition to the display modes, you can also preview aspects of your output, such as overprinting, color proofs and separations, and flattened artwork.

Change the Display View

1. Click the **Screen Mode** button on the Application bar or on the bottom of the Tools panel, and then select one of the following modes:

   ◆ **Normal.** Shows the guides, pasteboard, bleed, and slug areas.

   ◆ **Preview.** Shows the area inside the page boundaries.

   The pasteboard is replaced by a colored background, which you can change in Guides & Pasteboard preferences.

   ◆ **Bleed.** Shows the area inside the page boundaries and the bleed area.

   ◆ **Slug.** Shows the area inside the page boundaries and the slug area.

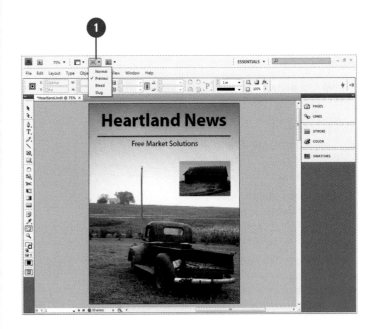

Did You Know?

You can temporarily hide all of InDesign's panels and Tools panel.
Press the Tab key to hide the panels. Press the Tab key a second time to display the hidden panels. Hold down the Shift key, and then press the Tab key to hide the panels, but not the Tools and Control panels.

Display Output Views

◆ **Overprint Preview Mode.** Displays an ink preview with blending, transparency, and overprinting in color separated output. Click the **View** menu, and then click **Overprint Preview**.

◆ **Separations Preview Mode.** Displays separations as they print. Click the **Window** menu, point to **Output**, and then click **Separations Preview**.

◆ **Flattener Preview Mode.** Displays and highlights artwork areas that are flattened when saved or printed. Click the **Window** menu, point to **Output**, and then click **Flattener Preview**.

◆ **Soft Proofs.** Displays your artwork as it will appear on a monitor or output device. Click the **View** menu, point to **Proof Setup**, and then select a proof type.

Did You Know?

You can rotate the Spread view and edit content. (**New!**) Display the two page spread you want to rotate, click the View menu, point to Rotate Spread, and then choose 90° CW (clockwise), 90° CCW (counter clockwise), or 180°. Edit the content you want. To restore the view, click Clear Rotation.

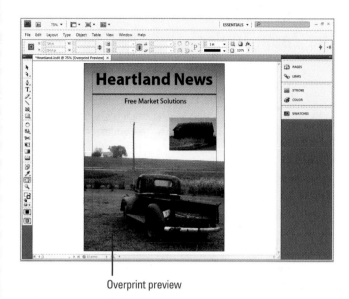

Overprint preview

Separations Preview panel

Separations preview

Changing the View with the Zoom Tool

Working with the Zoom tool gives you one more way to control exactly what you see in InDesign. The Zoom tool does not change the active image, but allows you to view the image at different magnifications. The Zoom tool is located towards the bottom of InDesign's Tools panel, and resembles a magnifying glass. The maximum magnification of an InDesign document is 4000%, and the minimum size is 5.0%. Large documents are difficult to work with and difficult to view. Many large documents, when viewed at 100%, are larger than the maximum size of the document window, requiring you to reduce the zoom in order to view the entire image. In addition to the Zoom tool, you can also select view options to fit the page or spread to the window, show the actual size, or show the entire pasteboard.

Zoom In the View of an Image

1. Select the **Zoom** tool on the Tools panel.

2. Use one of the following methods:

   ◆ **Click on the document.** The image increases in magnification centered on where you clicked.

   ◆ **Drag to define an area with the Zoom tool.** The image increases in magnification based on the boundaries of the area you dragged.

   ◆ **Set a specific view size.** Click the **Zoom Level** button on the Application bar, and then select a specific percentage size magnification.

   ◆ **Fit Page in Window.** Click the **View** menu, and then click **Fit Page In Window**.

   ◆ **Fit Spread in Window.** Click the **View** menu, and then click **Fit Spread In Window**.

   ◆ **Actual Size.** Click the **View** menu, and then click **Actual Size**.

   ◆ **Show Entire Pasteboard.** Click the **View** menu, and then click **Entire Pasteboard**.

2 Click and drag method

Zoom in

Zoom Out the View of an Image

1. Select the **Zoom** tool on the Tools panel.

2. Hold down the Alt (Win) or Option (Mac) key, and then click on the screen to reduce the magnification of the active document.

   TIMESAVER *Press Ctrl+= (Win) or ⌘+= (Mac) for Zoom In and press Ctrl+- (Win) or ⌘+- (Mac) for Zoom Out.*

   The zoom reduction centers at the spot where you click on the active document.

   IMPORTANT *The best way to really see what the printed results of your artwork will look like is to view the image (even if it is too big for the screen) at 100%.*

Did You Know?

You can zoom in or out using shortcut keys regardless of what tool you're currently using. To zoom in, press Ctrl+Spacebar (Win) or ⌘+Spacebar (Mac) and click or drag to define an area. To zoom out, press Ctrl+Spacebar+Alt (Win) or ⌘+Spacebar+Option (Mac) and click or drag to define an area.

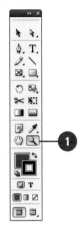

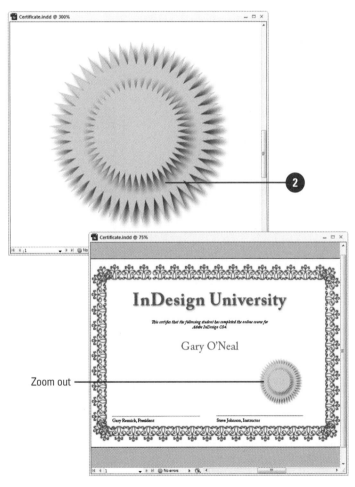

Zoom out

Viewing and Using Rulers

Carpenters know that precise measurements are essential to making things fit, so they have a rule: Measure Twice, Cut Once. The designers of InDesign also know that measurements are essential and give you several measuring systems—among them are the rulers. Rulers are located on the top and left sides of the active document window, and serve several purposes. Rulers start numbering at the top left corner of the page. You can move this point, known as the zero point, to another position. Rulers let you measure the width and height of the active image, they let you place guides on the screen to control placement of other image elements, and they create markers that follow your cursor as you move. As you can see, rulers are critical in the design of a document by helping you correctly align image design elements. The default measurement is in picas, which you can change in Preferences. You can also change the origin, which allows you to use rulers across spreads and spines.

Change Ruler Options

1. Click the **Edit** (Win) or **InDesign** (Mac) menu, point to **Preferences**, and then click **Units & Increments**.

2. Click the **Origin** list arrow, and then select an option:

   ◆ **Spread.** Displays rulers for two pages at a time, as in a book or magazine.

   ◆ **Page.** Displays rulers for one page at a time.

   ◆ **Spine.** Displays rulers for the area where two page spreads are bound together.

3. Click the **Horizontal** and **Vertical** list arrows, and then select a measurement from the available options.

   ◆ If you selected **Custom**, enter the number of points for each unit on the ruler.

4. Click **OK**.

   IMPORTANT *If the Rulers are not visible in the active document, click the View menu, and then click Show Rulers.*

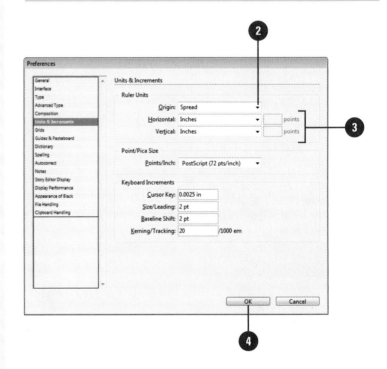

Work with Rulers

◆ **Show or Hide Rulers.** Click the **View** menu, and then click **Show Rulers** or **Hide Rulers**.

    TIMESAVER *Press Ctrl+R (Win) or* ⌘+R *(Mac).*

    ◆ You can also click the **View Options** menu (**New!**) on the Application bar, and then click **Rulers**.

◆ **Change Measurement Units.** Right-click (Win) or Option-click (Mac) a ruler, and then select a unit of measure.

◆ **Change Ruler Origin.** Point to the upper-left corner where the rulers intersect, and then drag the pointer to where you want the new ruler origin.

    When you change the ruler origin on a spine with facing pages, the X values are positive for right-sided pages and negative for left-sided pages (**New!**).

◆ **Reset Ruler Origin.** Double-click the upper-left corner where the rulers intersect.

Did You Know?

You can change the number of points per inch in InDesign. Points are used to measure font characters. In the Units & Increments Preferences dialog box, you can change the points per inch. Click the Edit (Win) or InDesign (Mac) menu, point to Preferences, click Units & Increments, specify an option, and then click OK.

Horizontal Ruler bar

Vertical Ruler bar

Using Guides

A guide is a nonprinting vertical or horizontal line that helps you align text and graphic objects. You can quickly show and hide guides, lock them in place, and align objects to them. With the Snap to Guides command, you can align an object to a guide. When the object's edge comes within a specified distance in pixels of a guide, it snaps to the guide point. When you no longer need one or all of the guides, you can quickly select and remove them.

Create and Move Guides

1. Click the **View** menu, and then click **Show Rulers** to display the ruler bars within the document window.

2. Move to the vertical or horizontal Ruler bar, and then click and drag into the document.

3. Return to the Ruler bar and continue to drag until you have all your guides properly set.

4. To lock the existing guides in place, click the **View** menu, point to **Grids & Guides**, and then click **Lock Guides**.

5. Click the **Selection** tool on the Tools panel to drag existing guides to a new position (make sure Lock Guides is not selected).

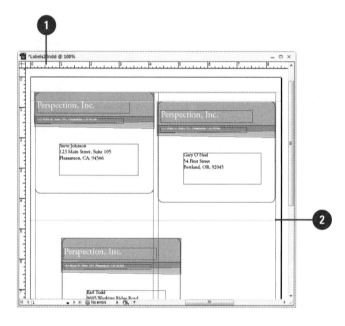

Work with Guides

◆ **Show or Hide Guides.** Click the **View** menu, point to **Grids & Guides**, and then click **Show Guides** or **Hide Guides**.

   TIMESAVER *Press Ctrl+; (Win) or* ⌘+; *(Mac).*

   ◆ You can also click the **View Options** menu (**New!**) on the Application bar, and then click **Guides**.

◆ **Lock/Unlock Guides.** Click the **View** menu, point to **Grids & Guides**, and then click **Lock Guides**.

   TIMESAVER *Press Alt+Ctrl+; (Win) or Option+*⌘*+; (Mac).*

◆ **Lock/Unlock Column Guides.** Click the **View** menu, point to **Grids & Guides**, and then click **Lock Column Guides**.

◆ **Snap Objects to Guides.** Click the **View** menu, point to **Grids & Guides**, and then click **Snap To Guides**.

   When you drag an object near a guide, the object snaps to it.

   TIMESAVER *Press Shift+Ctrl+; (Win) or Shift+*⌘*+; (Mac).*

◆ **Delete Guides.** Click the ruler guide with one of the Selection tools, and then press the Delete or Backspace key.

◆ **Delete All Guides.** Right-click (Win) or Ctrl-click (Mac) a ruler, and then click **Delete All Guides** (**New!**).

Guide   Snap to guide

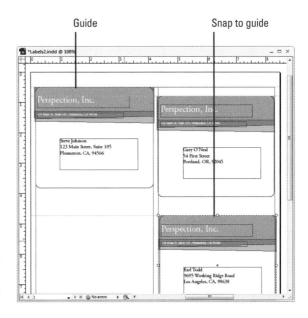

Changing Guides & Pasteboard Options

InDesign uses several different types of guides to show different areas of a document. Ruler guides are user-defined guides for moving and aligning objects. Margin guides show the current margins in the document. Column guides show current column settings for a page or master page. Bleed and Slug guides show the bleed and slug areas in a document. You can use Guides & Pasteboard preferences to set guide settings, such as color and display options, and pasteboard settings, such as color in Preview view and size above and below the document. You can also specify a snap to distance to align an object to a guide.

Change Guides & Pasteboard Preferences

① Click the **Edit** (Win) or **InDesign** (Mac) menu, point to **Preferences**, and then click **Guides & Pasteboard**.

② Select from the following Guides & Pasteboard options:

◆ **Margins.** Specify a guide color for margins.

◆ **Columns.** Specify a guide color for columns.

◆ **Bleed.** Specify a guide color for the bleed area.

◆ **Slug.** Specify a guide color for the slug area.

◆ **Preview Background.** Specify a color for the pasteboard background in Preview view.

◆ **Snap to Zone.** Enter a value to specify the distance in pixels when an object snaps to a guide.

◆ **Guides in Back.** Select to show guides in the background of text and objects.

◆ **Minimum Vertical Offset.** Enter a size to increase the pasteboard area above and below the document.

③ Click **OK**.

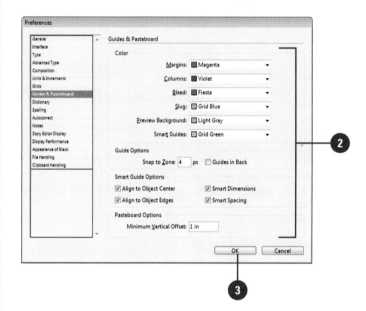

Change the Appearance of Ruler Guides

1. Click the **Layout** menu, and then click **Ruler Guides**.

2. Click the **Color** list arrow, and then select a color.

3. Click the **View Threshold** list arrow, and then select the lowest view percentage at which the ruler guides will be visible.

   When you increase the threshold, guides are hidden at low magnifications and are visible at high magnifications.

4. Click **OK**.

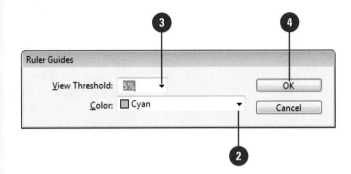

Using Smart Guides

InDesign gives you the ability to use Smart Guides (**New!**) to help align shapes and objects as you draw or drag to move, rotate, or resize. They appear automatically as you draw or move an element, and then disappear after the element is drawn or moved. They enable you to visually align one object to another with a minimum of effort. Smart Guides also display alignment and measurement information, known as Smart Dimensions (**New!**), such as distances between objects, angles of rotation, and whether an object matches the size of nearby objects, to make drawing and alignment even easier. You can also use Smart Spacing (**New!**) to evenly space multiple elements by snapping objects into position. Smart Guides are automatically turned on by default. You can use Guides & Pasteboard preferences to set color and information display options to customize your Smart Guides.

Use Smart Guides

1. Open or create a multi-layered document.

2. To turn Smart Guides on and off, click the **View** menu, point to **Grids & Guides**, and then click **Smart Guides**.

   ◆ You can also click the **View Options** menu (**New!**) on the Application bar, and then click **Smart Guides**.

3. To draw a shape and use Smart Guides, select a shape tool from the Tools panel, and then drag to draw the shape.

   As you draw the shape, Smart Guides appear to help you create shapes that match and align to other objects.

4. Select the **Selection** tool on the Tools panel, and then select and drag the objects you want to move and align.

   As you move the object, Smart Guides appear to help you align it with other objects.

5. Release the mouse and the guides disappear.

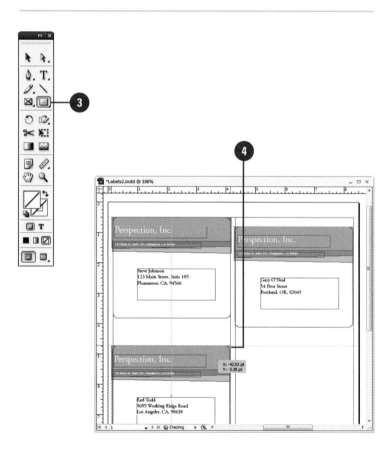

Change Smart Guide Preferences

1 Click the **Edit** (Win) or **InDesign** (Mac) menu, point to **Preferences**, and then click **Guides & Pasteboard**.

2 Click the **Smart Guides** list arrow, and then select a guide color.

3 Select from the following options:

◆ **Align to Object Center.** Select to display guides along the center of objects, art, and bleeds.

◆ **Align to Object Edges.** Select to display guides along edges of objects, artboard, and bleeds.

◆ **Smart Dimensions.** Select to enable the Smart Dimensions feature, which allows you to show width, height or rotation of an object, and indicate when the size or rotation matches nearby objects.

◆ **Smart Spacing.** Select to enable the Smart Spacing feature, which allows you to evenly space multiple items by snapping objects into position.

◆ **Snap to Zone.** Enter a value to specify the distance in pixels when an object snaps to a guide.

◆ **Guides in Back.** Select to show guides in the background of text and objects.

4 Click **OK**.

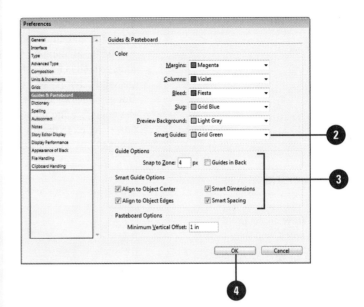

Using the Grid

ID 1.10

A grid is a checkerboard display that you can use to help you align text and graphic objects. There are two types of grids: Document and Baseline. The document grid displays a checkerboard pattern, which is helpful for aligning objects, while the baseline grid displays horizontal lines, which is helpful for aligning text. The grid appears behind your text and artwork, so it doesn't get in the way. With the Snap to Document Grid command, you can align an object to a gridline. When the object's edge comes within a specified number of pixels of a gridline, it snaps to the gridline point. You can use Grids preferences to set grid settings, such as color and spacing.

Work with the Grid

◆ **Show or Hide Document Grid.** Click the **View** menu, point to **Grids & Guides**, and then click **Show Document Grid** or **Hide Document Grid**.

> **TIMESAVER** *Press Ctrl+' (Win) or* ⌘+' *(Mac).*

◆ **Show or Hide Baseline Grid.** Click the **View** menu, point to **Grids & Guides**, and then click **Show Baseline Grid** or **Hide Baseline Grid**.

> **TIMESAVER** *Press Alt+Ctrl+' (Win) or Option+*⌘+' *(Mac).*

  ◆ You can also click the **View Options** menu (**New!**) on the Application bar, and then click **Baseline Grid**.

  ◆ When you use a measurement system other than points, baseline grid values still use points to match text size and leading (**New!**).

◆ **Snap Objects to Gridline.** Click the **View** menu, point to **Grids & Guides**, and then click **Snap To Document Grid**.

> **TIMESAVER** *Press Shift+Ctrl+' (Win) or Shift+*⌘+' *(Mac).*

When you drag an object near a gridline, it snaps to the gridline.

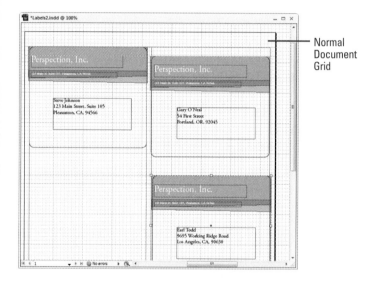

Normal Document Grid

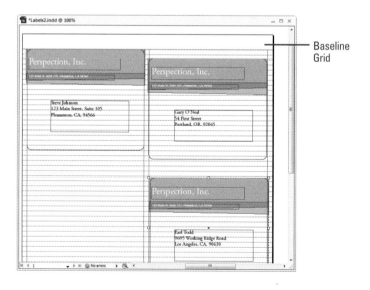

Baseline Grid

Change Grid Preferences

1. Click the **Edit** (Win) or **InDesign** (Mac) menu, point to **Preferences**, and then click **Grids**.

2. Select from the following Baseline Grid options:

   ◆ **Color.** Specify a grid color.

   ◆ **Start.** Specify a start value for the baseline.

   ◆ **Relative To.** Specify the location of the start value relative to the page or margin.

   ◆ **Increment Every.** Specify a measurement for the interval of gridlines. The default is 12 points.

   ◆ **View Threshold.** Specify the lowest view percentage at which the grid is visible.

3. Select from the following Document Grid options:

   ◆ **Color.** Specify a grid color.

   ◆ **Gridline Every (Horizontal and Vertical).** Specify a measurement for the interval of gridlines.

   ◆ **Subdivisions (Horizontal and Vertical).** Specify the number of grid subdivisions.

   ◆ **Grids in Back.** Select to show grids in the background of text and objects.

4. Click **OK**.

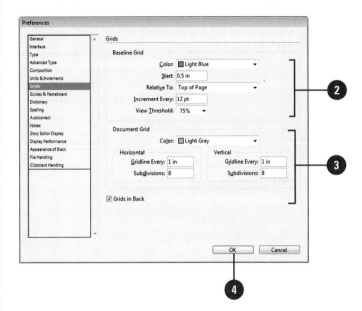

Moving Around with the Hand Tool

One of those little used, but handy, tools is InDesign's Hand tool. The Hand tool (so named because it resembles an open hand) lets you quickly move the active image within the document window without ever using the scroll bars. For example, you've zoomed the image beyond the size that fits within the document window and you need to change the visible portion of the document. It's a simple operation, but a handy one to know.

Move a Page Around in the Document Window

1. Select the **Hand** tool on the Tools panel.

2. Drag in the active document to move it.

3. Click and hold to zoom in. Release the mouse to return to the previous magnification.

Did You Know?

You can quickly access the Hand tool whenever you need it. Hold down the Spacebar to temporarily change to the Hand tool. Drag in the active document to the desired position, and then release the Spacebar. You're instantly returned to the last-used tool. It's important to note that you cannot use the Spacebar to access the Hand tool if you are currently using the Type tool.

See Also

See *"Changing the View with the Zoom Tool"* on pages 38-39 for more information on increasing and decreasing the view magnification.

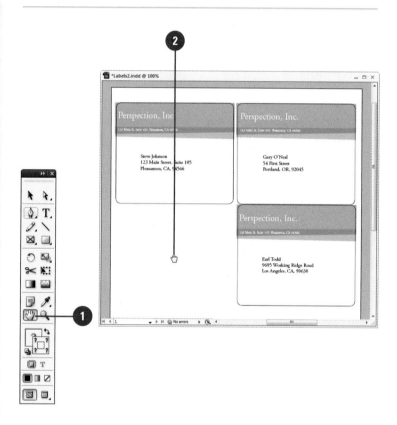

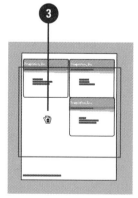

Working with the Info Panel

 ID 1.7

InDesign's Info panel gives you a wealth of data on the current document. The Info panel displays information on the x and y (horizontal/vertical) position of your mouse cursor within the active document window. In addition, when you're using one of InDesign's drawing, measuring, or transformation tools, the Info panel gives you up-to-date information on the size of the object you're creating. When an object is selected, the Info panel display the x and y position, width (w) and height (h). If you select multiple objects, only information that is the same for all selected objects appears in the Info panel. When you're using the Zoom tool, the Info panel displays the magnification factor and the x and y position. The Info panel also displays color information when you choose to show options.

Create a Specific Size Object

1. Select the **Info** panel.

2. Select a drawing tool on the Tools panel, and then drag to create a shape.

3. Release the mouse when the Info panel displays the desired dimensions.

4. To display color fill and stroke information for a selected object, click the **Options** menu, and then click **Show Options**.

5. To change cursor, fill or stroke information, click the related icon (with a small black triangle), and then select an option.

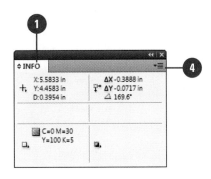

Did You Know?

You can measure the distance between objects. Select the Measure tool in the Tools panel, and then click two points, or click the first point and drag to the second point. Use Shift-drag to constrain the tool to multiples of 45 degrees. The Info panel displays the distances from the x and y axes, the absolute horizontal and vertical distances, the total distances, and the angle measured.

Creating and Displaying Workspaces

As you work with InDesign, you'll open, close, and move around windows and panels to meet your individual needs. After you customize the InDesign workspace, you can save the location of windows and panels as a workspace, which you can display by using the Workspace menu on the Application bar (**New!**) or the Workspaces submenu on the Window menu. You can create custom workspaces, or use one of the workspaces provided by InDesign, which are designed for space and workflow efficiency. The built-in workspaces include Essentials, Book, Interactivity, Printing and Proofing, and Typography (**New!**). If you no longer use a custom workspace, you can remove it at any time.

Create a Workspace

1. Open and position the panels and add the custom menus you want to include in the workspace.

2. Click the **Workspace** menu on the Application bar (**New!**) (the menu name displays the current workspace), and then click **New Workspace**.

   ◆ You can also click the **Window** menu, point to **Workspace**, and then click **New Workspace**.

   The New Workspace dialog box appears.

3. Type a name in the Name box.

4. Select or deselect check boxes to include **Panel Locations** and **Menu Customization**.

5. Click **OK**.

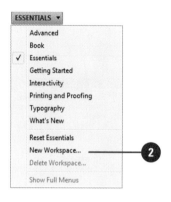

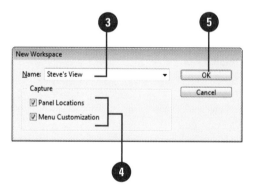

Did You Know?

You can hide a panel. Click the Window menu, and then click on a panel name to remove the check mark.

Display a Workspace

1. Click the **Workspace** menu on the Application bar (**New!**) (the menu name displays the current workspace), and then select a panel option:

   ◆ **Custom panel name.** Displays a custom panel layout that you created.

   ◆ **Advanced, Book, Essentials, Getting Started, Interactivity, Printing and Proofing, Typography, or What's New.** Displays panel layouts created by Adobe for specific purposes in InDesign (**New!**).

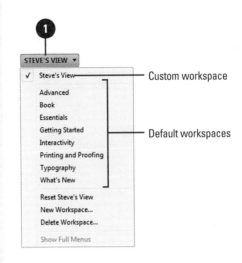

Custom workspace

Default workspaces

Delete a Workspace

1. Click the **Workspace** menu on the Application bar, and then click **Delete Workspace**.

   ◆ You can also click the **Window** menu, point to **Workspace**, and then click **Delete Workspace**.

   The Delete Workspace dialog box appears.

2. Select the workspace you want to delete.

3. Click **Delete**.

   The workspace is now deleted.

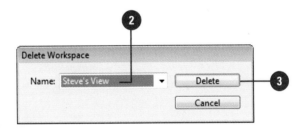

Using Undo and Redo

Probably one of the greatest inventions of the computer industry is the ability to Undo, and Redo. Now, if we could just figure out how to give real life an undo feature... that would be something. InDesign gives us the ability to undo our past mistakes, and redo something we wished we had not undone. However, you can no longer view actions, such as Set Preview and Show Guides with the undo feature (**New!**).

Undo or Redo One Action at a Time

◆ Click the **Edit** menu, and then click **Undo** to reverse your most recent action, such as typing a word or formatting a paragraph.

  TIMESAVER *Press Ctrl+Z (Win) or ⌘+Z (Mac) to undo.*

◆ Click the **Edit** menu, and then click **Redo** to restore the last action you reversed.

  TIMESAVER *Press Shift+Ctrl+Z to redo your undo.*

Click to Undo or Redo the previous command or action.

Managing Pages and Books

3

Introduction

Most documents are more than one page, so inserting new pages is a common practice in InDesign. You can quickly add a new blank page to a document using the Pages panel. The Pages panel allows you to visually display and navigate through all the pages in your document. When you work with multiple page documents, moving pages around is inevitable. You can simply drag pages in the Pages panel to rearrange them within a document or use the Move Page command on the Options menu to move them between documents. When you no longer need a page, you can quickly delete it from your document using the Pages panel.

A master page is one of the most important parts of creating an InDesign document. A master page holds and displays all the elements that you want to appear on every page in a document, such as headers, logos, page numbers, and footers. The master is like a background layer to a page. Everything on the background layer appears on the page in front of it. When you make a change to a master page, the change appears in all document pages unless you override the change.

Instead of creating long documents, you can break them up into smaller documents, like chapters, and then add them to a book. In InDesign, a book is not a single document. It simply keeps track of all the documents in the book and coordinates document page numbers, colors, and styles. When you create a book, you can synchronize page numbers, colors, and styles for all the documents in the book. Each book uses a file called the *style source* to control the style sheets, swatches, and master pages for all the documents in the book. When you make changes to the style source file, all the documents in the book are synchronized to the file.

What You'll Do

Use the Pages Panel

Insert Pages

Navigate Pages

Delete or Move Pages

Work with Page Spreads

Rotate Page Spreads

Create Master Pages

Work with Master Pages

Work with Page Numbers and Sections

Work with Chapter Numbers

Create and Use Text Variables

Create a Book

Manage Books

Create a Table of Contents

Adjust Layouts

Using the Pages Panel

The Pages panel allows you to visually display all the pages in your document. The Pages panel shows thumbnails for each page. At the top of the panel are the master pages for the document. A master page contains elements that are repeated on every page. When you're working with a multi-page document, the Pages panel is an essential part of working with pages. You can add and remove pages as well as navigate to and from pages. The Pages panel, like all panels, provides an Options menu where you can select page-related commands and Pages panel display options. The display options allow you to change page icons size, position, and location. In addition, you can also set options to show or hide icons for page transparency, transition, and spread rotation (**New!**).

Change the Pages Panel Display

1 Select the **Pages** panel.

◆ You can also click the **Window** menu, and then click **Pages**.

2 Click the **Options** menu on the panel, and then click **Panel Options**.

3 Select from the following Pages panel options:

◆ **Size.** Specify an icon size for Pages and Masters.

◆ **Show Vertically.** Select to show page or master page icons vertically.

◆ **Show Thumbnails.** Select to show page or master page icons as thumbnails.

4 Click the **Pages on Top** or **Masters on Top** option.

5 Click the **Resize** list arrow, and then select an option when you resize the Pages panel.

6 Click **OK**.

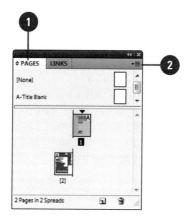

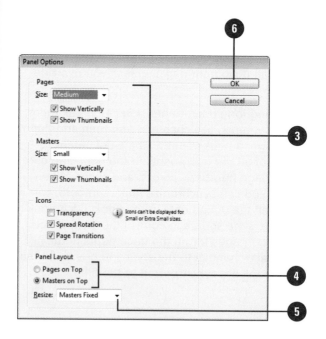

Show or Hide Pages Panel Icons

1. Select the **Pages** panel.

   ◆ You can also click the **Window** menu, and then click **Pages**.

2. Click the **Options** menu on the panel, and then click **Panel Options**.

3. Select from the following options for icon display:

   ◆ **Transparency.** Select to display icons when transparency is applied to a page or spread.

   ◆ **Spread Rotation.** Select to display icons when the spread view is rotated.

   ◆ **Page Transitions.** Select to display icons when page transitions are applied to a page or spread.

4. Click **OK**.

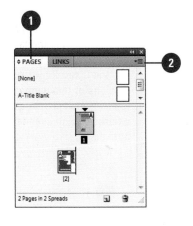

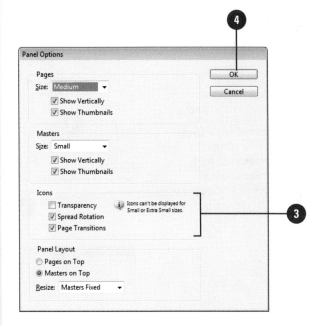

Inserting Pages

Most documents will be more than one page, so inserting new pages is a common practice in InDesign. You can quickly add a new blank page to a document using the Pages panel. You have several different methods to complete the task. You can use the New Page button on the page, drag a master page to the document area in the Pages panel, or use the Insert Pages command on the Options menu. If you're inserting only one or two pages, the first two methods work the best. If you want to insert multiple pages, the Insert Pages command is your best option, where you can use the Insert Pages dialog box to set additional options.

Insert Pages Using the Pages Panel

1. Select the **Pages** panel.

   ◆ You can also click the **Window** menu, and then click **Pages**.

2. Use any of the following methods to insert a page:

   ◆ Insert Page. Click the **Create New Page** button on the panel.

   ◆ Insert from Master Pages. Drag a master page or a nonmaster page from the master page area to the document page area of the panel.

3. Continue to insert pages as needed.

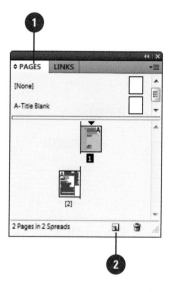

Did You Know?

You can duplicate a page. Select the Pages panel, select the pages or spreads you want to duplicate, and then drag the selected pages to the Create New Page button on the panel or use the Duplicate Spread command on the Options menu.

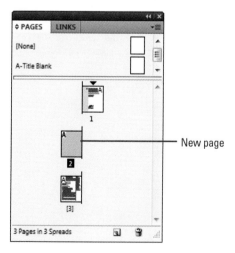

New page

Insert Multiple Pages Using the Insert Pages Dialog Box

① Select the **Pages** panel.

    ◆ You can also click the **Window** menu, and then click **Pages**.

② Click the **Options** menu, and then click **Insert Pages**.

③ Enter the number of pages that you want to insert.

④ Click the **Insert** list arrow, and then specify how you want to insert the pages:

    ◆ **After Page.** Inserts new pages after a specific page.

    ◆ **Before Page.** Inserts new pages before a specific page.

    ◆ **At Start of Document.** Inserts new pages at the start of the document.

    ◆ **At End of Document.** Inserts new pages at the end of the document.

⑤ Specify the specific page to use when you choose After Page or Before Page as your Insert option.

⑥ Click the **Master** list arrow, and then select a master or nonmaster page to use as the basis for the new pages.

⑦ Click **OK**.

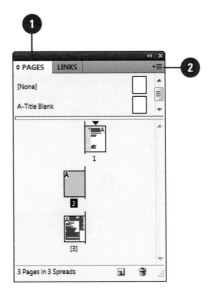

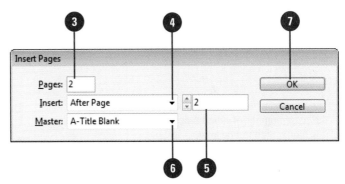

Navigating Pages

After you insert new pages into a document, you can use the Pages panel, Layout menu commands, and Status bar to navigate between them. As you work with pages in the Pages panel, there are two types of page selections. One targets a page and the other activates a page. A targeted page is a page selected in the Pages panel, while an activated page is a working page in the document window. When you target a page, you can apply a command in the Pages panel even though it may not be the current working page in the document window.

Target or Activate on a Page

1. Select the **Pages** panel.

   ◆ You can also click the **Window** menu, and then click **Pages**.

2. Use any of the following methods to select a page:

   ◆ Target a Page. Click a page in the Pages panel.

   The thumbnail is highlighted.

   ◆ Work on (Activate) a Page. Double-click a page in the Pages panel.

   The thumbnail is highlighted and the page number or name below it is highlighted in black.

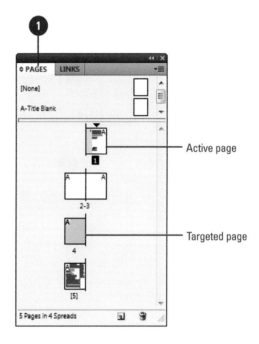

Active page

Targeted page

Navigate to Pages

◆ **Pages Panel.** Select the **Pages** panel, and then double-click the page in the panel that you want to work on.

◆ **Status Bar.** Use the navigation buttons on the Status bar to browse through pages or click the list arrow to select a specific page.

◆ **Layout Menu.** Click the **Layout** menu, and then select any of the following commands:

   ◆ **First Page.** Displays the first page in the document.

   ◆ **Previous Page.** Displays the previous page in the document.

   ◆ **Next Page.** Displays the next page in the document.

   ◆ **Last Page.** Displays the last page in the document.

   ◆ **Next Spread.** Displays the next spread of pages in the document.

   ◆ **Previous Spread.** Displays the previous spread of pages in the document.

   ◆ **Go To Page.** Displays the specified page in the document.

   ◆ **Go Back.** Displays the previously active page in the document.

   ◆ **Go Forward.** Displays the previously active page before the use of the Go Back command.

Pages panel

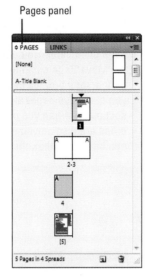

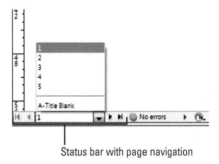

Status bar with page navigation

Layout menu with page navigation

Deleting or Moving Pages

When you no longer need a page, you can delete it from your document using the Pages panel. You can use the Delete Page or Delete Spread button on the panel or the same command on the Options menu. Moving and arranging pages is a common part of working with multiple page documents. You can simply drag pages in the Pages panel or use the Move Page command on the Options menu. When you drag pages, the cursor indicates new page location. With the Move Page command, you can move pages within the current document or to another open document. When you move the pages, objects in the slug and bleed areas are also moved (**New!**). Page numbers in the slug area display a number rather than the pasteboard index entry (**New!**).

Delete Pages

1. Select the **Pages** panel.

   ◆ You can also click the **Window** menu, and then click **Pages**.

2. Select the pages that you want to delete.

   ◆ You can use the Shift key to select contiguous pages or the Ctrl (Win) or ⌀⌘ (Mac) to select noncontiguous pages.

3. Click the **Delete Page** button on the panel.

   ◆ You can also click the **Options** menu, and then click **Delete Pages**.

   IMPORTANT *When you have a spread of pages selected, the button and command changes to Delete Spreads.*

4. Click **OK** to confirm the deletion.

   TIMESAVER *Hold down the Alt (Win) or Option (Mac) key, when you select the Delete Pages button or command to bypass the confirmation dialog box.*

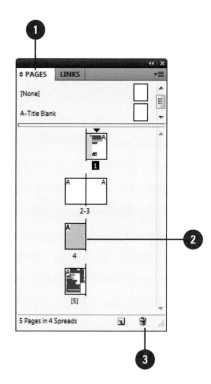

Move Pages by Dragging

1. Select the **Pages** panel.

2. Click the **Options** menu, and then select a move related option:

   ◆ **Allow Document Pages to Shuffle.** Enables or disables the shuffling of document pages.

   ◆ **Allow Selected Spread to Shuffle.** Enables or disables the shuffling of selected spread pages.

3. Drag a page next to or between spread pages.

   A straight black line indicates the move location with a shuffle. A bracket black line indicates the move location with attachment.

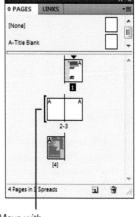

Move with attachment

Move Pages

1. Select the **Pages** panel.

2. Click the **Options** menu, and then click **Move Pages**.

3. Specify the pages that you want to move. Use a hyphen to designate a range, such as 1-4.

4. Click the **Destination** list arrow, select an option, and then enter a page number, if necessary.

5. Click the **Move To** list arrow, and then select a document location.

6. If you are moving the page(s) to a separate open file, select the **Delete Pages After Moving** check box if you want to delete the pages from the current document.

7. Click **OK**.

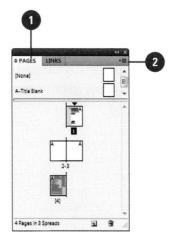

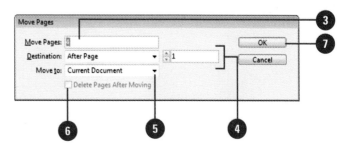

Working with Page Spreads

Most documents are either one or two page spreads. A single-page spread displays pages one at a time (top to bottom), while a two-page spread displays pages as facing pages (left and right). If you want to create a larger spread for a magazine foldout or a brochure, you can add more pages to a one or two page spread. These multiple-page spreads are also called **island spreads**. When you no longer want a larger spread, you can remove pages from the spread.

Add and Remove Pages from a Spread

① Select the **Pages** panel.

② Click the **Options** menu on the panel, and then click **Allow Document Pages to Shuffle** to deselect it.

③ To add pages, drag a page from the pages area, or a master page next to the spread where you want to add the page.

④ To remove pages, drag a page from the spread to outside of the spread, and then click **No**, if necessary.

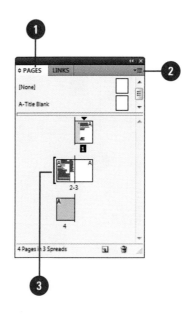

Did You Know?

You can keep pages in a spread together. Select the Pages panel, select the spread you want to protect, click the Options menu, and then click Allow Selected Spread To Shuffle to deselect it.

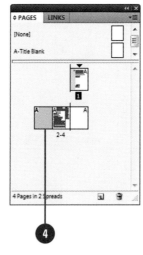

Rotating Page Spreads

If you need to work on non-horizontal design elements, such as a calendar, you can rotate the current spread in 90 degree increments (**New!**) to make it easier to work on. When you rotate the current spread view, you have full editing capabilities. When you're done, you can quickly clear the rotation to return to a normal view.

Rotate Page Spreads

1. Select the **Pages** panel.

2. Double-click the page numbers of the page spread you want to rotate.

3. Click the **Options** menu on the panel, point to **Rotate Spread View**, and then click **90° CW**, **90° CCW**, or **180°**.

   ◆ You can also click the **View** menu, point to **Rotate Spread**, and then click **90° CW**, **90° CCW**, or **180°**.

   A rotation icon appears next to the page indicating the spread is rotated.

4. Edit and modify the page spread the way you want.

5. Click the **Options** menu on the panel, point to **Rotate Spread View**, and then click **Clear Rotation**.

   ◆ You can also right-click (Win) or Control-click (Mac) the rotation icon to select a rotation spread command.

See Also

See "Using the Pages Panel" on pages 56-57 for more information on showing the spread rotation icon in the Pages panel.

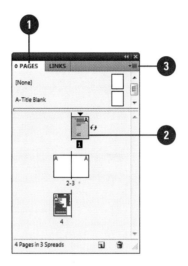

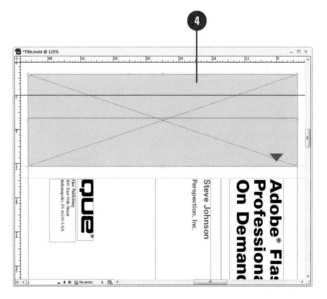

Creating Master Pages

ID 1.1, 2.11

A master page holds and displays all the elements that you want to appear on every page in a document, such as headers, logos, page numbers, and footers. The master is like a background layer to a page. Everything on the background layer appears on the page above it. Master elements appear on document pages surrounded by a dotted border to make them easy to identify. When you create a new document, you also create a master page. If you want to create additional master pages, you can create them from scratch or from an existing page or spread.

Add Objects to an Existing Master Page

1 Select the **Pages** panel.

◆ You can also click the **Window** menu, and then click **Pages**.

2 Double-click the master page in the master page area of the Pages panel.

The master page or two page spread appears in the document window.

3 Add text boxes, graphics, or any other elements you want on the page.

4 Double-click a page in the document page area of the Pages panel.

The elements added to the master page or spread appear on the document page.

Did You Know?

You can load master pages from another document. Select the Pages panel, click the Options menu, click Load Master Pages, select the file, and then click Open.

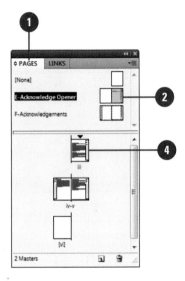

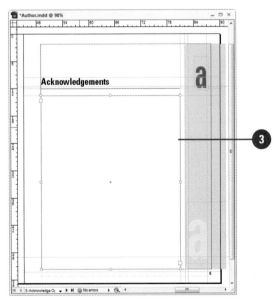

Create a Master Page from an Existing Page

1 Select the **Pages** panel.

- You can also click the **Window** menu, and then click **Pages**.

2 Drag a page or a spread from the document page area to the master page area.

- You can also select a page or spread, click the **Options** menu, and then click **Save As Master**.

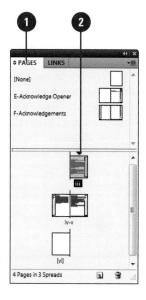
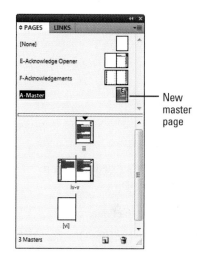

New master page

Create a Master Page from Scratch

1 Select the **Pages** panel.

- You can also click the **Window** menu, and then click **Pages**.

2 Click the **Options** menu on the panel, and then click **New Master**.

3 Select from the following Pages panel options:

- **Prefix.** Enter a prefix up to four characters. This identifies the applied master for each page.

- **Name.** Enter a name for the master page.

- **Based on Master.** Select an existing master on which to base the new master.

- **Number of Pages.** Enter the number of pages (1-10) you want in the master spread.

4 Click **OK**.

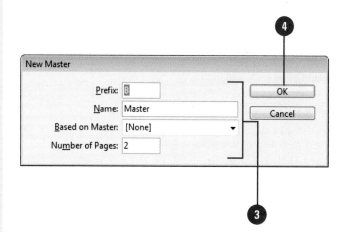

Working with Master Pages

ID 1.1, 2.11, 6.4

When you apply a master page to a document page, all the elements on the master page are attached and displayed on the document page. When you only want a selected number of elements from the master page on a document page, you can override or detach the elements you want. Overriding a master puts a copy of the master element on the document page and keeps the link, where you can make changes to it. The changes made on the document page don't affect the master; however, any changes to the same element on the master (separate from the document page) still appear from the master on the document page. Detaching a master overrides a master element and removes the link. Instead of overriding or detaching master elements, you have the option of hiding them

Apply a Master Page to a Document Page

1. Select the **Pages** panel.

    ◆ You can also click the **Window** menu, and then click **Pages**.

2. Drag a master page or spread from the master page area to a page or spread in the document page area.

3. To apply a master to multiple pages, select the pages in the document page area, and then Alt (Win) or Option (Mac) the master page you want to apply.

    ◆ You can also click the **Options** menu, click **Apply Master To Pages**, specify the options you want, and then click **OK**.

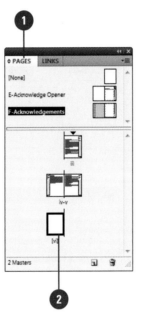

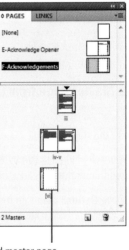

Selected master page applied to page

Did You Know?

You can change master page options. Select the Pages panel, select the master page, click the Options menu, click Master Options for *master page name*, specify the options you want, and then click OK.

Work with Master Pages

◆ **Delete Masters.** In the Pages panel, drag a master page you want to delete to the **Delete Selected Pages** button on the panel.

◆ **Copy Masters.** In the Pages panel, drag a master page you want to copy to the **Create New Page** button on the panel.

◆ **Hide Master Elements.** In the Pages panel, select the document page, click the **Options** menu, and then click **Hide Master Items**.

◆ **Override a Master Element.** In the Pages panel, click the **Options** menu, and then click **Allow Master Item Overrides On Selection** to select it. On a document page, Ctrl+Shift+click (Win) or ⌘+Shift+click (Mac) an element.

    ◆ You can also click the document page in the Pages panel, click the **Options** menu, and then click **Override All Master Page Items**.

◆ **Detach a Master Element.** On a document page, Ctrl+Shift+click (Win) or ⌘+Shift +click (Mac) an element to override it (see above). In the Pages panel, click the **Options** menu, and then click **Detach Selection From Master**.

    ◆ You can also click the **Options** menu, and then click **Detach All Objects From Master**.

◆ **Unassign Master.** In the Pages panel, drag the **[None]** master from the master page area to a page in the document page area.

All master elements are no longer attached to the document page.

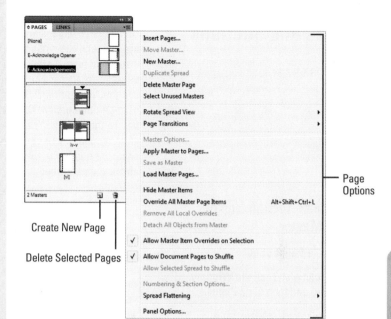

Create New Page

Delete Selected Pages

Page Options

Working with Page Numbers and Sections

ID 2.1, 2.11

One of the most common elements added to a master page is a page number. InDesign uses a special character to designate page numbers. On a master page, simply create a text box, place the insertion point in the box, and then insert the current page number marker. You can also insert and format additional text and variables in the text box to create a header or footer across the top or bottom of the page. You can also use the Numbering & Section Options dialog box to change the format of page numbers or the starting page number. If you want to insert text before the page number, you can specify a section prefix. In addition to page numbers, you can also define a section within a document with separate numbering. A section indicator icon (black triangle) appears above the page thumbnail in the Pages panel.

Add a Page or Section Number to a Page Master

1. Select the **Pages** panel.

   ◆ You can also click the **Window** menu, and then click **Pages**.

2. Double-click the master page in the master page area of the Pages panel.

   The master page or two page spread appears in the document window.

3. Select the **Type** tool on the Tools panel.

4. Click where you want to create a text box for the page or section number.

5. Click the **Type** menu, point to **Insert Special Character**, point to **Markers**, and then click **Current Page Number** or **Section Marker**.

   A special character marker appears in the text box. The current page or section number is the prefix for the master page.

6. For facing pages, repeat steps 3-5 for the other page.

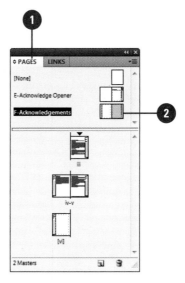

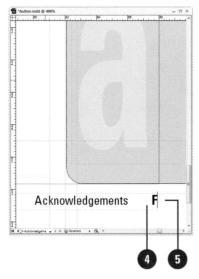

Set Page Numbering and Section Options

1 Select the **Pages** panel.

2 Double-click the page where you want to start the page numbering or section to start.

3 Click the **Layout** menu, and then click **Numbering & Section Options**.

4 Select the **Start Section** check box to start a new section.

5 Click the **Automatic Page Numbering** or **Start Page Numbering At** option.

6 If you selected the Start Page Numbering At option, specify the following options:

- ◆ **Section Prefix.** Enter a prefix that will appear before the page number, if desired.

- ◆ **Style.** Select a style for the page number.

- ◆ **Section Marker.** Enter text, such as *Section*, for a section within a document.

- ◆ **Include Prefix When Numbering Pages.** Select this option if you want to add the section prefix to the page number.

7 Click **OK**.

A section indicator icon (black triangle) appears above the page thumbnail in the Pages panel.

8 Double-click the page where you want the section to end, and then repeat steps 3-7 for section numbering (except, in this case, you will need to deselect the **Start Section** check box).

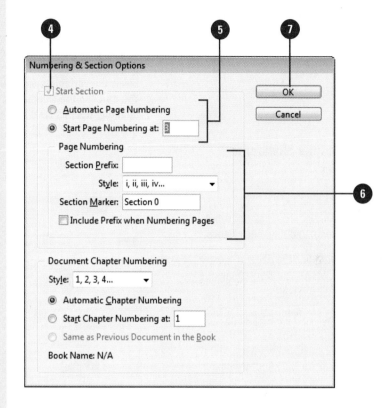

Working with Chapter Numbers

ID 6.5

Like page numbers, you can insert chapter numbers into documents that will be part of a book. Unlike a page number, a chapter number is a predefined text variable. The chapter number variable can be updated automatically and formatted as text. To insert a chapter number variable, create a text box, place the insertion point in the box, and then insert the variable using the Text Variable submenu on the Type menu. You can use the Numbering & Section Options dialog box to change updating options for chapter numbers.

Add a Chapter Number to a Document

1. Select the **Pages** panel.

   ◆ You can also click the **Window** menu, and then click **Pages**.

2. Double-click the page or master page where you want to place a chapter number.

3. Select the **Type** tool on the Tools panel.

4. Click where you want to create a text box for the chapter number.

5. Click the **Type** menu, point to **Text Variables**, point to **Insert Variable**, and then click **Chapter Number**.

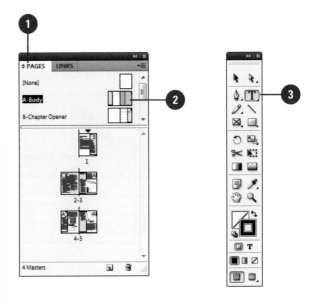

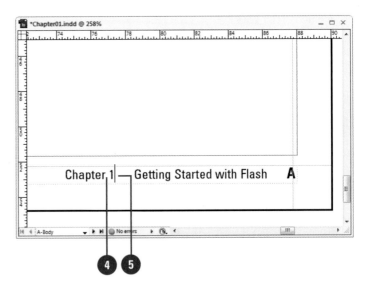

Set Chapter Numbering Options

1. Select the **Pages** panel.

2. Double-click the page where you want to start the chapter numbering.

3. Click the **Layout** menu, and then click **Numbering & Section Options**.

4. Click the **Style** list arrow, and then select a chapter numbering style.

5. Select one of the following options:

   ◆ **Automatic Chapter Numbering.**

   ◆ **Start Chapter Numbering At.** Enter a starting chapter number.

   ◆ **Same as Previous Document in the Book.**

6. Click **OK**.

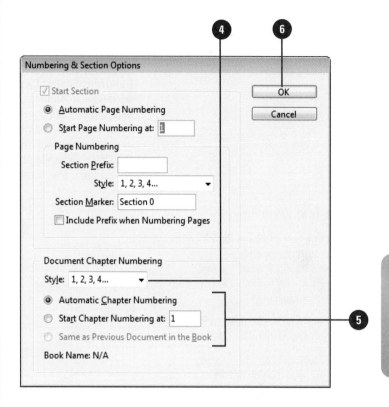

Creating and Using Text Variables

ID 2.11, 6.2, 6.5

A text variable is an element that varies based on circumstances in the document. You can use one of the preset text variables that comes with InDesign or you can create your own. Some of the preset variables include Running Header and Chapter Number. These are useful for adding information to master pages. Other variables, such as Creation Date, Modification Date, Output Date, and File Name, are useful for adding file information to the slug area for printing. To use a text variable, simply create a text box, place the insertion point in the box, and then insert the variable using the Text Variable submenu on the Type menu. You can also insert and format additional text along with the Running Header variable in the text box to create a header or footer across the top or bottom of the page on a document or master page.

Define a Text Variable

1. To define text variables for all documents, close all open documents. Otherwise, the text variable is only available for the current document.

2. Click the **Type** menu, point to **Text Variables**, and then click **Define**.

3. Click **New**, or select an existing variable, and then click **Edit**.

4. Type a name for the variable.

5. Click the **Type** list arrow, and then select a variable type.

6. Specify the options you want for the selected variable type.

    Options vary; some of the common options include:

    ◆ **Text Before or Text After.** Insert text to add before or after the text variable.

    ◆ **Style.** Select a style for the selected variable type.

7. Click **OK**.

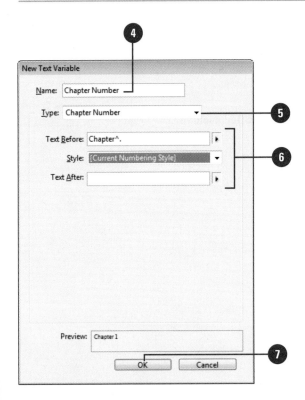

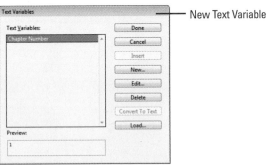

New Text Variable

Work with Text Variables

◆ **Insert Text Variables.** Click to place the insertion point where you want the text variable (on a document or master page), click the **Type** menu, point to **Text Variables**, point to **Insert Variable**, and then select a variable.

◆ **Delete Text Variables.** Click the **Type** menu, point to **Text Variables**, click **Define**, select the variable, and then click **Delete**.

◆ **Convert Text Variables to Text.** Select the text variable in the document, click the **Type** menu, point to **Text Variables**, and then click **Convert Variable to Text**.

   ◆ To convert all instances of the text variable, click the **Type** menu, point to **Text Variables**, click **Define**, select the variable, and then click **Convert To Text**.

◆ **Import Text Variables from Another Document.** Click the **Type** menu, point to **Text Variables**, click **Define**, click **Load**, double-click the document with the variables, select the variables that you want in the Load Text Variables dialog box, and then click **OK**.

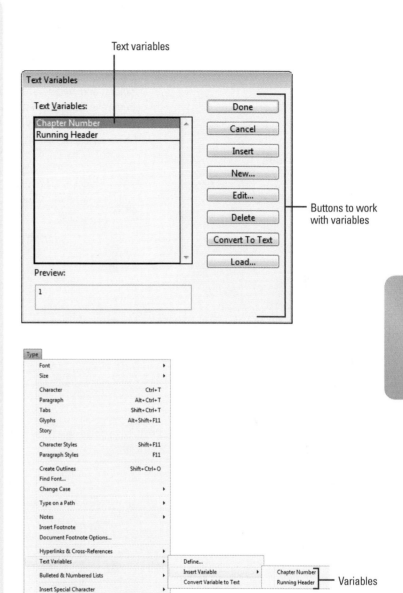

Text variables

Buttons to work with variables

Variables

Creating a Book

ID 6.2

Instead of creating long InDesign documents, you can break them up into smaller documents, like chapters, and then create a book to bring them all together. A book is not a document. It simply keeps track of all the documents in the book and coordinates document page numbers, colors, and styles. When you create a new book or open an existing book, the Book panel appears, displaying the book name in the title tab. In the Book panel, you can add, remove, move, or open documents.

Create a New Book

1. Click the **File** menu, point to **New**, and then click **Book**.

2. Enter a name for the book file.

3. Navigate to the drive or folder location where you want to save the book.

4. Click **Save**.

   The tab for the Book panel displays the name of the book.

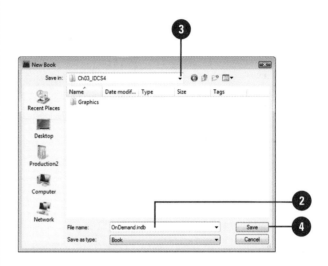

Open an Existing Book

1. Click the **File** menu, and then click **Open**.

2. Navigate to the drive or folder location where the book you want to open is stored.

3. Select the book you want to open.

4. Click **Open**.

   The Book panel opens.

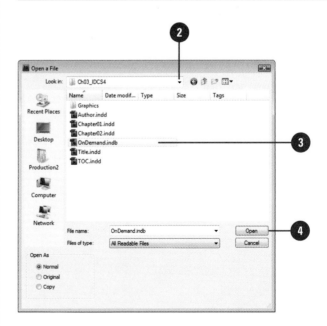

Add, Remove, Move, or Open Documents in a Book

1 Open the book you want to edit.

2 Do any of the following:

- ◆ **Add a Document.** Click the **Add Document** button on the panel, locate the document you want to add, and then click **Open**.

- ◆ **Remove a Document.** Select a document in the Book panel, and then click the **Remove Document** button at the bottom of the panel.

- ◆ **Move a Document.** Drag a document to a new position in the Book panel.

- ◆ **Open a Document.** Double-click a document in the Book panel. An open book icon appears, indicating the book is open.

3 Click the **Save Book** button on the panel.

4 Click the **Close** button to close the book.

Did You Know?

You can replace a document in a book. Open the book, select the document that you want to replace, click the Options menu, click Replace Document, select the replacement file, and then click Open.

You can print an entire book. Open the book, and then click the Print Book button on the panel.

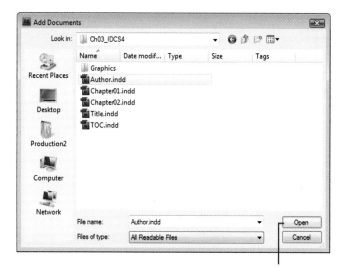

Open a document

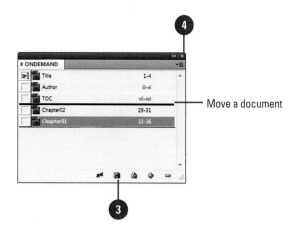

Move a document

Managing Books

 ID 6.2

When you create a book, you can synchronize page numbers, colors, and styles for all the documents in the book. Each book uses a file called the *style source* to control the style sheets (including character, paragraph, table, and object styles), swatches, conditional text, numbered lists, text variables, and master pages for all the documents in the book. When you make changes to the style source file, all or selected documents in the book are synchronized to the file. You can set synchronizing options to specify the features that you want to keep up-to-date in the Synchronize Options dialog box. With the Smart Match Style Groups synchronize option, you can synchronize a book without creating duplicate styles (**New!**) .

Synchronize Books

◆ **Synchronize Options.** Open the book, click the **Options** menu, click **Synchronize Options**, select the options you want to synchronize, and then click **OK**.

◆ **Set Style Source.** Open the book, and then click the **Style Source** box next to the name of the document.

◆ **Synchronize Style Source for a Book.** Open the book, click the **Synchronize Book** button on the panel.

◆ **Synchronize Style Source for a Document.** Open the book, select the document, click the **Options** menu, and then click **Synchronize Selected Documents**.

Did You Know?

You can set page numbers for each document in a book. Open the book, click the Options menu, click Document Numbering Options, specify the options you want, and then click OK. See "Working with Page Numbers," on page 71 for details about the page numbering options.

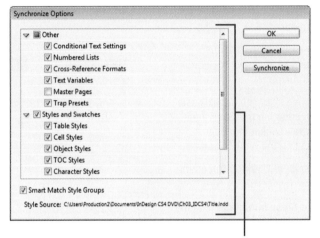

Synchronize options

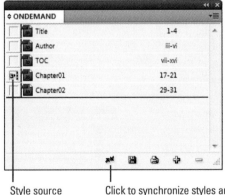

Style source   Click to synchronize styles and swatches with the Style Source

Set Page Numbering Options in a Book

1. Open the book you want to change.

2. Click the **Options** menu, and then click **Book Page Numbering Options**.

3. Select one of the following Page Order options:

   ◆ **Continue from previous document.** Starts new pages in sequence.

   ◆ **Continue on next odd page.** Starts new pages on an odd number.

   ◆ **Continue on next even page.** Starts new pages on an even number.

4. Select any of the following options:

   ◆ **Insert Blank Page.** Select to insert a blank page when using odd or even page numbers.

   ◆ **Automatically Update Page & Section Numbers.** Select to automatically adjust page numbers in book documents.

5. Click **OK**.

6. To update numbering in a book, click the **Options** menu, choose **Update Numbering**, and then click any of the following:

   ◆ **Update Page & Section Numbers.**

   ◆ **Update Chapter & Paragraph Numbers.**

   ◆ **Update All Numbers.**

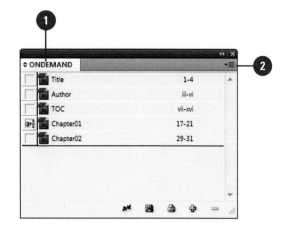

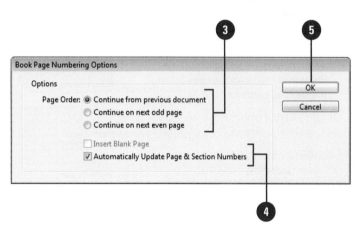

Creating a Table of Contents

ID 6.3, 7.3

A table of contents (TOC) appears at the beginning of a document, typically a long one, with page numbers associated with the beginning of main sections of the document. InDesign creates a table of contents based on the styles applied to paragraphs in the document. The table of content displays the text and page number associated with the paragraph styles. For example, when you apply different styles for chapter and topic titles in this book, you create a table of contents based on chapters and topics. So, before you can create a table of contents, you need to apply paragraph styles to text in your document.

Prepare for and Create a Table of Contents

1. To prepare for creating a table of contents, do the following:

   ◆ **Add Page for TOC.** Add a page for the table of contents.

   ◆ **Add Paragraph Styles.** Apply different paragraph styles to the text that you want to use in the table of contents.

2. Click the **Layout** menu, and then click **Table of Contents**.

3. Enter text for the title of the table of contents, and then use the Styles menu to select a style for the title text.

4. Select the paragraph styles that are applied to text in your document (under Other Styles), and then click **Add** to include them in the other list (under Include Paragraph Styles).

   ◆ To remove a style, select it (under Include Paragraph Styles), and then click **Remove**.

5. To format an entry in the table of contents, select the entry (under Include Paragraph Styles), click the **Entry Style** list arrow, and then select a style.

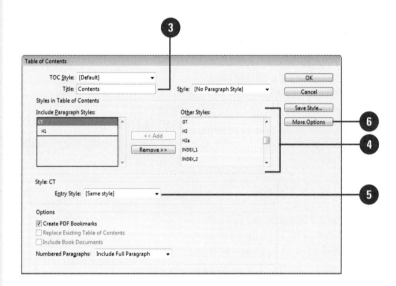

6. Click **More Options** to display additional options.

7. Select any of the following advanced options:

    ◆ **Page Number.** Select a position for the entry's page number.

    ◆ **Between Entry and Number.** Select a separator character between the entry and the number.

    ◆ **Sort Entries in Alphabetical Order.** Select to alphabetize the table of contents.

    ◆ **Level.** Select an indent level for each entry in the table of contents.

8. Select any of the following options:

    ◆ **Create PDF Bookmarks.** Select to add bookmarks to the PDF created from the table of contents.

    ◆ **Replace Existing Table of Contents.** Select to update or change the table of contents.

    ◆ **Include Book Documents.** Select to create a table of contents of all the documents in a book.

    ◆ **Numbered Paragraphs.** Select to format how paragraphs with auto numbering are formatted.

    ◆ **Run-In.** Select to create a single paragraph table of contents with each entry separated by a semicolon (;) and a space.

    ◆ **Include Text on Hidden Layers.** Select to use hidden text on layers.

9. Click **OK**.

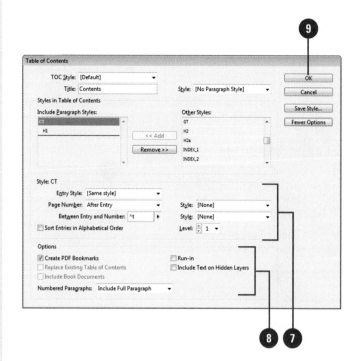

Adjusting Layouts

If you ever need to change the page size or margins after you have already added a document page or created a master page, you can enable the Layout Adjustment option to have InDesign adjust the layout and position of elements on document and master pages. The Layout Adjustment dialog box allows you to enable the option and set other related adjustment options, such as Allow Graphics and Groups to Resize and Ignore Object and Layer Locks.

Change Layout Adjustment Options

1. Click the **Layout** menu, and then click **Layout Adjustment**.

2. Select the **Enable Layout Adjustment** check box.

3. Select from the following options:

   - **Snap Zone.** Enter a distance value for snapping an object to a margin, column guide, or page boundary.

   - **Allow Graphics and Groups to Resize.** Select to allow graphics and groups to resize during the adjustment.

   - **Allow Ruler Guides to Move.** Select to allow ruler guides to move during the adjustment.

   - **Ignore Ruler Guide Alignments.** Select to keep objects from moving along ruler guides during the adjustment.

   - **Ignore Object and Layer Locks.** Select to move locked objects and layers during the adjustment.

4. Click **OK**.

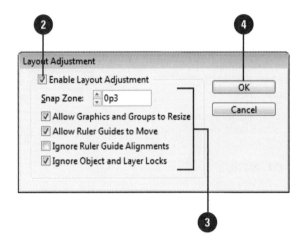

See Also

See "Setting Up a Document" on pages 34-35 for more information on changing the document page size and margins.

Working with Text

Introduction

InDesign comes with two main type tools: Type and Type on a Path. The Type tool allows you to create a rectangle text frame where you can store text in your document, while the Type on a Path tool allows you to add text along the inner or outer edge of a path.

Before you can work with text in InDesign, you need to select it. You can select the entire text frame or the characters in the text frame. You can use the type tools to select only the characters in the text frame, not the text frame itself, or use the Selection and Direct Selection tools to select both characters and the text frame. If you type, paste, or import more text than a text frame can hold, an overflow symbol (a tiny red plus sign in a square) appears on the edge of the text frame. You can reshape the text frame to accommodate the extra text or create a thread (link) to another text frame. You can thread overflow text from one text frame to a new or existing text frame.

InDesign provides two panels to modify characters and paragraphs. With the Character panel, you can change the font family (for example, Arial or Times New Roman) and style (Italic, Bold, or Condensed), as well as change other text attributes, such as size, kerning, scale, tracking, leading, and language. With the Paragraphs panel, you can change text alignment, indenting, and before and after spacing.

When integrating artwork and graphics with your text, you can wrap the text in a text frame around another object, such as a graphic. Another type effect, Create Outlines, allows you to convert characters in a text frame into a separate object with a path.

What You'll Do

Use Type Tools

Create Type

Create Path Type

Import and Flow Text

Work with Overflow Text

Use Smart Text Reflow

Type and Select Text

Edit Text with Autocorrect

Copy and Move Text

Change Fonts and Font Size

Lead, Kern, and Track Text

Scale and Skew Text

Align, Indent, and Space Paragraphs

Create a Drop Cap

Apply a Paragraph Rule

Set Tabs

Work with Glyphs

Insert Special Text Characters

Set Text Frame Options

Wrap Text Around an Object

Create Type Outlines

Add Page Numbers to Continued Text

Using Type Tools

 ID 1.9

InDesign comes with two main type tools: Type and Type on a Path. The Type tool allows you to create a rectangle text frame where you can store text in your document, while the Type on a Path tool allows you to add text along the inner or outer edge of a path. In addition to the type tools, you can also use the Frame tools—Rectangle, Ellipse, and Polygon—to add text to your document.

Use Type Tools

1. Click the Type tool slot on the Tools panel.

   ◆ Click the arrow on the right of the Type tools menu to create a detachable panel.

2. Click one of the following Type tools:

   ◆ **Type.** Creates a text frame box.

   ◆ **Type on a Path.** Creates text along the outer edge of an open or closed path.

3. For the Type tool, drag to draw a text box. For the Type on a Path tool, click on a path.

4. Type some text.

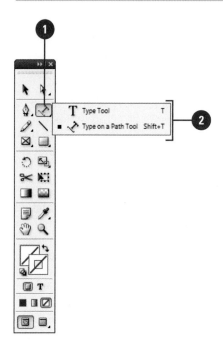

Adobe InDesign Type Tool —4

Creating Type in a Text Frame

With the Type tool, you can create a rectangle text box any size that you want. Simply, select the Type tool on the Tools pane, drag to create a text frame and then start typing. When you type text in a text frame, it automatically wraps to the size of the frame. If you type more text than the frame can hold, an overflow symbol (a tiny red plus sign in a square) appears on the edge of the rectangle box. You can reshape the text frame object to display the text or create a thread (link) to another text frame.

Create Type in a Text Frame

1. Select the **Type** tool on the Tools panel.

2. Drag to create a rectangle text box the size that you want.

   A flashing insertion point appears in the text frame.

3. Type some text. The text automatically wraps to the shape of the text frame. Press Enter (Win) or Return (Mac) if you want to start a new line.

   ◆ If the overflow symbol appears, deselect the text frame, select the **Direct Selection** tool on the Tools panel, and then drag a corner to reshape the text frame.

Adobe InDesign Type Tool

Creating Type Using Frame Tools

In addition to the Type tool, you can also use the Frame tools—Rectangle, Ellipse, and Polygon—to add text to your document. Instead of a rectangle shape for type, you can create irregular shapes to store text in your document. In addition to creating a polygon shape, you can also use the Polygon Frame tool to create a star shape for type. You can drag to create a frame box to the size that you want. If you need a frame box to be an exact size, you can click a blank area with the Rectangle and Ellipse tools or set width and height settings on the Control panel.

Create a Rectangle or Elliptical Frame for Type

1. Select the **Rectangle Frame** or **Ellipse Frame** tool on the Tools panel.

2. Drag to create a rectangle or elliptical frame the size that you want.

   ◆ To create a frame to an exact size, click a blank area, specify the width and height you want, and then click **OK**.

3. Select the **Type** tool on the Tools panel.

4. Click in the frame, and then type some text. The text automatically wraps to the shape of the text frame. Press Enter (Win) or Return (Mac) if you want to start a new line.

   ◆ If the overflow symbol appears, deselect the text frame, select the **Direct Selection** tool on the Tools panel, and then drag a corner to reshape the text frame.

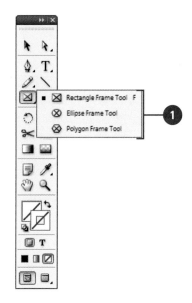

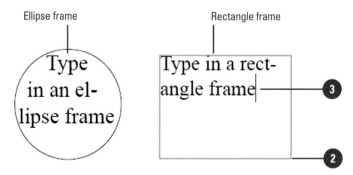

Ellipse frame

Type in an ellipse frame

Rectangle frame

Type in a rectangle frame

Create a Polygon Frame for Type

1. Double-click the **Polygon Frame** tool on the Tools panel.

2. Enter a **Number of Sides** value for the polygon.

3. Leave the **Star Inset** value at 0% to create a polygon.

4. Click **OK**.

5. Drag to create a polygon frame box the size that you want.

   ◆ As you drag, press the Up or Down arrow keys to increase or decrease the number of sides.

6. Click in the frame with the **Type** tool, and then type some text. The text automatically wraps to the shape of the text frame. Press Enter (Win) or Return (Mac) if you want to start a new line.

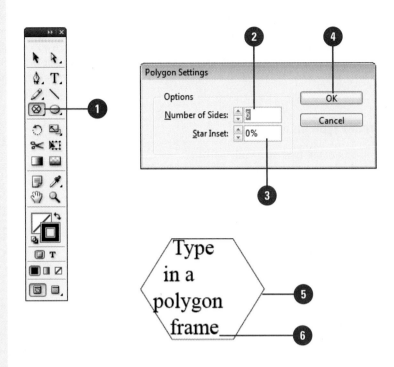

Create a Star Frame for Type

1. Double-click the **Polygon Frame** tool on the Tools panel.

2. Enter a **Number of Sides** value for the star.

3. Enter a **Star Inset** value. The higher the amount, the sharper the points.

4. Click **OK**.

5. Drag to create a star frame box the size that you want.

   ◆ As you drag, press the Up or Down arrow keys to increase or decrease the number of sides.

6. Click in the frame with the **Type** tool, and then type some text. The text automatically wraps to the shape of the text frame. Press Enter (Win) or Return (Mac) if you want to start a new line.

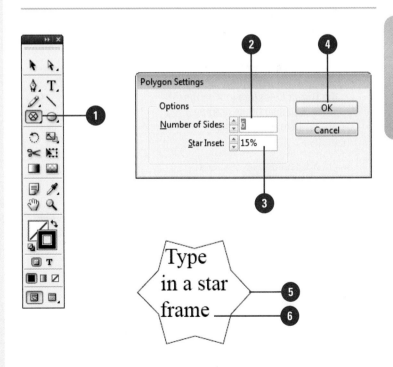

Creating Path Type

 ID 1.9

With the Type on a Path tools, you can add type along the inner or outer edge of a path. You can place the text on either side of the path, but not on both. If you initially place it on the inner part of the path, you can always move it to the outer part of the path later. When you select text on a path, brackets appear that you can drag to adjust the position and placement of the text.

Create Type on a Path

1. Select the **Type on a Path** tool on the Tools panel.

2. Click on the edge of the path (closed or open) to which you want to add type.

   A flashing insertion point appears in the text frame. Any fill or stroke on the object is removed.

3. Type some text. The text automatically wraps to the shape of the text frame. Don't press Enter (Win) or Return (Mac).

   The type appears along the edge of the object, conforms to its shape, and removes the fill and stroke.

   ◆ If the overflow symbol appears, deselect the text frame, select the **Direct Selection** tool on the Tools panel, and then drag a corner to reshape the text frame.

4. Select a selection tool or select the type tool again.

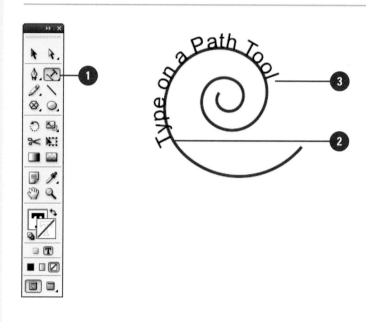

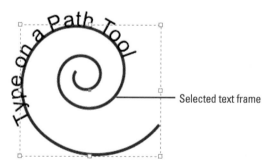

Selected text frame

Did You Know?

You can delete the text on a path. With a selection tool, select the text path frame, click the Type menu, point to Type On A Path, and then click Delete Type From Path.

Modify Type on a Path

1. Select the **Direct Selection** tool on the Tools panel.

2. Click on the type.

   Center, left, and right brackets appear around the type.

3. Drag the bracket (not the square) to adjust the position of the type on a path.

   ◆ **Swap Sides.** Drag the Center bracket to the other side to change the inner/outer position of the type along the path.

   ◆ **Left.** Drag to position the left side (or starting point) of the type along the path.

   ◆ **Center.** Drag left or right to position the type along the path.

   ◆ **Right.** Drag to position the right side (or ending point) of the type along the path.

   If the overflow symbol appears, deselect the text frame, select the **Direct Selection** tool on the Tools panel, and then drag a corner to reshape the text frame.

4. To change type on path options, click the **Type** menu, point to **Type on a Path**, and then click **Options**.

   ◆ Select the **Preview** check box to view your changes as you make them.

5. Specify the options (Effect, Flip, Align, To Path, and Spacing) you want, and then click **OK**.

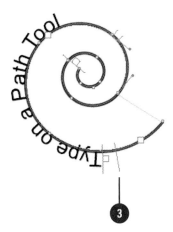

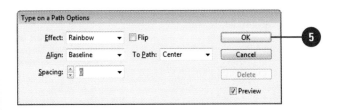

Importing Text

ID 2.8

If you have text from another document that you want to use in your InDesign document, you can use the Place command to import it. You can import text from the following text formats: plain text (TXT), Rich Text Format (RTF), Microsoft Word (DOC or DOCX), or Microsoft Excel (XLS or XLSX). When you import text using the Place command, InDesign allows you to place the text in a new text frame or an existing one.

Import Text

1. Click the **File** menu, and then click **Place**.

2. Click the **Files of Type** (Win) or **Enable** (Mac) list arrow, and then click **Importable Files** or select a text format:

   ◆ **Text Import.** Plain text.

   ◆ **Microsoft Word.** Microsoft Word 2003 (DOC) or earlier.

   ◆ **Microsoft Word 2007.** Microsoft Word 2007 (DOCX) or later.

   ◆ **RTF.** Rich Text Format (RTF).

   ◆ **Microsoft Excel.** Microsoft Excel 2003 (XLS) or earlier.

   ◆ **Microsoft Excel 2007.** Microsoft Excel 2007 (XLSX) or later.

3. Navigate to the drive or folder location with the text file you want to import.

4. Select the text file you want to place.

5. Select the **Replace Selected Item** check box to replace the selected item with the imported text.

6. Click **Open**.

   The imported text is placed in a loaded text cursor.

7. Click or drag a text frame with the loaded text cursor to place the text where you want it in your document.

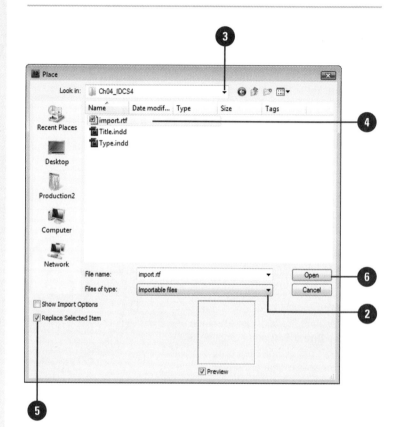

Imported text

Import Text with Options

1. Click the **File** menu, and then click **Place**.

2. Click the **Files of Type** (Win) or **Enable** (Mac) list arrow, and then click **Importable Files**.

3. Navigate to the drive or folder location with the text file you want to import.

4. Select the text file you want to place.

5. Select the **Show Import Options** check box to select import options.

6. Click **Open**.

7. Select the options you want. Options vary depending on the imported file format.

8. Click **OK**.

   The imported text is placed in a loaded text cursor.

9. Click or drag a text frame with the loaded text cursor to place the text where you want it in your document.

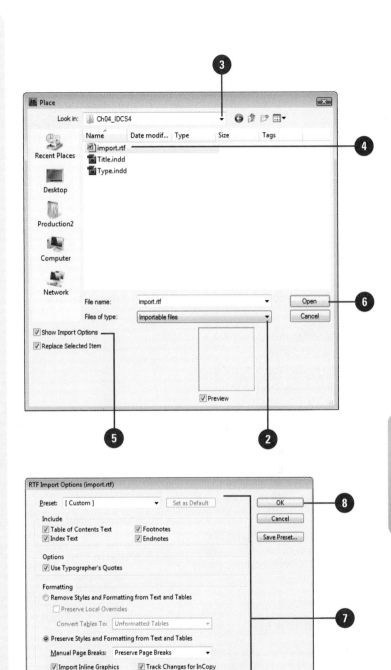

Flowing Imported Text

ID 2.4, 2.8

When you import text into your document, InDesign imports the text into a loaded text cursor with a small text icon and the first part of the text. When the text is loaded, you have several options to place the text into your document. You can create a new text frame or add the text to an existing text frame in a document or master page. When the loaded text cursor displays straight lines, the text will be placed in a new text frame. When the loaded text cursor displays curved lines, the text will be placed in an existing text frame. After you import the text, you can reflow the text manually with the overflow symbol (a tiny red plus sign in a square), or automatically with keyboard options.

Import and Flow Text

1. Click the **File** menu, and then click **Place**.

2. Navigate to and select the text file you want to place, and then click **Open**.

   The imported text is placed in a loaded text cursor.

3. Use any of the following to place the imported text in your document:

   ◆ **New Text Frame.** Drag to create a text frame the size you want.

   ◆ **New Text Frame within Margins.** Click to create a text frame the width of the margins.

   ◆ **Existing Text or Master Text Frame.** With the text or master text frame not selected, click inside the text frame.

Did You Know?

You can create a master text frame when you create a new document. Click the File menu, point to New, click Document, select the Master Text Frame check box, and then click OK.

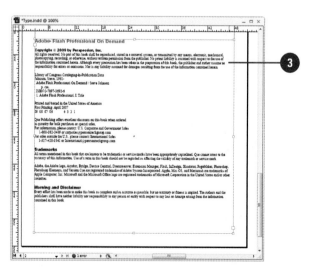

Import and Autoflow Text

1. Click the **File** menu, and then click **Place**.

2. Navigate to and select the text file you want to place, and then click **Open**.

   The imported text is placed in a loaded text cursor.

3. Use any of the following to place the imported text in your document:

   ◆ **Semi-Autoflow.** Hold down Alt (Win) or Option (Mac), and then click in an existing frame or drag a new frame. Continue to hold down Alt (Win) or Option (Mac), and then click or drag to create another text frame that is linked to the first.

   ◆ **Autoflow.** Hold down Shift, and then point to an existing frame or master frame (unselected) or click at the top-left corner of the margins, click to flow the text on the page and create as many additional pages as needed.

   ◆ **Autoflow on Fixed Pages.** Hold down Shift+Alt (Win) or Shift+Option (Mac), and then click in the master text frame or the margins of the page to flow text on the number of pages in the document.

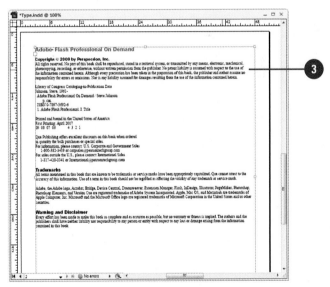

Working with Overflow Text

ID 2.4

If you type, paste, or import more text than a text frame can hold, an overflow symbol (a tiny red plus sign in a square) appears on the edge of the text frame. You can reshape the text frame to display the text or create a thread (link) to another text frame. You can thread overflow text from one text frame to a new or existing text frame. After you create a thread between two or more text frames, you can use the Show Text Threads command on the View menu to display the thread connection. If you no longer want to thread two or more text frames, you can unthread or disconnect them. When you unthread text frames, the text in the text frame remains in the first text frame (it may still overflow). When you disconnect text frames, the text in the text frames remains where it is.

Thread Overflow Text and Show Text Threads

1. Select the **Selection** tool on the Tools panel.

2. Select the text frame with the overflow text.

3. Click the **Out Port** icon on the selected object.

   TIMESAVER *Double-click an Out Port icon with the Selection tool to create a linked copy of the text frame.*

   The pointer changes to the Loaded Text cursor.

4. To create a new text frame for the overflow text, click a blank area or drag to create a text frame.

   To use an existing text frame, click in an existing text frame.

   Overflow text from the first text frame threads to the second text frame.

5. To display a text thread between text frames, select a threaded text frame, click the **View** menu, and then click **Show Text Threads**.

Adobe® Flash Professional On Demand

Copyright © 2009 by Perspection, Inc.
All rights reserved. No part of this book shall be reproduced, stored in a retrieval system, or transmitted by any means, electronic, mechanical, photocopying, recording, or otherwise, without written permission from the publisher. No patent liability is assumed with respect to the use of the information contained herein. Although every precaution has been taken in the preparation of this book, the publisher and author assume no responsibility for errors or omissions. Nor is any liability assumed for damages resulting from the use of the information contained herein.

Library of Congress Cataloging-in-Publication Data
Johnson, Steve, 1961-
  Adobe Flash Professional On Demand / Steve Johnson
    p. cm.
  ISBN 0-7897-3692-6
  1. Adobe Flash Professional. I. Title

Printed and bound in the United States of America
First Printing: April 2007
09 08 07 06   4 3 2 1

Unthread Text Frames

1. Select the **Selection** tool on the Tools panel.

2. Select a threaded text frame.

3. Double-click the **In Port** or **Out Port** icon on the selected object.

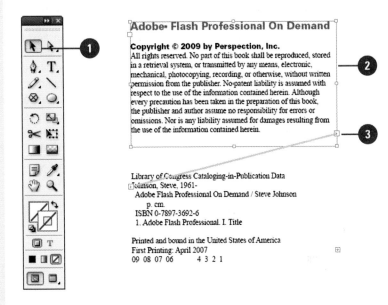

Change the Thread Between Frames

1. Select the **Selection** tool on the Tools panel.

2. Select a threaded text frame.

3. Click the **In Port** or **Out Port** icon on the selected object.

4. To create a new text frame for the overflow text, click a blank area or drag to create a text frame.

   To use an existing text frame, click in an existing text frame.

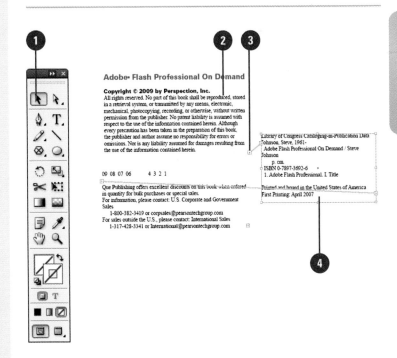

Using Smart Text Reflow

 ID 2.4

Set Smart Text Reflow Options

1 Click the **Edit** (Win) or **InDesign** (Mac) menu, point to **Preferences**, and then click **Type**.

2 Select the **Smart Text Reflow** check box to enable the feature.

3 Select from the following Smart Text Reflow options:

- **Add Pages To.** Specify where you want to add overflow pages.

- **Limit To Master Text Frames.** Select to only reflow text to master text frames. Deselect to reflow text in a threaded text frame from one page to another.

- **Preserve Facing-Page Spreads.** Select to add two page spreads for text reflow. Deselect to add a single page for text reflow and shuffle pages.

- **Delete Empty Pages.** Select to delete pages when an empty text frame is the only object on the page.

4 Click **OK**.

Smart Text Reflow (**New!**) allows you to automatically add or remove pages when you are typing and editing text. You can use Smart Text Reflow on master text frames (the default) and document text frames. When you want to reflow text in document text frames, the text frame needs to be threaded (linked) to another text frame on a different page. Before you reflow text, you can set Smart Text Reflow options in the Type preferences dialog box.

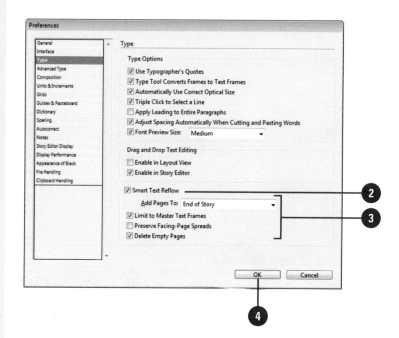

Use Smart Text Reflow

① In Type preferences, select the **Smart Text Reflow** and **Delete Empty pages** check boxes.

② Hold down Ctrl+Shift (Win) or ⌘+Shift (Mac), and then click the master text frame to override it.

③ Type text until you fill the text frame to automatically add a page, or delete enough text to automatically delete a page.

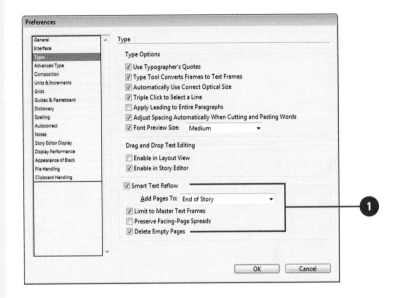

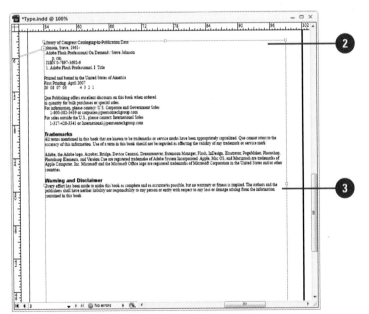

Typing and Selecting Text

ID 2.2

Before you can work with text in InDesign, you need to select it. You can select the entire text frame or the characters in the text frame. The selection tools (Selection and Direct Selection) allow you to select both characters and its object. You can use the type tools to select only the characters in the text frame, but not the object. When you add text to a text frame, pressing Enter (Win) or Return (Mac) creates a new paragraph. If you want to force a line break, known as a soft return, instead of a new paragraph, you can press Shift+Enter (Win) or Shift+Return (Mac).

Select Type and its Object

1. Select the **Selection** or **Direct Selection** tool on the Tools panel.

2. Use the appropriate selection method:

    ◆ **Type.** Click on the text.

    ◆ **Path Type.** Click on the path or text.

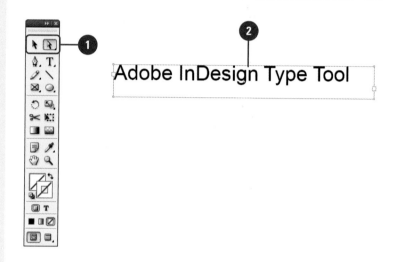

Type Text

1. Select the **Type** tool on the Tools panel.

    TIMESAVER *With a selection tool, double-click text to place the insertion point.*

2. Click to place the insertion point where you want to insert text.

3. Type some text. The text automatically wraps to the shape of the text frame.

4. Press Enter (Win) or Return (Mac) to create a new paragraph or press Shift+Enter (Win) or Shift+Return (Mac) to create a new line and not a new paragraph.

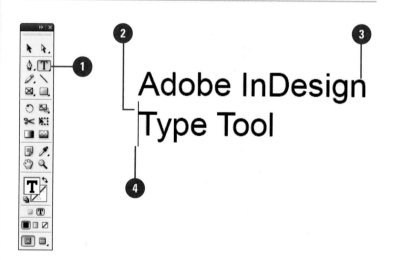

Select and Deselect Type Text

1. Select the **Type** tool on the Tools panel.

2. Do any of the following to select:

   ◆ **Text.** Drag the I-beam cursor to select and highlight a word or line of text.

   ◆ **Text Range.** Click to place the insertion point at the beginning of the text range, press Shift, and then click at the end of the text range.

   ◆ **Word.** Double-click a word of text.

   ◆ **Paragraph.** Triple-click a paragraph of text.

   ◆ **All Text.** Click to place the insertion point, click the **Edit** menu, and then click **Select All**.

   TIMESAVER *Click in a text frame, press Ctrl+A (Win) or ⌘+A (Mac) to select all the text.*

3. To deselect the text, click outside the text frame.

   ◆ You can also click the **Edit** menu, and then click **Deselect All**.

   TIMESAVER *Press Esc to return the text frame from text editing mode.*

Did You Know?

You can change what triple-clicking does. Click the Edit (Win) or InDesign (Mac) menu, point to Preferences, click Type, select the Triple Click To Select A Line check box, and then click OK.

Adobe InDesign Type Tool

Select all

Adobe InDesign Type Tool

Editing Text with Autocorrect

ID 2.2

InDesign's Autocorrect feature (**New!**) automatically corrects common capitalization and spelling errors as you type. Autocorrect comes with hundreds of text and symbol entries you can edit or remove. You can add words and phrases to the Autocorrect dictionary that you tend to misspell, or add often-typed words and save time by just typing their initials. You can use Autocorrect to quickly insert symbols. For example, you can type (c) to insert ©. You can enable Autocorrect and customize settings in the Autocorrect preferences dialog box.

Set Autocorrect Options

1. Click the **Edit** (Win) or **InDesign** (Mac) menu, point to **Preferences**, and then click **Autocorrect**.

2. Select the **Enable Autocorrect** check box to enable the feature.

3. Select from the following Autocorrect options:

    ◆ **Autocorrect Capitalization Errors.** Select to have InDesign automatically correct capitalization errors.

    ◆ **Language.** Choose the language dictionary you want InDesign to use when checking your text.

4. Do one of the following:

    ◆ **Add.** Type a misspelled word or an abbreviation to add it the list of words that will be autocorrected.

    ◆ **Edit.** Select any words you want to change.

    ◆ **Remove.** Select any words you want to delete.

5. Click **OK**.

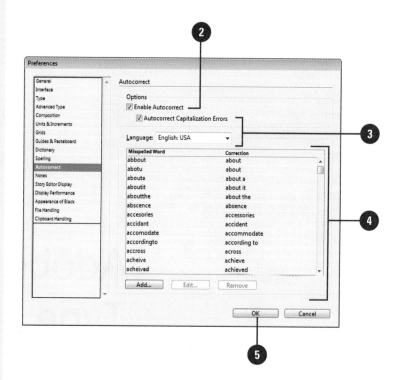

Copying and Moving Text

ID 2.2

Like most programs, you can copy and move text by using the Copy or Cut and Paste commands or drag-and-drop techniques. InDesign is no different. There are a couple of differences. When you paste text, you can paste it without formatting. Another difference is that InDesign allows you to inherit formatting from the destination text when you drag and drop text. You can use the Type preferences dialog box to enable drag and drop editing in Layout view and Story Editor.

Copy or Cut and Paste Text

1. Select the **Type** tool on the Tools panel, and then select the text you want to copy or cut (move).

2. Click the **Edit** menu, and then click **Cut** or **Copy**.

3. Click to place the insertion point where you want to place to the text.

4. Click the **Edit** menu, and then click **Paste** or **Paste Without Formatting**.

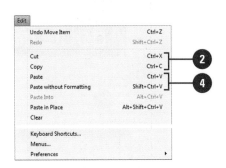

Drag Text

1. Select the **Type** tool on the Tools panel, and then select the text you want to move or copy. The cursor changes to an arrow with a T.

2. Use any of the following methods:

    ◆ **Move.** Drag the selected text to a new text frame location.

    ◆ **Copy.** Press Alt (Win) or Option (Mac) and drag the selected text to a new text frame location.

    ◆ **Inherit Formatting.** Press Shift and drag the selected text to a new text frame location. The text inherits the formatting of the of the text destination frame.

Copyright © 2009 by Perspection, Inc.
All rights reserved. No part of this book shall be reproduced, stored in a retrieval system, or transmitted by any means, electronic, mechanical, photocopying, recording, or otherwise, without written permission from the publisher. No patent liability is assumed with respect to the use of the information contained herein. Although every precaution has been taken in the preparation of this book, the publisher and author assume no responsibility for errors or omissions. Nor is any liability assumed for damages resulting from the use of the information contained herein.

Changing Fonts

A **font** is a collection of alphanumeric characters that share the same typeface, or design, and have similar characteristics. With the Character panel, you can change the font family (Arial or Times New Roman) and style (Italic, Bold, or Condensed), as well as change other type attributes, such as size, kerning, scale, tracking, leading, and language. You can also change these and other attributes by using the Type menu and Control panel. After you select the text that you want to change, you can change font attributes directly on the Control panel. For example, you can style text using All Caps, Small Caps, Underline, Strikethrough, Subscript and Superscript. As you can see, there are several ways to change font attributes. You can use any one of them.

Change Font Family and Style

1. Select the **Type** tool on the Tools panel, and then select the text that you want to change.

    ◆ You can also select the **Selection** tool, and then click the text frame to change all text in the frame.

2. Select the **Character** panel.

    ◆ Click the **Type** menu, and then click **Character**.

3. Click the **Font Family** list arrow, and then select a font.

    ◆ To see the font family in the style of the font, click the **Type** menu, point to **Font**, and then select a font.

4. Click the **Font Style** list arrow, and then select a font style, such as Italic, Bold, or Bold Italic.

Did You Know?

You can change the text language. Select the Character panel, click the Language list arrow, and then select the language that you want to use. You can also select text using any type tool, and then change the text language to something else.

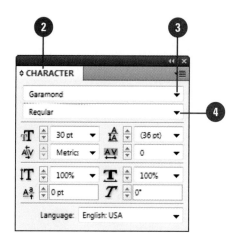

Type results

Adobe InDesign Type Tool

Apply Additional Font Styles

1 Select the **Type** tool on the Tools panel, and then select the text that you want to change.

◆ You can also select the **Selection** tool, and then click the text frame to change all text in the frame.

2 Select the **Character** panel.

◆ Click the **Type** menu, and then click **Character**.

◆ You can quickly access the following styles on the Options menu or the Control panel.

3 Click the **Options** menu, and then select the style you want:

◆ **All Caps.** Changes lowercase letters to all capitals.

◆ **Small Caps.** Changes lowercase letters to reduced capitals.

◆ **Superscript.** Reduces and raises the text above the baseline.

◆ **Subscript.** Reduces and lowers the text below the baseline.

◆ **Underline.** Underlines the text.

◆ **Strikethrough.** Adds a line through the text.

◆ **Underline Options.** Opens a dialog box, where you can change underline options.

◆ **Strikethrough Options.** Opens a dialog box, where you can change strikethrough options.

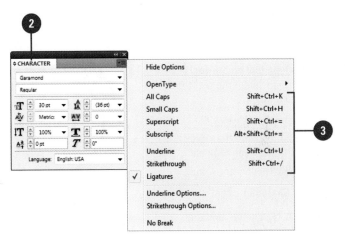

Style options on control panel

Changing Font Size

After setting the font family and style, the next attribute to set is the font size. The font size can range from 6 points to 72 points and beyond depending on the font. Open or TrueType fonts can be scaled to any size and still look and print well. Bitmap (screen fonts) fonts, on the other hand, cannot be scaled and you need to use the available sizes to print well. However, bitmap fonts are the best choice for commercial print jobs. An "O" appears next to an OpenType font, a "TT" appears next to a TrueType font, and an "a" appears next to a bitmap font on the Font submenu.

Change Font Size

1. Select the **Type** tool on the Tools panel, and then select the text that you want to change.

   ◆ You can also select the **Selection** tool, and then click the text frame to change all text in the frame.

2. Select the **Character** panel.

   ◆ Click the **Type** menu, and then click **Character**.

3. Enter a font point size, or click the **Font Size** list arrow, and then select a font size. Press Enter (Win) or Return (Mac) to apply the value.

   ◆ You can also hold down Ctrl+Shift (Win) or ⌘+Shift (Mac), and then press > to increase the point size or press < to decrease the point size.

   Use Ctrl+Alt-Shift (Win) or ⌘+Option+Shift to change the point size 5 sizes at a time.

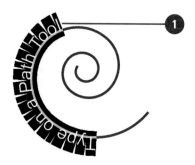

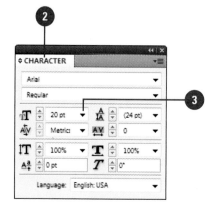

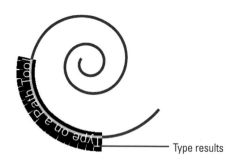

Did You Know?

What is a point? The size of each font character is measured in points (a point is approximately 1/72 of an inch). You can use any font that is installed on your computer in a document, but the default is 12-point Times New Roman.

Type results

Text Leading

Leading is the distance from the baseline of one line to the baseline of the next line and is measured in points. Each line of text can have a different leading size. You can specify a specific setting or use Auto, which is a percentage of the largest text size on each line. Leading is applied to horizontal text. If you want to change vertical spacing in text, you need to adjust horizontal tracking.

Change Text Leading

1. Select the **Type** tool on the Tools panel, and then select the text that you want to change.

   ◆ You can also select the **Selection** tool, and then click the text frame to change all text in the frame.

2. Select the **Character** panel.

   ◆ Click the **Type** menu, and then click **Character**.

3. Enter a leading point size, or click the **Leading** arrows, and then select a leading size. Press Enter (Win) or Return (Mac) to apply the value.

   ◆ You can also hold down Alt (Win) or Option (Mac), and then press the **down arrow** to increase the point size or press the **up arrow** to decrease the point size.

   The text increases or decreases by the Size/Leading value set in the Type preferences.

4. To shift characters up or down from the baseline, enter a baseline value, or click the **Baseline Shift** arrows, and then select a baseline value. A positive size adds space while a negative number removes space. Press Enter (Win) or Return (Mac) to apply the value.

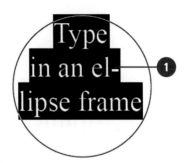

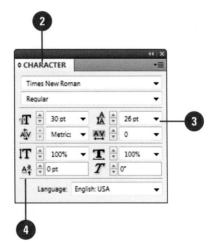

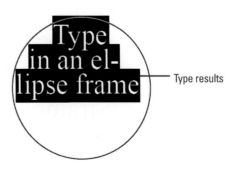

Type results

Text Kerning

Kerning is adding or removing space between pairs of characters in your text. Sometimes the space between two characters is larger than others, which makes the word look uneven. You can use the Character panel to change the kerning setting for selected characters. You can expand or condense character spacing to create a special effect for a title, or realign the position of characters to the bottom edge of the text—this is helpful for positioning copyright or trademark symbols.

Change Text Kerning

1. Select the **Type** tool on the Tools panel, and then click between the two characters of text you want to change.

2. Select the **Character** panel.

   ◆ Click the **Type** menu, and then click **Character**.

3. Enter a kerning size, or click the **Kerning** arrows, and then select a kerning size. A positive size adds space while a negative number removes space. Press Enter (Win) or Return (Mac) to apply the value.

   ◆ You can also hold down Alt (Win) or Option (Mac), and then press the **right arrow** to increase the point size or press the **left arrow** to decrease the point size.

   The text increases or decreases by the Tracking value set in the Type preferences.

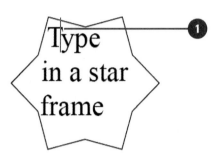

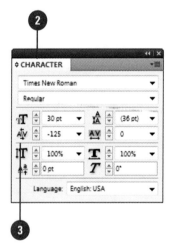

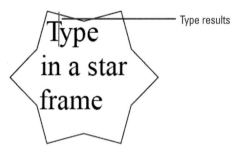

Type results

Text Tracking

Tracking is the adjustment of space between three or more characters. Typically, you'll track a line of text or a few words depending on the length and design application. This is useful for creating specialize text for a caption or short heading. To adjust space between two characters, kerning is the best choice. To track characters, you need to select them first and then set the Tracking option in the Character panel.

Change Text Tracking

① Select the **Type** tool on the Tools panel, and then select the text that you want to change.

◆ You can also select the **Selection** tool, and then click the text frame to change all text in the frame.

② Select the **Character** panel.

◆ Click the **Type** menu, and then click **Character**.

③ Enter a tracking size, or click the **Tracking** arrows, and then select a tracking size. A positive size adds space while a negative number removes space. Press Enter (Win) or Return (Mac) to apply the value.

◆ You can also hold down Alt (Win) or Option (Mac), and then press the **right arrow** to increase the point size or press the **left arrow** to decrease the point size.

The text increases or decreases by the Tracking value set in the Type preferences.

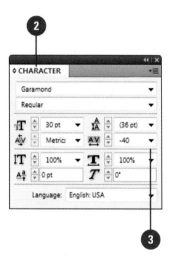

Type results

Scaling or Skewing Text

Scaling allows you to make text wider or narrower for horizontal text and taller or shorter for vertical text. You can use the Horizontal Scale and Vertical Scale options in the Character panel to modify text. **Skewing** allows you to distort the text at an angle to give it perspective. If the scaling or skewing doesn't look quite right, you can always use the Undo command to reverse the modification.

Scale and Skew Text

1. Select the text that you want to change.

   ◆ You can also select the **Selection** tool, and then click the text frame to change all text in the frame.

2. Select the **Character** panel.

   ◆ Click the **Type** menu, and then click **Character**.

3. To scale text, enter a horizontal or vertical percentage, or click the **Vertical Scale** or **Horizontal Scale** arrows. Press Enter (Win) or Return (Mac) to apply the value. Other ways of scaling text include:

   ◆ To scale a text frame, select the object, double-click the **Scale** tool on the Tools panel, specify a **Horizontal** and **Vertical** percentage, and then click **OK**.

   ◆ To scale a text frame, select the object, select the **Free Transform** tool on the Tools panel, and then drag a side handle on the bounding box.

4. To skew text, enter a degree value, or click the **Skew** arrows. Press Enter (Win) or Return (Mac) to apply the value.

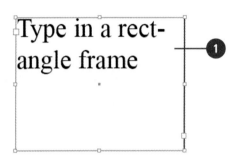

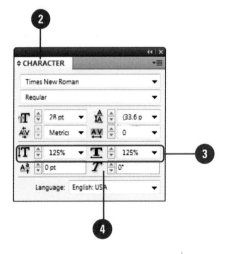

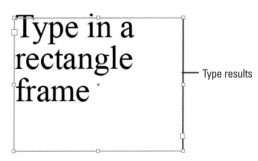

Type results

Aligning Paragraphs

When you press the Enter (Win) or Return (Mac) in a text frame, InDesign creates a paragraph. You can use the Paragraph panel to align and indent paragraphs in your document. At the top and bottom of the Paragraph panel is a set of buttons that you can use to align text in one or more paragraphs. The panel includes the typical options to align: left, center, right and justify. However, it also includes options to justify text with only the last line aligned left, center, or right.

Align Paragraphs

1. Select the **Type** tool on the Tools panel, and then click in a paragraph or select multiple paragraphs you want to align.

2. Select the **Paragraph** panel.

   ◆ Click the **Type** menu, and then click **Paragraph**.

3. Use any of the following alignment buttons on the panel:

   ◆ **Align Left**, **Align Center**, or **Align Right.** Click these buttons to align paragraph text left, center, or right.

   ◆ **Justify Left, Center, or Right.** Click these buttons to justify the paragraph text with only the last line aligned left, center, or right.

   ◆ **Justify.** Click to justify all lines.

   ◆ **Align Towards Spine.** Click to align the paragraph text towards the spine.

   ◆ **Align Away From Spine.** Click to align the paragraph text away from the spine.

   ◆ **Do Not Align To Baseline Grid.** Click to keep the paragraph text from aligning to the baseline grid.

   ◆ **Align To Baseline Grid.** Click to align the paragraph text to the baseline grid.

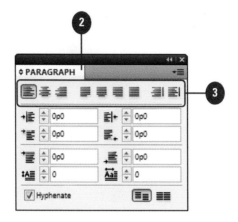

Left aligned

Dionsendiam nim augiam del ut at iustrud digna ad dolor at. Ut velit irit aliquis dolobore exero ero ex elendrer augait, con henim iliquam nibh et, quat vent ex exercing ea feumsan enim vel ut iure tat lore magniam, volore ver irit venit augiat. Sed tin ver iliquametum ipsustie consenibh er autetum

Dionsendiam nim augiam del ut at iustrud digna ad dolor at. Ut velit irit aliquis dolobore exero ero ex elendrer augait, con henim iliquam nibh et, quat vent ex exercing ea feumsan enim vel ut iure tat lore magniam, volore ver irit venit augiat. Sed tin ver iliquametum ipsustie consenibh er autetum

Center aligned

Right aligned

Dionsendiam nim augiam del ut at iustrud digna ad dolor at. Ut velit irit aliquis dolobore exero ero ex elendrer augait, con henim iliquam nibh et, quat vent ex exercing ea feumsan enim vel ut iure tat lore magniam, volore ver irit venit augiat. Sed tin ver iliquametum ipsustie consenibh er autetum

Dionsendiam nim augiam del ut at iustrud digna ad dolor at. Ut velit irit aliquis dolobore exero ero ex elendrer augait, con henim iliquam nibh et, quat vent ex exercing ea feumsan enim vel ut iure tat lore magniam, volore ver irit venit augiat. Sed tin ver iliquametum ipsustie consenibh er autetum qua

Justified

Indenting and Spacing Paragraphs

Quickly indent lines of text to precise locations from the left or right margin with the horizontal ruler. Indent the first or last line of a paragraph (called a **first-line** or **last-line indent**) as books do to distinguish paragraphs. Indent the second and subsequent lines of a paragraph from the left margin (called a **hanging indent**) to create a properly formatted bibliography. Indent the entire paragraph any amount from the left and right margins (called **left indents** and **right indents**) to separate quoted passages. In addition to indenting paragraphs, you can also set the spacing you want before or after a paragraph.

Indent and Space Paragraphs

1. Select the **Type** tool on the Tools panel, and then click in a paragraph or select multiple paragraphs you want to change.

2. Select the **Paragraph** panel.

   ◆ Click the **Type** menu, and then click **Paragraph**.

3. Enter a **Left Indent** and/or **Right Indent** value or use the up and down arrows to specify one. Press Enter (Win) or Return (Mac) to apply the value.

4. To create a first-line or last-line indent, enter a **First-Line Indent** or **Last-Line Indent** value or use the up and down arrows to specify one. Press Enter (Win) or Return (Mac) to apply the value.

   ◆ To create a hanging indent, enter a negative value in the First-line Left Indent box.

   ◆ To insert a manual indent, place the insertion point, click the **Type** menu, point to **Insert Special Character**, point to **Other**, and then click **Indent to Here**.

5. To add spacing between paragraphs, enter a **Space Before Paragraph** and/or **Space After Paragraph** value or use the up and down arrows to specify one. Press Enter (Win) or Return (Mac) to apply the value.

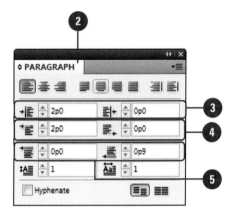

Left Indent

First-Line Indent

Dionsendiam nim augiam del ut at iustrud digna ad dolor at. Ut velit irit aliquis dolobore exero ero ex elendrer augait, con henim iliquam nibh et, quat vent ex exercing ea feumsan enim vel ut iure tat lore magniam, volore ver irit venit augiat. Sed tin ver iliquametum ipsustie consenibh er autetum quat lute modit dunt pratem veliquamet, quamet, veliquat in ute erat. Tat.

To od tat, consenit, cortinisi blaore tem zzrilis autpat. Ut niam, se conulla consequat. Ut inci blaor sit, susto core

Right Indent

Creating a Drop Cap

A few simple elements—drop caps, borders, and shading—make your newsletters and brochures look like a professional produced them. A **drop cap** is the enlarged first letter of a paragraph that provides instant style to a document. You can quickly achieve this effect in the Paragraph panel. You can change the drop cap position, font, and height, and then enter the distance between the drop cap and paragraph.

Create a Drop Cap

1. Select the **Type** tool on the Tools panel, and then click in a paragraph or select multiple paragraphs you want to change.

2. Select the **Paragraph** panel.

   ◆ Click the **Type** menu, and then click **Paragraph**.

3. Enter a **Drop Cap Number of Lines** value or use the up and down arrows to specify one. Press Enter (Win) or Return (Mac) to apply the value.

4. Enter a **Drop Cap One or More Characters** value or use the up and down arrows to specify one. Press Enter (Win) or Return (Mac) to apply the value.

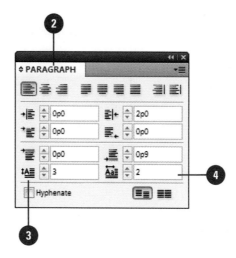

Drop cap

To od tat, consenit, cortinisi blaore tem zzrilis autpat. Ut niam, se conulla consequat. Ut inci blaor sit, susto core magna faciliscipit adignim nos ad tinibh et la consequi ex elit wisi.

Applying a Paragraph Rule

If you want a line above or below a paragraph, you can apply it to a paragraph, so the line stays with the paragraph as you add or delete text. A paragraph rule can also be applied as part of a style sheet. In the Paragraph Rules dialog box, you can set the weight, style type, color, width, and position of the paragraph rule line.

Apply a Paragraph Rule

1. Select the paragraph to which you want to apply a rule.

2. Select the **Paragraph** panel.

3. Click the **Options** menu, and then click **Paragraph Rules**.

4. Select the **Preview** check box to see changes as you make them.

5. Select **Rule Above** or **Rule Below** from the list arrow, and then select the **Rule On** check box.

   ◆ To set paragraph rules for both Rule Above and Rule Below, repeat Step 5.

6. Select any of the following appearance options:

   ◆ **Weight.** Specify the thickness of the line rule.

   ◆ **Type.** Specify the style of the line rule.

   ◆ **Color.** Specify the color of the line rule.

   ◆ **Tint.** Specify a tint for the line color.

   ◆ **Gap Color.** If you selected a type with a gap, specify a gap color for the line rule.

   ◆ **Gap Tint.** Specify a tint for the line gap color.

   ◆ **Overprint Gap.** Select to set the gap ink to overprint.

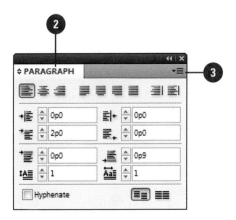

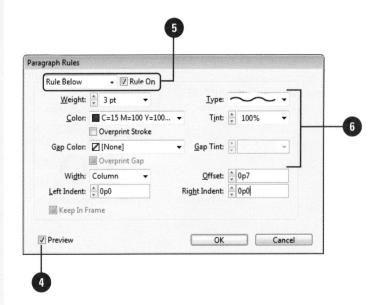

7 Select any of the following appearance options:

- **Width.** Select the rule line length equivalent to the column or the text.

- **Offset.** Specify the position above or below the baseline.

  By default, the paragraph rule is positioned on the baseline of the text.

- **Left and Right Indent.** Specify an indent value from the column or text margin.

8 To keep the rule in the text frame, select the **Keep In Frame** check box.

9 Click **OK**.

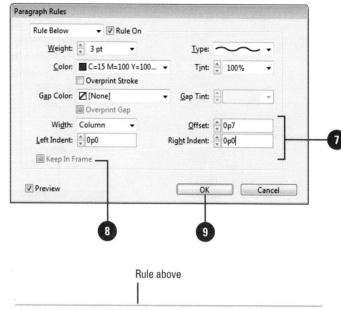

Rule above

Dionsendiam nim augiam del ut at iustrud digna ad dolor at. Ut velit irit aliquis dolobore exero ero ex elendrer augait, con henim iliquam nibh et, quat vent ex exercing ea feumsan enim vel ut iure tat lore magniam, volore ver irit venit augiat. Sed tin ver iliquametum ipsustie consenibh er autetum quat lute modit dunt pratem veliquamet, quamet, veliquat in ute erat. Tat.

Rule below

Adding Bullets and Numbering

ID 2.9

The best way to draw attention to a list is to format the items with bullets or numbers. For different emphasis, change any bullet or number style to one of InDesign's many predefined formats. For example, switch round bullets to check boxes or Roman numerals to lowercase letters. You can also customize the list style. If you move, insert, or delete items in a numbered list, InDesign sequentially renumbers the list for you.

Add Bullets or Numbering to a Paragraph

1. Select the paragraphs to which you want to add bullets or numbers.

2. Click the **Bulleted List** or **Numbered List** button on the Control panel.

   ◆ You can also click the **Type** menu, point to **Bulleted & Numbered Lists**, and then click **Apply Bullets** or **Apply Numbers**.

   The last used settings in the Bullets and Numbering dialog box are applied to the text.

Did You Know?

You can convert bullets or numbers to text. Select the text, click the Type menu, point to Bulleted & Numbered Lists, and then click Convert Bullets To Text or Convert Numbering To Text.

• Dionsendiam nim augiam del ut at iustrud digna ad dolor at. Ut velit irit aliquis dolobore exero ero ex elendrer augait, con henim iliquam nibh et, quat vent ex exercing ea feumsan enim vel ut iure tat lore magniam, volore ver irit venit augiat. Sed tin ver iliquametum ipsustie consenibh er autetum quat lute modit dunt pratem veliquamet, quamet, veliquat in ute erat. Tat.

• To od tat, consenit, cortinisi blaore tem zzrilis autpat. Ut niam, se conulla consequat. Ut inci blaor sit, susto core magna faciliscipit adignim nos ad tinibh et la consequi ex

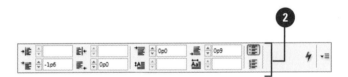

Format Bullets and Numbers

1. Select the **Paragraph** panel.

2. Click the **Options** menu, and then click **Bullets and Numbering**.

3. Select the **Preview** check box to see changes as you make them.

4. Click the **List Type** list arrow, and then select **Bullets** or **Numbers**.

5. For Bullets, select from the following options:

   ◆ **Bullet Character.** Select a bullet character. Add or remove specific characters from the list.

   ◆ **Text After.** Specify characters to separate the bullet and text.

   ◆ **Character Style.** Specify a bullet style.

6. For Numbers, select from the following options:

   ◆ **Format.** Specify a number format style.

   ◆ **Number.** Specify characters to separate the number and text.

   ◆ **Character Style.** Specify a number style.

   ◆ **Mode.** Specify a start number or sequence.

7. Select any of the following Bullet or Number Position options:

   ◆ **Alignment.** Specify an alignment.

   ◆ **Left Indent.** Specify an indent value.

   ◆ **First Line Indent.** Specify a first line indent value.

   ◆ **Tab Position.** Specify the position of the first character after the bullet or number.

8. Click **OK**.

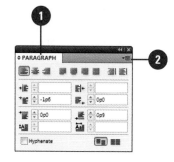

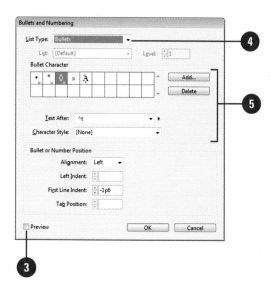

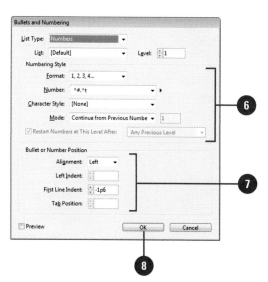

Setting Tabs

In your document, **tabs** determines how text or numerical data is aligned in relation to the document margins. A **tab stop** is a predefined stopping point along the document's typing line. Default tab stops are set every half-inch, but you can set multiple tabs per paragraph at any location. Choose from four types of text tab stops: left, right, center, and decimal (for numerical data). In the Tabs panel, you can view a ruler with the current tab setting for the selected text and add, move, or delete tab stops. When you press the Tab key with the insertion point active, the text shifts to the next tab stop.

Set Tabs

1. Select the **Type** tool on the Tools panel, and then click to place the insertion point in a text frame.

2. Select the **Tabs** panel.

   ◆ Click the **Type** menu, and then click **Tabs**.

   ◆ To use the default tabs, press the tab key to shift the text to the next default tab stop.

3. To move the panel next to the text, click the **Position Panel Above Text Frame** button on the panel.

4. Do any of the following:

   ◆ **Insert.** Click one of the tab stop buttons, and then click in the ruler where you want to place it. You can also enter a number in the X box to insert a tab at an exact position.

   ◆ **Move.** Drag the tab stop left or right or enter an exact position in the X box.

   ◆ **Delete.** Drag a tab stop down off the ruler.

   ◆ **Leader.** Enter a character that repeats in the tabbed space, such as a period.

   ◆ **Align On.** Enter a character that is used with the Decimal tab, such as a decimal point.

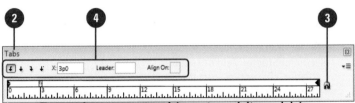

Dionsendiam nim augiam del ut at iustrud digna ad dolor at. Ut velit irit aliquis dolobore exero ero ex elendrer augait, con henim iliquam nibh et, quat vent ex exercing ea feumsan enim vel ut iure tat lore magniam, volore ver irit venit augiat. Sed tin ver iliquametum ipsustie consenibh er autetum quat lute modit dunt pratem veliquamet, quamet, veliquat in ute erat. Tat.

To od tat, consenit, cortinisi blaore tem zzrilis autpat. Ut niam, se conulla consequat. Ut inci blaor sit, susto core magna faciliscipit adignim nos ad tinibh et la consequi ex elit wisi.

Working with Glyphs

 ID 2.1

A glyph is a style variation—such as ligatures, ordinals, swashes, and fractions—for a given character in an OpenType font. OpenType fonts appear with an "O" next to the font name on the Font submenu. OpenType fonts are designed to work well on both Windows and Macintosh operating systems, which reduces font substitution problems when going back and forth between platforms. However, you can always add more character styles to extend the font format. For example, you can change fractions with numerals and slashes to properly formatted fractions. You can automatically insert alternate glyphs with the OpenType panel or insert them manually with the Glyphs panel to extend the font format.

Replace or Insert a Glyph

1 Select the **Type** tool on the Tools panel, and then select a character (to replace a glyph) or click in text (to insert a glyph).

2 Select the **Glyphs** panel.

◆ Click the **Type** menu, and then click **Glyphs**.

3 Select a different font and font style.

4 Click the **Show** list arrow, and then select a glyphs category.

Alternates for Selection or **Entire Font** are common choices.

5 Double-click the glyph that you want to replace or insert.

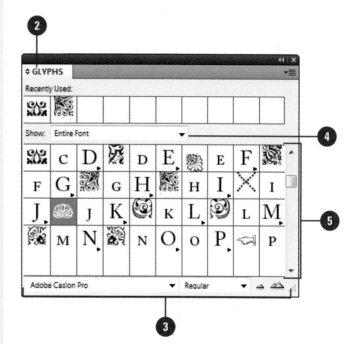

Did You Know?

You can use the OpenType panel to insert glyphs. Select the OpenType submenu from the Character Options menu, select the text that you want to change or deselect all text for the entire document, and then select the buttons with the options for glyphs that you want to apply, such as ligatures, swashes, titling, ordinals, and fractions.

Inserting Special Text Characters

 ID 2.1

In addition to inserting normal alphanumeric text, you can also insert special text characters, such as symbols, markers, hyphens, dashes, white space, and breaks. For example, you can insert text breaks to force a break between lines, or add white space, such as an Em or En space, between characters. If you want to keep two words together on the same line, you can insert a nonbreaking space. You can insert special characters, white space, and break characters by using submenus on the Type menu.

Insert Special Text Characters

1. Select the **Type** tool on the Tools panel.

2. Click to place the insertion point where you want to place the text.

3. To insert a break, click the **Type** menu, point to **Insert Break Character**, and then select a text break.

   ◆ Includes column, frame, page, paragraph return, and forced line break.

4. To insert special characters, click the **Type** menu, point to **Insert Special Character**, point to any of the following, and then select a special character:

   ◆ **Symbols.** Includes copyright and trademark.

   ◆ **Markers.** Includes page numbers and section markers.

   ◆ **Hyphens and Dashes.** Includes Em and En dashes.

   ◆ **Quotation Marks.** Includes double and single quotation marks.

   ◆ **Other.** Includes tabs and indents.

5. To insert a space, click the **Type** menu, point to **Insert White Space**, and then select a text break.

   ◆ Includes Em and En space, Hair, Thin, Punctuation, and Figure.

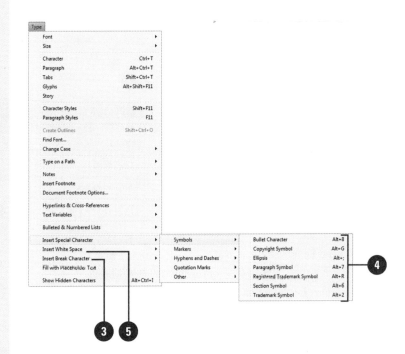

Working with Hidden Text

When you edit a document, sometimes it's hard to see the number of spaces between words. To make this job easier, you can show hidden characters, such as the Spacebar, Tab key, and Enter (Win) or Return (Mac) key. If you're still having trouble viewing the text, you can change the color of the hidden text by changing the color of the layer in the Layers panel. Hidden text is also hidden in Preview or Overprint Preview mode.

Show and Hide Text

◆ **Show Hidden Text.** Click the **Type** menu, and then click **Show Hidden Characters**.

◆ **Hide Hidden Text.** Click the **Type** menu, and then click **Hide Hidden Characters**.

Figure space

Adobe· Flash Professional On Demand¶
¶
Copyright © 2009 by Perspection, Inc.¶
All rights reserved. No part of this book shall be reproduced, stored in a retrieval system, or transmitted by any means, electronic, mechanical, photocopying, recording, or otherwise, without written permission from the publisher. No patent liability is assumed with respect to the use of the information contained herein. Although every precaution has been taken in the preparation of this book, the publisher and author assume no responsibility for errors or omissions. Nor is any liability assumed for damages resulting from the use of the information contained herein.¶
¶

Paragraph   Space

Setting Text Frame Options

IL 2.3, 2.4

If you need to make adjustments to all the text in a text frame, you can use the Text Frame Options dialog box to make all your changes in one place. You can create columns, adjust inset spacing and vertical justification, specify a first baseline offset, and add a baseline grid for a text frame. Inset spacing is the space between the text and the frame. Vertical justification controls the alignment of text in rectangle text frames from the top to the bottom. When you set vertical justification to Justify, you can set paragraph spacing limits. If you're working with wrapped text in a text frame, you can set an option to ignore it.

Set Text Frame Options

1. Select the text frame you want to change.

2. Click the **Object** menu, and then click **Text Frame Options**.

3. Select the **Preview** check box to see changes as you make them.

4. Click the **General** tab.

5. Select any of the following Columns options:

   ◆ **Number.** Specify the number of columns you want to create.

   ◆ **Width.** Specify the column width you want to use.

   ◆ **Gutter.** Specify the gutter space between the columns you want to use.

   ◆ **Fixed Column Width.** Select to keep a fixed column width.

6. Specify inset spacing values for **Top**, **Bottom**, **Left** and **Right**.

7. Select any of the following Vertical Justification options:

   ◆ **Align.** Specify an alignment option for a rectangle text frame.

   ◆ **Paragraph Spacing Limit.** When you select the Justify alignment option, specify a paragraph spacing limit.

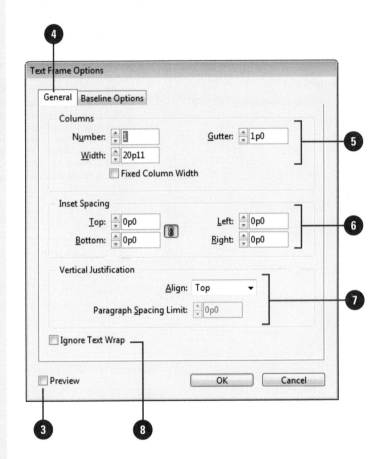

8 To ignore text wrapping for the selected text frame, select the **Ignore Text Wrap** check box.

9 Click the **Baseline Options** tab.

10 Click the **Offset** list arrow, select an option, and then specify a minimum offset space.

11 Select any of the following Baseline Grid options:

◆ **Use Custom Baseline Grid.** Select to create a baseline grid for the selected text frame.

◆ **Start.** Specify a start location for the baseline grid.

◆ **Relative To.** Specify a relative location where you want the baseline grid.

◆ **Increment Every.** Specify an interval for the baseline grid.

◆ **Color.** Select a color for the baseline grid.

12 Click **OK**.

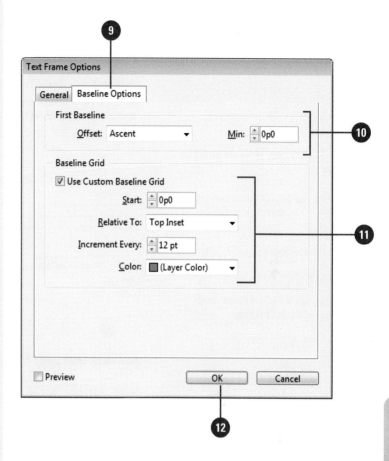

Wrapping Text Around an Object

When integrating graphics with your text, you can wrap the text around objects to create the results that you want. You can use the Text Wrap panel to quickly select button options to wrap text around an object. Some of the text wrapping options include No Wrap, Bounding Box, Object Shape, Jump Object, and Jump to Next Column. When you select Object Shape, you can select additional options to customize text wrapping around the object.

Wrap and Unwrap Text Around an Object

1. Arrange the object to be wrapped in front of the text frame. The objects should be overlapping.

2. Select the object to be wrapped.

3. Select the **Text Wrap** panel.

   ◆ Click the **Window** menu, and then click **Text Wrap**.

4. Select one of the following buttons:

   ◆ **No Text Wrap.** Text flows through the object.

   ◆ **Bounding Box.** Text wraps around the bounding box.

   ◆ **Object Shape.** Text wraps around the shape.

   ◆ **Jump Object.** Text wraps to the space under the object.

   ◆ **Jump to Next Column.** Text wraps to the next column or text frame.

5. Select the **Invert** check box to flow the text inside the object.

6. Enter offset values to specify the distance between the text and the object.

   ◆ Click the **Make All Settings the Same** button (chain icon) to set all the offset values to be the same. Click it again (broken chain icon) if you want to set different values.

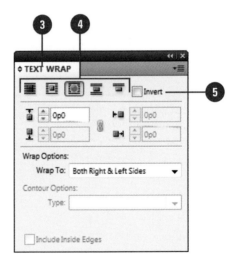

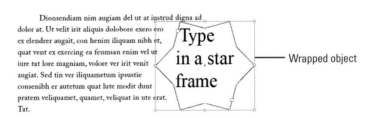

Wrapped object

Set Object Shape Wrap Options

1. Select the object to be wrapped.

2. Select the **Text Wrap** panel.

3. Click the **Object Shape** button.

4. Click the **Wrap Options** list arrow, and then select an option:

   - **Right Side.** Wraps around the right side.

   - **Left Side.** Wraps around the left side.

   - **Both Right & Left Sides.** Wraps to both sides.

   - **Side Towards Spine.** Wraps to the left or right side towards the spine.

   - **Side Away From Spine.** Wraps to the left or right side away from the spine.

   - **Largest Area.** Wraps to the side with the most space.

5. Click the **Contour Options** list arrow, and then select an option to control the shape of the wrap:

   - **Bounding Box.** Uses the bounding box rectangle.

   - **Detect Edges.** Uses the difference between the image pixels and the background.

   - **Alpha Channel.** Uses an embedded alpha channel.

   - **Photoshop Path.** Uses an embedded path.

   - **Graphic Frame.** Uses the frame of the graphic object.

   - **Same As Clipping.** Uses the clipping path shape for the graphic.

6. Select the **Include Inside Edges** check box to wrap text inside holes in the graphic, path, or alpha channel.

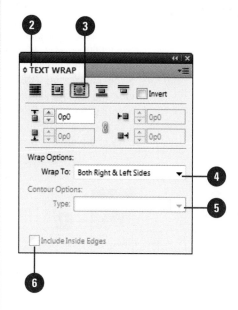

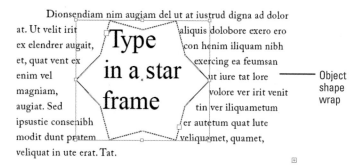

Object shape wrap

Creating Type Outlines

The Create Outlines command converts characters in a text frame into a separate object with a path. Some characters, such as "A" or "B," that contain an interior shape (known as a counter) are converted into compound objects. After you create an outline, you can reshape the path, use it as a mask object, fill it with a gradient or a mesh, or use it in a compound object. When you create outlines, the fill and stroke attributes and any appearances of the type are applied to the outlines. Before you use the Create Outlines command, it's a good idea to make a copy of the text frame or your document as a backup to preserve a copy of the original text frame.

Create Type Outlines

1. Select the **Selection** tool on the Tools panel.

2. Select the text frame or select characters.

3. Click the **Type** menu, and then click **Create Outlines**.

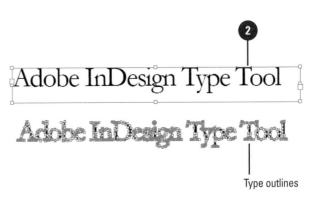

Type outlines

Adding Page Numbers to Continued Text

When you enter or import text for an article or story that you want to continue on another page, you can add a page number in a separate text frame to the bottom of the article or story as a jump line to where it continues. The continuation page number is typically put in a separate text frame, so the reflow of text doesn't move it. When you change pagination in a document, the continuation page numbers are automatically updated.

Add Page Numbers to Continued Text

1. Select the **Type** tool on the Tools panel.

2. Drag to create a text frame for the page number.

3. Select the **Selection** tool on the Tools panel, and then drag to move the text frame so that it touches or overlaps the frame containing the story you want to continue on another page.

4. Select the **Type** tool on the Tools panel, click in the text frame, and then type text you want to appear next to the page number, such as *Continued on* or *Continued from*.

5. Click the **Type** menu, point to **Insert Special Character**, point to **Marker**, and then click **Next Page Number** or **Previous Page number**.

6. Shift-click to select the text frame and the frame containing the story, click the **Object** menu, and then click **Group** to keep both together.

Adobe• Flash Professional On Demand

Copyright © 2009 by Perspection, Inc.
All rights reserved. No part of this book shall be reproduced, stored in a retrieval system, or transmitted by any means, electronic, mechanical, photocopying, recording, or otherwise, without written permission from the publisher. No patent liability is assumed with respect to the use of the information contained herein. Although every precaution has been taken in the preparation of this book, the publisher and author assume no responsibility for errors or omissions. Nor is any liability assumed for damages resulting from the use of the information contained herein.

Continued on 3

Adobe• Flash Professional On Demand

Copyright © 2009 by Perspection, Inc.
All rights reserved. No part of this book shall be reproduced, stored in a retrieval system, or transmitted by any means, electronic, mechanical, photocopying, recording, or otherwise, without written permission from the publisher. No patent liability is assumed with respect to the use of the information contained herein. Although every precaution has been taken in the preparation of this book, the publisher and author assume no responsibility for errors or omissions. Nor is any liability assumed for damages resulting from the use of the information contained herein.

Continued on 3

Placing and Working with Graphics

5

Introduction

You can use InDesign's Place command to insert artwork into an open document. InDesign lets you place graphic files saved in Illustrator AI, Photoshop PSD, JPEG, EPS, TIFF, PICT (Mac), and PDF (Portable Document Format) formats, to name a few. You can even place another InDesign INDD file into a document. With the Place command, you can place multiple graphics of different types at the same time. If you need more control over the import and placement of graphics in your document, you can display and use an import dialog box for the type of graphic that you want to place.

When you place graphics, InDesign loads them into a graphic preview cursor, which you can use to place them into a new or existing frame. When you place a graphic, InDesign creates a link to the original file. You can display and work with linked graphics in the Links panel.

Before you can work with the graphic in a frame, you need to select it first. You have several options depending on what you want to accomplish. You can select the frame and graphic, just the frame, or just the graphic. When you place a graphic into a frame, it doesn't always fit the way you want. You can automatically resize the graphic to fill the entire frame or proportionally fill the frame. In some cases you want to place a graphic on top of an existing graphic. This is called a nesting graphic. For example, you can place a graphic in a rectangle frame, and then place another graphic in a circle frame inside the rectangle frame.

When you place multiple graphics in a document, the display performance of your screen can slow down. You can change display resolution settings for the entire document or for individual graphics to improve performance.

What You'll Do

Place Graphics

Place Graphics with Options

Set Place Import Options

Place Multiple Graphics

Place Graphics from Adobe Bridge

Copy or Move Graphics

Use the Links Panel

Manage Linked Graphics

Edit a Linked Graphic

Display XMP Graphic Information

Create Specialty Frames for Graphics

Select and Move Frames and Graphics

Fit Graphics in Frames

Nest Graphics in Frames

Format Graphics in Frames

Control Graphics Display Performance

Placing Graphics

 ID 4.1

You can use InDesign's Place command to insert artwork into an open document. InDesign lets you place graphic files saved in Illustrator AI, Photoshop PSD, BMP, JPEG, EPS, PNG, TIFF, GIF, WMF, PICT (Mac), SCT, DCS, and PDF formats, to name a few. You can even place another InDesign INDD file into a document. You can place multiple graphics of different types at the same time. When you place graphics, InDesign loads them into a graphic preview cursor, which you can use to place them into a new or existing frame. When you draw a new frame, the frame constrains to the proportions of the graphic unless you hold down Shift. The scale is displayed as part of the loaded cursor (**New!**).

Place a Graphic

1. To place a graphic into an existing frame (rectangle, elliptical, or polygon), select the frame using the **Selection** or **Direct Selection** tool on the Tools panel.

2. Click the **File** menu, and then click **Place**.

3. Click the **Files of Type** (Win) or **Enable** (Mac) list arrow, and then click **Importable Files**, or select a specific file format.

4. Navigate to the drive or folder location with the file you want to import.

5. Select the graphic file you want to place.

6. Select the **Replace Selected Item** check box to replace the selected item with the imported graphic.

7. Click **Open**.

   The imported graphic is placed in a loaded preview cursor.

8. Click or drag a rectangle frame with the loaded cursor to place the graphic in a new frame, or click in an empty frame to place it in an existing frame.

   ◆ To place the graphic in an existing frame with a graphic, Alt (Win) or Option (Mac) click in the frame to add the graphic to it.

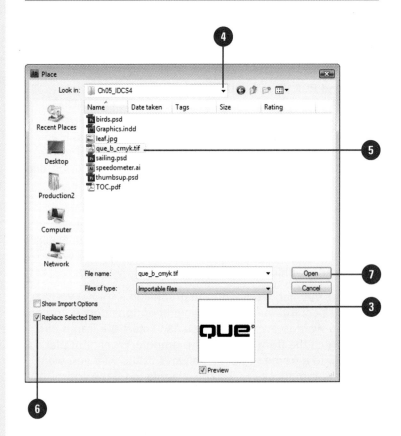

Placing Graphics with Options

 ID 4.1, 4.4

If you need more control over the import and placement of graphics in your document, you can display and use an import dialog box for the type of graphic that you want to place. For example, when you import Illustrator artwork, you can specify import options to select individual artboards (**New!**), layers, and a transparent background. When you import most images, such as TIFF and JPEG, you can specify import options to apply a clipping path along with an Alpha Channel and specify a color profile. For a Photoshop image, you can also select layers.

Place Graphics with Options

1. Click the **File** menu, and then click **Place**.

2. Click the **Files of Type** (Win) or **Enable** (Mac) list arrow, and then click **Importable Files**.

3. Navigate to the drive or folder location with the file you want to import.

4. Select the file you want to place.

5. Select the **Show Import Options** check box to select import options.

6. Click **Open**.

   ◆ If you don't select the Show Import Options check box, you can press Shift as you click the Open button to show import options.

7. Select the options you want. Options vary depending on the imported file format.

8. Click **OK**.

   The imported graphic is placed in a loaded cursor.

9. Click or drag a rectangle frame with the loaded cursor to place the graphic where you want it in your document.

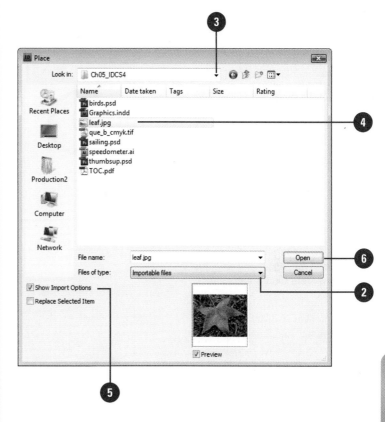

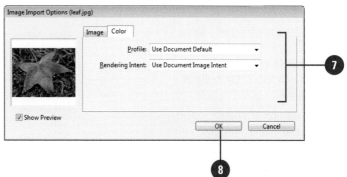

Setting Place Import Options

ID 4.1, 4.4

When you import graphics saved from Photoshop, Illustrator, or other compatible graphics programs, you can specify import options to use the same transparency as the original file, set the visibility of layers, and use clipping paths, which allows you to use only part of a graphic (the rest is transparent). If you save a Photoshop file with an Alpha Channel (white or shades of gray) as a PSD, TIFF or JPEG, or with a clipping path as a PSD, TIFF or EPS, you can import the graphic into your document and retain the Alpha Channel transparency or clipping path. For Photoshop, Illustrator, InDesign, and PDF files, you can specify which layers in the file you want to import into your document.

Import Layers or Transparency

1 Click the **File** menu, and then click **Place**.

2 Select the file (PSD, AI, INDD, or PDF) you want to place.

3 Select the **Show Import Options** check box to select import options.

4 Click **Open**.

The Image Import Options dialog box appears.

5 To set transparency, click the **General** tab, and then select the **Transparent Background** check box.

6 To set layer visibility, click the **Layers** tab, and then do any of the following:

◆ **Show or Hide Layers.** Click the visibility icon.

◆ **Update Links.** Select options to reset/use or maintain layer visibility overrides.

7 Click **OK**.

8 Click or drag a rectangle frame with the loaded cursor to place the graphic.

9 To edit the layers options, click the **Object** menu, and then click **Object Layer Options**.

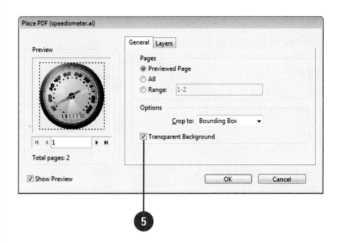

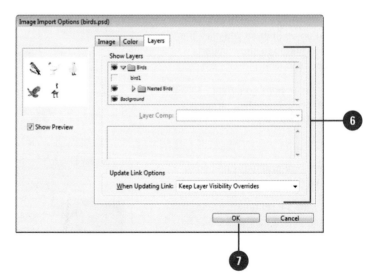

Import and Modify Clipping Paths or Alpha Channels

1. Click the **File** menu, and then click **Place**.

2. Select the file (PSD, TIFF, JPEG, or EPS) with the clipping path or Alpha Channel you want to place.

3. Select the **Show Import Options** check box to select import options.

4. Click **Open**.

   The Image Import Options dialog box appears.

5. Click the **Image** tab.

6. To import clipping paths, select the **Apply Photoshop Clipping Path** check box.

7. To select an Alpha Channel, click the **Alpha Channel** list arrow, and then select the one you want or select **None**.

8. Click **OK**.

9. Click or drag a rectangle frame with the loaded cursor to place the graphic.

10. To edit the clipping path, do any of the following:

    ◆ **Modify Path Shape.** Click the **Selection** tool, select the path, and drag points and handles.

    ◆ **Convert Path to a Frame.** Select the path, click the **Object** menu, point to **Clipping Path**, and then click **Convert Clipping Path to Frame**.

    ◆ **Set Path Options.** Click the **Object** menu, point to **Clipping Path**, and then click **Options**.

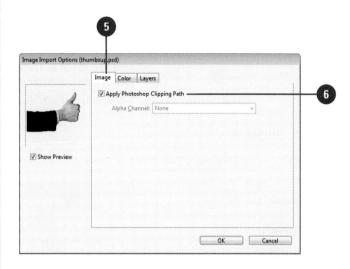

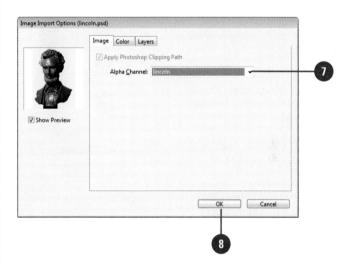

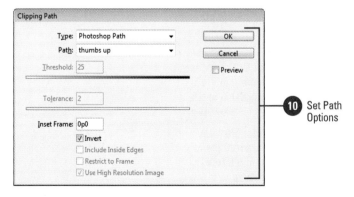

10 Set Path Options

Placing Multiple Graphics

With the Place command, you can place multiple graphics of different types at the same time. When you place graphics, InDesign loads them into a graphic preview cursor, which you can use to place them into a new or existing frame. A number appears in the loaded cursor indicating the number of loaded graphics. With the loaded cursor, you can also create a contact sheet to place multiple graphics in a grid arrangement (**New!**).

Place Multiple Graphics

1. Click the **File** menu, and then click **Place**.

2. Click the **Files of Type** (Win) or **Enable** (Mac) list arrow, and then click **Importable Files**.

3. Navigate to the drive or folder location with the files you want to import.

4. Select the graphic files you want to place.

   ◆ To select multiple files, use the Ctrl (Win) or ⌘ (Mac) key for individual files or the Shift key for a range of files.

5. Click **Open**.

   The imported graphic is placed in a loaded preview cursor. A number appears indicating the number of loaded graphics.

   ◆ Use the arrow keys to cycle through the graphic preview in the loaded cursor.

   ◆ Press Esc to delete the graphic in the preview of the loaded cursor.

   ◆ Use Alt (Win) or Option (Mac) to swap the element in the frame with the graphic in the loaded cursor.

6. Click or drag a rectangle frame with the loaded cursor to place each graphic in a new frame, or click in an empty frame to place the graphic in an existing frame.

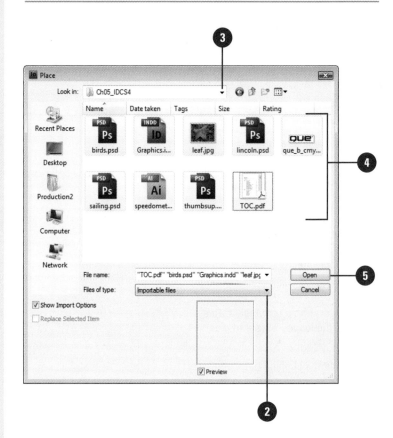

Place Multiple Graphics to Create a Contact Sheet

1. Click the **File** menu, and then click **Place**.

2. Click the **Files of Type** (Win) or **Enable** (Mac) list arrow, and then click **Importable Files**.

3. Navigate to the drive or folder location with the file you want to import.

4. Select the graphic files you want to place.

   ◆ To select multiple files, use the Ctrl (Win) or ⌘ (Mac) key for individual files or the Shift key for a range of files.

5. Click **Open**.

   The imported graphic is placed in a loaded preview cursor. A number appears indicating the number of loaded graphics.

   ◆ Use the arrow keys to cycle through the graphic preview in the loaded cursor.

   ◆ Press Esc to delete the graphic in the preview of the loaded cursor.

   ◆ Use Alt (Win) or Option (Mac) to swap the element in the frame with the graphic in the loaded cursor.

6. Ctrl (Win) or ⌘ (Mac)+Shift+drag a rectangle frame with the loaded cursor to place the graphics (**New!**).

   ◆ Before you release the mouse, use the arrow keys to adjust the number of rows and columns in the grid (**New!**).

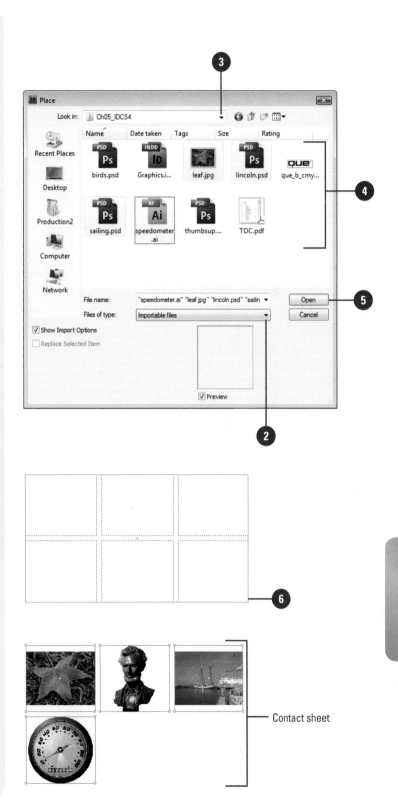

Contact sheet

Placing Graphics from Adobe Bridge

Adobe Bridge allows you to search, sort, filter, manage, and process files one at a time or in batches. You can open or place graphics directly into InDesign by using the Open With (Adobe InDesign) or Place (In InDesign) commands in Bridge from the File menu. You can also drag thumbnails from Bridge into an open InDesign document window.

Browse and Open Graphics with Adobe Bridge

1. Click the **Go to Bridge** button on the Application bar or click the **File** menu, and then click **Browse in Bridge**.

   Adobe Bridge opens, displaying files and folders on your computer.

2. Navigate to the drive or folder where the file is located.

3. Select the graphic thumbnail representing the file that you want to open in your InDesign document.

4. Click the **File** menu, point to **Open With**, and then click **Adobe InDesign CS4**.

Did You Know?

You can locate a linked graphic in Bridge from InDesign. In the Links panel, select the graphic name, click the Options menu, and then click Reveal In Bridge.

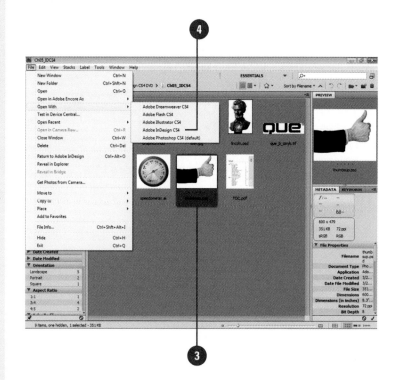

Place Graphics with Adobe Bridge

1️⃣ Click the **Go to Bridge** button on the Application bar or click the **File** menu, and then click **Browse in Bridge**.

Adobe Bridge opens, displaying files and folders on your computer.

2️⃣ Navigate to the drive or folder where the file is located.

3️⃣ Select the graphic thumbnail that represents the file you want to place in your InDesign document.

4️⃣ Click the **File** menu, point to **Place**, and then click **In InDesign**.

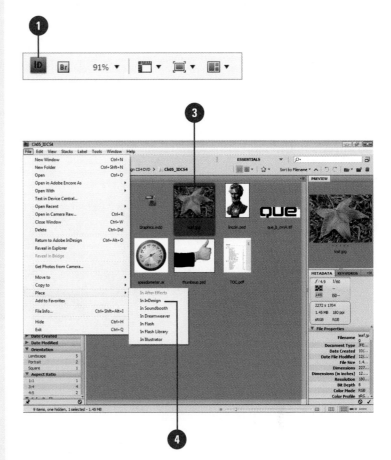

Copying or Moving Graphics

Instead of using the Place command, you can also copy and paste or drag-and-drop graphics from other programs directly into frames in your document. When you copy and paste graphics, InDesign converts the image to a compatible format during the transfer and embeds the graphic in your document at full resolution. **Embedding** inserts a copy from one document into another. An embedded graphic doesn't appear in the Links panel. When you drag-and-drop a graphic, InDesign creates a link just like when using the Place command.

Copy or Move Graphics

1. Open the program with the graphic that you want to copy or move into your InDesign document.

2. Select the graphic you want to use in InDesign.

3. Click the **Edit** menu, and then click **Copy** or **Cut**.

4. Close the program and switch back to InDesign.

5. Select the frame in which you want to place the graphic.

6. Click the **Edit** menu, and then click **Paste Into**.

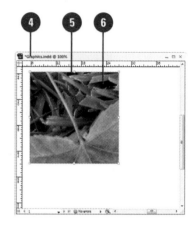

Drag and Drop Graphics

1. Open the program with the graphic that you want to copy into your InDesign document together with the InDesign program.

2. Select the graphic you want to use in InDesign.

3. Drag the graphic from the original program into your InDesign document.

Using the Links Panel

ID 4.3, 4.5

When you place a graphic, InDesign creates a link to the original file. **Linking** displays information stored in one document (the **source file**) in another (the **destination file**). You can edit the linked object from either file, although changes are stored in the source file. If you break the link between a linked object and its source file, the object becomes embedded. **Embedding** inserts a copy from one document into another. You can display and work with linked graphics in the Links panel. The Links panel allows you to relink a missing graphic, display a linked graphic, update a linked graphic, or edit a linked graphic in another program. Special icons appear next to linked graphics indicating a missing or modified link. You can also sort items (**New!**) and display information about a linked graphic, such as name, color space (mode), dimension (resolution), scale, format, and the path to the source in the Links panel.

Display Linked Graphic Information in the Links Panel

1 Select the **Links** panel.

◆ Click the **Window** menu, and then click **Links**.

   TIMESAVER *Press Shift+Ctrl+D (Win) or Shift+⌥⌘+D (Mac).*

2 Select the linked graphic for which you want to display information.

3 Click the **Show/Hide Link Information** button on the panel.

◆ You can click the **Next** and **Previous** button to view links.

4 Scroll down the list as needed to review the information for the selected linked graphic.

5 To sort items (**New!**) in the Links panel, click the **Name**, **Status** icon, **Page** icon, or **Type** icon at the top of the panel to sort items in the list. Click the icon again to change the sort order.

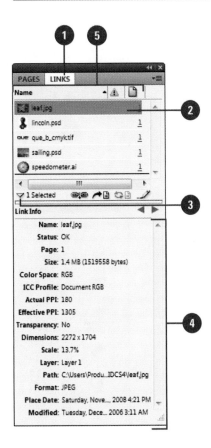

Managing Linked Graphics

ID 4.5

After you link or embed a graphic image file into an InDesign document, you can use the Links panel in InDesign to manage and work with the files. The Links panel displays a list of all the linked or embedded (contained within the document) files in your document. You can use the Links panel to update, replace, or relink a graphic image file. If a linked file is moved from its original location, you need to repair the link the next time you open the document. If a linked file needs to be updated, a warning icon appears in the Links panel to let you know.

Replace a Linked Graphic

1. Select the **Links** panel.

   ◆ Click the **Window** menu, and then click **Links**.

2. Select the linked graphic that you want to relink.

3. Click the **Relink** button on the panel.

4. Select the graphic file that you want to use as the replacement in the active document.

5. Click **Open**.

   ◆ You can also select the image in the document window, click the **File** menu, click **Place**, select a replacement image, select the **Replace Selected Item** check box, and then click **Open**.

Did You Know?

You can locate a placed graphic in your document. In the Links panel, select the graphic that you want to find, and then click the Go To Link button on the panel.

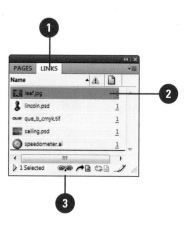

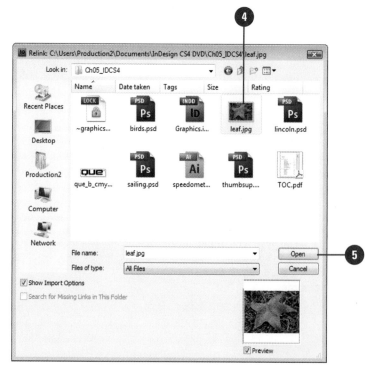

Work with Linked Graphics

1. Select the **Links** panel.

   ◆ Click the **Window** menu, and then click **Links**.

2. Select the linked graphic that you want to change.

3. Do any of the following:

   ◆ Update a Link. Click the **Update Link** button on the panel.

   ◆ Update All Links. Click the **Options** menu, and then click **Update All Links**.

   ◆ Go to Link. Click the **Go To Link** button on the panel.

   ◆ Edit Original. Click the **Edit Original** button on the panel to open the program that created the file and edit it.

   ◆ View Information. Double-click the graphic name, and then view the link information at the bottom of the panel.

   ◆ Change from Linked to Embedded. Click the **Options** menu, and then click **Embed Link**.

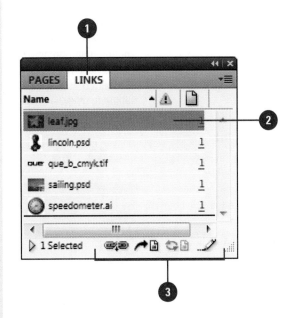

Did You Know?

You can change a linked graphic to an embedded graphic. Select the Links panel, select the linked graphic, click the Options menu, and then click Embed Link. If you prefer the graphic to be linked, select the embedded graphic (with the embedded icon), click the Options menu, click Unembed Link, and then click Yes.

Editing a Linked Graphic

 ID 4.5

When you link a graphic into an InDesign document, you need to edit the graphic in the source file using the original or a compatible program. You can open the program from Windows Explorer or the Finder and the open the graphic file, or you can have InDesign do it for you. You can use the Edit Original command to edit the file with the program associated with that particular file extension, or go to the Edit With submenu (**New!**) to select an editing program.

Edit a Linked Graphic in the Source

1. Select the **Links** panel.

   ◆ Click the **Window** menu, and then click **Links**.

2. Select the linked graphic that you want to edit.

3. Do any of the following:

   ◆ **Edit Original.** Click the **Edit Original** button on the Control panel.

   ◆ **Edit With.** Click the **Options** menu, point to **Edit With**, and then select an editing program.

   The editing program opens, displaying the linked graphic.

4. Make the changes you want to the linked graphic.

5. Click the **File** menu, and then click **Save**.

6. Click the **File** menu, and then click **Exit** or **Quit**.

   Your saved changes are updated in your document.

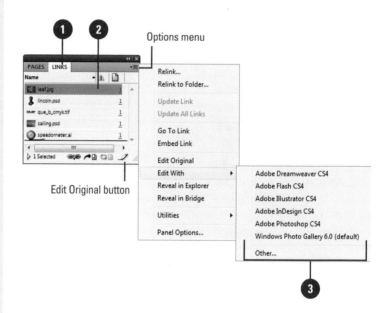

Options menu

Edit Original button

Displaying XMP Graphic Information

ID 4.2

When you place a graphic into an InDesign document, the graphic file includes information and data about itself. This data is saved with the file as metadata in the XMP format (Extensible Metadata Platform), and can be recognized and accessed by InDesign or any other application, such as Adobe Bridge, that reads XMP metadata. For example, if an image is a photograph, the metadata includes the type of image, where the image was shot, the camera used, shutter speed, f-stop, and other information, such as author and copyright. You can do the same with video and audio data, too.

Display XMP Metadata for a Linked Image

1. Select the **Links** panel.

   ◆ Click the **Window** menu, and then click **Links**.

2. Select the linked graphic for which you want to display information.

3. Click the **Options** menu, and then point to **Utilities**, and then click **XMP File Info**.

4. Click the different tabs to display information about the selected graphic.

5. Review the information and enter any new information (if available) you have related to the graphic.

6. Click **OK**.

See Also

See "Inserting File Information" on page 402 for more information on the types of information available in the File Information dialog box.

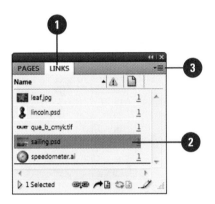

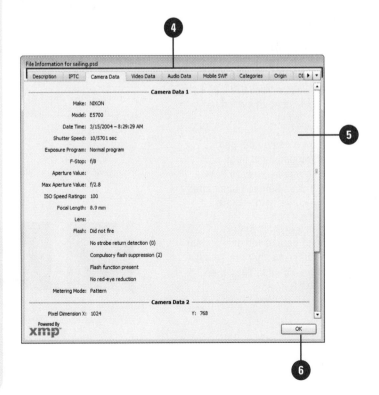

Creating Specialty Frames for Graphics

Instead of using the standard rectangle, ellipse, or polygon frames to place graphics, you can create and use specialty frames. A specialty frame is a vector-based compound path. You can create a compound path from one or more standard frames or text in InDesign, or you can import one from another vector-based program, such as Adobe Illustrator, that uses the AICB (Adobe Illustrator Clipboard). When you combine multiple frames into one compound path, the placed graphic appears across all the frames. You can unique specialty frames from text characters. The Create Outlines command converts characters in a text frame into a compound path. If you no longer want to use a compound path, you can use the Release Compound Path command to split the compound path up into individual frames.

Create and Release a Compound Path as a Frame

1. Select the **Selection** or **Direct Selection** tool on the Tools panel.

2. Select the frames that you want to use in the compound path.

   ◆ If the frames overlap, a transparent hole appears where the frames overlap.

3. Click the **Object** menu, point to **Paths**, and then click **Make Compound Path**.

   A compound path displays diagonal lines across the entire set of frames instead of individual frames.

4. To release a compound path, select the compound path, click the **Object** menu, point to **Paths**, and then click **Release Compound Path**.

   If there is a graphic in the compound path, it will only appear in the first frame after you release the compound path. The other frames will be empty.

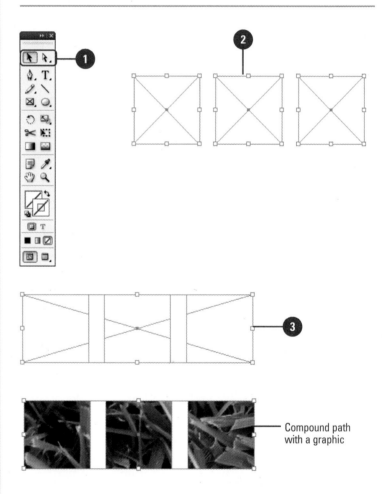

Compound path with a graphic

Create Type Outlines as Frames

1. Select the **Selection** tool on the Tools panel.

2. Select the text frame or double-click the text and then select characters.

3. Click the **Type** menu, and then click **Create Outlines**.

   InDesign creates a compound path from the text in the text frame.

   If you want to place different graphics in each of the letter frames, you need to ungroup (if needed) and release the compound path for the entire group first.

4. To release the compound path, click the **Object** menu, point to **Paths**, and then click **Release Compound Path**.

Import Paths as Frames

1. Open the program with the path that you want to copy into your InDesign document together with the InDesign program.

2. Drag the path from the original program into your InDesign document.

   When a black line appears around the boundaries of your document window, release the mouse to place the path.

Did You Know?

You can also use copy and paste. Instead of using drag-and-drop, you can also use copy and paste to import a path from another vector-based program.

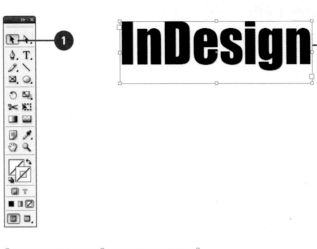

Outline with a graphic

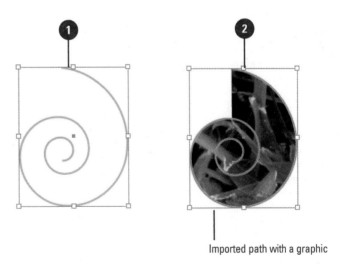

Imported path with a graphic

Selecting and Moving Frames and Graphics

Before you can work with the graphic in a frame, you need to select it first. There are two bounding boxes around the graphic. One for the frame (blue) and another for the graphic (brown). You have several options depending on what you want to accomplish. You can select the frame and graphic, just the frame, or just the graphic. If you want to resize the frame as well as the graphic inside, you need to select both. If you want to keep the frame the current size and resize the graphic, you need to just select the graphic and not the frame. The Selection and Direct Selection tools allow you to select the parts you want. If you want another option, you can also use the Position tool, which is a combination of the Selection and Direct Selection tools. After you select the parts you want, you can use options on the Control and Transform panels to modify the selection.

Select and Move Frames and Graphics

◆ **Select and Move the Frame and Graphic.** Select the **Selection** tool on the Tools panel, click the frame to show a bounding box, and then drag the selection.

  If you move quickly, only the bounding box appears as you reposition the frame. If you press down the mouse and pause for a moment before you drag, the graphic in the frame appears as you reposition the frame.

◆ **Select and Move the Frame.** Select the **Direct Selection** tool on the Tools panel, click the edge of the frame to show the points on the frame, Alt+click (Win) or Option (Mac)+click the frame edge again to select all the points, release the keys, and then drag the frame.

◆ **Select and Move the Graphic within the Frame.** Select the **Direct Selection** tool on the Tools panel, click inside the frame to show a bounding box with the Hand cursor, and then drag the graphic.

Frame selected

Graphic selected

Graphic moved

Use the Position Tool to Select and Move Frames and Graphic

1 Select the **Position** tool on the Tools panel.

There are two bounding boxes around the graphic. One for the frame and another for the graphic. The graphic bounding box appears in brown and the frame appears in blue by default. When you place a graphic the brown bounding box is on top of the blue bounding box.

2 Use any of the following methods:

◆ **Select the Frame.** Point to the edge of the frame (cursor changes to an arrow with a dot), and then click to select the bounding box.

A square handle appears on the corners and mid-points.

◆ **Resize the Frame.** Select the frame to display the square handles, and then drag to resize the frame.

◆ **Select the Graphic.** Point to the edge of the frame (cursor changes to a hand), and then click to select the graphic bounding box.

A square handle appears on the corners and mid-points.

◆ **Resize the Graphic and Not the Frame.** Select the graphic to display the square handles around the graphic, and then drag to resize the graphic.

◆ **Move the Graphic and Not the Frame.** Point to the graphic (cursor changes to a hand), and then drag the graphic to a new position in the frame bounding box.

Selected graphic

Selected frame

Fitting Graphics in Frames

When you place a graphic into a frame, it doesn't always fit the way you want. You can automatically resize the graphic to fill the entire frame or proportionally fill the frame. You can resize the graphic to fit the frame using buttons on the Control panel or commands on the Fitting submenu on the Object menu. If you want more control over how the graphic fits the frame, you can use the Frame Fitting Options dialog box.

Fit Graphics in Frames

1. Select the **Selection** or **Direct Selection** tool on the Tools panel.

2. Select the frame or the graphic.

3. Use any of the following methods:

   ◆ **Resize the Graphic to the Frame.** Click the **Fit Content to Frame** button on the Control panel.

   ◆ **Resize the Graphic Proportionally to the Frame.** Click the **Fit Content Proportionally** button on the Control panel.

   ◆ **Center the Graphic in the Frame.** Click the **Center Content** button on the Control panel.

   ◆ **Resize the Frame to the Graphic.** Click the **Fit Frame to Content** button on the Control panel.

      ◆ You can also double-click a frame handle to resize it to the graphic; a corner for proportional; a top or bottom for vertical; a right or left for horizontal.

   ◆ **Resize the Graphic to Fill the Frame.** Click the **Fill Frame Proportionally** button on the Control panel.

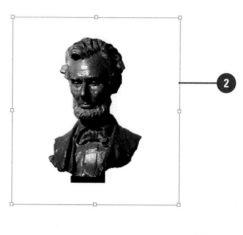

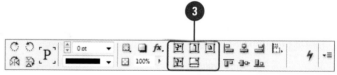

Resized graphic to fit frame

Fit Graphics in Frames Using Dialog Box Options

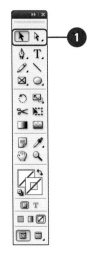

1 Select the **Selection** or **Direct Selection** tool on the Tools panel.

2 Select the frame or the graphic.

3 Click the **Object** menu, point to **Fitting**, and then click **Frame Fitting Options**.

4 Select the **Preview** check box to view your results in the document window.

5 Use any of the following methods:

◆ **Crop Amount.** Specify position values for Top, Bottom, Left, and Right to crop the graphic.

◆ **Reference Point.** Click the square you want to use as the positioning point for graphic fitting adjustments.

◆ **Fitting.** Select a fitting option to fit content to the frame, fit content proportionally to the frame, or to fill the frame proportionally.

6 Click **OK**.

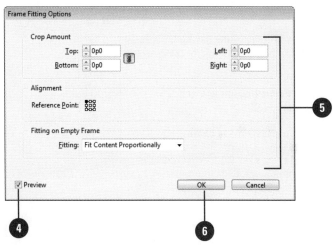

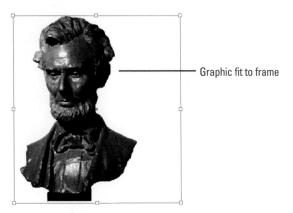

Graphic fit to frame

Nesting Graphics in Frames

In some cases you may want to place a graphic on top of an existing graphic. This is called a nesting graphic. For example, you can place a graphic in a rectangle frame, and then place another graphic in a circle frame inside the rectangle frame. You can also nest a text frame in a graphic frame. Frames can hold multiple levels of nested frames. After you nest graphics in a frame, you can use commands from the Select submenu on the Object menu to select the main container frame or nested frames.

Nest Graphics in a Frame

1. Select the **Selection** tool on the Tools panel.

2. Select the graphic or text frame that you want to place in a graphic frame.

3. Click the **Edit** menu, and then click **Cut** or **Copy**.

4. Select the graphic frame in which you want to place a graphic or text frame.

5. Click the **Edit** menu, and then click **Paste Into**.

6. To select frames, do any of the following:

   ◆ **Main Container.** Click the frame using the **Selection** tool on the Tools panel.

      ◆ You can drag the center point square (cursor changes to a black arrow) to move the object.

   ◆ **Nested Content.** Select the main container, click the **Object** menu, point to **Select**, and then click **Content**.

      ◆ To select other objects, click the **Object** menu, point to **Select**, and then click **Container**.

Formatting Graphics in Frames

If you place a grayscale graphic into your document, you can change the color of the graphic to create a different effect. A grayscale graphics uses black values to display the image, which you can change to a different color. With the Direct Selection tool, simply select the grayscale graphic, and then apply a fill color to it. If you want to lighten the effect, you can change the tint of the color. You can also use the same technique to change the color of the graphic frame fill or stroke.

Color a Grayscale Graphic

1. Select the **Direct Selection** tool on the Tools panel.

2. Select the grayscale graphic that you want to color.

3. Adjust the **Tint** in the Color panel.

4. Select a **Fill** color using the Tools or Color panel.

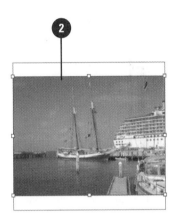

Did You Know?

You can color a graphic frame. Select the Selection tool on the Tools panel, select the graphic frame, and then select a Fill or Stroke color using the Tools or Color panel.

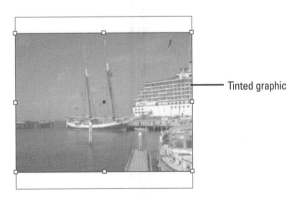

Tinted graphic

Controlling Graphics Display Performance

When you place multiple graphics in a document, the display performance of your screen can slow down. You can change display resolution settings for the entire document or for individual graphics to improve performance. You can set default display performance settings for all documents in the Display Performance preferences dialog box, for the current document on the Display Performance submenu on the View menu, or for individual graphics on the Display Performance submenu from the Object menu.

Change a Graphics Display Performance

1. Click the **View** menu, point to **Display Performance**, and then click **Allow Object-Level Display Settings** to select it.

2. Select the **Selection** or **Direct Selection** tool on the Tools panel.

3. Select the imported graphic.

4. Click the **Object** menu, point to **Display Performance**, and then select a performance option:

   ◆ **Fast Display.** Draws raster images or vector graphics as a gray box. Use to quickly page through documents with a lot of graphics. Best performance, lowest quality.

   ◆ **Typical Display.** Draws a low-resolution image (default). Use to quickly identify parts of a graphic.

   ◆ **High Quality Display.** Draws a high-resolution image. Use to view image details. Lowest performance, highest quality.

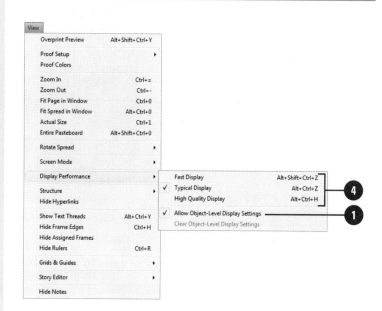

Set Default Display Performance Options

1. Click the **Edit** (Win) or **InDesign** (Mac) menu, point to **Preferences**, and then click **Display Performance**.

2. Click the **Default View** list arrow, and then select a performance option. See the previous page for details.

3. Select the **Preserve Object-Level Display Settings** check box to specify different display performance settings for individual objects.

4. Click the **Adjust View Settings** list arrow, and then select a performance option. See the previous page for details.

   If you want a custom setting, drag the sliders for **Raster Images**, **Vector Graphics**, and **Transparency**.

5. To specify text and graphic display performance with the Hand tool, drag the Hand Tool slider to the setting you want between better performance and higher quality.

6. Click **OK**.

Did You Know?

You can set document display performance. Click the View menu, point to Display Performance, and then select a performance option. See previous page for details.

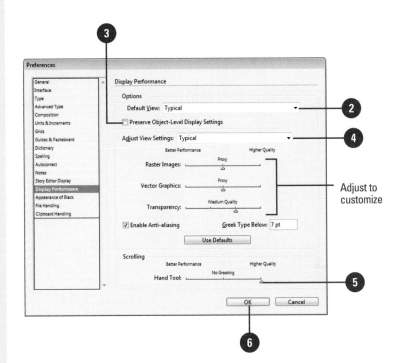

Adjust to customize

Working with Objects and Layers

6

Introduction

A frame is a container that holds graphics, text, and shapes. There are three types of frames: unassigned, graphic, and text. The unassigned frame is useful for adding fill and stroke color to a layout. You use the Rectangle, Ellipse, Polygon, and Line tools to create unassigned frames, while you use the Rectangle Frame, Ellipse Frame and Polygon Frame tools to create a graphic frame. A dot appears in the middle of an unassigned frame, while diagonal lines appear in a graphic frame. You can create shapes using unassigned or graphic shapes. You use the Type tool to create a text frame, which appears with small ports to thread text between frames.

With the transformation tools in InDesign, you can quickly move, scale (resize), shear (distort), and rotate an object. InDesign provides several ways to transform objects: tools (Rotate, Scale, and Shear) on the Tools panel, options on the Transform and Control panels, and commands on the Transform submenu on the Object menu.

Layers give you the ability to separate individual elements of your design, and then control how those elements appear. You can think of Layers as a group of transparent sheets stacked on top of each other, where each layer contains a separate aspect of the total design. Having multiple layers allows you to adjust and move each element independently.

What You'll Do

Create Shapes and Lines

Use the Selection Tool

Use the Direct Selection Tool

Resize and Move Objects

Duplicate Objects

Group and Combine Objects

Align and Distribute Objects

Arrange Object Stack Order

Transform Objects

Use the Free Transform Tool

Rotate, Scale, and Shear Objects

Repeat Object Transformations

Lock and Unlock Object Position

Create Inline Objects

Create Anchored Objects

Create and Delete Object Layers

Set Layer Options

Work with Layers

Use the Measure Tool

Creating Shapes

A frame is a container that holds graphics, text, and shapes. There are three types of frames: unassigned, graphic, and text. The unassigned frame is useful for adding fill and stroke color to a layout. You use the Rectangle, Ellipse, and Polygon tools to create unassigned frames, while you use the Rectangle Frame, Ellipse Frame and Polygon Frame tools to create a graphic frame. A dot appears in the middle of an unassigned frame, while diagonal lines appear in a graphic frame. You can create shapes using unassigned or graphic shapes. In addition to creating a polygon shape, you can also use the Polygon Frame tool to create a star shape for type. You can drag to create a frame box to the size that you want. If you need a frame box to be an exact size, you can click a blank area with the Rectangle and Ellipse tools or set width and height settings on the Control panel.

Create a Rectangle or Elliptical Shape

1. Select the **Rectangle** or **Rectangle Frame** tool or select the **Ellipse** or **Ellipse Frame** tool on the Tools panel.

   ◆ To create a frame to an exact size, click a blank area, specify the width and height you want, and then click **OK**.

2. Drag to create a rectangle or elliptical frame the size that you want.

   ◆ To draw the shape from the center, hold down Alt (Win) or Option (Mac) as you drag.

   ◆ To constrain the shape to a square or circle, hold down Shift as you drag.

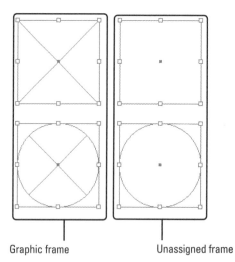

Graphic frame   Unassigned frame

Create a Polygon Shape

① Double-click the **Polygon** or **Polygon Frame** tool on the Tools panel.

② Enter a **Number of Sides** value for the polygon.

③ Leave the **Star Inset** value at 0% to create a polygon.

④ Click **OK**.

⑤ Drag to create a polygon frame box the size that you want.

◆ As you drag, press the Up or Down arrow keys to increase or decrease the number of sides.

◆ Use the Alt (Win) or Option (Mac) key as you drag to draw from center, or the Shift key to draw a proportional shape.

Create a Star Shape

① Double-click the **Polygon** or **Polygon Frame** tool on the Tools panel.

② Enter a **Number of Sides** value for the star.

③ Enter a **Star Inset** value. The higher the amount, the sharper the points.

④ Click **OK**.

⑤ Drag to create a star frame box the size that you want.

◆ As you drag, press the Up or Down arrow keys to increase or decrease the number of sides.

◆ Use the Alt (Win) or Option (Mac) key as you drag to draw from center, or the Shift key to draw a proportional shape.

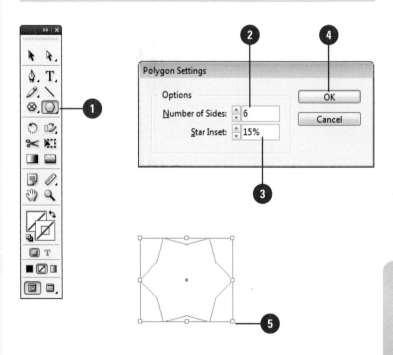

Creating Lines

The Line tool draws perfectly straight lines in any direction you drag your mouse. In InDesign, a line is called a stroke and there is a variety of thicknesses, styles, colors, and fills that can be applied to it using the Control, Stroke, and Color panels. You can also create your own line style for specific types of dashed, dotted or artistic lines. You can draw lines at precise 45- or 90-degree angles by holding down the Shift key as you drag.

Draw a Line

① Click the **Line** tool on the Tools panel.

The pointer becomes a crosshair that you can drag on the pasteboard.

② Select a line **Weight** on the Control panel.

③ Drag to create a line the size that you want.

◆ As you drag, hold down the Shift key, and then drag to draw a 45-, 90-, or 180-degree line.

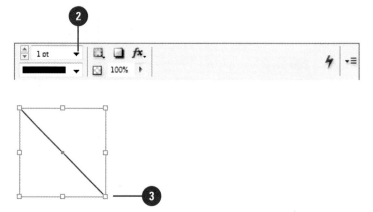

Using the Selection Tool

There are several ways to select objects in InDesign. The Selection tool selects entire objects, while the Direct Selection tool selects a point on an object or images inside objects. With the Selection tool, you can select an object's stroke or fill. After you select one or more objects, you can add or subtract objects to/from the selection. In addition, you can use the Selection tool and drag a marquee to select parts of the object or drag over a portion of it to create a selection rectangle.

Select an Object with the Selection Tool

1 Click the **Selection** tool on the Tools panel.

The pointer becomes a black arrow. When you point to a selectable object, a black dot appears on the bottom right.

2 Position the arrow on the edge or fill (if present) of the object and then click to select it.

◆ You can also drag a marquee across all or part of the object to select the entire object.

Square resize handles appear on each corner and midpoint line of the object.

3 To add or subtract objects from the selection, hold down the Shift key, and then click unselected objects to add or click selected objects to subtract them from the selection.

TIMESAVER *Click the Edit menu, and then click Select All or press Ctrl+A (Win) or ⌘+A (Mac) to select everything on the page.*

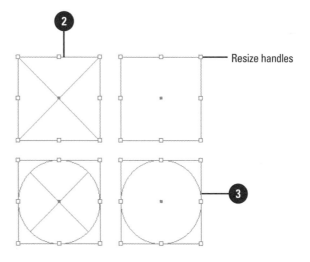

Resize handles

Did You Know?

You can delete an object. Select the object that you want to delete, and then press Delete, or click the Edit menu, and then click Clear.

Using the Direct Selection Tool

With the Direct Selection tool, you can select a point on an object or graphics inside an object. When you select an object with the Direct Selection tool, anchor points appear on the corners of the frame. You can select the object and one or more anchor points and drag to change the shape of the frame. With the Direct Selection tool, you can also select a graphic. There are two bounding boxes around a graphic frame. One for the frame (blue) and another for the graphic (brown). You can select the frame or graphic. When you select the frame, anchor points appear. When you select the graphic, square resizing handles appear on each corner and midpoint line. When you select a graphic, the Direct Selection tool works like the Selection tool.

Select a Graphic with the Direct Selection Tool

1. Click the **Direct Selection** tool on the Tools panel.

   The cursor becomes a white arrow. When you point to a graphic, the cursor changes to a hand.

   TIMESAVER *Press A to select the Direct Selection tool.*

2. Position the hand cursor on the graphic, then click to select it.

   Square resizing handles appear on each corner and midpoint line of the object.

3. Use any of the following to work with the selected graphic:

   ◆ To move the graphic in the frame, drag the graphic.

   ◆ To resize the graphic, drag the resize handles.

Frame selected

See Also

See "Selecting and Moving Frames and Graphics" on pages 144-145 for more information on using the Position tool.

Select an Object and Anchor Points with the Direct Selection Tool

1. Click the **Direct Selection** tool on the Tools panel.

   The cursor becomes a white arrow. When you point to a selectable point, a black dot appears near the white arrow. When you point to a selectable edge, a small line appears near the white arrow.

   TIMESAVER *Press A to select the Direct Selection tool.*

2. Position the arrow on the edge or fill (if present) of the object and then click to select it.

   ◆ You can also drag a marquee across all or part of the object to select the entire object.

   Small square anchor points appear on each corner of the object.

3. To select an anchor point, click the small square point to select it.

   The anchor point becomes solid.

4. To add or subtract anchor points or segments from the selection, hold down the Shift key, and then click unselected items to add them or selected items to subtract them from the selection.

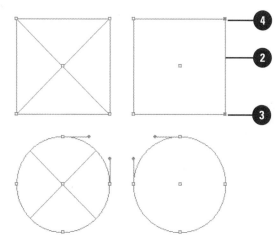

Resizing Objects

ID 1.6

When an object is too big or small for its location, you can resize the object to fit. When you select an object with the Selection tool, square resizing handles appears on the corner and midpoint, which you can drag to change the size of the object. If you drag quickly, you only see the bounding box for the object. If you press and hold down the mouse for a moment, and then drag, you see the object as you resize it. Resizing an object is different than scaling an object. Resizing an object changes the width and height, but the scaling remains the same. Scaling an object changes the width and height by a percentage.

Resize an Object

1. Select the **Selection** tool on the Tools panel.

2. Select one or more objects that you want to resize.

3. Drag a resizing handle to adjust the size of the object:

    ◆ Drag a corner handle to resize both width and height. Use the Shift key to keep the object proportional.

    ◆ Drag a side handle to resize only the width or height.

    If you drag quickly, you only see the bounding box for the object. If you press and hold down the mouse for a moment, and then drag, you see the object as you resize it.

4. Release the mouse to resize the object to the size you want.

Did You Know?

You can resize an object to an exact size with the Control panel. Select the object, and then enter width and height values in the Control panel.

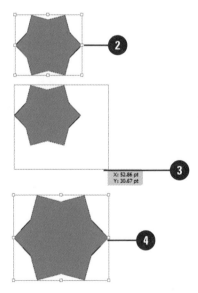

X: 52.86 pt
Y: 30.67 pt

Moving Objects

Moving an object or group of objects is very easy. The simplest way is to drag the edge or fill (if present) of an object. If you want to constrain the movement of the object in multiples of 45 degrees, then use the Shift key as you drag. When you drag an object with Smart Guides enabled, Smart Guides appear automatically to make it easier for you to align objects with other objects.

Move an Object

1. Select the **Selection** tool on the Tools panel.

2. Select one or more objects that you want to move.

3. Drag the edge or fill (if present) of an object.

   ◆ To constrain the movement of the object to multiples of 45 degrees, hold down the Shift key as you drag.

Did You Know?

You can enable Smart Guides. Click the View menu, point to Grids & Guides, and then click Smart Guides to select it (a check mark indicates the item is selected).

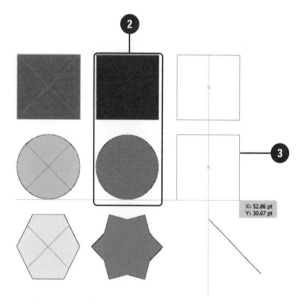

Duplicating Objects

Duplicating objects can be a powerful way of creating geometrical art-work. You can duplicate one or more selected objects by dragging them, using keys, copying to and pasting from the Clipboard, or using the Step and Repeat command. The Step and Repeat command dupli-cates copies of an object and positions them at specific horizontal and vertical intervals. For example, you can create a span of objects across the page, or a grid of objects.

Duplicate and Copy Objects

1 Select the **Selection** tool on the Tools panel.

♦ If the object is in a group, select the **Direct Selection** tool on the Tools panel.

2 Use any of the following methods:

♦ Copy and Paste. Select the object, click the **Edit** menu, and then click **Copy**. Click in the target document or area, click the **Edit** menu, and then click **Paste** or **Paste in Place**.

♦ Duplicate. Select the object, click the **Edit** menu, and then click **Duplicate**.

♦ Duplicate as You Drag. Hold down Alt (Win) or Option (Mac), and then drag the edge or fill of the object.

♦ Duplicate Between Documents. Open the documents side by side, and then drag the edge or fill of the object from one document to another.

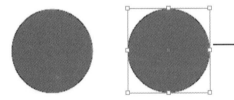

Duplicate Multiple Objects

1 Select the **Selection** tool on the Tools panel.

2 Select the object that you want to duplicate using the step and repeat process.

3 Click the **Edit** menu, and then click **Step and Repeat**.

4 Select the **Preview** check box to view your results in the document window.

5 Enter a **Repeat Count** value with the number of duplicates you want to create in the top row.

6 Enter a **Horizontal Offset** value with the horizontal distance you want between the duplicate objects.

7 Enter a **Vertical Offset** value with the vertical distance you want between the duplicate objects.

8 Click **OK**.

Did You Know?

You can create a grid with the Step and Repeat command. Select an object, click the Edit menu, and then click Step And Repeat. Enter the number of duplicates for the Repeat Count, enter zero for the Horizontal Offset, and then click OK. Select the entire row of objects, click the Edit menu, and then click Step And Repeat. Enter the number of rows for the Repeat Count, enter zero for the Vertical Offset, and then click OK.

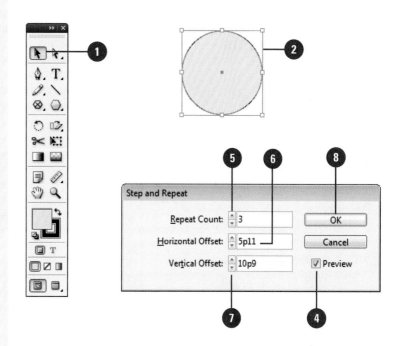

Step and Repeat

Repeat Count:	3	OK
Horizontal Offset:	5p11	Cancel
Vertical Offset:	10p9	☑ Preview

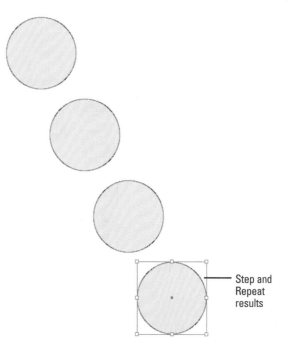

Step and Repeat results

Grouping and Combining Objects

Selecting and grouping objects makes it easier to work with multiple objects as if they were a single object. You can easily select, cut, copy, paste, move, recolor, and transform a grouped object. You can group all types of objects, yet still edit individual objects within the group as needed without having to ungroup them first by using the Direct Selection tool. If you no longer need to group objects, you can ungroup them. You can also use the Paste In command to combine objects.

Create a Group

1. Select the **Selection** tool on the Tools panel.

2. Use a selection method to select the objects that you want in the group.

3. Click the **Objects** menu, and then click **Group**.

   ◆ You can use the Group command again to group objects already in a group; this is known as a nested group.

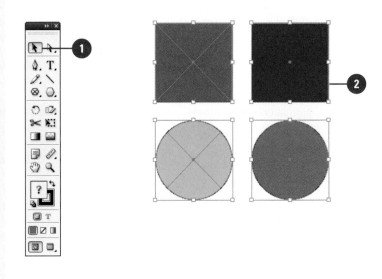

Ungroup Objects

1. Select the **Selection** tool on the Tools panel.

2. Select the grouped objects that you want to ungroup.

3. Click the **Objects** menu, and then click **Ungroup**.

   ◆ If you have nested groups within an object, you can use the Ungroup command again to ungroup them.

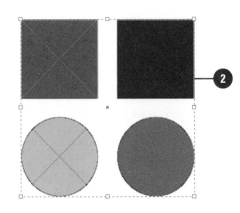

Select Objects in a Group

1. Select the **Selection** tool on the Tools panel.

2. Select the grouped object.

   TIMESAVER *Double-click to select an object in the group.*

3. Click the **Object** menu, point to **Select**, and then click **Content**.

   The topmost object in the group is selected.

4. Click the **Object** menu, point to **Select**, and then click **Previous Object** or **Next Object**.

   The previous or next object in the group is selected.

5. To select the group again, click the **Object** menu, point to **Select**, and then click **Container**.

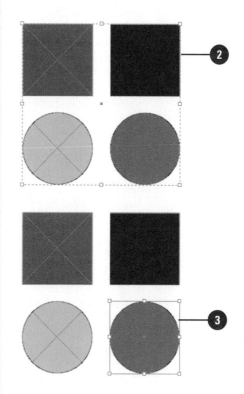

Combine Objects

1. Select the **Selection** tool on the Tools panel.

2. Select the object you want to combine into another object.

3. Click the **Edit** menu, and then click **Copy** or **Cut**.

4. Select the object with which you want to combine other objects.

5. Click the **Edit** menu, and then click **Paste Into**.

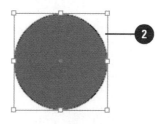

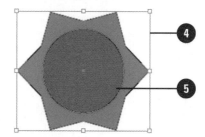

Did You Know?

You can remove a combined object.
Select the Direct Selection tool, select the pasted-in object, and then press Delete.

Aligning and Distributing Objects

In addition to using grids and guides to align objects to a specific point, you can align a group of objects to each other. The alignment buttons on the Align and Control panels make it easy to align two or more objects relative to each other or to the page. To evenly align several objects to each other across the document, either horizontally or vertically, select them and then choose a distribution option. Before you select an align command, specify how you want InDesign to align the objects. You can align the objects in relation to the page, margins, spread, or selection.

Align Objects

1. Select the **Selection** tool on the Tools panel.

2. Select two or more objects to align them.

3. Select the **Align** panel.

   ◆ Click the **Window** menu, point to **Object & Layout**, and then click **Align**.

4. Click the **Alignment** list arrow, and then select how you want to align the objects:

   ◆ **Align to Selection.** Aligns objects to themselves.

   ◆ **Align to Margins.** Aligns objects to the margin size.

   ◆ **Align to Page.** Aligns objects to the page size.

   ◆ **Align to Spread.** Aligns objects to the spread size.

5. If you want to align objects to an object, click the **Object** menu, and then click **Lock Position** to lock the object in place.

6. Use the alignment buttons on the Align or Control panel.

   ◆ **Align Top or Bottom Edges.**

   ◆ **Align Left or Right Edges.**

   ◆ **Align Horizontal or Vertical Centers.**

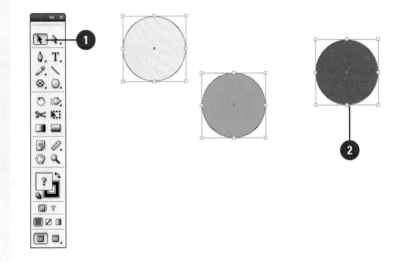

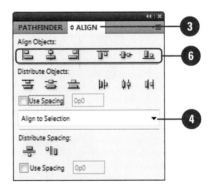

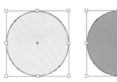

Results

Distribute Objects

①　Select the **Selection** tool on the Tools panel.

②　Select three or more objects to distribute them.

③　Select the **Align** panel.

◆ Click the **Window** menu, point to **Object & Layout**, and then click **Align**.

④　To apply a spacing distance, select the **Use Spacing** check box, and then enter a spacing value for tops, centers, bottoms, or sides.

⑤　Use the distribution buttons on the Align panel.

◆ **Distribute Top or Bottom Edges.**

◆ **Distribute Left or Right Edges.**

◆ **Distribute Horizontal or Vertical Centers.**

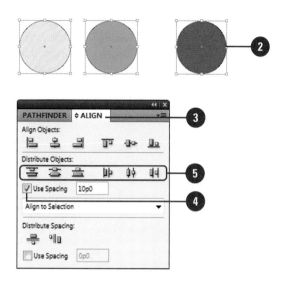

Results

Distribute Objects with Spacing

①　Select the **Selection** tool on the Tools panel.

②　Select two or more objects to distribute them.

③　Select the **Align** panel.

◆ Click the **Window** menu, point to **Object & Layout**, and then click **Align**.

④　To apply a spacing distance, select the **Use Spacing** check box, and then enter an object spacing value.

⑤　Use the **Distribute Horizontal Space** or **Distribute Vertical Space** buttons on the Align panel.

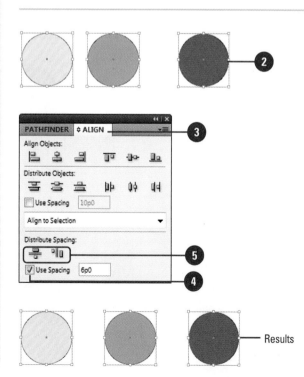

Results

Arranging Object Stack Order

Multiple objects on a document appear in a stacking order, like layers of transparencies. Stacking is the placement of objects one on top of another. In other words, the first object that you draw is on the bottom and the last object that you draw is on top. You can change the order of this stack of objects by using Bring to Front, Send to Back, Bring Forward, and Send Backward commands on the Arrange submenu from the Object menu.

Arrange a Stack of Objects

1. Select the **Selection** tool on the Tools panel.

2. Select the objects you want to arrange.

3. Click the stacking option you want.

   ◆ Click the **Object** menu, point to **Arrange**, and then click **Bring to Front** or **Bring Forward** to move an object to the top of the stack or up one location in the stack.

   ◆ Click the **Object** menu, point to **Arrange**, and then click **Send to Back** or **Send Backward** to move an object to the bottom of the stack or back one location in the stack.

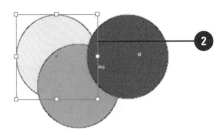

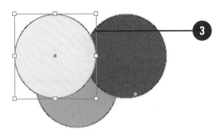

Transforming Objects

With the transformation tools in InDesign, you can quickly move, scale (resize), shear (distort), and rotate an object. InDesign provides several ways to transform objects: tools (Rotate, Scale, and Shear) on the Tools panel, options on the Transform and Control panels, and commands on the Transform submenu on the Object menu. All transformations are performed based on a reference point; center is the default, however, you can change it on the Control or Transform panel. When you perform a transformation on an object, InDesign remembers it, which allows you to repeat the last transformation by using commands on the Transform Again submenu on the Object menu. If you don't like a transformation, you can use the Clear Transformation command to remove it.

Transform Objects

1. Select the **Selection** tool on the Tools panel.

2. Select one or more objects to transform.

3. Use any of the following methods:

   ◆ **Transform Tools.** Select a transform tool (Rotate, Scale, and Shear) on the Tools panel, and then drag to apply the transformation.

   ◆ **Transform Panel.** Click the **Window** menu, point to **Object & Layout**, and then click **Transform**. Enter desired values to apply the transformation.

   ◆ **Transform Menu.** Click the **Object** menu, point to **Transform**, and then select a transform option.

      ◆ Click **Clear Transformations** to remove a transformation.

   ◆ **Transform Again.** Select a different object to apply the same transformation. Click the **Object** menu, point to **Transform Again**, and then select a transform again option.

   ◆ **Reference Point.** Select an object, and then click a square reference point on the Control or Transform panel.

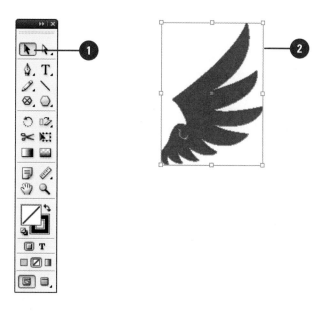

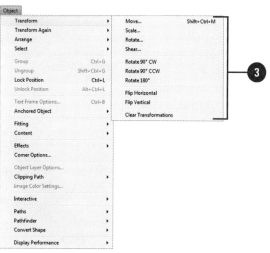

Using the Free Transform Tool

ID 1.6

The Free Transform tool allows you to rotate, scale (resize), or shear (slant) an object. However, you cannot copy an object or move the reference point. As you drag to transform an object, you can use keyboard keys to alter the results of a transformation. Free Transform makes it easy to transform an object by using the mouse to visually get the results that you want. The Free Transform tool works just like the one in Illustrator and Photoshop (**New!**). If you need to use exact values for a transformation, you can use the Control or Transform panel.

Transform an Object with the Free Transform Tool

1. Select the **Free Transform** tool on the Tools panel.

2. Select one or more objects to transform.

3. Use any of the following methods:

   ◆ Scale. Drag a corner handle to scale along two axes; drag a side handle to scale along one axis; Shift-drag to scale proportionally; hold down Alt (Win) or Option (Mac), and then drag to scale from the center. Or, hold down Shift to scale from the center proportionally.

   ◆ Rotate. Point slightly outside a corner handle (pointer changes to a double arrow), and then drag in a circular motion. To rotate in 45-degree increments, Shift-drag.

   To rotate an object 180 degrees, drag a corner handle diagonally all the way across the object.

   ◆ Shear. Drag a side handle and then hold down Ctrl (Win) or ⌘ (Mac) as you continue to drag. To constrain the movement, also press Shift. To shear from the center, add the Alt (Win) or Option (Mac) key.

Shear

Scale

Rotate

Rotating Objects

ID 1.6

After you create an object, you can change its orientation by rotating it. For a freeform rotation, when you want to rotate the object in other than 90-degree increments, you can use the Rotate tool. You can transform the object from its center or the reference point. To rotate an object in 90-degree increments or flip it horizontally or vertically, you can use easy access buttons on the Control panel. If you want to rotate an object with an exact angle value, you can use the Control or Transform panel, which is available on the Object & Layout submenu on the Window menu.

Free Rotate an Object

1. Select the **Selection** tool on the Tools panel.

2. Select one or more objects to transform.

3. Select the **Rotate** tool on the Tools panel.

4. To move the reference point, click a new point.

5. Drag in a circular motion.

   ◆ To rotate in 45-degree increments, Shift-drag.

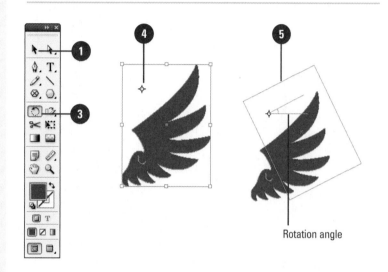

Rotation angle

Rotate or Flip an Object

1. Select the **Selection** tool on the Tools panel.

2. Select one or more objects to transform.

3. Use any of the following methods:

   ◆ Rotate Value. Enter a **Rotation Angle** on the Control or Transform panel.

   ◆ Rotate 90° Intervals. Click the **Rotate 90° Clockwise** or **Rotate 90° Counter-clockwise** button on the Control panel.

   ◆ Flip. Click the **Flip Horizontal** or **Flip Vertical** button on the Control panel.

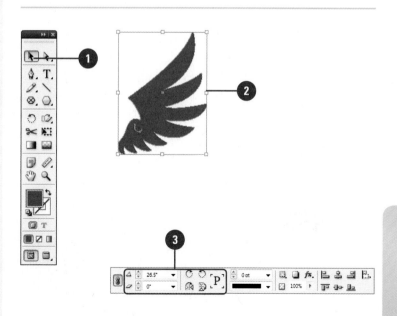

Scaling Objects

ID 1.6

After you create an object, you can change its size by scaling it. To resize an object, either smaller or larger, you can use the Scale tool. You can transform the object from its center or the reference point. If you want to scale an object using exact percentages, you can use the Transform panel, which is available from the Object & Layout submenu on the Window menu.

Scale an Object

① Select the **Selection** tool on the Tools panel.

② Select one or more objects to transform.

③ Select the **Scale** tool on the Tools panel.

④ To move the reference point, click a new point.

⑤ Use any of the following methods:

◆ Scale. Drag away from or toward the object. Shift-drag to scale proportionally; hold down Alt (Win) or Option (Mac), and then drag to scale from the center. Or, hold down Shift to scale from the center proportionally.

◆ Scale and Flip. Drag across the entire object.

◆ Scale and Copy. Hold down Alt+Shift (Win) or Option+Shift (Mac), and then drag.

⑥ To scale an object using exact percentages, use the Control or Transform panel.

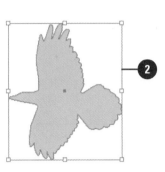

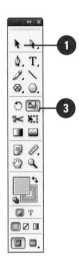

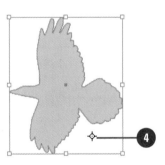

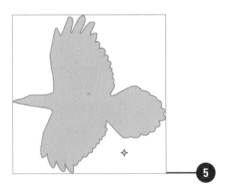

Shearing Objects

ID 1.6

The Shear tool on the Tools panel allow you to be creative as you transform object by creating a slanted version of that object. You can transform the object from its center or the reference point. If you want to shear an object using exact angle values, you can use the Control panel or the Transform panel, which is available on the Object & Layout submenu on the Window menu.

Shear an Object

1. Select the **Selection** tool on the Tools panel.

2. Select one or more objects to transform.

3. Select the **Shear** tool on the Tools panel.

4. To move the reference point, click a new point.

5. Drag away from the object.

6. To shear an object using exact angle values, use the Control or Transform panel.

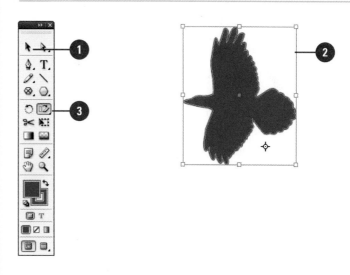

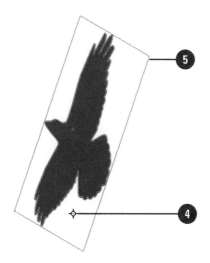

Repeating Object Transformations

When you perform a transformation on an object, InDesign remembers your choices, which allows you to repeat the transformation again on another object. With the commands on the Transform Again submenu on the Object menu, you can repeat transformations individually or as a sequence. Experiment with the different options to create varied results. If you don't like a transformation, you can use the Clear Transformation command from the Transform submenu on the Object menu to remove it.

Repeat Object Transformations

1. Select the **Selection** tool on the Tools panel.

2. Select one or more objects to transform.

3. Use any of the transformation commands on an object.

4. Select a different object.

5. Click the **Object** menu, point to **Transform Again**, and then select one of the following commands:

   - **Transform Again.** Applies the last single transform command to the selection as a whole.

   - **Transform Again Individually.** Applies the last single transform command to each object in the selection.

   - **Transform Sequence Again.** Applies the last set of transform commands to the selection as a whole.

   - **Transform Sequence Again Individually.** Applies the last set of transform commands to each object in the selection.

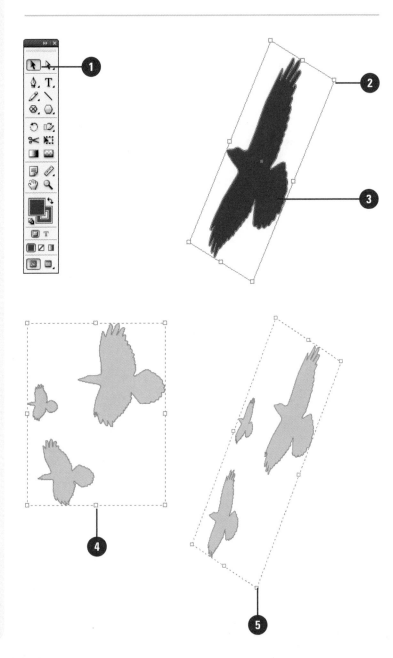

Locking and Unlocking Object Position

After you've spent a lot of time laying out objects in your document, you may want to lock everything into place. The Lock Position command allows you to lock the position of one or more selected objects. A locked object can still be selected and text or graphics inside the object can still be modified. However, the position of the object cannot be changed. If you want to move a locked object, you need to unlock it first.

Lock or Unlock Object Position

1. Select the **Selection** tool on the Tools panel.

2. Select one or more objects to lock or locked objects to be unlocked.

3. Click the **Object** menu, and then click **Lock Position** or **Unlock Position**.

   When you try to move the object, the cursor changes to a lock icon, and the object doesn't move.

Creating Inline Objects

An inline object is a shape or graphic that is pasted into a text frame. The object is pasted into a text frame in the same way as a text. When the object is placed in a text, you can adjust the object in the frame by using the Direct Selection tool or move the object in the text frame by using the Selection tool. You can also use any of the Text Wrap command in the Text Wrap panel to wrap text around the object.

Create an Inline Object

1. Select the **Selection** tool on the Tools panel.

2. Select a text frame into which you want to paste a shape or graphic.

3. Click to place the insertion point in the text where you want to place the inline object by using the **Type** tool.

4. Click the **Edit** menu, and then click **Paste**.

5. To adjust the object in the frame, drag the object using the **Direct Selection** tool. To move the object in the text frame, drag the object by using the **Selection** tool.

Did You Know?

You can place an inline graphic object. Click to place the insertion point where you want the inline graphic, click the File menu, click Place, select the graphic file, and then click Open.

See Also

See "Wrapping Text Around an Object" on pages 122-123 for more information on wrapping text around an object.

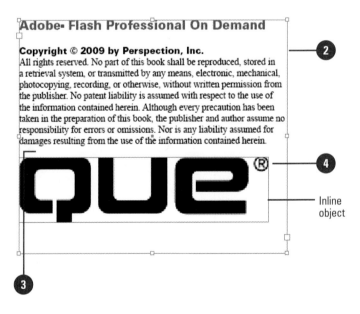

Inline object

Creating Anchored Objects

An anchored object is an object that is attached to a text frame using specific options. The Insert Anchored Object dialog box allows you to control how, where, and what type an object is placed in a text frame. After you specify the options that you want, an anchored object frame with an anchor symbol appears next to the text frame. If you no longer want the anchored object, you can release it from the text frame.

Create an Anchored Object

1. Click to place the insertion point in the text where you want to place the anchored object by using the **Type** tool.

   You can change this location later if you want.

2. Click the **Object** menu, point to **Anchored Object**, and then click **Insert**.

3. Specify the following options you want:

   ◆ **Object Options.** Specify options for content type, object and paragraph style, and height and width.

   ◆ **Position.** Select the **Custom** or **Inline or Above Line** option, and then specify options that relate to your choice.

4. Click **OK**.

   An anchored object frame with an anchor symbol appears next to the text frame.

5. To change options for the anchored object, select it, click the **Object** menu, point to **Anchored Object**, and then click **Options**.

6. To release an anchored object from a text frame, select the object, click the **Object** menu, point to **Anchored Object**, and then click **Release**.

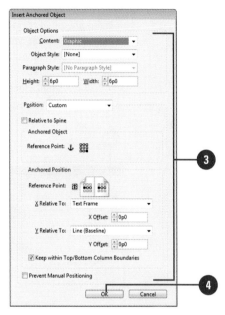

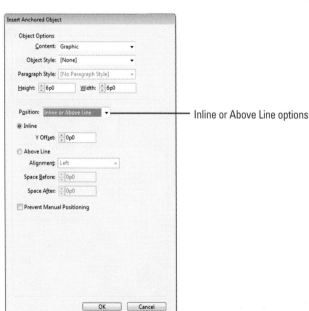

Inline or Above Line options

Creating and Deleting Object Layers

ID 1.3

You can think of Layers as a group of transparent sheets stacked on top of each other, where each layer can contain a separate aspect of the total design. Layers give you control over the design elements of your document. When you open a document, a default layer is already there for you to work on. Everything you create in the document appears on the default layer until you create a new one. You can quickly create a new layer or duplicate an existing one using a button or selecting options in a dialog box. When you create a new layer, it's given a color, which is used to highlight object frames and paths. When you duplicate a layer, any objects on the layer are also duplicated. When you no longer need a layer, you can quickly delete it. Remember that once you've deleted a layer and saved the document, there is no way to recover the deleted layer. However, while the document is open, you can use the Undo command to recover a deleted layer.

Create and Rename a New Layer

1. Select the **Layers** panel.

   ◆ Click the **Window** menu, and then click **Layers**.

2. Click the **New Layer** button on the panel.

   ◆ To create a new layer and specify the options you want, click the **Options** menu, click **New Layer**, specify options, and then click **OK**.

   A new layer appears in the panel.

3. To rename the layer, double-click the layer, enter a name, and then click **OK**.

Did You Know?

You can create a new layer while you paste. Select the Layers panel, click the Options menu, and then select Paste Remembers Layers. With this option selected, InDesign creates a new layer when you paste, or drag and drop objects from another document.

Layer name

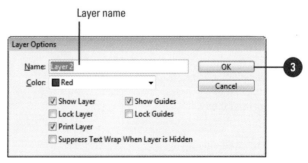

Duplicate a Layer

1. Select the **Layers** panel.

   ◆ Click the **Window** menu, and then click **Layers**.

2. Drag the layer that you want to duplicate onto the **New Layer** button on the panel.

   InDesign creates an exact copy of the layer and appends the word *copy* at the end of the original layer name.

3. To rename the layer, double-click the layer, enter a name, and then click **OK**.

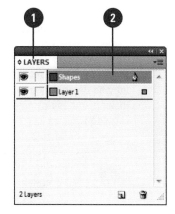
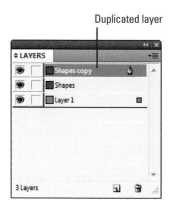

Duplicated layer

Delete Layers

1. Select the **Layers** panel.

   ◆ Click the **Window** menu, and then click **Layers**.

2. Select the layers that you want to delete.

   ◆ Hold down the Ctrl (Win) or ⌘ (Mac) key, and then click to select multiple items.

3. Click the **Delete Layer** button.

4. Click **OK** to delete any objects on the layer.

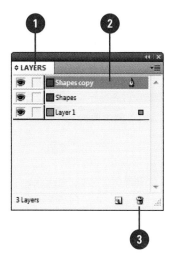
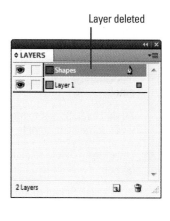

Layer deleted

Did You Know?

You can delete all unused layers. Select the Layers panel, click the Options menu, and then click Delete Unused Layers.

Setting Layer Options

ID 1.3

When you create a layer, it's given a generic name, (Layer 1, Layer 2, etc.) and a distinctive color. The color is used to highlight object frames and paths. To avoid confusion, it's a good idea to specify names for layers in a document. You can quickly rename and set layer options by double-clicking the layer you want to change. In the Layer Options dialog box, you can set options for color, showing and hiding layers, locking and unlocking layers, printing layers, showing and hiding guides, locking and unlocking guides, and suppressing text wraps when a layer is hidden.

Set Layer Options

1. Select the **Layers** panel.

   ◆ Click the **Window** menu, and then click **Layers**.

2. Double-click an existing layer or click the **Options** menu, and then click **New Layer**.

3. Select or deselect any of the following options:

   ◆ **Name.** Enter a name for the layer.

   ◆ **Color.** Specify a color for the layer. This color is used to highlight object frames and paths.

   ◆ **Show Layer.** Select to show the layer or deselect to hide it.

   ◆ **Lock Layer.** Select to lock the layer or deselect to unlock it.

   ◆ **Print Layer.** Select to print the layer or deselect to prevent printing.

   ◆ **Suppress Text Wrap When Layer is Hidden.** Select to prevent text wrapping on hidden layers.

   ◆ **Show Guides.** Select to show guides on the layer.

   ◆ **Lock Guides.** Select to lock guides on the layer.

4. Click **OK**.

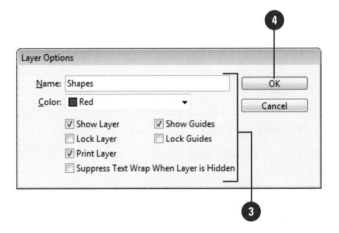

Showing and Hiding Layers and Objects

ID 1.3

When you have a lot of objects in the document window, it can be hard to keep track of them. In the Layers panel, you can hide layers and objects to reduce the clutter and make it easier to work with the layers and objects that you want. When you click the visibility (first) column in the Layers panel, an eye icon appears indicating the layer is visible. To hide a layer, you simply click the eye icon to remove visibility. Hidden objects don't print and don't appear in the document window. When you save, close, and reopen your document, any hidden objects remain hidden until you show them.

Show and Hide Layers and Objects in the Layers Panel

1. Select the **Layers** panel.

   ◆ Click the **Window** menu, and then click **Layers**.

2. Use any of the following:

   ◆ **Show/Hide Individual.** Click the visibility (first) column for each layer that you want to show or hide.

   ◆ **Show/Hide Multiple.** Click and drag the visibility (first) column.

   ◆ **Show/Hide Except One.** Alt+click (Win) or Option+click (Mac) the visibility (first) column for a top-level layer to show/hide all the other top-level layers except the one you clicked.

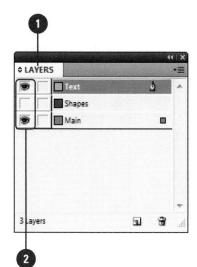

Locking Layers and Objects

ID 1.3

When you don't want an object to be moved or modified, you can lock it in the Layers panel. When you lock a layer, the objects remain visible in the document window. When you click the lock (second) column in the Layers, a padlock icon appears, indicating the layer is locked. When you lock a layer, all the objects on the layer are locked. To unlock a layer, you simply click the padlock icon to remove it. You can lock/unlock individual layers and multiple layers.

Lock and Unlock Layers and Objects in the Layers Panel

1. Select the **Layers** panel.

   ◆ Click the **Window** menu, and then click **Layers**.

2. Use any of the following:

   ◆ **Lock/Unlock Individual.** Click the lock (second) column for each layer that you want to lock or unlock.

   ◆ **Lock/Unlock Multiple.** Click and drag the lock (second) column.

   ◆ **Lock/Unlock Except One.** Alt+click (Win) or Option+click (Mac) the lock (second) column for a layer to lock/unlock all the other layers except the one you clicked.

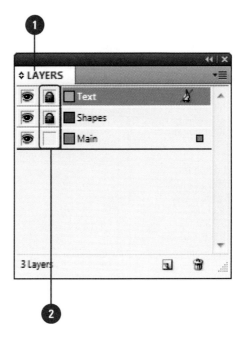

Merging Layers and Groups

Adobe Certified Expert ID 1.3

Merge Layers in the Layers Panel

1. Select the **Layers** panel.

   ◆ Click the **Window** menu, and then click **Layers**.

2. Select two or more layers that you want to merge.

   ◆ Hold down the Ctrl (Win) or ⌘ (Mac) key, and then click to select multiple items.

3. Click the last layer into which you want to merge the selected layers.

4. Click the **Options** menu, and then click **Merge Layers**.

Did You Know?

You can reorder layers. Select the Layers panel, and then drag one layer above or below another layer to the new position that you want. A thick black line appears, indicating the new position.

If you have objects on multiple layers and want to consolidate them onto one layer, you can merge them together. You can merge two or more layers. However, you can't merge an object with another object. If a layer is locked or hidden, you can still use it in a merge. Before you use the Merge Layers command, it's a good idea to make a copy of your document as a backup to preserve a copy of the separate layers.

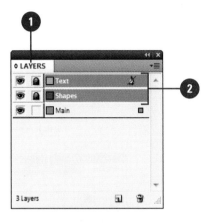

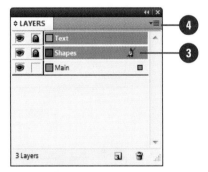

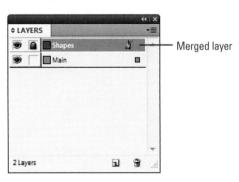

Merged layer

Working with Objects on Layers

ID 1.3

After you have created more than one layer, you can create objects on the new layers or move objects from one layer to another. To work with a layer, all you need to do is select an object on the layer in the document window or select a layer in the Layers panel. The color of an object's frame indicates the layer on which it is located. Blue is the default color of the first layer when you create a new document. This makes it easy to identify objects and layers. When you select an object, a square object icon appears in the Layers panel. A quick way to move an object from one layer to another is to drag the square object icon from one layer to another in the Layers panel.

Work with Objects on Layers

◆ **Select a Layer with Objects.** Select an object in the document window with the same color frame as the layer color.

◆ **Select a Layer in the Layers Panel.** Select the Layers panel, and then click a layer.

◆ **Move an Object Between Layers.** Select an object in the document window, select the Layers panel, and then drag the square object icon from the selected layer to another layer.

◆ **Copy an Object Between Layers.** Select an object in the document window, select the Layers panel, hold the Alt (Win) or Option (Mac) key, and then drag the square object icon from the selected layer to another layer.

◆ **Reorder Layers.** Select the Layers panel, then drag a layer from one position to another. A thick black line appears, indicating the new position.

Layer selected

Objects on Main layer

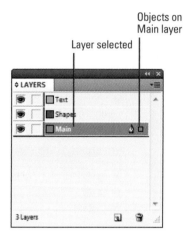

Objects selected on Main layer

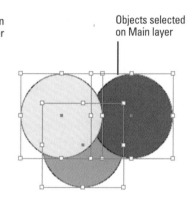

Objects moved to Shapes layer

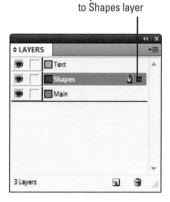

Objects on a new layer

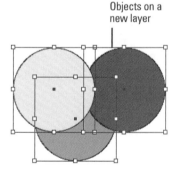

Using the Measure Tool

The Measure tool allows you to find out the size of items or measure the distance between objects. The Measure tool displays measurement information in the Info panel. The panel shows you the horizontal and vertical position, distance and angle of the measurement line, and width and height of the bounding box.

Measure Distances and Angles with the Measure Tool

① Select the **Info** panel.

- ◆ Click the **Window** menu, and then click **Info**.

② Click the **Measure** tool on the Tools panel.

③ Point to the start point of what you want to measure, and then drag to draw a line to the end point.

④ To create an angle, point to the start or end point, hold the Alt (Win) or Option (Mac) key, and then drag a new line to the angle you want.

⑤ To move a measurement line, drag the line (not the end points) to a new position.

⑥ To adjust the start and end points on the measurement line, drag the start or end point to a new position.

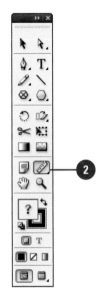

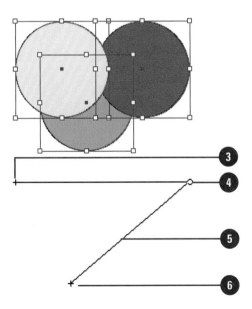

Applying and Managing Color

7

Introduction

Color management is an important part of working with InDesign. Setting up document and graphic image color settings in the right way will make it easier for a printer to produce the results that you want.

InDesign does its best to manage color for you. However, sometimes there are color conflicts or you have specific color requirements that you want to use. If a document's profile doesn't match the current working color space or is not assigned a color profile, you can use the Assign Profile dialog box to change or remove a profile to avoid conflicts. A working space is a temporary color space used to define and edit color in Adobe programs. Each color mode has a working space profile. InDesign's color modes are Lab, RGB (Red, Green, and Blue), and CMYK (Cyan, Magenta, Yellow, and Black). Color modes not only define the working color space of the active document, they also represent the color space of the output document. You can use the Color Settings dialog box to select a working space profile.

InDesign not only lets you select virtually any colors you desire in the Color panel, it also lets you store those colors for future use in the Swatches panel. You can also create swatches with color tints, gradients, and mixed inks. If you're not sure what colors to use, you can use the swatch libraries from color systems, such as Trumatch and Pantone, to select colors with predictable results.

After you create the colors and swatches you want, you can apply them to objects in your documents. The Tools panel provides color boxes to make it easy for you to apply fill and stroke colors and the Eyedropper tool on the Tools panel makes it easy to quickly pick up a color from one area of your artwork and apply it to another area.

What You'll Do

Change Color Settings

Change Color Profiles

Work with Color Modes

Apply Colors

Use the Eyedropper Tool

Work with the Color Panel

Work with the Swatches Panel

Manage Color Swatches

Work with Swatch Libraries

Create Tint Swatches

Create Gradient Swatches

Create Mixed Inks

Use Colors from the Kuler Panel

Overprint Colors

Proof Colors on the Screen

Changing Color Settings

ID 5.5

InDesign does its best to manage color for you. However, sometimes there are color conflicts or you have specific color requirements that you want to use. When you create or open a document, InDesign creates or looks for a color profile, which specifies color usage in the document. The Color Settings dialog box allows you to specify color settings and select options to deal with conflicts. The two main color settings are Working Space and Color Management Policies. Working Space controls how RGB and CMYK colors are used in a document that doesn't have an embedded profile, while Color Management Policies controls how InDesign works with color when opening files that don't have a color profile or one that doesn't match your current color settings from the RGB and CMYK menus. If you need to convert colors between color spaces, use Advanced mode.

Change Color Settings

1. Click the **Edit** menu, and then click **Color Settings**.

2. Click the **Settings** list arrow, and then select from the following preset color settings:

   ◆ **Monitor Color.** Useful for video and onscreen content. Sets the RGB working space to your current monitor space.

   ◆ **North America General Purpose 2.** Useful for screen and print content in North America.

   ◆ **North America Prepress 2.** Useful for common printing conditions in North America. The default RGB color space is set to Adobe RGB.

   ◆ **North America Web/Internet.** Useful for non-print content on the Web in North America.

3. Click **OK** to use the defined settings, or select your own custom settings:

   ◆ **Working Spaces.** Controls how RGB and CMYK colors are used in a document that doesn't have an embedded profile.

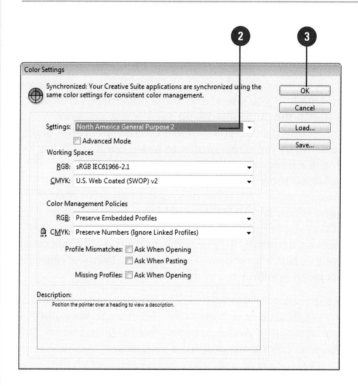

Select **Monitor RGB** for onscreen output; **Adobe RGB** for photo inkjet printers (converts RGB images to CMYK images); **ProPhoto RGB** for inkjet printers; and **sRGB IEC61966-2.1** for web output.

◆ **Color Management Policies.** Controls how InDesign works with color when opening files that don't have a color profile or one that doesn't match your current color settings from the RGB and CMYK menus.

Select **Off** to prevent the use of color management, **Preserve Numbers** to preserve the document color profile for CMYK documents, **Preserve Embedded Profiles** to preserve links to color profiles, or **Convert to Working Space** to use the working space color (useful for the web).

Select the appropriate check boxes to choose if and when InDesign will warn you of profile mismatches (no warning, when opening the file, or when pasting) or missing profiles (when opening a file or no warning).

4 Click **OK**.

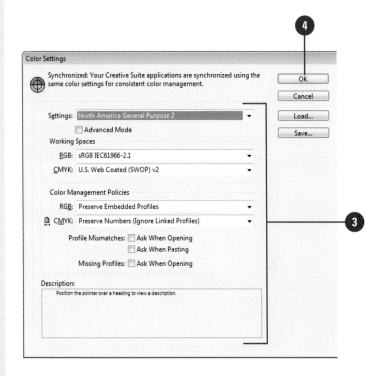

For Your Information

Synchronizing Color Settings Using Bridge

If you're using Adobe Creative Suite, you can use Adobe Bridge to synchronize your color settings for all programs in the suite. When you synchronize your color settings, you can avoid color profile conflicts. In Adobe Bridge, click the Edit menu, click Creative Suite Color Settings, select one of the settings, and then click Apply.

Changing Color Profiles

 ID 5.5

When you create or open a document, InDesign creates or looks for a color profile, which specifies color usage in the document. If a document's profile doesn't match the current working color space or is missing an assigned color profile, you can use the Assign Profile dialog box to change or remove a profile to avoid conflicts. You can also specify rendering intent (object display or print) for the transition from one color space to another. When you change a color profile, color in your document may shift to match the new color profile.

Change or Remove Color Profiles

1. Click the **Edit** menu, and then click **Assign Profile**.

2. Select one of the following RGB or CMYK Profile options:

   ◆ **Discard (use current working space).** Select to remove a color profile from your document and use the current working color settings.

   ◆ **Assign Current Working Space.** Select when your document doesn't have an assigned profile or its profile is different from the current working space.

   ◆ **Assign Profile.** Select to assign a different profile to your document.

3. Select any of the following options:

   ◆ **Solid Color Intent.** Specify a rendering intent for vector objects.

   ◆ **Default Image Intent.** Specify a rendering intent for bitmap images.

   ◆ **After-Blending Intent.** Specify a rendering intent for the proofing or final color space for colors (from transparency interactions).

4. Click **OK**.

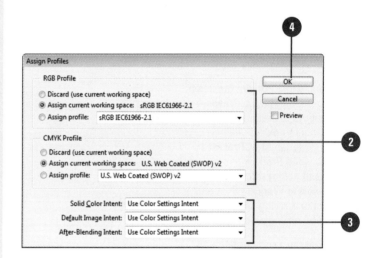

Convert Document Colors to Another Profile

1. Click the **Object** menu, and then click **Image Color Settings**.

2. Click the **RGB Profile** and **CMYK Profile** list arrow, and then select a profile.

3. Click the **Engine** list arrow, and then select an option:

   ◆ **Engine.** Specify the color management module used to map the gamut of one color space to the gamut of another.

   ◆ **Intent.** Specify rendering intent (object display or print) for the transition from one color space to another.

     ◆ **Perceptual.** Use to preserve the visual look of colors; useful for photographs. The standard in Japan.

     ◆ **Saturation.** Use to create vivid color in an image; useful for graphics and charts.

     ◆ **Relative Colorimetric.** Use to shift out-of-gamut colors to the closest color in the destination color space. The standard in North America and Europe.

     ◆ **Absolute Colorimetric.** Use to leave out-of-gamut colors unchanged in the destination color space.

   ◆ **Use Black Point Compensation.** Select to preserve shadow detail in images. Use when printing to ensure the detail.

4. Click **OK**.

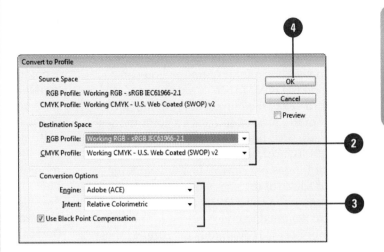

For Your Information

Changing Profiles for Imported Bitmap Images

If you import a bitmap image into your document, you can view, override, or disable profiles assigned to it. For cases when an image doesn't have a profile, you can assign one. Select the imported bitmap image, click the Object menu, click Image Color Settings, select a Profile option, select a Rendering Intent option (optional), and then click OK.

Working with Color Modes

Color modes define the colors represented in the active document. Although you can change the color mode of a document, it is best to select the correct color mode at the start of the project. InDesign's color modes are Lab, RGB (Red, Green, and Blue), and CMYK (Cyan, Magenta, Yellow, and Black). Color modes not only define the working color space of the active document, they also represent the color space of the output document. It's the document output (print, press, or monitor) that ultimately determines the correct document color mode. Color modes do not just determine what colors the eye sees; they represent how the colors are mixed, and that's very important because different output devices use different color mixes.

Lab Mode

The Lab color mode is an old color measuring system. Created in France, its purpose was to measure color based on visual perception. Since personal computers had not been created at that time, the Lab mode is not based on a particular computer or operating system, and so Lab color is device independent. The Lab mode measures color using a lightness channel, an "a" channel (red to green), and a "b" channel (blue to yellow). Lab Color works well for moving images between operating systems (Mac to Win), and for printing color images to PostScript Level 2 or 3 devices. Because of its ability to separate the gray tones of an image into an individual channel (lightness), the Lab color mode is excellent for sharpening, or increasing the contrast of an image without changing its colors.

RGB Mode

The RGB color mode is probably the most widely used of all the color modes. RGB gen-erates color using three 8-bit channels: 1 red, 1 green, and 1 blue. Since each channel is capable of generating 256 steps of color, mathematically, that translates into 16,777,216 possible colors per image pixel. The RGB color mode (sometimes referred to as Additive RGB) is the color space of computer monitors, televisions, and any electronic display. This also includes PDAs (Personal Digital Assistants), and cellular phones. RGB is considered a device-dependent color mode. Device independent means that the colors in images created in the RGB color mode will appear differently on various devices. In the world of computer monitors and the Web, what you see is very seldom what someone else sees; however, understanding how InDesign manages color information goes a long way to gaining consistency over color.

CMYK Mode

The CMYK color mode is the color mode of paper and press. Printing presses (sometimes referred to as 4-color presses) convert an image's colors into percentages of CMYK (Cyan, Magenta, Yellow, and Black), which eventually become the color plates on the press. One at a time, the plates apply color to a sheet of paper, and when all 4 colors have been applied, the paper contains an image similar to the CMYK image created in InDesign. The CMYK color mode can take an image from a computer monitor to a printed document. Before converting an image into the CMYK mode, however, it's important to understand that you will lose some color saturation during the conversion. The colors that will not print are defined as being out of gamut. **Out of gamut** means that the current RGB or Lab color doesn't have a CMYK equivalent, which means you can't use it on a commercial project unless you select a substitute color close to a CMYK equivalent.

Applying Colors

The Tools panel provides color boxes to make it easy for you to apply fill and stroke colors. The color box in the foreground is the Fill box and the outlined box in the background is the Stroke box. When you select an object, fill, or stroke, the color boxes (also known as thumbnails), on the Tools panel display the current colors. To change the fill or stroke color, select an object, fill or stroke, select the Fill or Stroke box, and then select a color from the Color or Swatches panel.

Apply Colors to an Object, Fill or Stroke

1. Select an object, fill, or stroke using a selection tool.

2. Click the **Fill** or **Stroke** color box on the Tools panel to choose the color's destination.

3. Click the **Apply Color** button on the Tools panel to apply a color or click **Apply None** to apply no color.

4. Use any of the following methods to change the active fill or stroke colors:

   ◆ Select the **Swatches** panel, and then click a color swatch to change the color.

   ◆ Select the **Color** panel, and then specify a color using the sliders or the color spectrum.

   ◆ Double-click the **Fill** or **Stroke** color box to open the Color Picker dialog box, select a color or enter color values, and then click **OK**.

   ◆ To set the default colors of black and white, click the **Default Fill and Stroke** icon on the Tools panel.

   ◆ To switch the current fill and stroke color, click the **Swap Fill and Stroke** icon on the Tools panel.

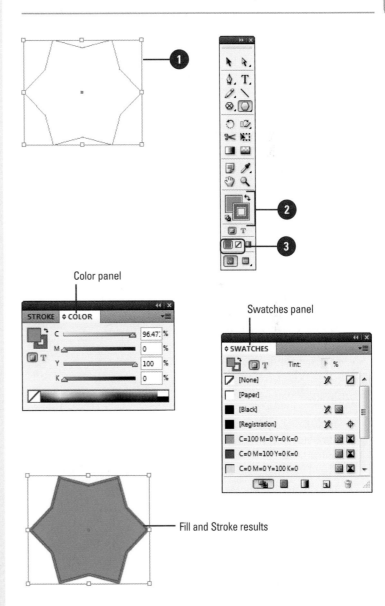

Color panel

Swatches panel

Fill and Stroke results

Using the Eyedropper Tool

The Eyedropper tool on the Tools panel makes it easy to quickly pick up a color from one area of your artwork and apply it to another area. When you click an object with the Eyedropper tool, it picks up the object's color and stroke attributes and displays them in the Tools, Color, and Stroke panels. You can pick up attributes from any type of object, even a graphic image, and the object doesn't even need to be selected. If an object is selected, the color and stroke attributes are applied to the selected object. The Eyedropper tool also provides options for you to customize the attributes—such as Stroke, Fill, Character, Paragraph, and Object—that you want to pick up with the tool.

Apply Colors and Attributes with the Eyedropper Tool

1. If you want to apply the acquired color and attributes to one or more objects, then select them first.

2. Select the **Eyedropper** tool on the Tools panel.

   The eyedropper appears white, ready to sample object attributes.

3. Click an object that contains the color and attributes that you want to pick up and apply.

   The eyedropper appears black, filled with object attributes. If an object is selected, the attributes are applied to the object.

4. Click an object to apply the attributes.

   ◆ To pick up different object attributes, Alt+click (Win) or Option+click (Mac) another object.

   ◆ To have the Eyedropper tool only pick up an object's color and not other attributes, click the Fill or Stroke box on the Tools or Color panel, and then Shift+click the color to be picked up.

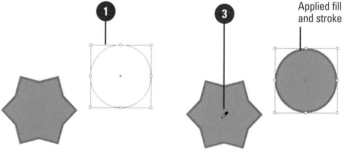

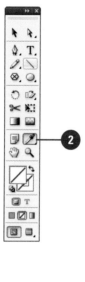

Applied fill and stroke

Change Eyedropper Options

1. Double-click the **Eyedropper** tool on the Tools panel.

2. Click the **Expand** arrow to display individual options for the main settings (Stroke, Fill, Character, Paragraph, or Object).

3. Select the check boxes for the options that you want the Eyedropper to pick up and deselect the ones you don't.

4. Click **OK**.

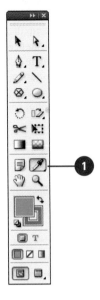

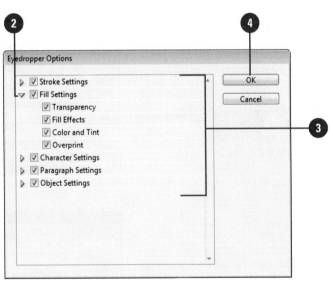

Working with the Color Panel

The Color panel gives you access to InDesign's color-generation tools. This single panel lets you select a color mode (Lab, RGB, or CMYK), create colors using different sliders, spectrum color selectors, and an option that lets you create a color ramp for the current fill and stroke colors. For example, the CMYK spectrum displays a rainbow of colors in the CMYK color gamut. Moving the eyedropper into the spectrum box and clicking lets you select any color and gives you a visual representation of the relationships between various colors.

Select Color Modes with the Color Panel

1. Select the **Color** panel.

   ◆ Click the **Window** menu, and then click **Color**.

2. Click the **Options** menu.

3. Select from the following type of Color Sliders:

   ◆ **Lab.** Creates three sliders (L, a, and b). The L slider has a possible value from 0 to 100, and the a and b sliders have a possible value from-128 to 127.

   ◆ **CMYK.** Creates four subtractive sliders (cyan, magenta, yellow, and black). Each slider has a possible value from 0 to 100. Converts the lower portion of the Color panel to the CMYK spectrum. Clicking anywhere in the spectrum changes the active color.

   ◆ **RGB.** Creates three sliders (red, green, and blue). Each slider has a possible value from 0 to 255. Converts the lower portion of the Color panel to the RGB spectrum. Clicking anywhere in the spectrum changes the active color.

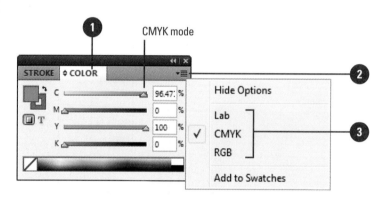

CMYK mode

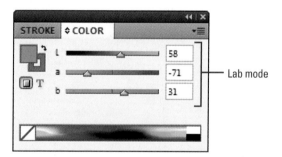

Lab mode

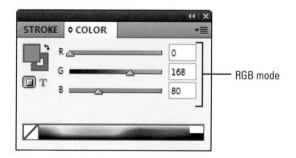

RGB mode

Work with the Color Panel

1. Select the **Color** panel.

   ◆ Click the **Window** menu, and then click **Color**.

2. To change a color, click a color box, use a slider, enter specific color values, or click a color in the spectrum. The box with the red diagonal line is the None color.

   ◆ Hold the Shift key while you drag a slider to have all the other sliders move too.

   ◆ You can also drag a color directly from the Color panel onto objects.

3. To change a color using the Color Picker, double-click a color box, select a color using the color range or color mode options, and then click **OK**.

4. To add the current color to the Swatches panel, drag it to the Swatches panel, or click the **Options** menu, and then click **Add To Swatches**.

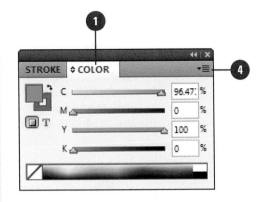

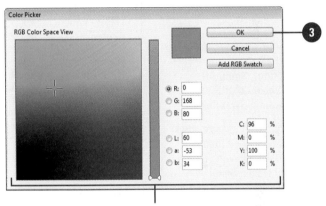

Select options or click the color range to select a color.

Did You Know?

You can identify out-of-gamut colors. If an out-of-gamut warning icon (a triangle with an exclamation point) appears below the color boxes on the Color panel, it indicates that the current RGB or Lab color doesn't have a CMYK equivalent, which means you can't use it in a commercial project.

You can convert out-of-gamut colors. If an out-of-gamut warning icon (a triangle with an exclamation point) appears below the color boxes on the Color panel, click the small square next to the out-of-gamut symbol to convert the color to the closest process-color equivalent.

Working with the Swatches Panel

InDesign not only lets you select virtually any colors you desire, it also lets you store those colors for future use in the Swatches panel. Where the Color panel lets you select virtually any color you need, the Swatches panel lets you save and re-use specific colors that you use often. In the Swatches panel, you can point to a color box to display a tooltip indicating the color's settings. If you want to view more information, you can change the Swatches panel display to make it easier to view and work with colors. To help you find the swatches you need, you can display them by type or you can adjust the size of the swatch.

Change the Swatches Panel Display

1. Select the **Swatches** panel.

   ◆ Click the **Window** menu, and then click **Swatches**.

2. To display different types of swatches, click one of the following buttons: **Show All Swatches**, **Show Color Swatches**, or **Show Gradient Swatches**.

3. To display swatches by size, click the **Options** menu, and then choose from the following options: **Name**, **Small Name**, **Small Swatch**, or **Large Swatch**.

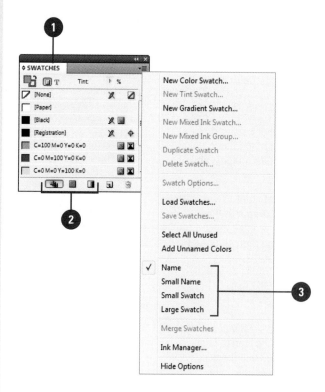

Did You Know?

You can duplicate a color swatch from the Swatches panel. Select the Swatches panel, select a color swatch, and then click the New Swatch button on the panel. The duplicate color swatch appears at the bottom of the list with the word *copy* at the end of the name.

Add or Edit a Color Swatch

1. Select the **Swatches** panel.

   ◆ Click the **Window** menu, and then click **Swatches**.

2. Click the **Options** menu, and then click **New Color Swatch** to add a new color swatch, or double-click the swatch to edit it.

   TIMESAVER *Alt+click (Win) or Option+click (Mac) the New Swatch button on the panel to add a color swatch.*

   ◆ To add a color, you can also drag a color from the color boxes on the Tools or Color panel to the Swatches panel.

3. To enter a color swatch name, deselect the **Name with Color Value** check box, and then enter a name.

4. Click the **Color Type** list arrow, and then click one of the following:

   ◆ **Process.** Colors printed using small dots of the CMYK inks to create color combinations.

   ◆ **Spot.** Colors printed using color-specific inks.

5. Click the **Color Mode** list arrow, and then select a color mode.

6. Adjust the color sliders to create the color you want.

7. Click **OK**.

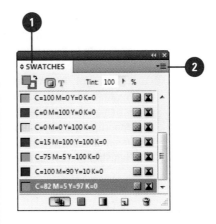

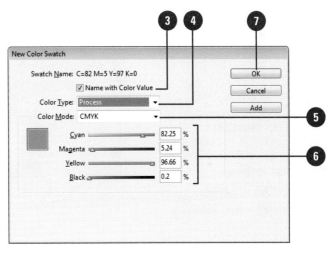

Did You Know?

You can delete a color swatch from the Swatches panel. Select the Swatches panel, display and select the color you want to delete, and then click the Delete Swatch button.

Managing Color Swatches

ID 5.1

In addition to adding and editing swatches, you can also move, delete, duplicate, merge, save, load, rename, and name unnamed color swatches in the Swatches panel. Unnamed colors are colors that are applied to objects using the Color panel or Color Picker, while named colors are applied from the Swatches panel. If you no longer use a color or you want to change the use of a color, you can use the Delete Swatches button on the Swatches panel. If a color is not in use, InDesign simply deletes it. If the color is in use, InDesign gives you an opportunity to delete the color and use another one or specify the color as unnamed. The default swatches for None, Paper, Black, and Registration cannot be edited or deleted.

Delete Color Swatches

1. Select the **Swatches** panel.

   ◆ Click the **Window** menu, and then click **Swatches**.

2. Select the swatches you want to delete.

   ◆ To select multiple swatches, hold the Shift key to select the first and last swatch in a contiguous range, or hold the Ctrl (Win) or ⌘ (Mac) key to select noncontiguous swatches.

3. Click the **Delete Swatch** button on the panel.

   If the swatch is being used, an alert dialog box appears.

4. Click the **Defined Swatch** option, and then select a color, or click the **Unnamed Swatch** option.

5. Click **OK**.

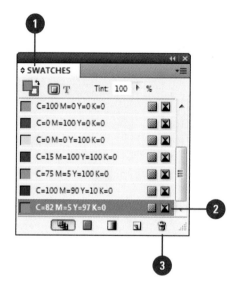

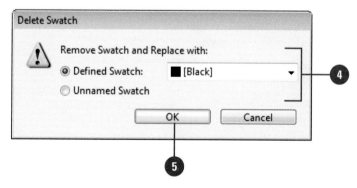

Did You Know?

You can delete all unused color swatches. Select the Swatches panel, click the Options menu, click Select All Unused, and then click the Delete Swatch button on the panel.

Work with Swatches

◆ **Select Swatches.** Hold the Shift key to select the first and last swatch in a contiguous range, or hold the Ctrl (Win) or ⌘ (Mac) key to select noncontiguous swatches.

◆ **Move Swatches.** Select a swatch in the **Swatches** panel, and then drag the swatch to a new position. A thick black line appears, indicating the new position.

◆ **Duplicate Swatches.** Select a swatch in the **Swatches** panel, and then click the **New Swatch** button on the panel.

◆ **Merge Swatches.** Select the **Swatches** panel, click the first color (which is the merge into color), hold the Ctrl (Win) or ⌘ (Mac) key, and then click to select other swatches for the merge. Click the **Options** menu, and then click **Merge Swatches**.

◆ **Save Swatches.** Select the swatches you want to save in the **Swatches** panel, click the **Options** menu, click **Save Swatches**, specify a name and location, and then click **Save**. Swatches are saved with the Adobe Swatch Exchange (ASE) file format.

◆ **Load Swatches.** Select the **Swatches** panel, click the **Options** menu, click **Load Swatches**, select the ASE swatches file, and then click **Open**.

◆ **Add All Unnamed Colors to the Swatches Panel.** Unnamed colors are colors that are applied to objects using the Color panel or Color Picker. Select the **Swatches** panel, click the **Options** menu, and then click **Add Unnamed Colors**. The unnamed colors are named with color percentage values.

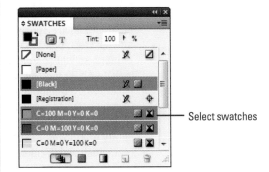

Select swatches

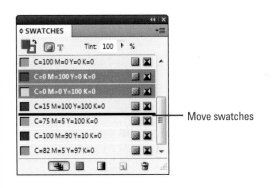

Move swatches

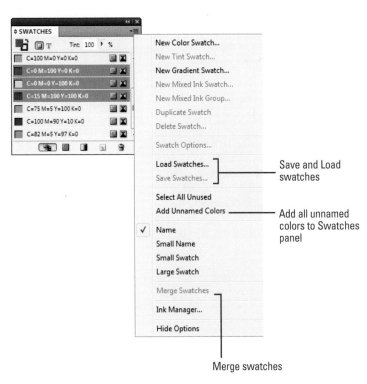

Save and Load swatches

Add all unnamed colors to Swatches panel

Merge swatches

Working with Swatch Libraries

Instead of creating your own color swatches, you can use the swatch libraries from color systems, such as Trumatch and Pantone. Trumatch and Pantone are common color libraries in North America for prepress and desktop color printing. These color systems are universally used by printers, so you can produce consistent results. Other color libraries include ANPA (commonly used for newspapers), DIC (commonly used in Japan), Focoltone (commonly used in France and Great Britain), HKS (commonly used in Europe), System (Macintosh), System (Windows), Toyo (commonly used in Japan), and Web. Web is a common color library of 216 web-safe colors for use on the web by both the Macintosh and Windows operating systems.

Add Colors from Swatch Libraries

1. Select the **Swatches** panel.

   ◆ Click the **Window** menu, and then click **Swatches**.

2. Click the **Options** menu, and then click **New Color Swatch** to add a new color swatch, or double-click the swatch to edit it.

3. Click the **Color Mode** list arrow, and then select a swatch library.

4. Select a color in the library.

5. Click **OK**.

Did You Know?

You can import swatches from other documents. Select the Swatches panel, click the Options menu, click Load Swatches, navigate to and select the InDesign or Illustrator document, and then click Open.

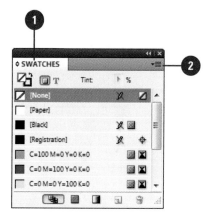

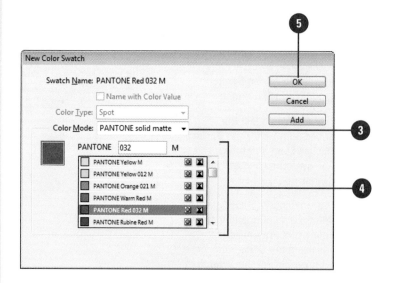

Creating Tint Swatches

A tint is a shade of a base color. The base color is a 100% tint. You can adjust the tint of a color by lowering the percentage from 1% to 99%. You can create a new tint swatch by using a dialog box or the Tint option at the top of the Swatches panel. I like the dialog box method better. After you create a new tint color swatch, it appears in the Swatches panel list with the new tint percentage in the name. If you need to edit a tint swatch, simply double-click the swatch to open the Swatch Options dialog box to make the changes you want.

Create and Edit a Tint Swatch

1. Select the **Swatches** panel.

   ◆ Click the **Window** menu, and then click **Swatches**.

2. Do either of the following:

   ◆ **New.** Select a base color in the Swatches panel as the basis for the color tint, click the **Options** menu, and then click **New Tint Swatch**.

   ◆ **Edit.** Double-click the tint swatch.

3. Enter a **Tint** percentage value or drag the slider to create a tint screen of the color.

4. Click **OK**.

   The new tint swatch appears in the Swatches panel list with the new tint percentage.

Did You Know?

You can create a tint swatch without the dialog box. Select the Swatches panel, select a color as the basis, enter a tint percentage in the Tint control at the top of the Swatches panel, and then click the New Swatch button on the panel.

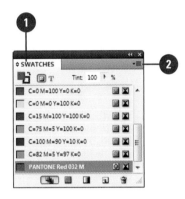

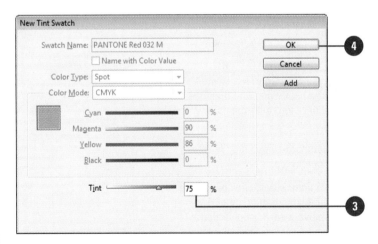

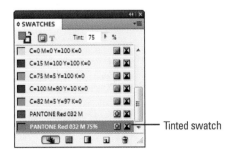

Tinted swatch

Creating Gradient Swatches

ID 5.2

A gradient is a smooth transition between two or more colors in an object. You can create and save a gradient of your own by using the Swatches panel. You can create a gradient with two or more colors. There are two types of gradients: Radial (circular) and Linear (horizontal). You can adjust the number and blend of gradient colors by adding or changing color stops. After you create a gradient, you can apply it to objects just like any other swatch in the Swatches panel. In addition to the Swatches panel, you can also create a gradient by using the Gradient panel. The gradient is unnamed and not saved unless you store it as a swatch.

Create a Gradient Swatch

1. Select the **Swatches** panel.

   ◆ Click the **Window** menu, and then click **Swatches**.

2. Click the **Options** menu, and then click **New Gradient Swatch**.

3. Enter a name for the gradient swatch.

4. Click the **Type** list arrow, and then select a gradient type: **Radial** or **Linear**.

5. Click the left color stop.

6. Click the **Stop Color** list arrow, select a color type, and then use the sliders to create the color you want.

7. Repeat the previous step for the right color stop.

8. To add color stops, click below the gradient spectrum in a blank area. To remove a color stop, drag it down and away from the gradient spectrum.

9. To adjust the amount of each color in the gradient, drag the diamond above the gradient spectrum.

10. Click **Add** to add the gradient to the Swatches panel and continue to add gradients, or click **OK**.

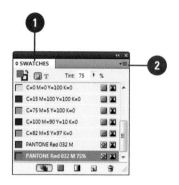

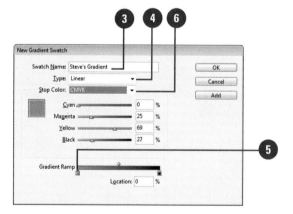

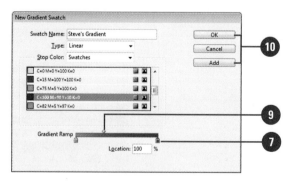

Create a Gradient with the Gradient Panel

1 Select the **Gradient** panel.

◆ Click the **Window** menu, and then click **Gradient**.

2 Click the **Type** list arrow, and then select a gradient type: **Radial** or **Linear**.

3 Click the left color stop.

4 Use the color spectrum and sliders in the Color panel to create the color you want.

5 Repeat the previous step for the right color stop.

6 To add color stops, click below the gradient spectrum in a blank area. To remove a color stop, drag it down and away from the gradient spectrum.

7 To adjust the amount of each color in the gradient, drag the diamond above the gradient spectrum.

8 Enter an **Angle** value to set the angle of the gradient.

9 To reverse the position of the color stops, click the **Reverse** button.

10 To save the gradient, drag the gradient preview box to the Swatches panel or click the **New Swatch** button on the Swatches panel.

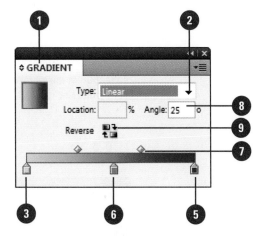

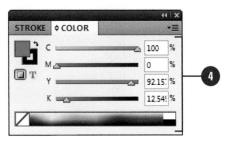

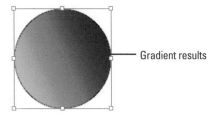

Gradient results

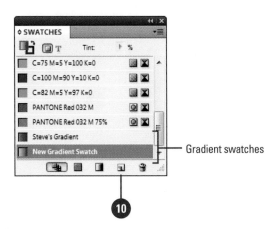

Gradient swatches

Creating Mixed Inks

ID 5.3, 5.5

Mixed inks combine a spot color with other spot colors or process colors to give you more color options for your custom designs. Mixed inks can be useful when you want a darker shade of a color to make it stand out in your design or to create a new spot color from two other existing spot colors. You can even use a mixed ink group to create a collection of mixed inks. This is useful when you want to create a series of color mixes.

Create a Mixed Ink

1. Select the **Swatches** panel.

   ◆ Click the **Window** menu, and then click **Swatches**.

2. Click the **Options** menu, and then click **New Mixed Ink Swatch**.

3. Enter a name for the mixed ink swatch.

4. Click two or more ink controls to select the colors you want to use in the mixed ink swatch.

5. Drag the sliders to adjust the inks to achieve the color you want.

6. Click **OK**.

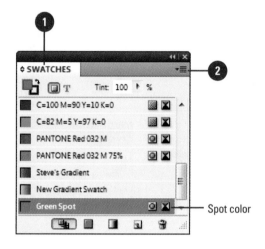

Spot color

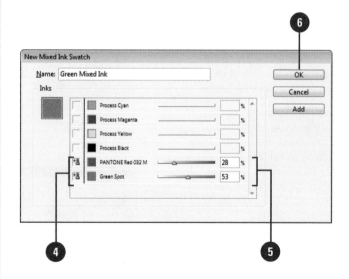

Create a Mixed Ink Group

1. Select the **Swatches** panel.

   ◆ Click the **Window** menu, and then click **Swatches**.

2. Click the **Options** menu, and then click **New Mixed Ink Group**.

3. Enter a name for the mixed ink group.

4. Click two or more ink controls to select the colors you want to use in the mixed ink group.

5. Enter an **Initial** value to define the color amount for the first instance of an ink.

6. Enter a **Repeat** value to set the number of mixed inks in the new color.

7. Enter an **Increment** value to set the increment value for each new mixed ink.

8. Click **Preview Swatches** to see the results of the grouping.

9. Click **OK**.

Did You Know?

You can edit a mixed ink group. Select the Swatches panel, and then double-click the mixed ink group. Select the ink controls to remove colors, or use the list arrows to change colors. Choose Swatch Options from the Options menu and then select the Convert Mixed Ink Swatches To Process check box to change all the colors in the mixed ink swatches to their process color equivalents. When you're done, click OK.

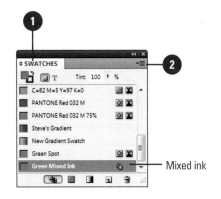

Mixed ink

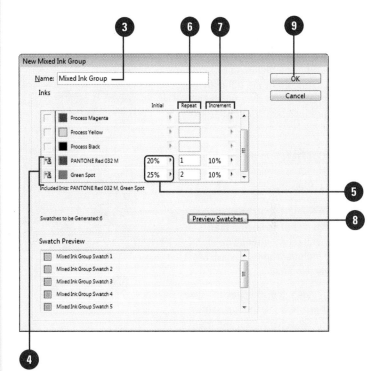

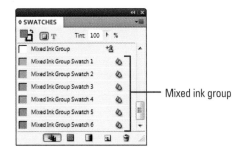

Mixed ink group

Using Colors from the Kuler Panel

The Kuler panel (**New!**) is an extension to InDesign that allows you to use groups of color, or themes in your projects. You can use the panel to browse thousands of color themes, create your own using the complementary harmony rules, and share them with others in the Kuler community. After you find or create the theme you want, you can add it to the Swatches panel for use in your project. You can access the Kuler panel by using the Extensions submenu on the Window menu. The Kuler panel is also available in the CS4 version of Photoshop, Flash, Illustrator, and Fireworks.

Browse Themes and Add to the Swatches Panel

1. Click the **Window** menu, point to **Extensions**, and then click **Kuler**.

2. Click the **Browse** tab.

3. To search for a theme, click in the Search box, enter the name of the theme, a tag, or a creator, and then press Enter (Win) or Return (Mac).

   IMPORTANT *In a search, use only alphanumerical characters (Aa-Zz, 0-9).*

4. To narrow down the browse list, click the list arrows, and then select the filter options you want. Some include Highest Rated, Most Popular, Newest.

   ◆ To save a search, click the first list arrow, click **Custom**, enter your search criteria, and then click **Save**.

5. To browse for a theme, click the **View Previous Set Of Themes** or **View Next Set Of Themes** button.

6. Select a theme in the panel.

7. To add the theme to the Swatches panel, click the **Add Selected Theme To Swatches** button.

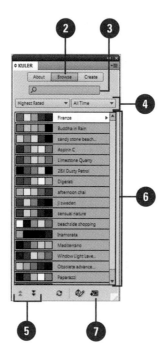

Create or Edit a Theme

① Click the **Window** menu, point to **Extensions**, and then click **Kuler**.

② To create or edit a theme, do either of the following:

◆ **Create a theme.** Click the **Create** tab.

◆ **Edit a theme.** Click the **Browse** tab, select the theme you want to edit, and then click **Edit Theme in Create Panel**.

③ Click the **Select Rule** list arrow, and then select a harmony rule or **Custom**.

The harmony rule uses the base color as the basis for generating the colors in the color group, so you can create a theme with complementary colors.

④ Select a color box, and then use the sliders and the color wheel to display the color you want.

⑤ Use the buttons below the color boxes to add/remove the theme color, add the current stroke/fill color as the base color, or adjust the other colors.

◆ Double-click a color box to set the active color in InDesign.

⑥ Upon completion, do any of the following:

◆ **Save theme.** Click **Save Theme**, name the theme, and then click **Save** to create a new one.

◆ **Add to Swatches Panel.** Click the **Add This Theme To Swatches** button.

◆ **Upload to Kuler.** Click the **Upload Theme To Kuler** button.

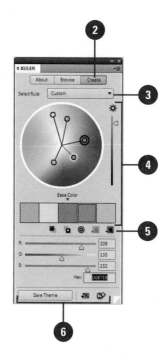

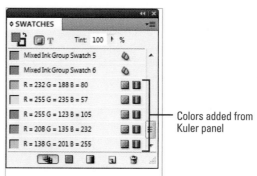

Colors added from Kuler panel

Overprinting Colors

ID 5.5

Overprinting allows you to set the color of one object to mix with any colors underneath. For example, when you have a red object overlapping a blue object, the red object knocks out the overlapped area underneath in the blue object. When you set the red object to overprint, the red object mixes with the blue object underneath to create another color. You can individually set fill, stroke, and gap colors to overprint. After you set overprint options for an object, you can preview your results by using Overprint Preview.

Set a Fill or Stroke to Overprint and Preview the Results

1 Select the object.

2 Select the **Attributes** panel.

◆ Click the **Window** menu, and then click **Attributes**.

3 Select from the following options:

◆ **Overprint Fill.** Select to set the object's fill color to overprint.

◆ **Overprint Stroke.** Select to set the object's stroke color to overprint.

◆ **Overprint Gap.** Select to set the gap color applied to stroke effects to overprint.

◆ **Nonprinting.** Select to not print the object.

4 To preview overprinting, click the **View** menu, and then click **Overprint Preview**.

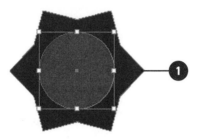

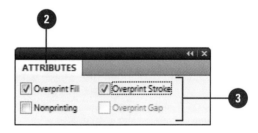

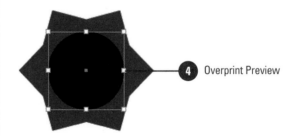

Overprint Preview

Proofing Colors on the Screen

ID 5.5

As you start to use color in your document, it's important to see how your color settings appear. It would be nice to see a printed copy in color to see the actual colors. However, that is not always possible. Instead, you can view a soft proof on your screen to quickly see how your colors will appear. A soft proof simulates the output of your actual device and media, such as a printer with a specific type of paper.

Display a Soft Proof

1. Click the **View** menu, and then point to **Proof Setup**.

2. Select from one of the available output devices to simulate, or click **Custom** to set up your own.

3. For a custom soft proof setup, select from the following options:

   ◆ **Device to Simulate.** Select a target device to simulate.

   ◆ **Preserve CMYK Numbers.** Select to use colors as they are and not convert them to the working color space. Deselect to use a rending intent option to display colors.

   ◆ **Simulate Paper Color.** Select to simulate white paper.

   ◆ **Simulate Black Ink.** Select to simulate dark gray instead of black.

4. Click **OK**.

5. Click the **View** menu, and then click **Proof Colors**.

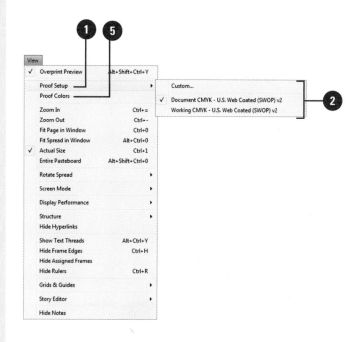

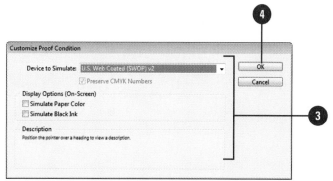

Applying Fills, Strokes, and Effects

8

Introduction

After you draw an object, you can apply fills, strokes, gradients, and other effects to enhance your documents. The Tools panel provides color boxes to make it easy for you to apply fill and stroke colors to objects. The Stroke panel provides additional options to quickly change stroke attributes, such as weight (width), position on the path, and stroke style. In addition to the typical stroke styles found in the Stroke panel, you can create and use custom stroke styles with stripes, dashes, and dots. For example, you can create a custom dashed stroke where you can specify the length of the dashes and gaps.

A gradient is a smooth transition between two or more colors in an object. You can apply a gradient from the Swatches or Gradient panel. The Gradient and Gradient Feather tools on the Tools panel allows you to change how a gradient appear for an object. You can specify how gradient colors blend, the angle of a linear gradient, and the location of the center for a radial gradient with a drag of the mouse over the gradient fill.

If you want to create a cool effect, you can apply blending modes, transparency, and other effects—shadow, glow, bevel and emboss, satin, and feather—to objects. A blend mode allows you to apply colors and shades to one object and have the effect interact with the objects underneath. InDesign comes with a variety of blend modes, including Overlay, Soft Light, Hard Light, Darken, Lighten, and Color. Transparency allows you to create see-through objects. Other special effects allow you to be creative without even knowing how to draw.

If you always create an object with a certain fill or stroke attribute, you can make those settings the default. InDesign has its own default fill and stroke settings of a black stroke and no fill. These are separate from the any defaults that you may set.

What You'll Do

Apply Fill and Stroke Colors

Change Stroke Attributes

Create Stroke Styles

Apply Gradients

Use the Gradient Tool

Use the Gradient Feather Tool

Create Blends and Effects

Apply Shadow Effects

Apply Glow Effects

Apply Bevel and Emboss Effects

Apply Feather Effects

Apply Corner Object Effects

Convert Shape Objects

Set Object Defaults

Applying Fill and Stroke Colors

 ID 5.4

The Tools panel provides color boxes to make it easy for you to apply fill and stroke colors. The color box in the foreground is the Fill box and the outlined box in the background is the Stroke box. When you select an object, fill, or stroke, the color boxes (also known as thumbnails), on the Tools panel display the current colors. To change the fill or stroke color, select an object, fill or stroke, select the Fill or Stroke box, and then select a color from the Color and Swatches panel, or use the Eyedropper to apply a color from the active document.

Apply Colors to an Object, Fill or Stroke

1. Select an object, fill, or stroke using the appropriate selection tool.

2. Click the **Fill** or **Stroke** color box on the Tools or Color panel to choose the color's destination.

3. Click the **Color** button on the Tools panel to apply a color or click **None** to apply no color.

   ◆ A fill or stroke of None makes the item in the object transparent.

4. Use any of the following methods to change the active fill or stroke colors:

   ◆ Select the **Swatches** panel, and then click a color swatch to change the color.

   ◆ Select the **Color** panel, and then specify a color using the controls.

   ◆ Select the **Eyedropper** tool on the Tools panel, and then click anywhere in the active document to change the color.

   ◆ Double-click the **Fill** or **Stroke** color box to open the Color Picker dialog box, select a color or enter color values, and then click **OK**.

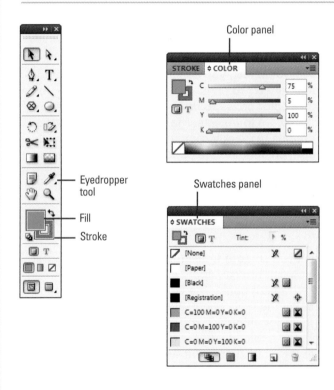

Color panel

Eyedropper tool

Fill

Stroke

Swatches panel

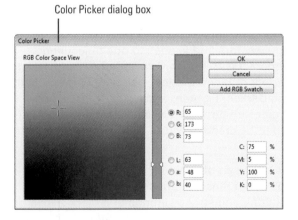

Color Picker dialog box

Use Default Colors and Switch the Fill and Stroke Colors

1. Click the **Default Fill and Stroke** button to revert the fill and stroke colors to their default values of no fill and a black stroke.

2. Click the **Swap Fill and Stroke Colors** button to switch current colors.

   TIMESAVER *Press D to change the fill and stroke colors to their default values of no fill and a black stroke, and press X to switch the current colors.*

Did You Know?

You can add colors from the Color Picker to the Swatches panel. Open the Color Picker dialog box, select the color you want to add to the Swatches panel, click Add To Swatches, type a name for the color, and then click OK.

Changing Stroke Attributes

ID 5.4

The Stroke panel makes it easy to change stroke attributes, such as weight (width), position on the path, and stroke style. The weight of a stroke represents the thickness of the line. A weight smaller than .25 may not print and a weight of 0 completely removes the stroke. In addition to the width of a stroke, you can also specify the position (known as alignment) of the stroke on the path (either center, inside, or outside) as well as specify the stroke cap, end join, and miter limit. You can apply these options to any object, even a text object (**New!**). Style is what stands out on the page. You can change the stroke style by applying dashes and endpoints, such as arrows, circles, and squares.

Change the Weight of a Stroke

1. Select one or more objects.

2. Select the **Stroke** panel.

3. Specify or enter a weight in the Stroke or Control panel.

   ◆ Click the up or down arrow, or Shift+click to change the weight by a larger interval.

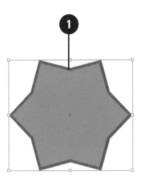

Change the Alignment of a Stroke on the Path

1. Select one or more closed objects.

2. Select the **Stroke** panel.

3. Click one of the following alignment buttons:

   ◆ **Align Stroke to Center.**

   ◆ **Align Stroke to Inside.**

   ◆ **Align Stroke to Outside.**

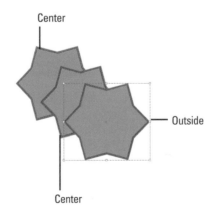

Center

Outside

Center

216

Change Stroke Caps or Joins

1. Select one or more objects.

2. Select the **Stroke** panel.

3. To change the endpoints, click one of the following buttons:

   ◆ **Butt Cap.** Creates a square-edged end.

   ◆ **Round Cap.** Creates a rounded end.

   ◆ **Projecting Cap.** Creates a square-edged end that extends past the endpoint.

4. To change the bends on corner points, click one of the following:

   ◆ **Miter Join.** Creates a pointed join point.

   ◆ **Round Join.** Creates a rounded join point.

   ◆ **Bevel Join.** Creates a beveled (cut off) join point.

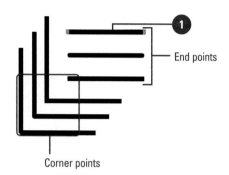

End points

Corner points

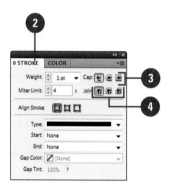

Style a Stroke

1. Select one or more objects.

2. Select the **Stroke** panel.

3. Specify any of the following:

   ◆ **Type.** Select a line style.

   ◆ **Start.** Select a style for the start point of the line.

   ◆ **End.** Select a style for the end point of the line.

   ◆ **Gap Color.** Select a color for the gap in dashed or dotted lines.

   ◆ **Gap Tint.** Select a tint percentage for the gap color.

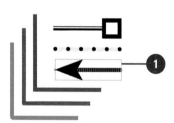

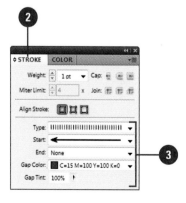

Creating Stroke Styles

In addition to the typical stroke styles found in the Stroke panel, you can create and use custom stroke styles with stripes, dashes, and dots. For example, you can create a custom dashed stroke where you can specify the length of the dashes and gaps. In the Stroke Styles dialog box, you can create, edit, delete, save, and load stroke styles. After you create a custom stroke style, the saved stroke style appears in the Stroke panel for use in the future.

Apply a Custom Dashed Stroke

1. Select one or more objects.

2. Select the **Stroke** panel.

3. Click the **Type** list arrow, and then click **Dashed** (at the bottom).

   The Stroke panel expands to display options for corners, dashes, and gaps.

4. Enter a value in the first Dash box.

   If you don't enter any more values, the value in the first box is used for the rest of the boxes.

5. Enter a value in the first Gap box.

6. Fill in the remaining boxes.

7. To adjust the dashes and gaps, click the **Corners** list arrow, and then select an option:

   ◆ **None.** No changes.

   ◆ **Adjust Dashes.** Adjusts corner dashes to be equal.

   ◆ **Adjust Gaps.** Adjusts gap lengths to be equal.

   ◆ **Adjust Dashes and Gaps.** Adjusts corner dashes and gap lengths to be equal.

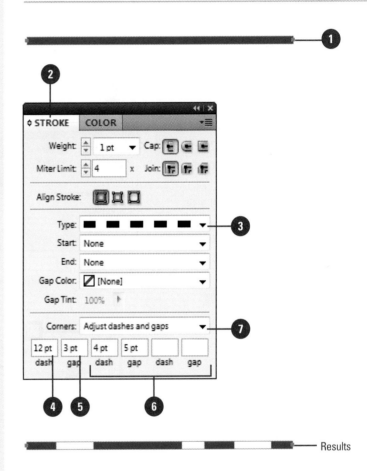

Results

Create a Custom Stroke Style

1. Select the **Stroke** panel.

2. Click the **Options** menu, and then click **Stroke Styles**.

   The Stroke Styles dialog box appears, where you can create, edit, save, and load stroke styles.

3. To use an existing style as the base for a new style, select it.

4. Click **New**.

   The New Stroke Style dialog box appears, where you can create a stroke style.

5. Enter a name for the stroke style.

6. Click the **Type** list arrow, and then select a stroke type: **Stripe**, **Dotted**, or **Dash**.

   The dialog box varies depending on the stroke type that you choose.

7. Adjust the options to create the style that you want.

8. View the preview at the bottom of the dialog box and adjust the **Preview Weight** to view the custom stroke style.

9. Click **OK**.

   ◆ To continue adding stroke styles, click **Add**.

10. To delete a custom stroke style, select it, and then click **Delete**.

11. To save stroke styles to a file, or load stroke styles from a file, click **Save** or **Load**.

12. Click **OK**.

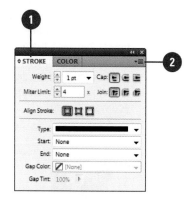

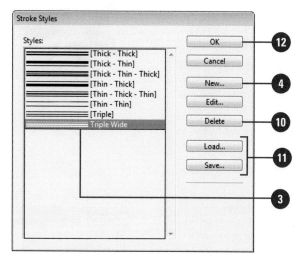

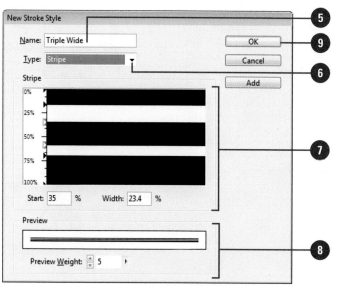

Applying Gradients

ID 5.2

A gradient is a smooth transition between two or more colors in an object. You can apply a gradient from the Swatches or Gradient panel. After you apply a gradient, you can edit it. You can edit a gradient in an object and keep the gradient in the Swatches panel unchanged or you can edit the gradient in the Swatches panel and keep the gradient in an object unchanged. Editing a gradient is similar to creating one. The techniques are the same. All you need to do is select the element that you want to edit.

Apply a Gradient to an Object

1. Select an object.

   - For a fill, click the **Fill** box on the Tools panel.

   - For a stroke, click the **Stroke** box on the Tools panel.

   - For type, convert it to outlines (click the Type menu, and then click Create Outlines), and then apply a gradient Fill or Stroke.

2. Click the **Apply Gradient** button on the Tools panel.

3. Or, do one of the following to apply a gradient:

   - **Swatches Panel.** Select the **Swatches** panel, and then click a gradient on the panel.

   - **Gradient Panel.** Select the **Gradient** panel, select a color stop, and then use the color spectrum and sliders in the Color panel to create a color gradient.

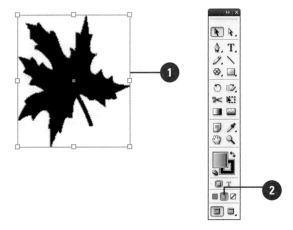

Gradient panel

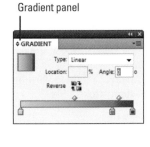

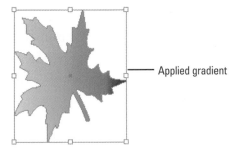

Applied gradient

See Also

See "Creating Gradient Swatches" on pages 204-205 for more information on creating gradients using the Swatches and Gradient panels.

Edit a Gradient

1. Select an object with a gradient.

2. Select the **Gradient** panel.

    ◆ To edit a gradient in the Swatches panel, select the **Swatches** panel, double-click a gradient swatch, edit the options as shown below, and then click **OK**.

3. To change the gradient type, click the **Type** list arrow, and then select a gradient type: **Radial** or **Linear**.

4. Do any of the following:

    ◆ **Add color stops.** Click below the gradient spectrum in a blank area.

    ◆ **Remove color stops.** Drag the stop down and away from the gradient spectrum.

    ◆ **Move color stops.** Drag the stop or enter a **Location** value.

    ◆ **Duplicate color stops.** Alt+drag (Win) or Option+drag (Mac) a color stop.

    ◆ **Adjust color amount.** Drag the diamond above the gradient spectrum.

    ◆ **Reverse color stops.** Click the Reverse button on the Gradients panel.

5. To save the edited gradient, click the **New Swatch** button on the Swatches panel.

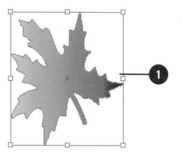

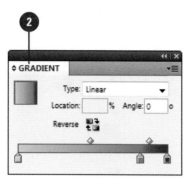

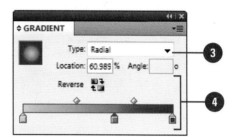

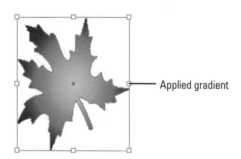

Applied gradient

Using the Gradient Tool

ID 5.2

The Gradient tool on the Tools panel allows you to change how a gradient appears for an object. You can change how gradient colors blend, the angle of a linear gradient, and the location of the center for a radial gradient with a drag of the mouse over the gradient fill. You can double-click the Gradient tool to display the Gradient panel and create a gradient, or drag across an existing gradient to adjust the gradient fill.

Use the Gradient Tool to Change a Gradient

1. Select an object with a gradient that you want to change.

2. Click the **Gradient** tool on the Tools panel.

3. To manually apply or adjust a gradient, double-click the **Gradient** tool on the Tools panel, and then specify any of the following options in the Gradient panel.

   ◆ Type. Specify the type: **Radial** or **Linear**.

   ◆ Angle. Specify the gradient angle.

   ◆ Add color stops. Click below the gradient spectrum in a blank area.

   ◆ Remove color stops. Drag stops down and away from the gradient spectrum.

   ◆ Duplicate color stops. Alt+drag (Win) or Option+drag (Mac) a color stop.

   ◆ Reverse color stops. Click the **Reverse** button on the Gradients panel.

4. To adjust the gradient angle and color stops, drag across the gradient in the object.

   The first drag point is the first color stop and the last drag point is the last color stop.

5. To save the edited gradient, click the **New Swatch** button on the Swatches panel.

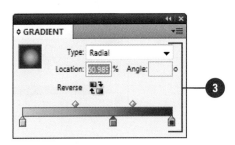

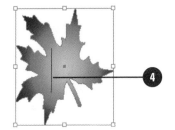

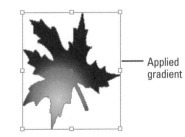

Applied gradient

Using the Gradient Feather Tool

ID 5.2, 5.4

The Gradient Feather tool on the Tools panel allows you to add an opacity, or transparency, to a gradient for an object. The Gradient Feather tool works just like the Gradient tool. You can change how gradient colors blend, the angle of a linear gradient, and the location of the center for a radial gradient with a drag of the mouse over the gradient fill. You can double-click the Gradient Feather tool to display the Effects dialog box, where you can adjust gradient feather options.

Use the Gradient Feather Tool to Change a Gradient

1. Select an object with a gradient that you want to change.

2. Click the **Gradient Feather** tool on the Tools panel.

3. To manually apply or adjust a gradient feather, double-click the **Gradient Feather** tool on the Tools panel, specify any of the following options in the Effects dialog box, and then click **OK**.

   ◆ Type. Specify the type: **Radial** or **Linear**.

   ◆ Angle. Specify the gradient angle.

   ◆ Add color stops. Click below the gradient spectrum in a blank area.

   ◆ Remove color stops. Drag stops down and away from the gradient spectrum.

   ◆ Reverse color stops. Click the **Reverse** button on the Gradients panel.

4. To apply or adjust a gradient feather, drag across the gradient in the object.

   The first drag point is the first color stop and the last drag point is the last color stop.

5. To save the edited gradient, click the **New Swatch** button on the Swatches panel.

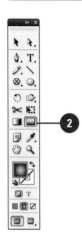

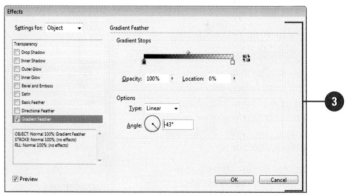

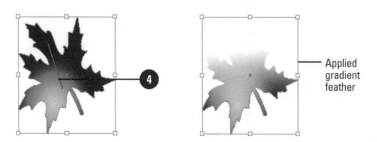

Applied gradient feather

Creating Blends and Effects

ID 5.4, 5.5

Blend mode allows you to apply colors and shades to one object and have the effect interact with the objects underneath. InDesign comes with a variety of blend modes, including Overlay, Soft Light, Hard Light, Darken, Lighten, and Color. Experiment with them to find out what works best for you. When you work with groups of objects, you can set options to apply blending modes and opacity settings with the objects in the group or not. The Knockout Group option doesn't apply settings to object groups, but it does to objects not in the group, while the Isolate Blending option does apply settings to object groups. You can set options in the Effects panel or Effects dialog box for Transparency.

Create a Blend Effect

1. Select an object that appears on top of another object.

2. Select the **Effects** panel.

    ◆ Click the **Window** menu, and then click **Effects**.

3. Click the **Blend Mode** list arrow, and then select a blend mode.

4. To add object transparency, enter an **Opacity** percentage or drag the slider to adjust it.

5. Choose any of the following:

    ◆ Isolate Blending. Objects in a group display their blending mode and transparency with each other. Group and select the objects that you want to use, and then select the **Isolate Blending** check box.

    ◆ Knockout Group. Objects in a group display their blending mode and transparency with other objects, but not each other. Group and select the objects that you want to use, and then select the **Knockout Group** check box.

    ◆ Add an Effect. Click the **fx** button to specify effect options for the selected object.

    ◆ Clear All Effects. Click the **Clears All Effects** button on the panel to clear all effects for the selected object.

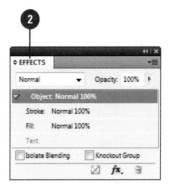

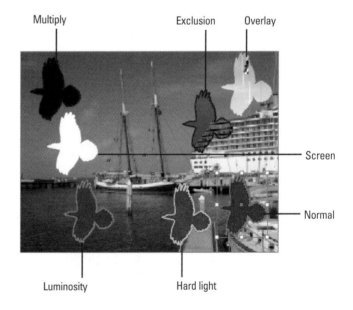

224

Create a Transparency Effect

① Select one or more objects.

② Select the **Effects** panel.

◆ Click the **Window** menu, and then click **Effects**.

◆ You can also click the **Object** menu, point to **Effects**, and then click **Transparency** to use a dialog box.

③ Enter an **Opacity** percentage or drag the slider to adjust it.

See Also

See "Controlling Graphics Display Performance" on pages 150-151 for more information on setting transparency preferences for the onscreen quality of transparent objects in a new document.

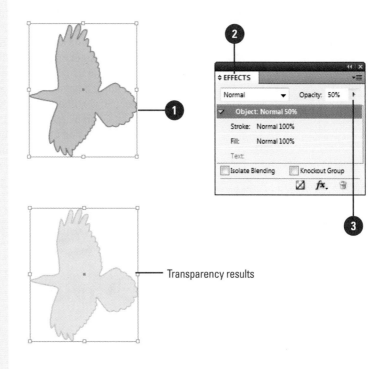

Transparency results

Select a Color Space for Blending Transparent Objects

① Click the **Edit** menu, and then point to **Transparency Blend Space**.

② Select a document's color space, such as Document RGB or Document CMYK.

This converts the colors of all objects to a common color space (RGB or CMYK) for blending. This avoids color mismatches between objects in different color spaces.

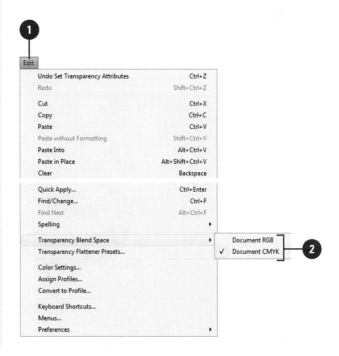

Applying Shadow Effects

ID 5.4

The Drop Shadow style is probably the most common effect used (next to Bevel and Emboss). The Inner Shadow style applies a shadow to the inside of an object. When you apply the Inner Shadow style, the shadow effect appears on the inside edges—like a reverse drop shadow. In addition to the distance and angle of the drop shadow, you can apply a blending mode and transparency. Other options include Global Light, Choke (inner), Spread (outer), and Noise. The Use Global Light option allows you to simulate the same light source on objects. The Spread and Choke options determine the amount of transparency used for the outer or inner part of the shadow. The Noise option introduces a random shift to the colors of the drop shadow.

Apply a Shadow Effect

1. Select one or more objects.

2. Click the **Object** menu, point to **Effects**, and then click **Drop Shadow** or **Inner Shadow**.

3. Do any of the following:

   ◆ **Blending options.** Select a blending mode and opacity for the shadow effect.

   ◆ **Position options.** Specify **Distance**, **Angle**, and **Offset** (X and Y) values to position the shadow in relation to the object.

   Select the **Use Global Light** check box to simulate the same lighting angle for all effects.

   ◆ **Other options.** Specify size and other options for the shadow; options vary depending on the type of shadow.

   The **Spread** and **Choke** options determine the amount of transparency used for the outer or inner part of the shadow. The **Noise** option introduces a random shift to the colors of the drop shadow.

4. Click **OK**.

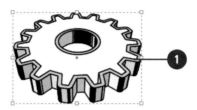

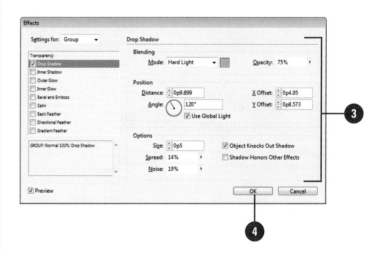

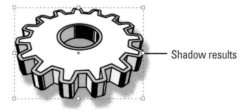

Shadow results

Applying Glow Effects

 ID 5.4

Outer Glow applies a glow in any color you choose to all selected objects. The Outer Glow style is an excellent way to create a neon effect for text. The Inner Glow style applies a glow to the inside of an object. When you apply the Inner Glow style, the effect appears on the inside edges—like a reverse outer glow. In addition to the technique (softer or precise) of the glow, you can apply specific blending modes and transparency. Other options include choke (inner), spread (outer), and Noise. The Spread and Choke options determine the amount of transparency used for the outer or inner part of the glow. The Noise option introduces a random shift to the colors of the glow.

Apply a Glow Effect

1. Select one or more objects.

2. Click the **Object** menu, point to **Effects**, and then click **Outer Glow** or **Inner Glow**.

3. Do any of the following:

   ◆ **Blending options.** Select a blending mode and opacity for the glow effect.

   ◆ **Other options.** Specify a **Technique** (softer or more precise glow) and **Size** of the glow; options vary depending on the type of glow.

   The **Spread** and **Choke** options determine the amount of transparency used for the outer or inner part of the glow. The **Noise** option introduces a random shift to the colors of the glow.

4. Click **OK**.

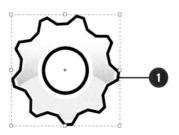

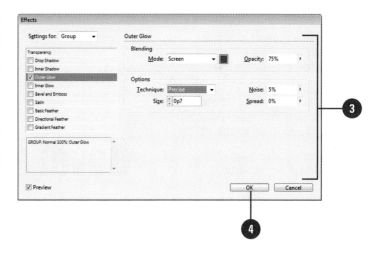

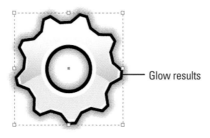

Glow results

Did You Know?

You can apply the satin effect. The satin effect applies a textured appearance to an object. Select one or more objects, click the Object menu, point to Effects, click Satin, specify angle, distance, size, and invert options, and then click OK.

Applying Bevel and Emboss Effects

Apply a Bevel and Emboss Effect

1. Select one or more objects.

2. Click the **Object** menu, point to **Effects**, and then click **Bevel and Emboss**.

3. Do any of the following:

   ◆ **Structure options.** Specify a **Style** (inner or outer bevel, emboss or pillow emboss), **Technique** (smooth, chisel hard, chisel soft), **Direction**, and **Size** for the effect.

   ◆ **Shading options.** Specify the **Angle** and **Altitude** values to position the effect in relation to the object.

   Select the **Use Global Light** check box to simulate the same lighting angle for all effects.

   Select a blending mode for **Highlight** and **Shadow**.

4. Click **OK**.

Did You Know?

You can set the global light. The global light allows you to simulate the same lighting angle for all effects. You can set the angle and altitude options to create shadows. Click the Object menu, point to Effects, and then click Global Light.

The Bevel and Emboss style, second only to Drop Shadow in popularity, creates a 3D illusion of roundness to a flat surface. You can apply the Bevel effect to outline text to get the impression of 3D text. If the object you're applying the Bevel and Emboss has no transparent areas, the style will be applied to the outer edge of the image, and if you want to experiment beyond the standard rounded bevel, you can use a Chisel Hard option that makes text appear as if it's carved out of stone.

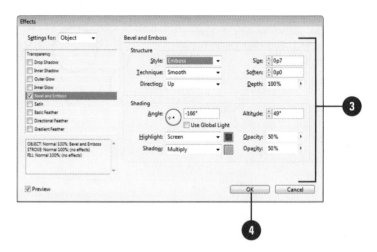

Bevel and Emboss results

Applying Feather Effects

ID 5.4

A feather effect softens the edges of an object to appear transparent. InDesign provides three different feather effects: Basic, Directional, and Gradient. The Basic Feather effect creates a soft edge around the outside of objects. The Directional Feather effect creates soft edges for the top, bottom, left, or right sides of objects. The Gradient Feather effect creates soft edges in a gradient. Instead of making a transition from one color to another, a gradient feather makes a transition from a color to a transparent fade. Some common feather options include Choke (inner) and Noise. The Choke option determines the amount of transparency used for the inner part of the feather. The Noise option introduces a random shift to the colors of the feather.

Apply a Feather Effect

1. Select one or more objects.

2. Click the **Object** menu, point to **Effects**, and then click **Basic Feather**, **Directional Feather**, or **Gradient Feather**.

3. Specify the options for the type of feather effect you selected:

   - **Basic Feather.** Specify a **Feather Width**, **Choke**, **Corners** (sharp, rounded, or diffused), and **Noise** for the effect.

   - **Directional Feather.** Specify a **Feather Width** for top, bottom, left, or right, **Noise**, **Choke**, **Shape**, and **Angle** for the effect.

   - **Gradient Feather.** Specify **Opacity** and **Location** for color stops, and **Type** and **Angle** for the gradient.

4. Click **OK**.

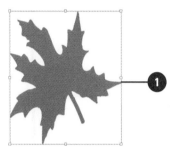

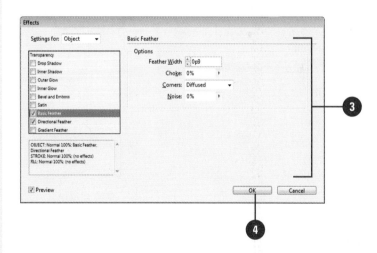

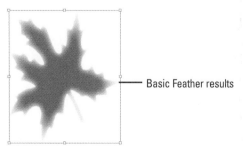

Basic Feather results

Applying Corner Object Effects

If you have an object with corners, you can change the shape of the object by applying corner object effects in the Corner Options dialog box. The effects include Fancy, Bevel, Inset, Inverse Rounded, and Rounded. In addition to specifying a corner effect, you can also specify a size for the effect. If you're not satisfied with the end result, you can always open the dialog box and adjust the corner effect and size.

Apply Corner Object Effects

1. Select an object that you want to change.

2. Click the **Object** menu, and then click **Corner Options**.

3. Select the **Preview** check box to view your results in the document window.

4. Click the **Effect** list arrow, and then select an effect.

   ◆ **Fancy.**

   ◆ **Bevel.**

   ◆ **Inset.**

   ◆ **Inverse Rounded.**

   ◆ **Rounded.**

5. Specify a **Size** value for the effect.

6. Click **OK**.

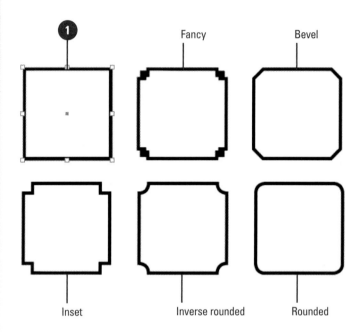

Fancy

Bevel

Inset

Inverse rounded

Rounded

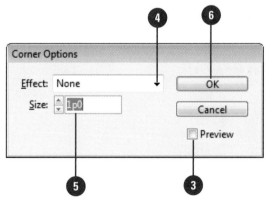

Converting Shape Objects

Sometimes when you create a shape with a certain look you just need to change the shape. Instead of creating a new shape, you can convert the shape to another shape by using Convert Shape buttons in the Pathfinder panel. The Pathfinder panel provides several different types of shapes: rectangle, rounded rectangle, beveled rectangle, inverted rounded rectangle, ellipse, triangle, polygon, and line. Some of the rectangle shapes use the radius value in the Corner Options dialog box to complete the conversion, so you can customize the shape.

Convert Shape Objects

1. Select one or more objects.

2. Select the **Pathfinder** panel.

   ◆ Click the **Window** menu, point to **Object & Layout**, and then click **Pathfinder**.

3. Select from the following Pathfinder Convert Shape buttons:

   ◆ **Rectangle.** Converts selection to a rectangle.

   ◆ **Rounded Rectangle.** Converts selection to a rounded rectangle using the radius from the Corner Options dialog box.

   ◆ **Beveled Rectangle.** Converts selection to a beveled rectangle using the radius from the Corner Options dialog box.

   ◆ **Inverted Rounded Rectangle.** Converts selection to an inverted rounded rectangle using the radius from the Corner Options dialog box.

   ◆ **Ellipse.** Converts selection to an ellipse.

   ◆ **Triangle.** Converts selection to a triangle.

   ◆ **Polygon.** Converts selection to a polygon.

   ◆ **Line.** Converts selection to a line.

   ◆ **Vertical or Horizontal Line.** Converts selection to a vertical or horizontal line.

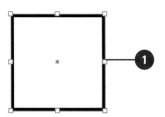

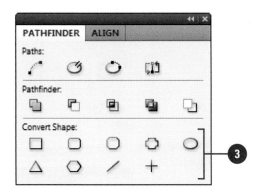

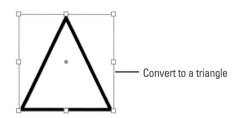

Convert to a triangle

Setting Object Defaults

If you always create an object with a certain fill or stroke attribute, you can make those settings the default. I find it useful to set the stroke weight to 1 point. Then I don't have to do it every time I create a new object. You can set the object defaults for the current document or for all new documents. InDesign has its own default fill and stroke settings of no fill and a black stroke. These program defaults are separate from the defaults you set.

Set Object Defaults

◆ **Document Defaults.** Open a document, deselect all objects, and then specify the defaults you want in the Stroke or other panels.

◆ **All New Document Defaults.** Close all documents, and then specify the defaults you want in the Stroke or other panels.

◆ **Apply InDesign Defaults.** Click the **Default Fill and Stroke** button on the Tools panel.

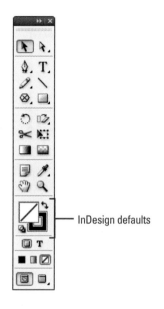
— InDesign defaults

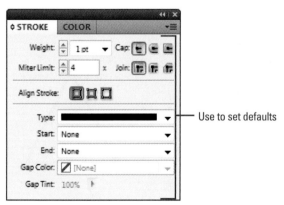
— Use to set defaults

Working with Points and Paths

9

Introduction

When you use InDesign's vector drawing or pen tools, InDesign creates a path to store that information. Paths are defined mathematically using anchor points and segments. Once created, they can be precisely modified to fit any design situation.

Working with the various Pen tools, it's possible to create precise paths, and even create complicated selections around virtually any shape. Once the path is created, it's a simple matter to subtract anchor points, and add new or modify existing anchor points to produce complex paths. It's even possible to convert straight segments (the visible line that connects two anchor points together) into elegantly curved segments, or you can remove the curve from a segment with a single click.

Paths can be used to precisely guide a brush stroke, or the interior of a path can be filled with any color or gradient available in InDesign using Color, Stroke and Gradient panels. Paths can even be used as a clipping mask, which is an object whose shape masks out everything except the contents behind the shape.

What You'll Do

Draw with the Pen Tool

Select and Move Points and Segments

Convert Points

Add and Delete Anchor Points

Split Paths

Join Anchor Points

Use the Smooth Tool

Use the Pencil Tool

Erase to Reshape Paths

Work with Pathfinder

Create a Compound Path

Work with Clipping Paths

Drawing with the Pen Tool

When you work with InDesign's Pen tool, you're creating a path. The path consists of curved and straight segments connected by anchor points. When you click with the Pen tool, you create corner points and straight segments. When you drag with the Pen tool, you can create smooth points and curve segments, which have direction handles you can use to change the curved segment. The shape of the curve segment is defined by the length and direction of the direction handles. As you create drawings with the Pen tool, you can turn on Smart Guides to help you align the segments.

Draw a Polygon with the Pen Tool

1. Click the **Fill** box on the Tools panel, and then click the **Color** or **None** button to specify whether you want to fill the object or not.

2. Select the **Pen** tool on the Tools panel.

3. Click to create the first anchor point.

   ◆ To draw segments constrained to 45 degrees, hold down Shift while you click.

4. Click to create the second anchor point at another location.

   A line segment appears between the two anchor points.

5. Continue to add anchor points.

6. Do any of the following to complete the shape as a:

   ◆ **Open Path.** Click the Pen tool or any other tool on the Tools panel, or Ctrl+click (Win) or ⌘+click (Mac) outside the new shape to deselect it.

   ◆ **Closed Path.** Point to the starting anchor point, and then click it.

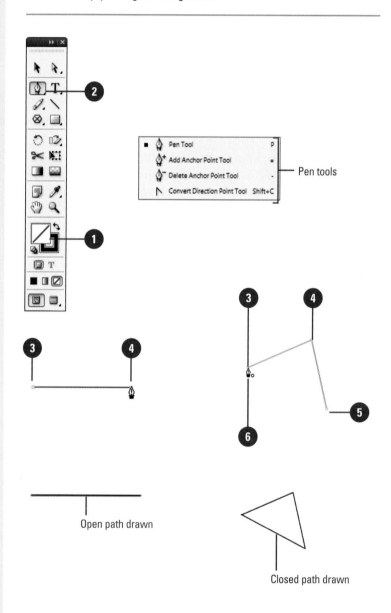

Open path drawn

Closed path drawn

Draw Curves with the Pen Tool

① Click the **Fill** box on the Tools panel and then click the **Color** or **None** button to specify whether you want to fill the object or not.

② Select the **Pen** tool on the Tools panel.

③ Click and drag to create the first anchor point.

As you drag, the direction handles move.

④ Release the mouse, and then move to where you want the second point.

⑤ Click and drag to create the second anchor point and a smooth curve.

   ◆ To create the second anchor point and corner curves, hold the Alt (Win) or Option (Mac) key as you drag.

   A curve segment appears between the two anchor points. As you drag, the direction handles move, which changes the the curve segment.

   The shape of the curve segment is defined by the length and direction of the direction handles.

⑥ Continue to add anchor points and direction handles.

⑦ Do any of the following to complete the shape as a:

   ◆ **Open Path.** Click the Pen tool or any other tool on the Tools panel, or Ctrl+click (Win) or ⌘+click (Mac) outside the new shape to deselect it.

   ◆ **Closed Path.** Point to the starting anchor point, and then click it.

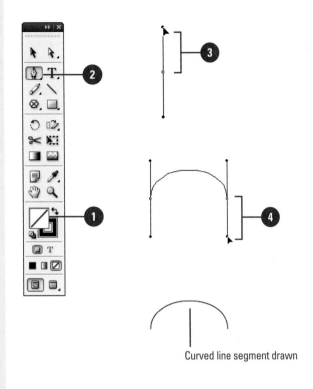

Curved line segment drawn

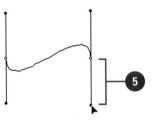

S-Curve drawn

Selecting and Moving Points and Segments

It's hard to draw a segment right the first time. Moving anchor points and segments is all part of the process of creating artwork. When you move an anchor point, the segments that are connected to it change. When you move a straight segment, the anchor points on the segment move with it. When you move a curve segment, the curve changes, but the connecting anchors remain the same. You can also change a curve segment by adjusting a direction point on the direction handle.

Select, Move, and Reshape Anchor Points or Segments

1. Select the **Direct Selection** tool on the Tools panel.

2. Click a blank area to deselect all points.

   ◆ To select and move multiple anchor points and segments, hold the Shift key, and then click the anchor points or segments you want, or drag a rectangle marquee around the ones you want.

3. Drag an anchor point or drag the middle of a segment.

   ◆ For a smaller move, click the anchor point or segment, and then press an arrow key.

   ◆ To constrain the movement of anchor points or segments to 45 degrees, hold down Shift while dragging.

4. To reshape a curve segment, click an anchor point or a curve segment, and then drag a direction point at the end of the direction handle.

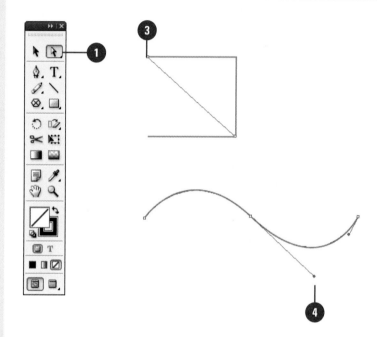

Converting Points

When you create a curve with the Pen tool, the curve segment after the second anchor point appears on the opposite side as the first curve segment. If you want the second curve segment to appear on the same side as the first, you need to convert the anchor point from a smooth point to a corner point. You can make this conversion as you create the curve segment with the Pen tool or you can do it later with commands on the Paths submenu (**New!**) or with the Convert Direction Point tool.

Convert Points on a Path

1. Select the **Direct Selection** tool on the Tools panel.

2. Select one or more points on a path to convert.

3. Click the **Object** menu, point to **Paths**, point to **Convert Point**, and then click **Line End**, **Corner**, **Smooth**, or **Smooth Symmetrical**.

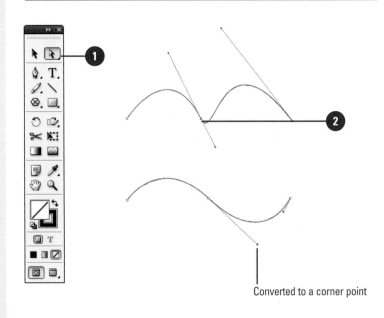

Converted to a corner point

Convert Points on a Path Using the Convert Direction Point Tool

1. Select the **Direct Selection** tool on the Tools panel, and then select a path to convert points.

2. Select the **Convert Direction Point** tool on the Tools panel.

3. Do any of the following to convert a point on a path:

   ◆ Drag a corner point to create a smooth point with no handles.

   ◆ Click a smooth curve point to create a corner point with no handles.

   ◆ Drag one of the handles of a smooth curve point to create a corner curve.

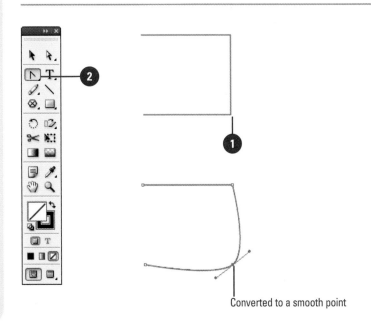

Converted to a smooth point

Adding and Deleting Anchor Points

Creating a path is not necessarily the end of the job; in fact, there are many ways you can modify a path once it's been created. For example, you can add, subtract, or delete anchor points on an existing path. You can also modify those points to conform to any desired shape. In addition, existing anchor points can be modified to change the segments connecting the points. Just like anything else in InDesign, paths are flexible. They can be modified to meet whatever design considerations are needed to make the job successful.

Add Anchor Points

1. Select the **Direct Selection** tool on the Tools panel.

2. Select the object to which you want to add an anchor point.

3. Select the **Add Anchor Point** tool on the Tools panel.

4. Click once on the path to add a new anchor point.

   When you add an anchor point to a curve segment, a smooth point appears on the path. When you add an anchor point to a straight segment, a corner point appears.

5. Click and drag on the path to add to and modify the segment.

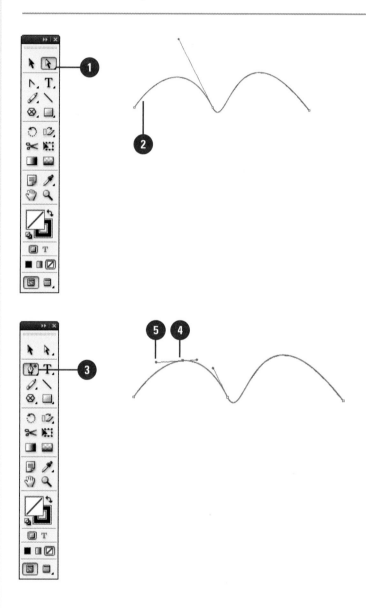

Add Anchor Points to an Open Path

① Select the **Pen** tool on the Tools panel.

② Point to the endpoint to which you want to add an anchor point.

A slash appears next to the Pen pointer.

③ Click the endpoint to make it a corner point or drag it to make a smooth point.

④ Click once on the path to add a new anchor point.

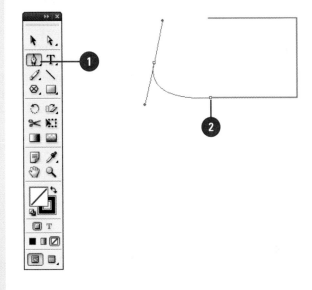

Delete Anchor Points

① Select the **Direct Selection** tool on the Tools panel.

② Select the object from which you want to delete an anchor point.

③ Select the **Delete Anchor Point** tool on the Tools panel.

④ Click once on an existing anchor point to remove it from the path.

The anchor points on either side of the deleted point are now used to define the segment.

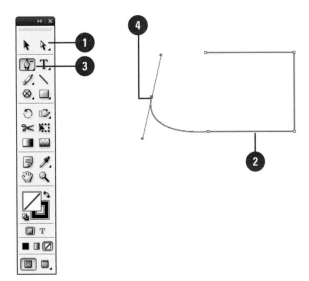

Did You Know?

You can delete a segment. Select the Direct Selection tool, click to select the segment, and then press the Delete key or click the Edit menu, and then click Clear.

Splitting Paths

The Scissors tool on the Tools panel allows you to split an open path into two paths or open a closed path. If you just want to open a closed path, you can also use the Open Path button (**New!**) on the Pathfinder panel or the same command on the Paths submenu. You can split a path at an anchor point or in the middle of a segment. The Scissors tool creates two points, one on top of the other. You can use the Direct Selection tool to move one point away from the other. If a path contains text, you cannot split it into two segments.

Split a Path

1. Select the **Direct Selection** tool on the Tools panel.

2. Select the object with the path that you want to split.

3. Select the **Scissors** tool on the Tools panel.

4. Click the object's path where you want to split it.

   If you click on a closed path, it turns into an open path. If you click on an open path, it splits it into two paths.

   If you click a line segment, two endpoints appear, one on top of the other.

5. To move the endpoints, select the **Direct Selection** tool, and then drag the selected endpoint to display the endpoint below it.

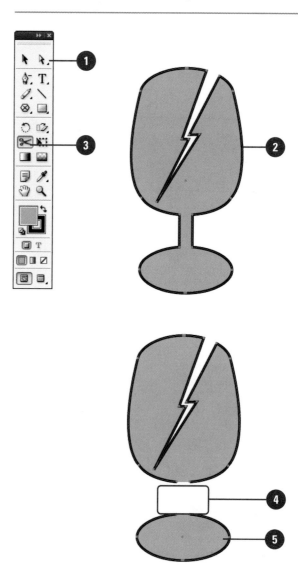

240

Open a Closed Path

1. Select the **Direct Selection** tool on the Tools panel.

2. Select the anchor point or segment where you want to open a closed path.

3. Select the **Pathfinder** panel.

   ◆ Click the **Window** menu, point to **Object & Layout**, and then click **Pathfinder**.

4. Click the **Open Path** button on the panel.

   The closed path turns into an open path.

5. To move the endpoints, select the **Direct Selection** tool, and then drag the selected endpoint to display the endpoint below it.

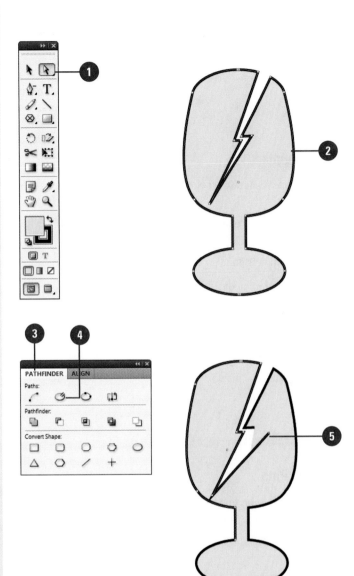

Did You Know?

You can reverse the direction of a path. Select the Direct Selection tool, select the path you want to reverse, and then click the Reverse button (**New!**) on the Pathfinder panel, or click the Object menu, point to Paths, and then click Reverse Path.

Joining Anchor Points

If you have an open path with two endpoints that you want to connect, you can use the Join or Close Path (**New!**) buttons on the Pathfinder panel to connect them with a straight line. You can also use the Join or Open Path commands from the Paths submenu on the Object menu. With the Join command, you need to select the two anchor points that you want to connect. With the Close Path command, all you need to do is select the open path.

Join Anchor Points

1 Select the **Direct Selection** tool on the Tools panel.

2 Select the two anchor points on a path you want to join.

3 Select the **Pathfinder** panel.

◆ Click the **Window** menu, point to **Object & Layout**, and then click **Pathfinder**.

4 Click the **Join Path** button on the panel.

The anchor points are joined together.

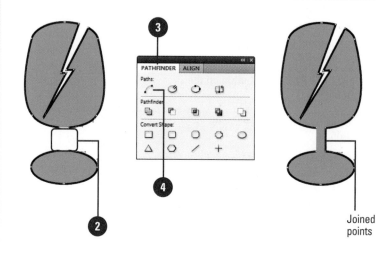

Joined points

Close an Open Path

1 Select the **Direct Selection** tool on the Tools panel.

2 Select the open path you want to close.

3 Select the **Pathfinder** panel.

◆ Click the **Window** menu, point to **Object & Layout**, and then click **Pathfinder**.

4 Click the **Close Path** button on the panel.

The open path becomes closed.

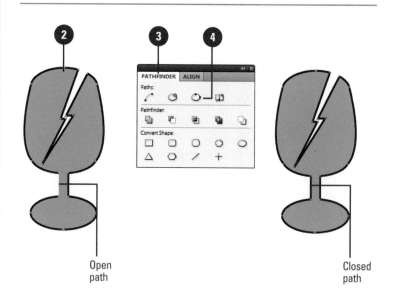

Open path

Closed path

Using the Smooth Tool

If you create a path with some jagged edges, you can use the Smooth tool to remove extra anchor points to smooth it out. Simply select the Smooth tool on the Tools panel, and then drag along a selected path. You can customize the way the Smooth tool works by setting preferences in the Smooth Tool Preferences dialog box.

Use the Smooth Tool

① Select the **Direct Selection** tool on the Tools panel.

② Select the path you want to smooth out.

③ Select the **Smooth** tool on the Tools panel.

④ Drag along the path to smooth it out.

The path is reshaped with fewer points.

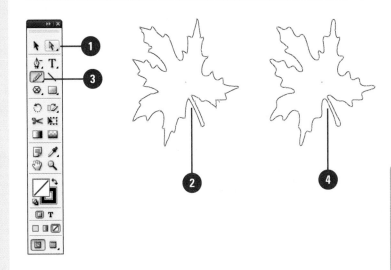

Set Smooth Tool Options

① Double-click the **Smooth** tool on the Tools panel.

② Drag the slider or enter a **Fidelity** value (.5-20). Fidelity determines how far the mouse must move before an anchor point is added. A higher value creates fewer anchor points and a smoother path while a lower value creates more anchor points and a rougher path.

③ Drag the slider or enter a **Smoothness** value (0-100). A high value creates a smoother curve, while a low value creates bends.

④ Select the **Keep Selected** check box to keep paths selected after you draw them.

⑤ Click **OK**.

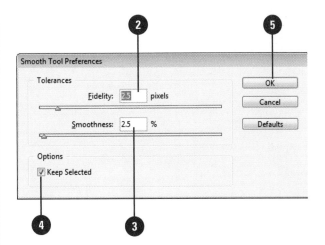

Using the Pencil Tool

The Pencil tool is exactly what its name implies...a pencil. If you like to draw freehand or sketch objects, especially with a drawing tablet, the Pencil tool is right for you. You can use the Pencil tool in several ways. You can draw new line segments to create a path, reshape a path, or add to a path. You can customize the way the Pencil tool works by setting preferences in the Pencil Tool Preferences dialog box.

Use the Pencil Tool

1. Select the **Pencil** tool on the Tools panel.

2. Select a stroke color and weight and a fill of **None** on the Tools or Stroke panels.

3. Use any of the following methods:

   ◆ **New Path.** Drag in a blank area to create an open or closed path. To create a closed path, hold down Alt (Win) or Option (Mac) while you finish drawing.

   ◆ **Reshape Path.** Drag along the edge of a selected open or closed path.

   ◆ **Add to Path.** Drag from an endpoint of an open path.

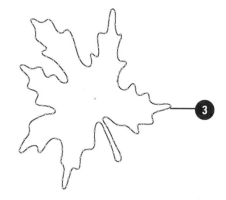

Set Pencil Tool Options

1. Double-click the **Pencil** tool on the Tools panel.

2. Drag the slider or enter a **Fidelity** value (.5-20). Fidelity determines how far the mouse must move before an anchor point is added. A higher value creates fewer anchor points and a smoother path while a lower value creates more anchor points and a rougher path.

3. Drag the slider or enter a **Smoothness** percentage value (0%-100%). A high value creates a smoother curve, while a low value creates bends.

4. Select or deselect any of the following check boxes:

   ◆ **Keep Selected.** Select to keep pencil paths selected after you draw them.

   ◆ **Edit Selected Paths.** Select to enable Reshaping for the Pencil tool within the specified pixel range (2-20).

5. To revert settings back to the defaults, click **Defaults**.

6. Click **OK**.

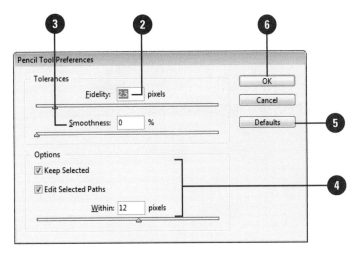

Erasing to Reshape Paths

Instead of selecting and deleting individual anchor points to reshape a path, you can use the Eraser tool on the Tools panel to delete parts of a path. When you use the Eraser tool to remove parts of a closed path, InDesign creates an open path. If you remove parts of an open path, InDesign creates two separate open paths. When you erase inside of filled path, InDesign creates a compound path. This is useful when you want to simplify a complex drawing or remove a background.

Erase Parts of Paths

1. Select the objects that you want to reshape with the Eraser tool.

2. Select the **Eraser** tool on the Tools panel.

3. Drag across the parts of the object that you want to erase.

   The remaining parts of the path reconnect to close the path.

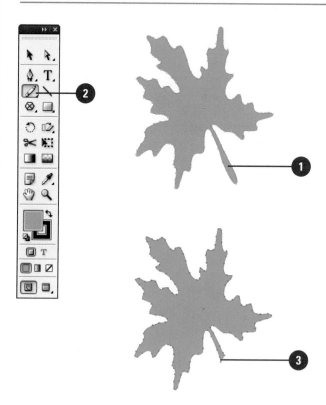

Working with Pathfinder

If you have overlapping objects, you can use buttons on the Pathfinder panel to create compound shapes, which are editable and releasable (restoring original attributes). You can use Pathfinder buttons (Add, Subtract, Intersect, Exclude Overlap, or Minus Back) on almost any object, except placed or rasterized images, mesh objects, or a single group.

Apply a Pathfinder Command

1. Select two or more overlapping objects.

2. Select the **Pathfinder** panel.

   ◆ Click the **Window** menu, point to **Object & Layout**, and then click **Pathfinder**.

3. Select from the following Pathfinder buttons:

   ◆ **Add.** Use to join the outer edges of selected objects into a compound shape.

   ◆ **Subtract.** Use to remove objects in front of other objects and still preserve paint attributes.

   ◆ **Intersect.** Use to preserve object areas that intersect.

   ◆ **Exclude Overlap.** Use to change overlapping areas to transparency.

   ◆ **Minus Back.** Use to remove objects in the back, leaving only part of the frontmost object.

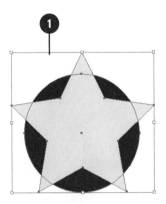

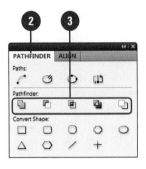

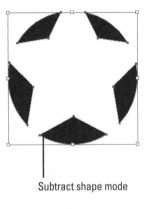

Subtract shape mode

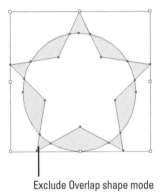

Exclude Overlap shape mode

Did You Know?

You can release a compound shape to restore object attributes. Select the Selection tool on the Tools panel, select the compound shape, click the Object menu, point to Paths, and then click Release Compound Path.

Creating a Compound Path

A compound path is a single object made up from two or more objects. In overlapping areas, a compound path removes the overlapping space displaying the attributes of the backmost object behind it. Think of it like a cookie cutter. After you create a compound path, you can release (restore) it at any time. However, the results are not exact. If you want to add another object to the compound path, you need to arrange the object in front or back of the compound object, select them both, and then reuse the Make Compound Path command.

Create a Compound Path

1. Arrange your objects so that the frontmost object will be cut out to reveal the attributes of the backmost object.

2. Select all the objects that you want to include in the compound path.

3. Click the **Object** menu, point to **Paths**, and then click **Make Compound Path**.

4. To add another object to the compound path, arrange the object in front or back of the compound object, select them both, and then click the **Object** menu, point to **Path**, and then click **Make Compound Path**.

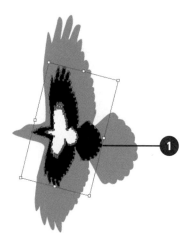

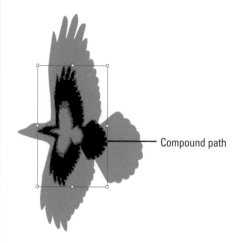

Compound path

Reverse an Object's Fill in a Compound Path

1. Click in a blank area to deselect the compound path.

2. Select the **Direct Selection** tool on the Tools panel.

3. Click the edge of the object for which you want to reverse the fill.

4. Select the **Pathfinder** panel.

   ◆ Click the **Window** menu, point to **Object & Layout**, and then click **Pathfinder**.

5. Click the **Reverse Path** button on the panel.

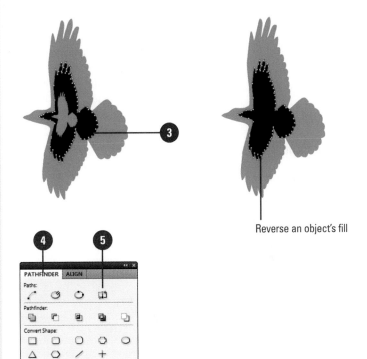

Reverse an object's fill

Release a Compound Path

1. Select the compound path.

2. Click the **Object** menu, point to **Paths**, and then click **Release Compound Path**.

   The single object reverts back to individual objects. All the objects are selected and painted with the attributes from the compound path, not their original attributes.

Released compound path

Working with Clipping Paths

A clipping path, or clipping mask, is a path whose shape masks out everything except the image contents behind the shape. You can create one in Adobe Photoshop and then place it into your InDesign document with the Apply Photoshop Clipping Path option in the Import Options dialog box, or you can have InDesign try to create a clipping path from the edges of an image. Once you have a clipping path, you can select and modify it like any other path using the Direct Selection tool and change options using the Clipping Path dialog box.

Modify a Clipping Path from a Graphic Image

1. Select the clipping path.

2. Click the **Object** menu, point to **Clipping Path**, and then click **Options**.

3. Select the **Preview** check box to view your results in the document window.

4. Click the **Type** list arrow, and then click **Detect Edges**.

5. Specify a **Threshold** value to define the color used as the area outside the clipping path and **Tolerance** value to apply small color variations and smooth out the path.

6. Click **OK**.

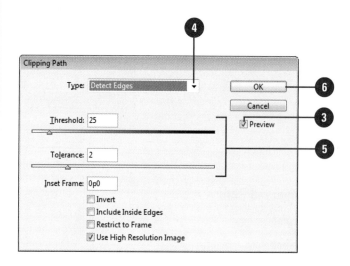

Did You Know?

You can convert a clipping path into a frame. Select the clipping path, click the Object menu, point to Clipping Path, and then click Convert Clipping Path To Frame.

See Also

See "Setting Place Import Options" on pages 130-131 for more information on importing and modifying clipping paths or alpha channels.

Select a Path or Alpha Channel as the Clipping Path

1 Select the clipping path.

2 Click the **Object** menu, point to **Clipping Path**, and then click **Options**.

3 Select the **Preview** check box to view your results in the document window.

4 Click the **Type** list arrow, and then click **Photoshop Path** or **Alpha Channel**.

The list arrow below it changes to Path for Photoshop Path or Alpha for Alpha Channel.

5 Specify a **Threshold** value to define the color used as the area outside the clipping path and **Tolerance** value to apply small color variations and smooth out the path.

6 Specify any of the following:

- ◆ **Inset Frame.** Use to enlarge (negative values) or shrink (positive values) the path in the image.

- ◆ **Invert.** Select to switch the visible and non-visible areas.

- ◆ **Include Inside Edges.** Select to add areas to the clipping path in the image.

- ◆ **Restrict to Frame.** Select to prevent the clipping path frame from displaying areas outside the frame.

- ◆ **Use High Resolution Image.** Select to create the path from the high resolution version of the image.

7 Click **OK**.

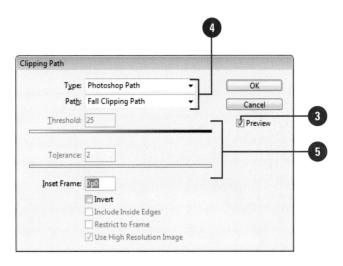

Alpha Channel

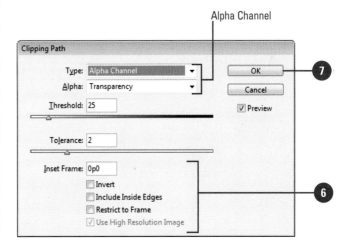

Working with Tables

10

Introduction

There are times when typing a paragraph will not do your text justice. Creating a bulleted or numbered list might better show your information. Another way to organize items in a document is with a table. A **table** is an object that is inserted into the document that displays text in rows and columns. You can set up your table with existing or imported text, or create a blank table and enter in new text. Once created, you can adjust the cells (where the text is contained in the rows and columns). You can also adjust the table to insert or delete rows, columns or individual cells, or change the alignment of text or graphics in cells.

In InDesign, a table is placed in a text frame, which might be larger or smaller than the table. You can drag the corner of the text frame to adjust the frame. If the text frame is smaller than the table, an overflow symbol appears in the bottom right corner. The overflow symbol works the same for tables as it does for normal text. When a table overflows, you can repeat the first (header) and last (footer) rows of a table when it appears in a different text frame on the same or different page. The information you enter in the header and footer automatically appears in the repeated headers and footers.

When you create a table, InDesign automatically creates strokes around cells to format it. You can remove or customize the strokes or add fills by using the Strokes and Fills tab on the Cell Options dialog box. If that is not enough, you can apply a border to the table. If you want to take formatting to the next level, you can add an alternating pattern to rows or columns to make it easier to read information in a table.

What You'll Do

Create Tables

Import Text into Tables

Enter and Edit Text in a Table

Modify a Table

Adjust Table Rows and Columns

Adjust Table Cells

Align Content in Table Cells

Create Table Headers and Footers

Add Strokes and Fills

Alternate Fills and Strokes

Add Diagonal Lines in Cells

Add a Border to a Table

Adjust Tables in the Text Frames

Creating Tables

ID 3.3

A table organizes your information into rows and columns. The intersection of a row and column is called a **cell**. You can create a blank table, and then enter text, or make a table from existing text separated by paragraphs, tabs, or commas. The first row in the table is good for column headings, whereas the leftmost column is good for row labels. Knowing how to select the rows and columns of a table is also essential to working with the table itself. If you want create a table within a table, you can create **nested tables**. If you decide a particular table is not really necessary after all, you can convert it to text.

Create a New Table

1. Click to place the insertion point where you want to create a table.

   ◆ To insert a table within a table, click to place the new table insertion point in a table cell.

2. Click the **Table** menu, and then click **Insert Table**.

3. Specify the following table dimensions:

   ◆ **Body Rows.** Enter a number to specify the number of rows you want in the table.

   ◆ **Columns.** Enter a number to specify the number of columns you want in the table.

   ◆ **Header Rows.** Enter a number to set the number of headers rows at the top of the table.

   ◆ **Footer Rows.** Enter a number to set the number of footer rows at the bottom of the table.

4. Click the **Table Style** list arrow, and then select a table style.

5. Click **OK**.

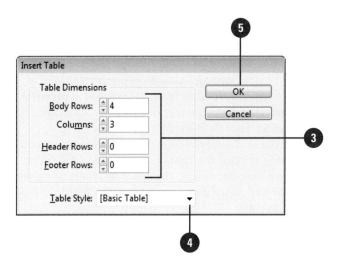

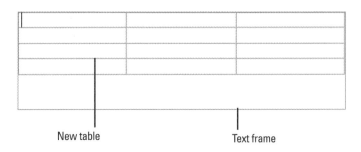

New table   Text frame

Did You Know?

You can delete a table. Click inside the table you want to delete, click the Table menu, point to Delete, and then click Table.

Convert Text to a Table

1. Select the text that you want to convert into a table.

2. Click the **Table** menu, and then click **Convert Text to Table**.

3. Click the **Column Separator** list arrow, and then select a separator: **Tab**, **Comma**, or **Paragraph**.

4. Click the **Row Separator** list arrow, and then select a separator: **Tab**, **Comma**, or **Paragraph**.

5. Enter a **Column** number to set the number of columns in the table.

6. Click the **Table Style** list arrow, and then select a table style.

7. Click **OK**.

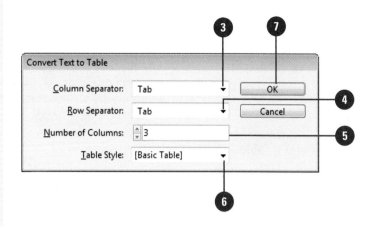

Convert a Table into Text

1. Click to place the insertion point inside any cell in the table.

2. Click the **Table** menu, and then click **Convert Table to Text**.

3. Click the **Column Separator** list arrow, and then select a separator: **Tab**, **Comma**, or **Paragraph**.

4. Click the **Row Separator** list arrow, and then select a separator: **Tab**, **Comma**, or **Paragraph**.

5. Click **OK**.

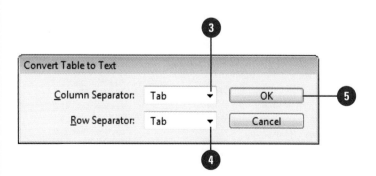

Importing Text into Tables

ID 3.3, 3.4

In addition to creating a table from text in an InDesign document, you can copy tabbed text from other programs and paste it into a table in your document. If you have a table in Microsoft Word or a spreadsheet in Microsoft Excel that you want to use in a document, you can import the table by using the Place command on the File menu. During the import process, you can specify import options to place the information you want in the way you want. A red dot inside a table cell indicates there is overflow text.

Import Text into a Table

1. Open the program where you want to copy text for a table.

   ◆ You can also copy text from another table to paste into an InDesign table.

2. Select and copy text that has tab separators.

3. Switch back to InDesign.

4. Select the cells in the table where you want to paste text.

5. Click the **Edit** menu, and then click **Paste**.

   The text appears in the selected cells. Any additional text appears in new cells.

Did You Know?

You can import a graphic into a table cell. Click to place the insertion point in the cell where you want the graphic, click the File menu, click Place, select the graphic file, and then click OK. The graphic is linked to the document in the table cell. You can use the Links panel to update or relink the graphic. See Chapter 5, "Placing and Working with Graphics" for details.

You can adjust table options. Click inside the table, click the Table menu, point to Table Options, click Table Setup, specify the options you want, and then click OK.

Import a Table from Word or Excel

1. Click the **File** menu, and then click **Place**.

2. Navigate to the drive or folder location with the file you want to import.

3. Select the file you want to place.

4. Select the **Show Import Options** check box to select import options.

5. Click **Open**.

6. Specify the following options:

   ◆ **For Word.** Select options from the Microsoft Word Import Options dialog box.

      ◆ **Preset and Include.** Select an import preset and select check boxes to include Word elements.

      ◆ **Formatting.** Select formatting options to Remove or Preserve Styles and Formatting from Text and Tables, or Import Styles Automatically.

   ◆ **For Excel.** Select options from the Microsoft Excel Import Options dialog box.

      ◆ **Sheet, View, and Cell Range.** Select an Excel sheet, view, and cell range. You can also import hidden cells not saved in view.

      ◆ **Formatting.** Select formatting options for table, style, cell alignment, the number of decimal places to use, and typographer's quotes.

7. Click **OK**.

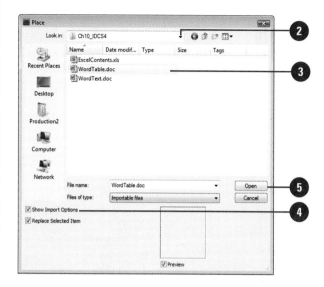

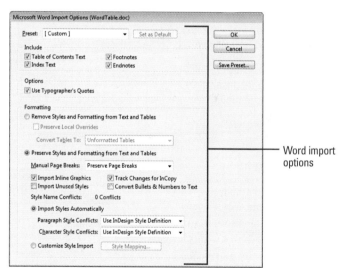

Word import options

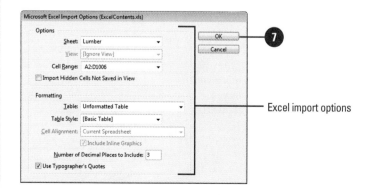

Excel import options

Entering and Editing Text in a Table

ID 3.1, 3.2

Once you create your table, you enter text into cells just as you would in a paragraph, except in a table, pressing Tab moves you from cell to cell. As you type in a cell, text wraps to the next line, and the height of a row expands as you enter text that extends beyond the column width. Before you can edit text directly in a table, you need to know how to select the rows and columns of a table. If you want to focus solely on table text, you can use the Story Editor, which displays text in sequential columns and rows for easy editing (**New!**).

Enter Text and Navigate a Table

1. The insertion point shows where text that you type will appear in a table. After you type text in a cell:

   ◆ Press Enter (Win) or Return (Mac) to start a new paragraph within that cell.

   ◆ Press Tab or Shift+Tab to move the insertion point to the next or previous cell (or to the first cell in the next or last row).

   ◆ Press the arrow keys or click in a cell to move the insertion point to a new location.

Press Tab to move to the next cell.

Press Tab to move to the first cell in the next row.

Decorating with Paint	13.99	Foxworthy
Simple Kids Rooms	9.49	Collar
Using Tile	10.75	Lamb
Grilling Indoor	19.97	Mills
Fireplaces	14.00	Panico

Press Tab to create a new row.

Select Table Elements

Refer to this table for methods of selecting table elements, including:

   ◆ The entire table

   ◆ One or more rows and columns

   ◆ One or more cells

Did You Know?

You can delete contents within a cell. Select the contents of the cell you want to delete, and then press Delete.

Selecting Table Elements

To Select	Do This
The table	Click the top left corner of the table and then click ↗ or click in the table, click the Table menu, point to Select, and then click Table.
One or more columns	Click just above the first column you want to select, and then drag with ↓ to select the columns you want.
The column or row with the insertion point	Click in the column or row, click the Table menu, point to Select, and then click Column or Row.
A single cell	Drag a cell or click the cell with ↗ , or click the Table menu, point to Select, and then click Cell.
More than one cell	Drag with ↗ to select a group of cells.

Select and Edit Text

1 Move the I-beam pointer to the left or right of the text you want to select.

2 Drag the pointer to highlight the text, or click in the document to place the insertion point where you want to make a change.

3 Perform one of the following editing commands:

◆ To replace text, type your text.

◆ To delete text, press the Backspace key or the Delete key.

◆ Drag the selection to the new location.

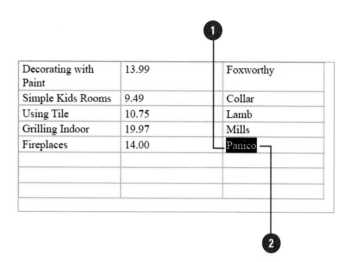

Edit Table Elements in the Story Editor

1 Click in the table you want to edit using Story Editor.

2 Click the **Edit** menu, and then click **Edit in Story Editor**.

3 Drag the pointer to highlight the text, or click in the document to place the insertion point where you want to make a change.

4 Perform one of the following editing commands:

◆ To replace text, type your text.

◆ To delete text, press the Backspace key or the Delete key.

◆ Drag the selection to the new location.

5 Click the **Close** button.

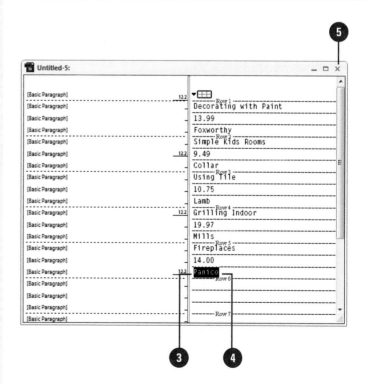

Modifying a Table

ID 3.1

As you begin to work on a table, you might need to modify table contents by using options available on the Control and Table panels and Table menu. You can modify the table's structure by adding more rows, columns, or cells to accommodate new text, graphics, or other tables. The table realigns as needed to accommodate the new structure. When you insert rows or columns, the existing rows shift down and the existing columns shift right. Similarly, when you delete unnecessary rows or columns from a table, the table automatically realigns.

Modify Tables Using the Control or Table Panels

① Select the cells, rows, or columns you want to modify.

The Control panel displays options for the current selection.

② Select the **Table** panel.

③ Use the following Control and Tables panel options:

◆ **Number of Rows or Columns.** Specify a number.

◆ **Row Height or Column Width.** Specify a number.

◆ **Align Top, Center, Bottom, and Justify.** Click a button.

◆ **Rotate 0°, 90°, 180°, 270°.** Click a button.

◆ **Cell Inset Top, Bottom, Right or Left.** Specify a number for spacing between cell edge and cell contents.

Additional Control panel options include:

◆ **Merge and Unmerge.** Click a button to combine or uncombine cells.

◆ **Stroke Weight.** Enter a line thickness.

◆ **Stroke Style.** Select a line style.

◆ **Proxy Cell Line Preview.** Select which lines to which you want to apply settings.

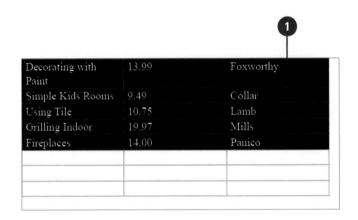

Table options

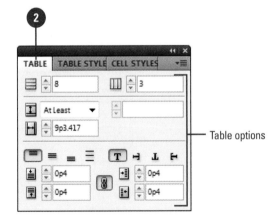

Table options

Insert Additional Rows or Columns

① Select the row or column next to where you want the new ones.

TIMESAVER *Drag the last row or column, and then press Alt (Win) or Option (Mac) as you drag to insert new rows or columns.*

② Drag to select the number of rows or columns you want to insert.

③ Click the **Table** menu, point to **Insert**, and then click **Rows** or **Columns**.

④ Specify the number of rows or columns, and then select an option for the position.

⑤ Click **OK**.

Insert rows

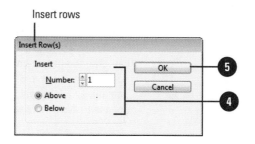

Insert columns

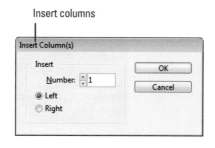

Delete Rows and Columns

① Select the rows or columns you want to delete.

② Click the **Table** menu, point to **Delete**, and then click **Row** or **Column**.

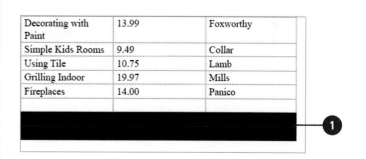

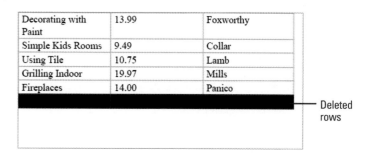

Deleted rows

Adjusting Table Rows and Columns

After you insert and delete rows and columns in a table, you can adjust them to any size you want. If you want to create evenly sized rows and columns, you can use the Distribute Rows Evenly or Distribute Columns Evenly command to quickly do the job. If you want custom sizes, you can drag the row or column borders to the size you want or set exact sizing in the Rows and Columns tab in the Cell Options dialog box. Sometimes a long table doesn't fit in a text frame. You can also set cell options to keep rows together.

Distribute Row or Column Spacing Evenly

1. Specify the content position of the rightmost column or bottommost row that you want to use as the model for the row or column spacing.

2. Select the columns or rows in which you want the content distributed to match the model row or column.

3. Click the **Table** menu, and then click **Distribute Rows Evenly** or **Distribute Columns Evenly**.

Evenly distributed columns

Adjust Row Heights and Column Widths

◆ **Adjust Rows.** Point to a row border (cursor changes to a double-arrow), and then drag to adjust the height of the row.

◆ **Adjust All Rows.** Point to the bottom row border (cursor changes to a double-arrow), and then drag to adjust the height of all rows.

◆ **Adjust Columns.** Point to a column border (cursor changes to a double-arrow), and then drag to adjust the width of the column.

Adjust Row and Column Options

1 Select the cells you want to adjust.

2 Click the **Table** menu, point to **Cell Options**, and then click **Rows and Columns**.

3 Specify the following row and column options.

◆ **Row Height.** Enter a row height value for the **At Least** or **Exactly** option.

◆ **Column Width.** Enter a column width.

◆ **Start Row.** Select an option to control when and how the rows of a table break across text frames.

◆ **Keep with Next Row.** Select to keep the selected row with the one following it across text frames.

4 Click **OK**.

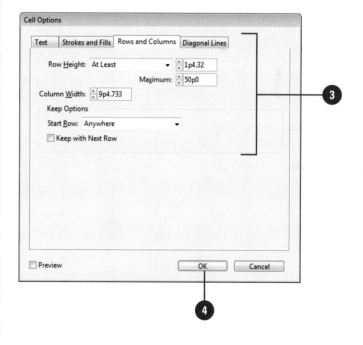

Drag to adjust columns

Decorating with Paint	13.99	Foxworthy		
Simple Kids Rooms	9.49	Collar		
Using Tile	10.75	Lamb		
Grilling Indoor	19.97	Mills		
Fireplaces	14.00	Panico		

Adjusting Table Cells

Often, there is more to modifying a table than adding or deleting rows or columns; you need to make cells just the right size to accommodate the text or graphics you are entering in the table. For example, a title in the first row of a table might be longer than the first cell in that row. To spread the title across the top of the table, you can merge (combine) the cells to form one long cell. Sometimes, to indicate a division in a topic, you need to split (or divide) a cell into two. You can also split one table into two at any row. Moreover, you can modify the width of any column and height of any row to better present your data.

Merge Table Cells

1. Select the two or more cells you want to merge into a single cell.

2. Drag to select the number of rows you want to insert.

3. Click the **Table** menu, and then click **Merge Cells**.

4. To unmerge table cells, click in the single merged cell, click the **Table** menu, and then click **Unmerge Cells**.

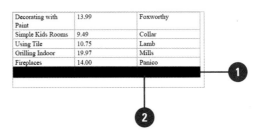

Split Table Cells

1. Click the cell you want to split into two cells.

2. Click the **Table** menu, and then click **Split Cell Horizontally** or **Split Cell Vertically**.

Aligning Content in Table Cells

 ID 3.2

Adjust the Spacing of Text and Graphics in a Cell

1. Select the cells you want to adjust.

2. Click the **Table** menu, point to **Cell Options**, and then click **Text**.

3. Select the **Preview** check box to view your results in the document window.

4. Specify any of the following options:

   ◆ **Cell Insets.** Enter the spacing sizes for the top, bottom, left and right inside areas of the cell.

   ◆ **Vertical Justification.** Specify an alignment position for vertical text in the cell.

   ◆ **Paragraph.** Enter an amount for the space between the lines or paragraphs in the cell.

   ◆ **First Baseline.** Specify an option to control where the first text baseline appears in the cell.

   ◆ **Clipping for Graphics.** Select the **Clip Contents to Cell** check box to restrain the graphic content to the size of the cell. Deselect it to allow the graphic to appear outside of cell boundaries.

   ◆ **Text Rotation.** Specify a rotation angle for the contents of the cell.

5. Click **OK**.

After you enter or insert text and graphics into cells in a table, you can adjust the spacing of the content to position it where you want in a cell. You can control how text is positioned vertically or horizontally in the cell as well as the text baseline. A graphic appears in a table as an inline graphic, so you can adjust its position like you would text. If the graphic is larger than the cell, you can set the Clip Content to Cell option to crop the image to the cell boundaries.

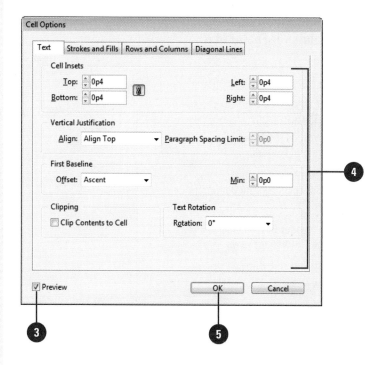

Creating Table Headers and Footers

Table headers are the first row in a table and footers are the last row. Sometimes a long table doesn't fit in a text frame. You can repeat the first and last rows of a table when they appear in a different text frame on the same or a different page. The information you enter in the header and footer automatically appears in the repeated headers and footers. If you already have text in the table that you want to use as a header or footer, you can convert the rows into a table header or footer. On the flip side, you can also convert header or footer rows into normal rows.

Insert a Header or Footer in a Table

1. Click in the table you want to add a header or footer.

2. Click the **Table** menu, point to **Table Options**, and then click **Headers and Footers**.

3. Select the **Preview** check box to view your results in the document window.

4. Enter a **Header Rows** value to set a number for header rows.

   ◆ To disable header rows, set the value to zero.

5. Enter a **Footer Rows** value to set a number for footer rows.

   ◆ To disable footer rows, set the value to zero.

6. Click the **Repeat Header** or **Repeat Footer** list arrow, and then specify a repeat option.

   ◆ **Every Text Column.** Repeat everywhere in the table.

   ◆ **Once Per Frame.** Repeat only once in the same frame.

   ◆ **Once Per Page.** Repeat only once in the same page.

7. Select **Skip First** or **Skip Last** check box to display the header or footer only after the first or last use.

8. Click **OK**.

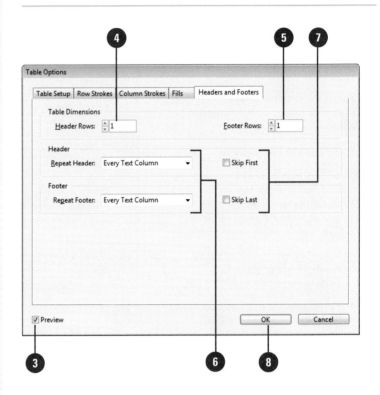

Book	Price	Author
Decorating with Paint	13.99	Foxworthy
Simple Kids Rooms	9.49	Collar
Using Tile	10.75	Lamb
Grilling Indoor	19.97	Mills
Fireplaces	14.00	Panico
	Average	

Convert Cells into a Table Header or Footer

1. Select the rows that you want to convert into a header or footer.

2. Click the **Table** menu, point to **Convert Rows**, and then click **To Header** or **To Footer**.

   If you already have text in a header or footer, the new header or footer text is added to the bottom (for a header) or top (for a footer) of the existing cells.

Book	Price	Author
Decorating with Paint	13.99	Foxworthy
Simple Kids Rooms	9.49	Collar
Using Tile	10.75	Lamb
Grilling Indoor	19.97	Mills
Fireplaces	14.00	Panico
	Average	

Convert a Header or Footer into Cells

1. Select the header or footer row that you want to convert into normal body rows of table cells.

2. Click the **Table** menu, point to **Convert Rows**, and then click **To Body**.

Book	Price	Author
Decorating with Paint	13.99	Foxworthy
Simple Kids Rooms	9.49	Collar
Using Tile	10.75	Lamb
Grilling Indoor	19.97	Mills
Fireplaces	14.00	Panico
	Average	

Adding Strokes and Fills

 ID 3.2

When you create a table, InDesign automatically creates strokes around cells. You can remove or customize the strokes, and even add custom fills by using the Strokes and Fills tab on the Cell Options dialog box. In the dialog box, you select cell lines in a proxy preview to specify to which actual lines in the cell you want to apply formatting. When you mix and match stroke colors and styles in a table, you also need to specify stroke drawing order to determine how the table should be drawn. After you apply formatting once, you don't need to reselect the proxy preview lines the next time you want to apply formatting changes to the same cells (**New!**).

Set Stroke Drawing Order

1. Select the cells in the table you want to format.

2. Click the **Table** menu, point to **Table Options**, and then click **Table Setup**.

3. Select the **Preview** check box to view your results in the document window.

4. Click the **Draw** list arrow, and then select a stroke drawing order option:

  ◆ **Best Joins.** Allows InDesign to choose the best way to display strokes.

  ◆ **Row Strokes in Front.** Displays the strokes from rows in front of strokes from columns.

  ◆ **Column Strokes in Front.** Displays strokes from columns in front of strokes from rows.

  ◆ **InDesign 2.0 Compatibility.** Uses a combination of Best Joins for the table border and Row Strokes for interior cells.

5. Click **OK**.

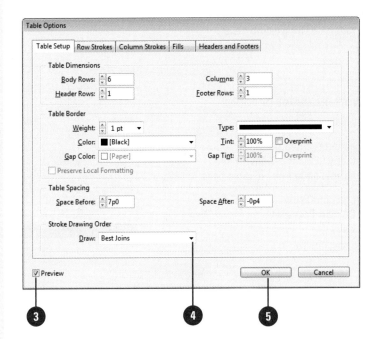

Add Strokes or Fills to Cells

1. Select the cells in the table you want to format.

2. Click the **Table** menu, point to **Cell Options**, and then click **Strokes and Fills**.

3. Select the **Preview** check box to view your results in the document window.

4. Click the lines in the cell proxy preview to select (they will turn blue) the edges that you want to format.

5. Specify the following Cell Stroke and Fill options:

   - **Weight.** Enter a value to set the thickness of the stroke.

   - **Type.** Specify a style for the stroke.

   - **Color and Tint.** Specify a color and tint for the stroke. Select the Overprint Stroke check box to apply it.

   - **Gap Color and Tint.** If you selected a stroke type with dashes or dots, specify a gap color (for the space between the lines) and tint for the stroke. Select the Overprint Gap check box to apply it.

   - **Color and Tint for Fill.** Specify a color and tint for the fill. Select the Overprint Fill check box to apply it.

6. Click **OK**.

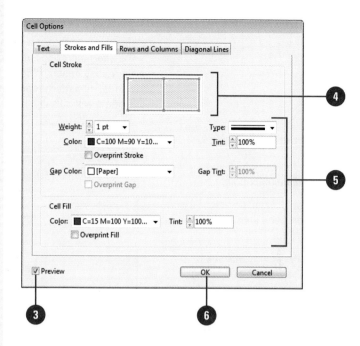

Applied fills

Alternating Fills and Strokes

ID 3.2

Alternating rows or columns with a color or a pattern can make it easier to read information in a table. With this thought in mind, InDesign allows you to format a table with repeating alternating fills and strokes. The alternating fills and strokes remain in place until you change the alternating option to None. If you insert or delete a row or column, the alternating pattern reapplies to the table. You can create alternating patterns with fills in a table and strokes in a row or column.

Alternate Fills in Table Cells

1. Click in the table to which you want to add alternating fills.

2. Click the **Table** menu, point to **Table Options**, and then click **Alternating Fills**.

3. Select the **Preview** check box to view your results in the document window.

4. Click the **Alternating Pattern** list arrow, and then select a pattern option.

5. Specify the following options on the left for the first set of columns or rows, and on the right for the second set of columns or rows:

   ◆ **First** or **Next**. Enter a value to set the number of rows in the alternating pattern.

   ◆ **Color and Tint.** Specify a color and tint for the fill. Select the Overprint check box to apply it.

   ◆ **Skip First** or **Skip Last.** Enter a value to omit the number of rows or columns at the start or end of the alternating fills.

   ◆ **Preserve Local Formatting.** Select to use the cell formatting instead of the border formatting. Deselect to use the border formatting.

6. Click **OK**.

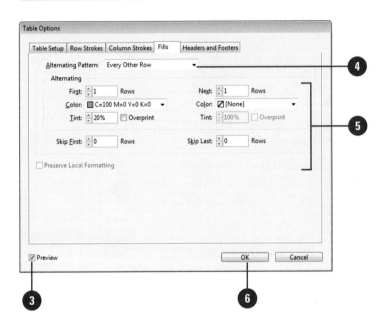

Book	Price	Author
Decorating with Paint	13.99	Foxworthy
Simple Kids Rooms	9.49	Collar
Using Tile	10.75	Lamb
Grilling Indoor	19.97	Mills
Fireplaces	14.00	Panico
	Average	

Alternating fills

Alternate Strokes for Rows or Columns in Table Cells

1. Click in the table to which you want to add alternating fills.

2. Click the **Table** menu, point to **Table Options**, and then click **Alternating Row Strokes** or **Alternating Column Strokes**.

3. Select the **Preview** check box to view your results in the document window.

4. Click the **Alternating Pattern** list arrow, and then select a pattern option.

5. Specify the following options on the left for the first set of columns or rows, and on the right for the second set of columns or rows:

    ◆ **First** or **Next**. Enter a value to set the number of rows in the alternating pattern.

    ◆ **Weight**. Enter a value to set the thickness of the stroke.

    ◆ **Type**. Specify a style for the stroke.

    ◆ **Color and Tint**. Specify a color and tint for the stroke. Select the Overprint check box to apply it.

    ◆ **Gap Color and Tint**. If you selected a stroke type with dashes or dots, specify a gap color (for the space between the lines) and tint for the stroke. Select the Overprint check box to apply it.

    ◆ **Skip First** or **Skip Last**. Enter a value to omit the number of rows or columns at the start or end of the alternating strokes.

6. Click **OK**.

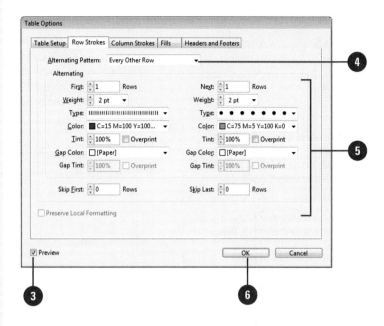

Book	Price	Author
Decorating with Paint	13.99	Foxworthy
Simple Kids Rooms	9.49	Collar
Using Tile	10.75	Lamb
Grilling Indoor	19.97	Mills
Fireplaces	14.00	Panico
	Average	

Alternating strokes

Adding Diagonal Lines in Cells

 ID 3.2

Diagonal lines or X's in a table cell can be an effective formatting tool to indicate no data is available or the data in the cell needs to reviewed or changed. You can use the Diagonal Lines tab in the Cell Options dialog box to quickly add a diagonal line to one cell or a range of cells in a table. You can specify the color, weight (width), and style you want. Even after you add a diagonal line to a cell, you can still add information to it and specify which item appears in front.

Add Diagonal Lines in Cells

1. Select the cells in the table to which you want to add diagonal lines.

2. Click the **Table** menu, point to **Cell Options**, and then click **Diagonal Lines**.

3. Select the **Preview** check box to view your results in the document window.

4. Click a button to select the type of diagonal line you want to apply.

5. Specify the following Line Stroke options:

    ◆   **Weight.** Enter a value to set the thickness of the line.

    ◆   **Type.** Specify a style for the line.

    ◆   **Color and Tint.** Specify a color and tint for the line. Select the Overprint Stroke check box to apply it.

    ◆   **Gap Color and Tint.** If you selected a line type with dashes or dots, specify a gap color (for the space between the lines) and tint for the line. Select the Overprint Gap check box to apply it.

    ◆   **Draw.** Specify how you want to show the line: Content in Front or Diagonal in Front.

6. Click **OK**.

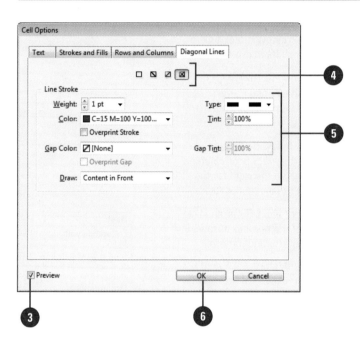

Book	Price	Author
Decorating with Paint	13.99	Foxworthy
Simple Kids Rooms	9.49	Collar
Using Tile	10.75	Lamb
Grilling Indoor	19.97	Mills
Fireplaces	14.00	Panico
	Average	

Diagonal lines

Adding a Border to a Table

 ID 3.2

A border is the line around a table. A border is a good way to add definition to the outside of a table and make it stand out. You can use the Table Setup tab in the Table Options dialog box to to quickly add a border and specify the color, weight (width), and style you want. If you applied a stroke to a cell that is also a border edge, you can select an option to preserve the formatting already applied to the cell.

Add a Border to a Table

1. Click in the table to which you want to add a border.

2. Click the **Table** menu, point to **Table Options**, and then click **Table Setup**.

3. Select the **Preview** check box to view your results in the document window.

4. Specify the following Table Border options:

   ◆ **Weight.** Enter a value to set the thickness of the border line.

   ◆ **Type.** Specify a style for the border line.

   ◆ **Color and Tint.** Specify a color and tint for the border line. Select the Overprint check box to apply it.

   ◆ **Gap Color and Tint.** If you selected a border type with dashes or dots, specify a gap color (for the space between the lines) and tint for the border line. Select the Overprint check box to apply it.

   ◆ **Preserve Local Formatting.** Select to use the cell formatting instead of the border formatting. Deselect to use the border formatting.

5. Click **OK**.

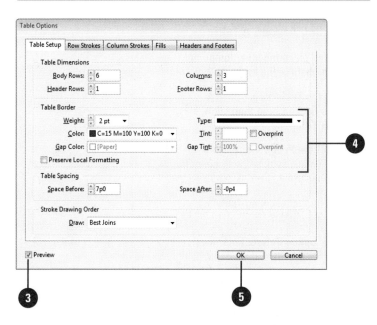

Applied border

Adjusting Tables in the Text Frame

A table is placed in a text frame, which might be larger or smaller than the table. You can drag the corner of the text frame to adjust the frame. If the text frame is smaller than the table, an overflow symbol appears in the bottom right corner. The overflow symbol works the same for tables as it does for normal text. You can adjust the space around the table in the text frame by setting options in the Table Setup tab in the Table Options dialog box.

Set Spacing Around a Table

1. Click to place the insertion point somewhere in the table.

2. Click the **Table** menu, point to **Table Options**, and then click **Table Setup**.

3. Select the **Preview** check box to view your results in the document window.

4. Specify the following Table Spacing options:

   ◆ **Space Before.** Enter a value to set the distance that appears before the table.

   ◆ **Space After.** Enter a value to set the distance that appears after the table.

5. Click **OK**.

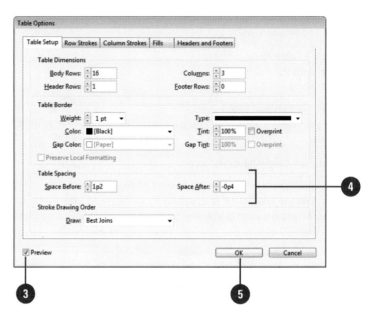

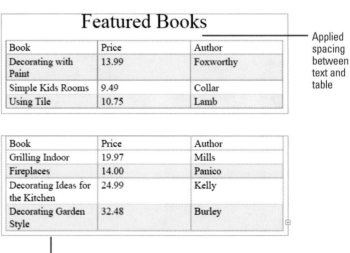

Featured Books		
Book	Price	Author
Decorating with Paint	13.99	Foxworthy
Simple Kids Rooms	9.49	Collar
Using Tile	10.75	Lamb

Applied spacing between text and table

Book	Price	Author
Grilling Indoor	19.97	Mills
Fireplaces	14.00	Panico
Decorating Ideas for the Kitchen	24.99	Kelly
Decorating Garden Style	32.48	Burley

Table in two text frames

Working with Styles

11

Introduction

A style is a group of format settings that you can create or modify to get the exact look you want. In InDesign, you can create two types of styles, character and paragraph. Character styles apply formatting to only character attributes, while paragraph styles apply formatting for both characters and paragraphs attributes.

The styles panels for paragraphs, characters, objects, tables, and cells are centralized places to work with the different types of styles in InDesign. The panels display the current styles in the InDesign document. You can use buttons on the bottom of the panel to quickly create a new style group, clear overrides in a selection, create a new style, and delete styles. If you have styles in one InDesign document that you want to use in another, you can transfer them from one document into another. If you have styles in a word processing document, such as Microsoft Word, you can import them into an InDesign document, too.

After you create styles, you can use any of the style panels or keyboard shortcuts to apply them. However, you can also use the Quick Apply button. The Quick Apply button provides an easy way to apply any style in your InDesign document. You can even use keyboard shortcuts to speed up the process. After you apply a style, you can still apply additional formatting, known as local or override formatting, by using the Control, Paragraph, or Character panels. Instead of applying individual character styles for a line of text, you can create and apply a nested style to do it for you. A nested style is useful for a list of predictable elements on a line, such as a name, address, and phone number.

What You'll Do

Use the Paragraph Styles or Character Styles Panel

Change the Basic Paragraph Style

Create Paragraph Styles

Create Character Styles

Create GREP Styles

Create Style Groups

Load and Import Styles

Apply and Override Styles

Create Nested Styles

Create Object Styles

Create Table and Cell Styles

Use Quick Apply

Using the Paragraph Styles or Character Styles Panel

The Paragraph Styles and Character Styles panels are centralized places to work with paragraph and character styles in InDesign. The panels display the current paragraph and character styles in the InDesign document. You can use buttons on the bottom of the panel to quickly create a new style group, clear overrides in a selection (Paragraph only), create a new style, and delete styles. You can also use the Options menu to duplicate and edit styles, as well as sort styles in the panel by name.

Use the Paragraph Styles or Character Styles Panel

1. Select the **Paragraph Styles** or **Character Styles** panel.

   ◆ Click the **Type** menu, and then click **Paragraph Styles** or **Character Styles**.

2. Use any of the following buttons or commands to perform an operation:

   ◆ **Create a New Style Group.** Click the **Create New Style Group** button to create a folder to organize styles. Double-click the style group, enter a name, and then click **OK**.

   ◆ **Clear Style Overrides.** Select the style, and then click the **Clear Overrides** button.

   ◆ **Create a New Style.** Click the **Options** menu, click **New Paragraph** or **Character Style**, make changes to the style, and then click **OK**.

   ◆ **Delete a Style or Group.** Select the style or group, and then click the **Delete Selected Style/Groups** button.

   ◆ **Edit a Style.** Select the style, click the **Options** menu, click **Style Options**, make changes to the style, and then click **OK**.

   ◆ **Duplicate a Style.** Select the style, click the **Options** menu, click **Duplicate Style**, enter a name, and then click **OK**.

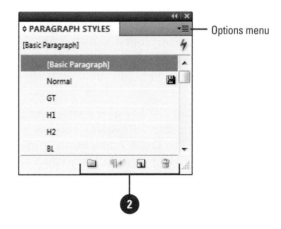

Options menu

Changing the Basic Paragraph Style

The **Basic Paragraph** style is the default style for the document and all new text uses this style. You can modify the Basic Paragraph style, or create a new style. To modify the Basic Paragraph style or any style for that matter, adjust the formatting settings for the existing style. When you see a plus (+) sign after the name, it means that the text with the applied style also contains other formatting, which you can redefine.

Redefine the Basic Paragraph Style

1. Select the **Type** tool on the Tools panel, and then select text that uses the Basic Paragraph style.

   ◆ You can use the same method to redefine any style.

2. Use the Control, Character, and Paragraph panels to change text attributes.

3. Select the **Paragraph Styles** panel.

   ◆ Click the **Type** menu, and then click **Paragraph Styles**.

   A plus (+) sign appears next to the style name.

4. Click the **Options** menu, and then click **Redefine Style**.

   The plus (+) sign disappears.

5. To manually change style attributes, select the Basic Paragraph style, and then do the following:

   ◆ Click the **Options** menu, and then click **Style Options**.

   ◆ View the current settings and make any changes that you want.

   ◆ Click **OK**.

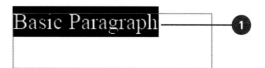

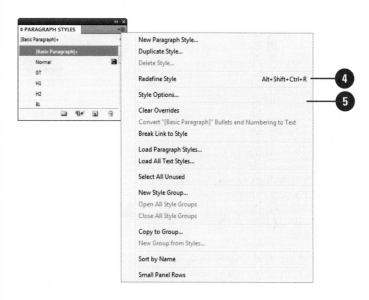

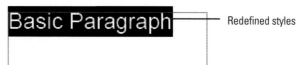

Redefined styles

Creating Paragraph Styles

 ID 2.5

A paragraph style is a group of paragraph and character format settings that can be applied to text. You can create a new paragraph style from the formatting of existing text or use the New Paragraph Styles dialog box to specify the formatting and other attributes you want. When you create a new paragraph style with the New Paragraph Styles dialog box, you can create a new style from scratch or base the new style on an existing style and then modify to it. You can also select a style for the next paragraph. When you press Enter (Win) or Return (Mac), InDesign automatically switches from the current style to the next style. If you like using keyboard shortcuts, you can attach a shortcut to the style to make it easy to apply.

Create a Paragraph Style from Existing Text

1. Select the **Type** tool on the Tools panel, and then select the text that you want to use as the style.

   ◆ You can use the Control, Character, and Paragraph panels to change text attributes.

2. Select the **Paragraph Styles** panel.

   ◆ Click the **Type** menu, and then click **Paragraph Styles**.

3. Click the **Create New Style** button on the panel.

4. To rename the style, double-click the style, enter a name, and then click **OK**.

Did You Know?

You can delete paragraph styles. Select the Paragraph Styles panel, select the styles you want to delete, and then click the Delete Selected Style button on the panel. If the style is in use, select a replacement style, and then click OK. To select all unused styles to delete, click the Options menu, and then click Select All Unused.

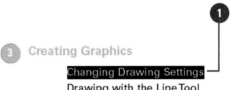

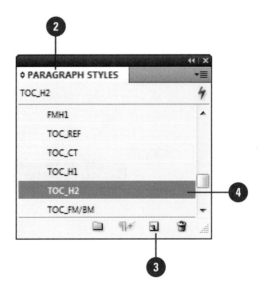

Create a Paragraph Style

① Select the **Paragraph Styles** panel.

◆ Click the **Type** menu, and then click **Paragraph Styles**.

② Click the **Options** menu, and then click **New Paragraph Style**.

③ Enter a name for the style.

④ Select the **General** category, and then specify the following:

◆ **Based On.** Select a style to use as the base for the new style.

◆ **Next Style.** Select a style to use as the style for the next paragraph when you press Enter (Win) or Return (Mac).

◆ **Shortcut.** Press a keyboard combination to create a shortcut for the style.

⑤ Select each category to set text attributes.

◆ **Basic Character Formats.**
◆ **Advanced Character Formats.**
◆ **Indents and Spacing.**
◆ **Tabs.**
◆ **Paragraph Rules.**
◆ **Keep Options.**
◆ **Hyphenation.**
◆ **Justification.**
◆ **Drop Caps and Nested Styles.**
◆ **GREP Style.**
◆ **Bullets and Numbering.**
◆ **Character Color.**
◆ **OpenType Features.**
◆ **Underline Options.**
◆ **Strikethrough Options.**

⑥ View the current settings and make any changes that you want.

⑦ Click **OK**.

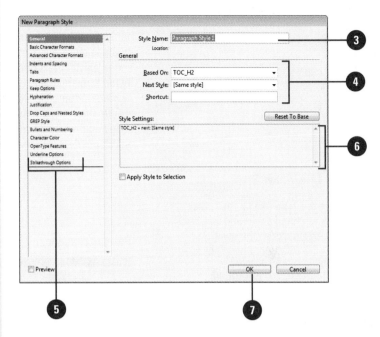

Creating Character Styles

ID 2.5

A character style is a group of format settings that is applied to any block of text. Rather than formatting text from the Control or Character panels, using the character styles features allows you to quickly make changes later. You can create a new character style from the formatting of existing text or use the New Character Style dialog box to specify the formatting and other attributes you want. When you create a new character style with the New Character Style dialog box, you can create a new style from scratch or base the new style on an existing style and then modify it. If you like using keyboard shortcuts, you can attach a shortcut to the style to make it easy to apply.

Create a Character Style

1. Select the **Type** tool on the Tools panel, and then select the text that you want to use as the style.

   ◆ You can use the Control, Character, and Paragraph panels to change text attributes.

2. Select the **Character Styles** panel.

   ◆ Click the **Type** menu, and then click **Character Styles**.

3. Click the **Create New Style** button on the panel.

4. To rename the style, double-click the style, enter a name, and then click **OK**.

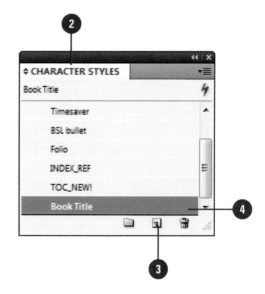

Did You Know?

You can delete character styles. Select the Characters Styles panel, select the styles you want to delete, and then click the Delete Selected Style button on the panel. If the style is in use, select a replacement style, select the Preserve Formatting check box to convert the style into local formatting, and then click OK. To select all unused styles to delete, click the Options menu, and then click Select All Unused.

Create a Character Style

1. Select the **Character Styles** panel.

   ◆ Click the **Type** menu, and then click **Character Styles**.

2. Click the **Options** menu, and then click **New Character Style**.

3. Enter a name for the style.

4. Select the **General** category, and then specify the following:

   ◆ **Based On.** Select a style to use as the base for the new style.

   ◆ **Shortcut.** Press a keyboard combination to create a shortcut for the style.

5. Select each category to set text attributes.

   ◆ **Basic Character Formats.**
   ◆ **Advanced Character Formats.**
   ◆ **Character Color.**
   ◆ **OpenType Features.**
   ◆ **Underline Options.**
   ◆ **Strikethrough Options.**

6. View the current settings and make any changes that you want.

7. Click **OK**.

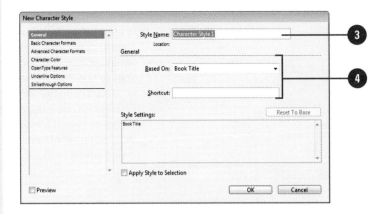

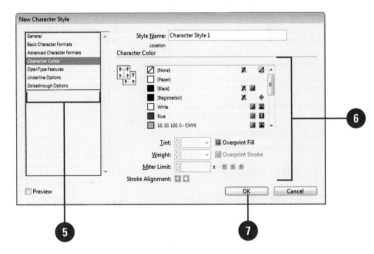

Creating GREP Styles

A **GREP expression** is an advanced method for locating text and special characters in a document. GREP (Global Regular Expression Print) is used by the Find/Change dialog box to find and replace text and special characters, such as tabs, ends of paragraphs, white space, variables, and wildcards. You can create a style to apply a character style to text that conforms to a GREP expression (**New!**). A GREP style is a Character style with a GREP expression. When text matches the GREP expression, the character style is applied to the text. In the GREP Styles and Find/Change dialog boxes (where you can select a character or paragraph style), you can create a style without having to exit the dialog box (**New!**).

Create a GREP Style

1. Select the **Paragraph Styles** panel.

   ◆ Click the **Type** menu, and then click **Paragraph Styles**.

2. Click the **Options** menu, and then click **New Paragraph Style**.

   ◆ To add a GREP expression to an existing style, select the style, click the **Options** menu, and then click **Style Options**.

3. Enter a name for the style.

4. Select each category to set text attributes.

5. Select the **GREP Style** category.

6. Click **New GREP Style**.

7. Click to the right of *Apply Style*, and then select a character style or click **New Character Style** to create one.

8. Click to the right of *To Text*, and then enter a search expression or click the **Special Character For Search** icon to the right to display a menu. Choose options from the **Locations**, **Repeat**, **Match**, **Modifiers**, and **Posix** submenus to help construct the GREP expression.

9. Click **OK**.

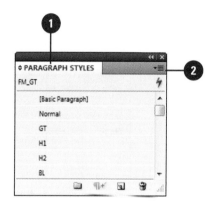

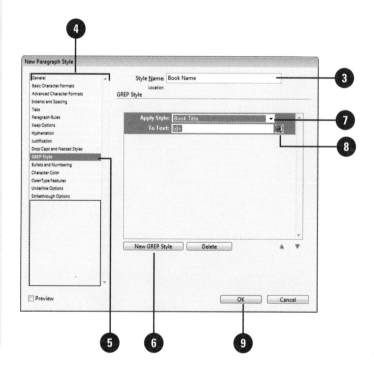

Creating Style Groups

As you continue to create styles, the list in the Paragraph and Character panels can become long and difficult to use. A style group is a folder you can use to organize styles in the Paragraph or Character panels. This can help you reduce the clutter in the panels and make it easier to find and work with the styles you want. After you create a style group, you can drag styles into it, just like you drag files into a folder in Windows Explorer (Win) or Finder (Mac).

Create a Style Group and Move Styles into the Group

1. Select the **Paragraph Styles** or **Character Styles** panel.

   ◆ Click the **Type** menu, and then click **Paragraph Styles** or **Character Styles**.

2. Click the **Create New Style Group** button on the panel.

   ◆ You can also select styles, click the **Options** menu, and then click **New Group from Styles**.

   ◆ You can also Alt+click (Win) or Option+click (Mac) the **Create New Style Group** to display the New Style Group dialog box.

3. Double-click the new style group.

4. Enter a name for the style group.

5. Click **OK**.

6. To move styles into the group, select a style, and then drag it into the new style group.

7. To copy styles into the group, select a style, click the **Options** menu, click **Copy to Group**, select the group, and then click **OK**.

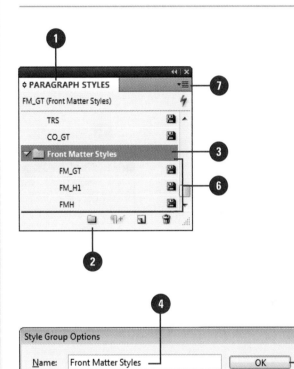

Loading and Importing Styles

If you have styles in one InDesign document that you want to use in another, you can transfer (or load) them from one document into another. If you have styles in a word processing document, such as a Microsoft Word file, you can import them into an InDesign document, too. When you place text from a word processing document, the styles associated with the text are added to the Paragraph or Character panels in the InDesign document. When you add styles to an InDesign document, there may be times when style names are the same. In this case, you need to resolve the conflict between the styles. Style names are case-sensitive, so the name *Header text* is different than *header text*. If you want text with an imported style to be used by a current style, you can map the incoming style to the current style. This way, you don't have to reapply the text style.

Load Styles from an InDesign Document

1. Select the **Paragraph Styles** or **Character Styles** panel.

    ◆ Click the **Type** menu, and then click **Paragraph Styles** or **Character Styles**.

2. Click the **Options** menu, and then click **Load Character Styles** or **Paragraph Styles**, or **Load All Text Styles**.

3. Navigate to the document with text styles that you want to open.

4. Click the file you want to open.

5. Click **Open**. If a conflict occurs, the Load Styles dialog box appears.

6. Select the check boxes for the styles you want to load and deselect the check boxes for the styles you don't want to load.

7. For each checked style, click the **Conflict With Existing Style** list arrow, and then select an option:

    ◆ **Auto-Rename.** Add a suffix to create a new style name.

    ◆ **Use Incoming Definition.** Changes the existing style to match the imported style.

8. Click **OK**.

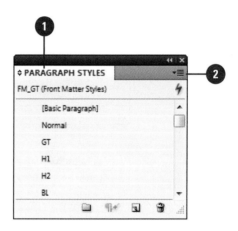

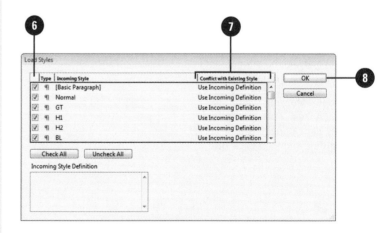

Import Styles from a Word Processing Document

1. Click the **File** menu, and then click **Place**.

2. Navigate to the document with text styles that you want to open.

3. Click the file you want to open.

4. Select the **Show Import Options** check box.

5. Click **Open**.

6. Click the **Preserve Styles and Formatting from Text and Tables** option.

7. To resolve style conflicts automatically, click the **Import Styles Automatically** option, and then select conflict options:

   ◆ **Use InDesign Style Definition.** Select to have InDesign styles override incoming styles.

   ◆ **Redefine InDesign Style.** Select to have incoming styles override InDesign styles.

   ◆ **Auto Rename.** Select to add incoming styles to the list of InDesign styles.

8. To map styles, click the **Customize Style Import** option, click **Style Mapping**, select a style under the InDesign Style column for each incoming Word style, and then click **OK**.

9. Click **OK**.

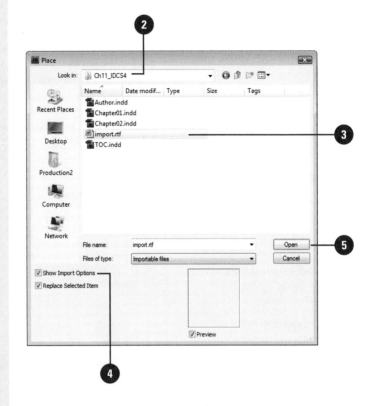

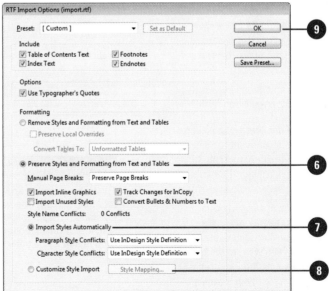

Applying and Overriding Styles

ID 2.5

After you create paragraph and character styles, you can use the Paragraph Styles and Character Styles panels or keyboard shortcuts to apply styles to text. For a GREP style, you can use the GREP styles dialog box to apply styles to selected paragraphs. After you apply a style, you can still apply additional formatting, known as **local** or **override formatting**, by using the Control, Paragraph, or Character panels. When the applied style also contains other formatting, a plus sign (+) appears after the style name, which you can remove to redefine the style. You can use the Clear Override button on the Paragraph Styles panel to remove formatting overrides in a text selection.

Apply Styles

1 Select the **Type** tool on the Tools panel, and then select the text that you want to change.

For paragraph styling, select a text frame or select paragraphs. For character styling, select specific text, not a text frame.

◆ You can also select the **Selection** tool, and then click the text frame to change all text in the frame.

2 Select the **Character Styles** or **Paragraph Styles** panel.

3 Click a style name in one of the panels, or press the keyboard shortcut defined for the style.

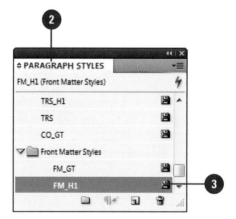

Applied style

Did You Know?

You can apply the next style. Select the text to which you want to apply the next style, select the Paragraph Styles panel, right-click (Win) or Control-click (Mac) the next style, click Apply "name of style" then Next Style.

You can break the link to a style. Click to place an insertion point in the paragraph in which you want to break, click the Options menu in the Paragraph Styles or Character Styles panel, and then click Break Link To Style.

Apply GREP Styles

1. Select the **Type** tool on the Tools panel, and then select the paragraphs for which you want to change styles.

   For paragraph styling, select a text frame or select paragraphs.

2. Click the **Control panel** menu, and then click **GREP Styles**.

3. Select a GREP style.

4. Click **OK** to apply the style.

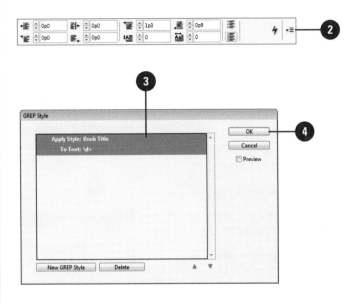

Clear Style Overrides

1. Select the **Type** tool on the Tools panel, and then select the text that you want to clear.

2. Select the **Paragraph Styles** panel.

3. Use any of the following:

   ◆ **Clear Local Formatting in a Selection.** Click the **Clear Overrides** button on the panel.

   ◆ **Clear Local Character Formatting in a Selection.** Ctrl+click (Win) or ⌘+click (Mac) the **Clear Overrides** button on the panel.

   ◆ **Clear Local Paragraph Formatting in a Selection.** Ctrl+Shift+click (Win) or ⌘+Shift+click (Mac) the **Clear Overrides** button on the panel.

We invite you to visit the Perspection Web site at:

www.perspection.com

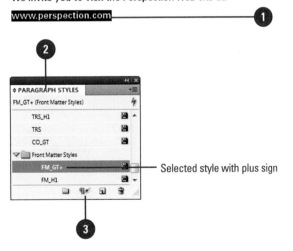

Selected style with plus sign

Style override

Creating Nested Styles

 ID 2.5

Instead of applying individual character styles for a line of text, you can create and apply a nested style to do it for you. A nested style is useful for a list of predictable elements, such as a name, address, and phone number, on a line. You can also create and use nested inline styles to apply complex character formatting through the end of a line (**New!**). Before you create a nested style, you need to create the individual characters that you want to make up the nested style. If you want a nested style to end at a certain place in the text, you can insert the End Nested Style Here special character.

Create a Nested Line Style

1. Select the **Paragraph Styles** panel.

    ◆ Click the **Type** menu, and then click **Paragraph Styles**.

2. Click the **Options** menu, and then click **New Paragraph Style**.

3. Enter a name for the style.

4. Select the **Drop Caps and Nested Styles** category.

5. Click **New Line Style**.

6. Click the **Nested Line Styles** list arrow for each line style, and then select a line style or click **New Line Style** to create one.

    ◆ To loop two or more nested styles, select **Repeat** from the list arrow.

7. Enter a value for the number of repeating lines for each line style.

8. To move a style up or down the list, click the **Up** or **Down** arrow.

9. To remove a style, select it, and then click **Delete**.

10. Click **OK**.

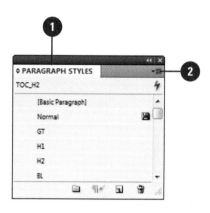

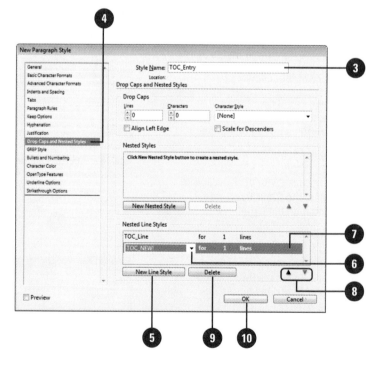

Create a Nested Style

1. Select the **Paragraph Styles** panel.
   - Click the **Type** menu, and then click **Paragraph Styles**.
2. Click the **Options** menu, and then click **New Paragraph Style**.
3. Enter a name for the style.
4. Select the **Drop Caps and Nested Styles** category.
5. Click **New Nested Style**.
6. Click the **Nested Styles** list arrow for each nested style, and then select a nested style or click **New Nested Style** to create one.
   - To loop two or more nested styles, select **Repeat** from the list arrow.
7. Click the **Duration** list arrow for each nested style, and then click **Through** to include the repeating elements or **Up to** to not include the repeating elements.
8. Enter a value for the number of repeating elements for each nested style.
9. Click the **Repeating Element** list arrow for each nested style, and then select which element controls the nested style.
10. To move a style up or down the list, click the **Up** or **Down** arrow.
11. To remove a style, select it, and then click **Delete**.
12. Click **OK**.

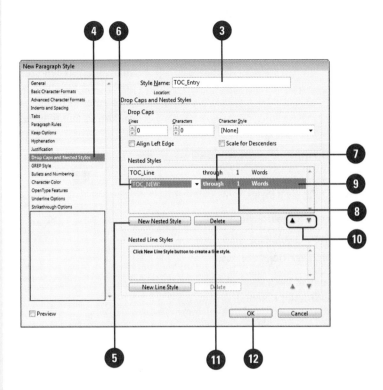

For Your Information

Inserting the End Nested Style Here Character

The End Nested Style Here special character allows you to control where a nested style ends. To insert the special character, click to place the insertion point where you want to the nested style to end, click the Type menu, point to Insert Special Character, point to Other, and then click End Nested Style Here. This special character is a hidden character. Click the Type menu, and then click Show Hidden Characters to show hidden characters.

Creating Object Styles

ID 1.8

In the same way you create paragraph and character styles, you can also create and modify styles for objects. InDesign comes with two default objects styles, one for a graphics frame and another for a text frame. There is also a style for None, which removes all formatting from an object. You can create and modify object styles in the Object Styles panel. Just as when using text styles, when the applied style also contains other formatting, a plus sign (+) appears after the style name, which you can remove, redefine, or clear.

View and Apply Object Styles

① Select the object to which you want to apply a style.

② Select the **Object Styles** panel.

◆ Click the **Window** menu, and then click **Object Styles**.

③ Click one of the built-in styles [**Basic Graphics Frame**], [**Basic Text Frame**], or [**None**] or a custom style.

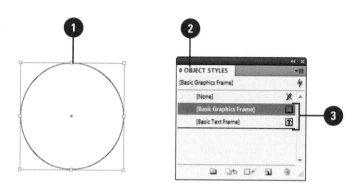

Modify the Default Object Styles

① Select the object to which you want to apply a style.

② Select the **Object Styles** panel.

◆ Click the **Window** menu, and then click **Object Styles**.

③ Double-click [**Basic Graphics Frame**] or [**Basic Text Frame**].

④ Select each main attribute to set individual object attributes.

⑤ Select the **General** category, and then view Style Settings to see a description of the completed style.

⑥ Click **OK**.

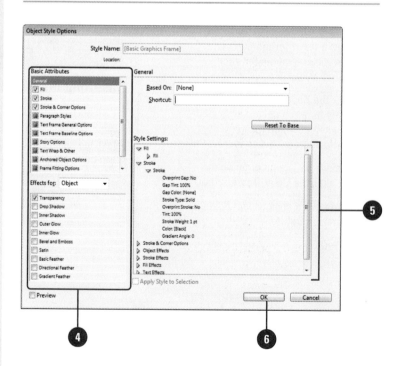

Create an Object Style

① To create an object style by using an object, select the object.

② Select the **Object Styles** panel.

◆ Click the **Window** menu, and then click **Object Styles**.

③ Click the **Options** menu, and then click **New Object Style**.

◆ You can also Alt+click (Win) or Option+click (Mac) the **New Object Style** button on the panel.

④ Enter a name for the style.

⑤ If you didn't select an object, select each main attribute to set individual object attributes.

⑥ Select the **General** category, and then view Style Settings to see a description of the completed style.

⑦ Click **OK**.

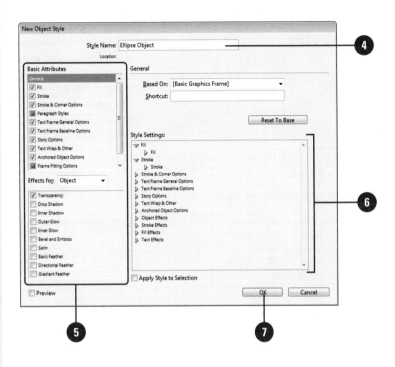

Clear Object Style Overrides

① Select the object that local formatting applied.

② Select the **Object Styles** panel.

◆ Click the **Window** menu, and then click **Object Styles**.

③ Use any of the following:

◆ **Clear Local Formatting Not Defined in the Style.** Click the **Clear Attributes Not Defined by Style** button on the panel.

◆ **Clear Local Formatting in a Selection.** Click the **Clear Overrides** button on the panel.

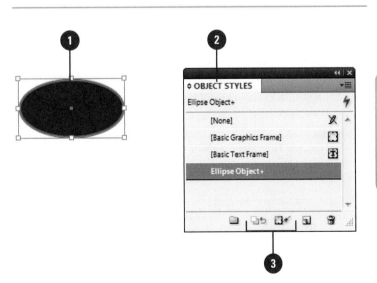

Creating Table and Cell Styles

You can use the Table Styles or Cell Styles panels to create, apply, import, modify, and organize table and cell styles. In the Table Styles and Cell Styles panels, you can perform the same operations as in other style panels, including creating a style group, clearing overrides, creating a new style, and deleting styles. You can also use the Options menu to duplicate and edit styles, select all unused styles, as well as sort styles in the panel by name. When you create a table style, you can use cell styles, so you should create your cell styles before you create table styles.

Create Cell Styles

1. Select the **Cell Styles** panel.

   ◆ Click the **Window** menu, point to **Type & Tables**, and then click **Cell Styles**.

2. Click the **Options** menu, and then click **New Cell Style**.

   ◆ You can also Alt+click (Win) or Option+click (Mac) the **Create New Style** button on the panel.

3. Enter a name for the style.

4. Select the **General** category, and then specify the following:

   ◆ **Based On.** Select a style to use as the base for the new style.

   ◆ **Shortcut.** Press a keyboard combination to create a shortcut for the style.

   ◆ **Paragraph Styles.** Select a default paragraph style for the table cells.

5. Select each main category (**Text, Strokes and Fills**, and **Diagonal Lines**) to set individual cell attributes.

6. Select the **General** category, and then view Style Settings to see a description of the completed style.

7. Click **OK**.

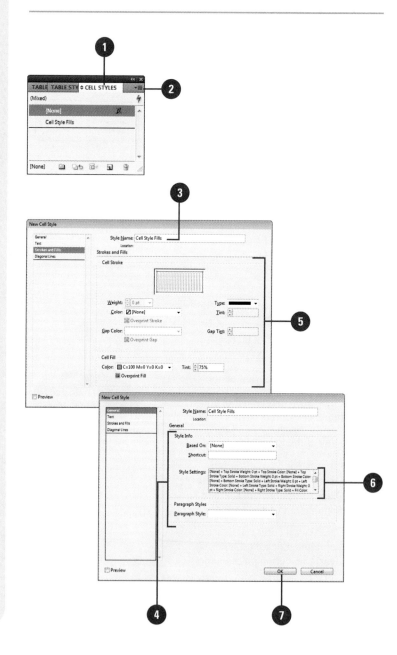

Create Table Styles

1. Select the **Table Styles** panel.
   - Click the **Window** menu, point to **Type & Tables**, and then click **Table Styles**.

2. Click the **Options** menu, and then click **New Table Style**.
   - You can also Alt+click (Win) or Option+click (Mac) the **Create New Style** button on the panel.

3. Enter a name for the style.

4. Select the **General** category, and then specify the following:
   - **Based On.** Select a style to use as the base for the new style.
   - **Shortcut.** Press a keyboard combination to create a shortcut for the style.
   - **Cell Styles.** Select a default cell style for the table cells.

5. Select each main category (**Table Setup**, **Row Strokes**, **Column Strokes**, and **Fills**) to set individual table attributes.

6. Select the **General** category, and then view Style Settings to see a description of the completed style.

7. Click **OK**.

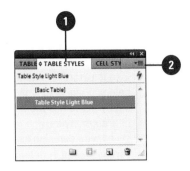

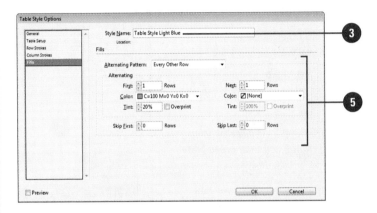

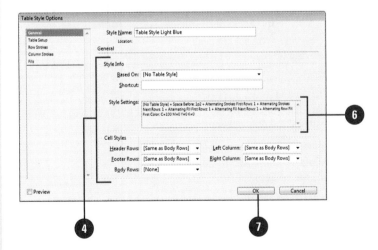

Did You Know?

You can delete and clear table and cell styles. In the Table Styles or Cell Styles panel, select the styles, and then click the Delete Selected Style/Groups or Clear Overrides button on the panel.

Using Quick Apply

 ID 1.2

The Quick Apply button that is available on the right side of the Control panel and any of the style panels provides an easy way to apply any style in your InDesign document. You can use all available keyboard shortcuts to speed up the process. If you want to edit a style, you can access the style dialog box to make changes. If the list of styles is so long it is hard to find the one you want, you can use the Search box to help you find a style by name or style prefix. The prefixes are internally set by InDesign. The prefixes include *p:* for paragraph styles, *c:* for character styles, and *o:* for object styles, to name a few. In addition to styles, you can also use Quick Apply to apply menu commands, text variables, and scripts.

Use Quick Apply

1. Select the text, table, or object to which you want to apply the style.

2. Click the **Quick Apply** button on the Control panel or any of the style panels.

   TIMESAVER *Press Ctrl (Win) or ⌘ (Mac), and then press Enter (Win) or Return (Mac).*

   ◆ Quick Apply remembers your last selected style, so you can simply press Enter (Win) or Return (Mac) to apply it.

3. To narrow down the list of styles, type the first letters in the style name.

4. Use the Up and Down arrow keys to move up and down the list of styles to find the one you want.

5. Click the style you want to apply or press Enter (Win) or Return (Mac) to apply the selected style.

   The Quick Apply dialog box closes.

6. To apply a style without closing the Quick Apply dialog box, press Shift+Enter (Win) or Shift+Return (Mac).

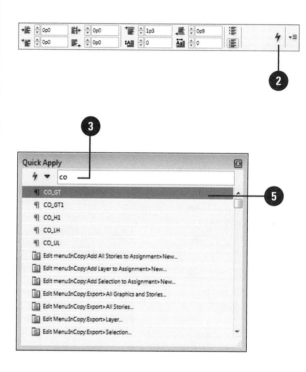

Edit Styles with Quick Apply

1. Click the **Quick Apply** button on the Control panel or any of the style panels.

2. To narrow down the list of styles, type the first letters in the style name.

3. Use the Up and Down arrow keys to move up and down the list of styles to find the one you want.

4. Press Ctrl+Enter (Win) or ⇧⌘+Return (Mac) to open the dialog box for the selected style.

5. Make the changes you want, and then click **OK**.

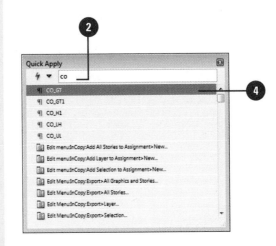

Use Letter Commands with Quick Apply

1. Click the **Quick Apply** button on the Control panel or any of the style panels.

2. To narrow down the list of styles, click the Down Arrow, and then select (check) or deselect (uncheck) the styles you want to view in the list.

3. Type the prefix for the style type (see illustration for prefixes) and then continue to type the first letters in the style name.

4. Use the Up and Down arrow keys to move up and down the list of styles to find the one you want.

5. Press Enter (Win) or Return (Mac) to apply the selected style.

Finalizing a Document

12

Introduction

Finalizing your document is an important thing to do prior to printing. Of course, no document should be printed without first going through the spell checker to check your spelling. You can add personalized names, terms, and company information to a user dictionary, so that when you are using the spell checker, there won't be unnecessary stops on words that are spelled and used correctly. If you need to make text fit in text frames and on pages, you can adjust the hyphenation, choose to keep lines together, and change justification options to help you finalize your document.

Sometimes you use a certain font in a document, but later you decide to change it. Instead of manually changing each use of the font, you can use the Find Font command to quickly find and change every instance of the font in your document. You can also use the Find/Change dialog box to find and replace elements—including text, GREP expressions, glyphs, and objects—in your document. The dialog box provides powerful features to find and change special characters, including tabs, line breaks, end of paragraph returns, symbols, markers, hyphens and dashes, white space, variables, and wildcards to name a few.

If you want to focus solely on the text in your document, the Story Editor is the tool for you. The Story Editor displays text and tables in a separate window with unformatted sequential columns and rows for easy editing. Any graphics, shapes, text formatting, and other design elements in your document do not appear in the Story Editor.

When you work with more than one person on a document, it's important to communicate changes and other information with each other. Notes are a great way to communicate and record the notes along with the document.

Using Spell Check

There's nothing more embarrassing than creating a document that contains misspelled words. InDesign includes a fully functional spell checking system, which lets you make sure all of your words are spelled correctly. Instead of using Spell Check, you can also use dynamic spelling, which displays misspelled or unrecognized words in your document with a red underline as you type. You can right-click (Win) or Control-click (Mac) the word to select a correction on the context menu.

Use Spell Check on a Document

1. Click the **Edit** menu, point to **Spelling**, and then click **Check Spelling**.

   TIMESAVER *Ctrl+I (Win) or* ⌘+I *(Mac).*

2. Click **Start**, if necessary.

3. When InDesign encounters a word not in the dictionary, it displays that word, and allows you to choose one of the following options:

   ◆ **Skip.** Leaves the word alone and moves on.

   ◆ **Change.** Changes the word, based on the selected suggestion.

   ◆ **Ignore All.** Ignores all instances of this word in the document.

   ◆ **Change All.** Changes all occurrences of the word, based on the selected suggestion.

   ◆ **Dictionary.** Opens the Dictionary dialog box.

   ◆ **Add.** Adds the word to the selected dictionary. Click the Add To list arrow to select a dictionary.

   InDesign continues to highlight misspelled and other incorrectly used words until the document is completely scanned.

4. When you're finished, click **Done**.

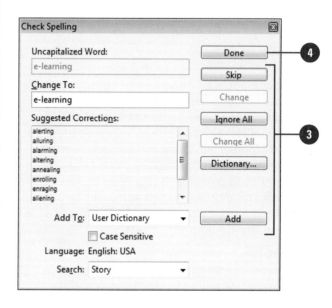

Use Spell Check Options

1. To spell check a text frame, click to place the insertion point.

2. Click the **Edit** menu, point to **Spelling**, and then click **Check Spelling**.

3. Click the **Search** list arrow, and then select a search option:

   ◆ **All Documents.** Checks all open documents.

   ◆ **Document.** Checks the active document.

   ◆ **Story.** Checks all the linked frames of the selected text.

   ◆ **To End of Story.** Checks from the insertion point to the end of the story.

   ◆ **Selection.** Checks only the selected text.

4. Select the **Case Sensitive** check box to require a match of lower and uppercase characters.

5. When you're finished, click **Done**.

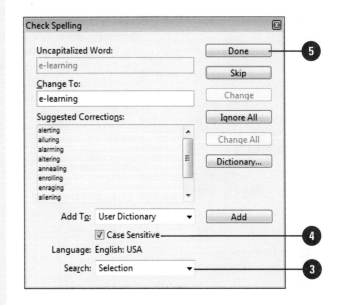

Use Spell Check Options

1. To enable dynamic spelling, click the **Edit** menu, point to **Spelling**, and then click **Dynamic Spelling**.

2. Right-click (Win) or Control-click (Mac) a word with a red underline, and then select a word correction or an option to **Ignore All** or **Add "*Word*" To User Dictionary**.

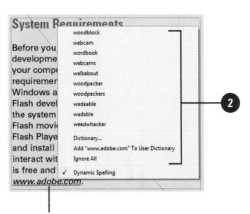

"Misspelled" Word found with Dynamic Spelling

Using Custom Dictionaries

InDesign comes with a custom dictionary for the spell checker. If you need to manage dictionary content, you can use the Edit Custom Dictionary dialog box to add, delete, or edit words. The ability to edit the dictionary becomes useful when you accidentally enter a word that you don't want in the dictionary, or you have some specialty words that you want to enter in all at once. When you add a custom word, name, or phrase to a custom dictionary, all languages treat the item as correctly spelled (**New!**).

Use a Custom Dictionary

1. Click the **Edit** menu, point to Spelling, and then click **Dictionary**.

   ◆ You can also click **Dictionary** in the Check Spelling dialog box.

2. Click the **Target** list arrow, and then select the dictionary you want to use.

3. Click the **Language** list arrow, and then select the language you want to use.

4. Click the **Dictionary List** list arrow, and then click **Added Words**, **Removed Words**, or **Ignored Words**.

5. Select the **Case Sensitive** check box to specify a match of lower and uppercase characters.

6. Type the word you want to add or select the word you want to remove or be ignored by the spell checker.

7. Click **Add** or **Remove**.

8. If you want to export or import dictionary entries, click **Export** to name and save the file or click **Import** to locate and open (import) the file.

9. When you're finished, click **Done**.

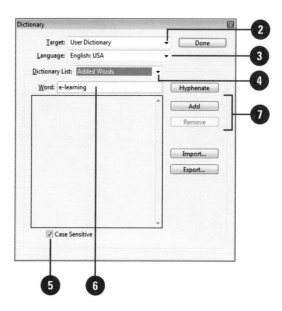

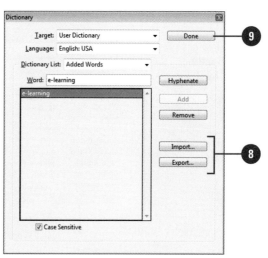

Finding and Changing Fonts

Say you create some text using a certain font. After customer or client reviews, you're asked to change it. Instead of manually changing each use of the font, you can use the Find Font command to quickly find and change every instance of the font in your document. If you're not sure what fonts are used in your document, the Find Font dialog box gives you a list.

Find or Change a Font

1. Click the **Type** menu, and then click **Find Font**.

   The fonts in the top list are the ones currently used in your document. The list at the bottom displays fonts in your document or on your computer, depending on your setting.

2. To find a specific font, select it in the top list.

3. To replace the font in the top list, click the **Font Family** and **Font Style** list arrows, and then select a replacement font and style.

4. Select the **Redefine Style When Changing All** check box to redefine the replaced style for Change All.

5. Click **Find Next** to display the first instance of the font, and then click **Change** to replace it, or click **Change All** to replace all uses of the font in your document.

6. When you're done, click **Done**.

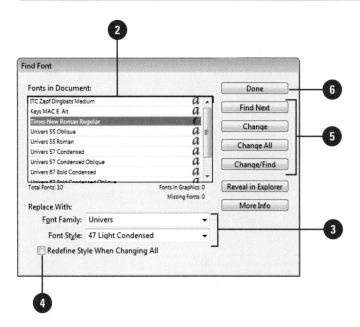

Using Find and Change

The Find/Change command on the Edit menu allows you to find and change text, font characters, or object attributes in a document. You can use tabs to search for specific elements in a document, including text, GREP patterns, glyphs, and objects. I'll focus on the basics of using the Find/Change dialog box in this topic. Other topics in this chapter go into specifics for each search type. After you create a search, you can save it as a query for later use. InDesign also comes with some built-in queries that you can use.

Use Find and Change

1. Click the **Edit** menu, and then click **Find/Change**.

   TIMESAVER *Ctrl+F (Win) or* ⌘+F (Mac).

2. To use a search query, click the **Query** list arrow, and then select a built-in or custom query.

3. Click one of the following tabs to specify the type of search you want to perform:

   ◆ **Text.** Finds and changes text and text formatting.

   ◆ **GREP.** Finds and changes search expressions for patterns within text.

   ◆ **Glyph.** Finds and changes glyphs using unicode or GID/CID values.

   ◆ **Object.** Finds and changes objects with specific formatting.

4. Specify what you want to find. The method varies depending on the search type.

5. Specify what you want to change the find item to. The method varies depending on the search type.

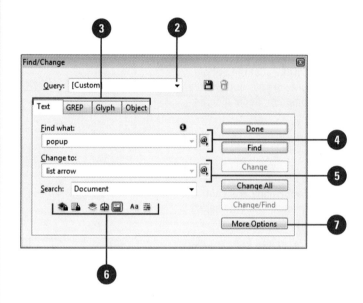

6 Click the following buttons, which toggle on and off, to allow or not allow a search in the specified area:

◆ **Locked Layer.** Searches on locked layers. You can't make changes on a locked layer.

◆ **Locked Stories.** Searches in locked stories. You can't make changes in locked stories.

◆ **Hidden Layers.** Finds and changes in hidden layers.

◆ **Master Pages.** Finds and changes in master pages.

◆ **Footnotes.** Finds and changes in footnotes.

7 To display more options, if available, click **More Options**.

The button toggles to Fewer Options.

8 Use the following buttons to find or change the search items:

◆ **Find.** Starts the search for the specified find items.

◆ **Change.** Changes the selected find item to the specified change.

◆ **Change All.** Changes all find items to the specified change.

◆ **Change/Find.** Changes the selected find item to the specified change, and then continues the search for the next find item.

9 To save a search as a query for use in the future, click the **Save Query** button, enter a name, and then click **OK**.

10 To delete a custom query, select it, and then click the **Delete Query** button.

11 When you're finished, click **Done**.

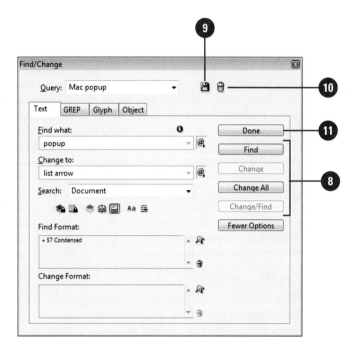

Searching for Text

The Find/Change command on the Edit menu allows you to find and change text, text formatting, and special characters in a document. The special characters, known as **metacharacters**, include tabs, line breaks, end of paragraph returns, symbols, markers, hyphens and dashes, white space, variables, and wildcards to name a few. Wildcards allow you to create more general searches. You can select special characters from a menu in the Find/Change dialog box. The special characters appear in the Find/Change dialog box as a character code. In addition to text, you can also find and change text formatting. You can specify the same formatting find and change options as the ones for creating styles.

Search for Text

1. To find and change text in a specific text frame, click to place the insertion point in the text.

2. Click the **Edit** menu, and then click **Find/Change**.

    TIMESAVER Ctrl+F (Win) or ⌘+F (Mac).

3. Click the **Text** tab.

4. Specify what you want to find in the **Find What** box, and then specify what you want to change the find item to in the **Change To** box.

    ◆ **Include Special Characters.** Click the @ menu, and then use the menus to select the special characters you want to add to the find. A character code appears for the special character in the Find What and Change To boxes.

    ◆ **Include Wildcards.** Click the @ menu, point to **Wildcards**, and then click **Any Digit**, **Any Letter**, **Any Character**, or **Any White Space**.

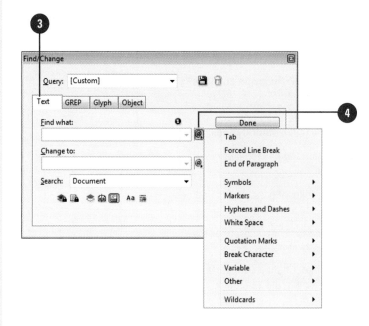

5 Click the **Search** list arrow, and then select a search option:

- **All Documents.** Searches all open documents.
- **Document.** Searches the active document.
- **Story.** Searches all the linked frames of the selected text.
- **To End of Story.** Searches from the insertion point to the end of the story.
- **Selection.** Searches only the selected text.

6 Click the **Case Sensitive** button to require a match of lower and uppercase characters.

7 Click the **Whole Word** button to ignore text contained within other words.

8 To display more options, if available, click **More Options**.

The button toggles to Fewer Options.

9 To find and change formatting, click the **Format** button for Find or Change, select the formatting options that you want, and then click **OK**.

- To delete a formatting search, click the **Delete** button.

10 Use the Find and Change buttons to perform the search and make changes.

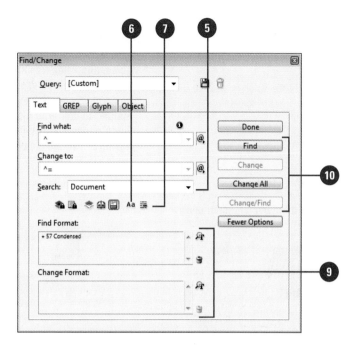

See Also

See "Using Find and Change" on pages 302-303 for information on common Find/Change dialog box options.

Searching Using GREP

 ID 2.6

GREP stands for Global Regular Expression and Print. The Find/Change command on the Edit menu allows you to to find and replace text and special characters, such as tabs, end of paragraph, white space, variables, and wildcards. In the Find What and Change To boxes, you can build GREP search expressions for patterns within text. For example, you could build a search to find any text variable, and then change the formatting to bold. You can select a character or paragraph style in the Find/Change and GREP Styles dialog boxes and create a style without having to exit the dialog box (**New!**).

Search Using GREP

1. Click the **Edit** menu, and then click **Find/Change**.

   TIMESAVER *Ctrl+F (Win) or* ⌘*+F (Mac).*

2. Click the **GREP** tab.

3. Specify what you want to find in the **Find What** box, and then specify what you want to change the find item to in the **Change To** box.

4. Click the @ menu for **Find What** and **Change To**, and then use the menus to select the special characters you want to add to the find. A character code appears for the special character in the Find What and Change To boxes.

5. Specify the other text search options. See "Searching for Text" on pages 304-305 for details on text search options.

6. Use the Find and Change buttons to perform the search.

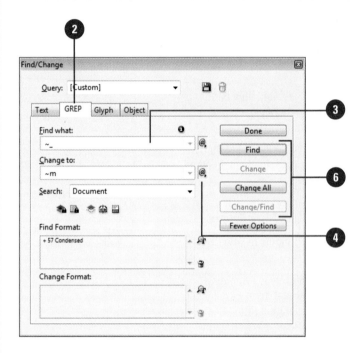

See Also

See "Using Find and Change" on pages 302-303 for information on common Find/Change dialog box options.

Searching for Glyphs

A glyph is a style variation—such as ligatures, ordinals, swashes, and fractions—for a given character in an OpenType font. For example, you can change fractions with numerals and slashes to properly formatted fractions. You can automatically insert alternate glyphs with the OpenType panel or insert them manually with the Glyphs panel to extend the font format. In the Find/Change dialog box, you can search for alternate glyphs using special ID codes or symbols.

Search for Glyphs

1. Click the **Edit** menu, and then click **Find/Change**.

   TIMESAVER *Ctrl+F (Win) or* ⌘+F (Mac).

2. Click the **Glyph** tab.

3. Specify the following options for Find Glyph and Change Glyph:

   - **Font Family.** Select a font typeface.

   - **Font Style.** Select a font style.

   - **ID.** Select the Unicode or GID/CID numbering system, and then enter a code for the glyph you want to find or change.

   - **Glyph.** Select a glyph symbol from the display panel.

4. Specify the other search options.

5. To clear all the information from the glyph field, click **Clear Glyphs**.

6. Use the Find and Change buttons to perform the search.

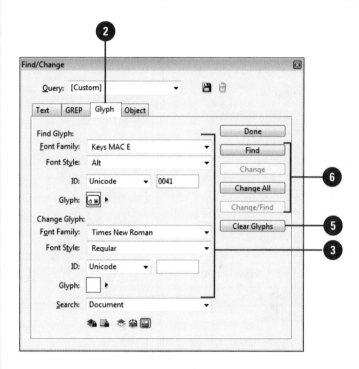

See Also

See "Using Find and Change" on pages 302-303 for information on common Find/Change dialog box options.

Searching for Objects

In addition to text-related searches, you can also use the Find/Change dialog box to search for objects with certain formatting and then apply other attributes. You can specify the formatting that you want to find for all or specific types of objects, such as text frames, graphic frames, or unassigned frames.

Search for Objects

1. Click the **Edit** menu, and then click **Find/Change**.

   TIMESAVER *Ctrl+F (Win) or* ⌘+F *(Mac)*.

2. Click the **Object** tab.

3. To find and change formatting, click the **Format** button for Find or Change, select the formatting options that you want, and then click **OK**.

   ◆ To delete a formatting search, click the **Delete** button.

4. Click the **Search** list arrow, and then select a search option.

5. Click the **Type** list arrow, and then select a frame option: **All Frames**, **Text Frames**, **Graphic Frames**, or **Unassigned Frames**.

6. Use the Find and Change buttons to perform the search.

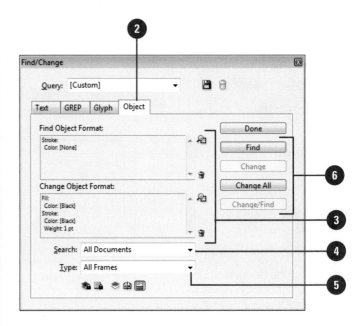

See Also

See "Using Find and Change" on pages 302-303 for information on common Find/Change dialog box options.

Working with Hyphenation

ID 2.12

When you select the Hyphenate check box in the Paragraph panel, InDesign automatically adds hyphenation as you need it based on the options set in the Hyphenation dialog box. If you want to manually set hyphenation, deselect the check box. The Hyphenation options allow you to specify how long a word needs to be before hyphenation takes place, the maximum number of hyphens you can use, and what balance you want between better spacing and fewer hyphens.

Change Hyphenation Options

1. Click in the text frame where you want to enable hyphenation.

2. Select the **Paragraph** panel.

3. To enable hyphenation, select the **Hyphenate** check box.

4. Click the **Options** menu, and then click **Hyphenation**.

5. Specify the following options:

   ◆ **Words With At Least.** Enter the minimum number of characters in a word before hyphens are added.

   ◆ **After First.** Enter the minimum number of characters that can occur before a hyphen.

   ◆ **Before Last.** Enter the minimum number of characters that can occur after a hyphen on the next line.

   ◆ **Hyphen Limit.** Enter the maximum number of hyphens in a row (0-25).

   ◆ **Hyphenation Zone.** Drag the slider to adjust the balance of hyphenation between better spacing and fewer hyphens.

   ◆ **Hyphenate Capitalized Words.** Select to hyphenate capitalized words.

   ◆ **Hyphenate Across Column.** Select to hyphenate across columns.

   ◆ **Hyphenate Last Word.** Select to hyphenate the last word.

6. Click **OK**.

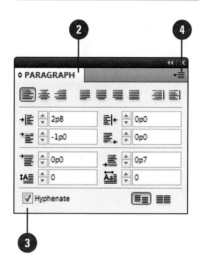

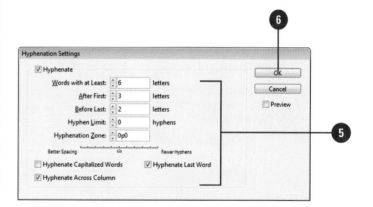

Keeping Lines Together

 ID 2.12

When you choose Keep Options from the Paragraph panel, InDesign automatically keeps paragraphs together based on the number of lines that you want, instead of allowing them to break naturally into other columns or on to other pages. The Keep Lines Together options allow you to specify the number of lines in a paragraph that you want to stay in the same column or page, and where you want paragraph lines to move, such as Anywhere, In Next Column, In Next Frame, or On Next Page.

Change Keep Options

1. Click in the text frame for which you want to set keep options.

2. Select the **Paragraph** panel.

3. Click the **Options** menu, and then click **Keep Options**.

4. Enter a **Keep with Next** value to force the last line in a paragraph to stay in the same column or page with a specified number of lines.

5. Select the **Keep Lines Together** check box.

6. Click the **All Lines in Paragraph** option to keep all paragraph lines together or click the **At Start/End of Paragraph** option to specify the number of lines that you want to remain with the paragraph.

7. Click the **Start Paragraph** list arrow, and then select an option to indicate where the lines should appear.

8. Click **OK**.

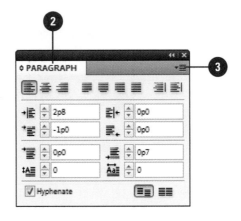

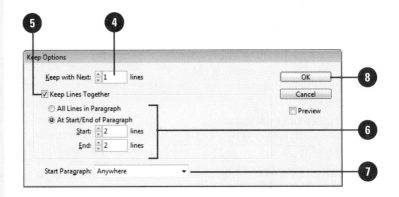

Did You Know?

You can balance uneven line breaks. Select the text, select the Paragraph panel, click the Options menu, and then select Balance Ragged Lines.

Changing Justification Options

 ID 2.12

When you use Justify buttons on the Control panel or Paragraph panel, you can further adjust settings in the Justification dialog box. The justification settings allow you to specify how lines fit between margins in a document. In InDesign, there are three justification controls: word spacing, letter spacing, and glyph spacing. For each control, you can set a minimum, desired, and maximum percentage to specify the justification levels you want. The default percentages are recommended for most uses. However, if you need to make information fit on a page, you can change the percentage values. The best way to adjust justification setting is to use the Preview option to view your changes in the document window.

Change Justification Options

1. Click in the text frame for which you want to set justification options.

2. Select the **Paragraph** panel.

3. Click the **Options** menu, and then click **Justification**.

4. Select the **Preview** check box to view your results in the document window.

5. Specify the following options:

   ◆ **Word Spacing.** Specifies the spacing between words.

   ◆ **Letter Spacing.** Specifies the spacing between characters.

   ◆ **Glyph Scaling.** Specifies the horizontal scaling for glyphs.

   ◆ **Auto Leading.** Specifies how much space to use between lines for the Auto Leading option.

   ◆ **Single Word Justification.** Select an option to specify how you want to justify a single word on a line.

   ◆ **Composer.** Select an option to specify the best way to justify text, either as a line or an entire paragraph.

6. Click **OK**.

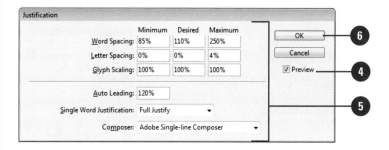

For Your Information

Setting Optical Margin Alignment

If you have punctuation along a margin with justified text, you can set optical margin adjustment to create a more uniform appearance for the edge of the text. This moves the punctuation slightly outside of the text margin to so the type appears aligned. To set the option, select the text, click the Type menu, click Story, select the Optical Margin Alignment check box in the Story panel, and then enter a size value for adjustment.

Changing Case

If there are paragraphs with inconsistent use of capitalization in your document, you can use change case options to fix them. You can set options to create text as UPPERCASE, lowercase, Title Case, or Sentence case. Title Case capitalizes each word in a title, while Sentence case capitalizes the first word in the sentence.

Change Case

1. Select the type for which you want to change case.

2. Click the **Type** menu, and then point to **Change Case**.

3. Select one of the following:

   ◆ **UPPERCASE**.

   ◆ **lowercase**.

   ◆ **Title Case**.

   ◆ **Sentence case**.

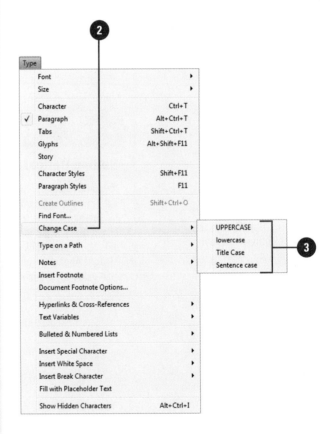

To perform a standard application install, insert the Adobe Flash Professional installation disc into the drive on your computer, and then follow the on-screen instructions. Because the setup process is different for Macintosh OS X and Windows platforms, general steps are provided to help you get started, and the on-screen instructions will guide you through the rest. Make sure to have your serial number handy because you'll be asked to enter it during the installation process. If you're updating from a previous version of Flash, you'll be required to verify the older version with your serial number for the previous version. The Flash installation includes all the components you need, including the Flash Player, to develop Flash content. The Flash Player is software installed on a user's computer that allows them to view published Flash movies (SWFs) in a Web page or through the player.

Using the Story Editor

ID 2.2

If you want to focus solely on text in your document, the Story Editor is the tool for you. The Story Editor displays text and tables (**New!**) in a separate window with unformatted sequential columns and rows for easy editing. Any graphics, shapes, text formatting, or other design elements in your document do not appear in the Story Editor. The left side of the Story Editor displays the paragraph style, while the right side displays the editable text. You don't have to close the Story Editor to work in layout view. You can switch back and forth by clicking in the layout window. You can change the display of the Story Editor window by changing Story Editor Display preferences.

Edit Text and Tables in the Story Editor

1. Click in the text frame that you want to edit using Story Editor.

2. Click the **Edit** menu, and then click **Edit in Story Editor**.

3. Drag the pointer to highlight the text, or click in the document to place the insertion point where you want to make a change.

4. Perform one of the following editing commands:

   ◆ To replace text, type your text.

   ◆ To delete text, press the Backspace key or the Delete key.

   ◆ Drag the selection to a new location.

5. Click the **Close** button.

See Also

See "Setting Story Editor Display Preferences" on page 422 for more information on setting Story Editor preferences.

Style for text frame

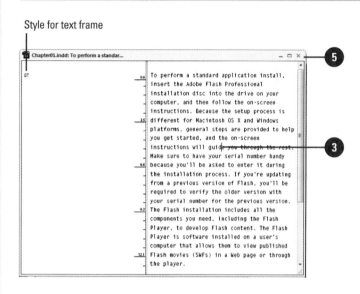

Adding Footnotes

A footnote is a note placed at the bottom of a text frame to cite a reference in the text. Footnote reference marks appear numeric characters (1, 2, 3, etc.). InDesign provides you with various options in order to customize the reference marks. If you'd like to change your footnotes to alpha characters (a, b, c, etc.) or Roman numerals (i, ii, iii, etc.), you can do that through the Footnote Options dialog box. You can also have InDesign renumber your footnotes after each page, section, or spread in your document, and change the style and other formatting for reference marks.

Add Footnotes

1. Click to place the insertion point where you want the footnote reference to appear.

2. Click the **Type** menu, and then click **Insert Footnote**.

3. Type or paste the text for the footnote.

Did You Know?

You can import footnotes and endnotes from Microsoft Word. When you place a Word document with footnotes and endnotes into an InDesign document, you can include them when importing the text by using the Import Options dialog box. Footnotes from Word are converted to InDesign footnotes, while endnotes are converted to normal text.

and Windows. Flash is the world's most pervasive software platform, used by over one million professionals and reaching more than 97% of Web-enabled desktops worldwide, as well as a wide range of consumer electronic devices, such as PDAs and mobile phones. — **1**

and Windows. Flash is the world's most pervasive software platform, used by over one million professionals and reaching more than 97% of Web-enabled desktops worldwide, as well as a wide range of consumer electronic devices, such as PDAs and mobile phones[1].

Flash operates virtually the same on both Macintosh and Windows versions, except for a few keyboard commands that have equivalent functions. You use the [Ctrl] and [Alt] keys in Windows, and the [⌘] and [Option] keys on a Macintosh computer. Also, the term *popup* on the Macintosh and *list arrow* in Windows refer to the same type of option.

1 World Marketing Research data: 2006 — **3**

Change Footnote Options

1. Click the **Type** menu, and then click **Document Footnote Options**.

2. Click the **Numbering and Formatting** tab.

3. Select the various options you want to use:

   ◆ **Numbering.** Specify a style, start number, and select options to restart numbering and show and specify prefix or suffix characters.

   ◆ **Footnote Reference Number in Text.** Specify a position and character style.

   ◆ **Footnote Formatting.** Specify a paragraph style and special character separator.

4. Click the **Layout** tab.

5. Select the various options you want to use:

   ◆ **Spacing Options.** Specify options for spacing before the first footnote and between footnotes.

   ◆ **First Baseline.** Specify an offset for the baseline shift.

   ◆ **Placement Options.** Specify options to place end of story footnotes at bottom of text and allow split footnotes in different columns.

   ◆ **Rule Above.** Specify options to create a rule line above the footnote.

6. Click **OK**.

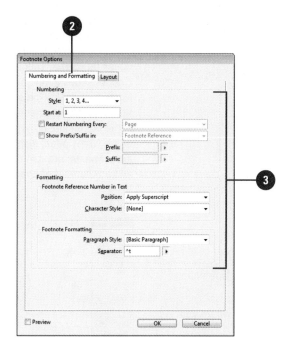

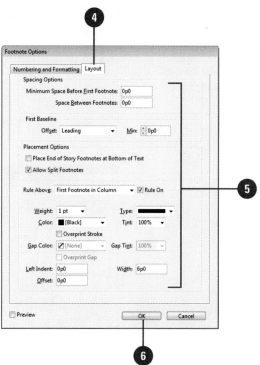

Creating and Working with Notes

ID 3.2

When you work with more than one person on a document, it's important to communicate changes and other information with each other. Notes are a great way to communicate with others and record the notes along with the document. You can add inline notes in text and tables (**New!**) to collaborate more effectively. Notes are linked to specific locations in text and tables. When you create a note with the Notes tool on the Tools panel, you type text directly in the Notes panel. In the Notes panel, you can show and hide notes, go to the note anchor in the document, browse notes, create notes, and delete notes. The top of the Notes panel displays information about the active note, including author name, created date, modified date, story location, page number, and the number of characters and words in the note.

Create Notes

1. Select the **Notes** tool on the Tools panel.

   The cursor changes to a notepad icon.

2. Click in the text or table where you want to insert an note.

   The Notes panel appears.

3. Type the notes you want in the Notes panel window.

4. To create additional notes, click in the text or table where you want to insert a note, and then type the notes you want.

Did You Know?

You can convert text to a note. Select the text you want to convert, select the Notes panel, click the Options menu, and then click Convert To Note.

See Also

See "Setting Notes Preferences" on page 420 for more information on setting Notes preferences.

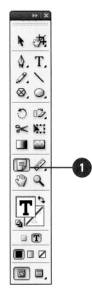

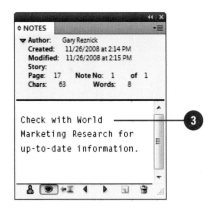

Work with Notes in the Notes Panel

1. Select the **Notes** panel.

   ◆ Click the **Window** menu, point to **Type & Tables**, and then click **Notes**.

2. Use any of the following buttons or commands to perform an operation:

   ◆ **Identify Note Color.** The icon on the bottom of the panel to the left shows you the color of the note.

   ◆ **Show or Hide Notes.** Click the **Show/Hide** button on the panel.

   ◆ **Go to Note Location.** Click the **Go to Note Anchor** button on the panel.

   ◆ **Display Previous or Next Notes.** Click the **Go to Previous Note** or **Go to Next Note** button on the panel.

   ◆ **Create a Note.** Click to place the insertion point where you want the note, and then click the **New Note** button on the panel.

   ◆ **Delete a Note.** Display the note you want to delete, and then click the **Delete Note** button on the panel.

      ◆ To remove all notes, click the **Options** menu, and then click **Remove All Notes**.

   ◆ **Convert a Note to Text.** Display the note you want to convert, click the **Options** menu, and then click **Convert to Text**.

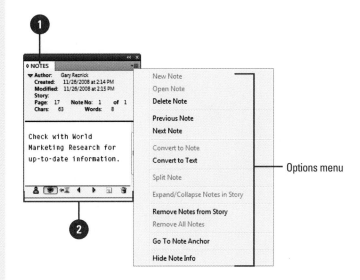

— Options menu

and Windows. Flash is the world's most pervasive software platform, used by over one million professionals and reaching more than 97% of Web-enabled desktops worldwide, as well as a wide range of consumer electronic devices, such as PDAs and mobile phones. ——————————— Note indicator

Flash operates virtually the same on both Macintosh and Windows versions, except for a few keyboard commands that have equivalent functions. You use the [Ctrl] and [Alt] keys in Windows, and the ⌘ and [Option] keys on a Macintosh computer. Also, the term *popup* on the Macintosh and *list arrow* in Windows refer to the same type of option.

Creating an Interactive Document

13

Introduction

In the past, desktop publishing was exclusively considered a print-based medium. However, with the introduction of the PDF (Portable Document Format) file format and the Adobe Reader, interactive documents are more popular than ever. Instead of creating a document just for printing, you can now create an interactive document with hyperlinks, bookmarks, and buttons for presentations. You can even add page transitions, such as a wipe or dissolve, when you turn a page and insert sounds and movies into an InDesign document in addition to graphics.

With the Hyperlinks panel, you can create hyperlinks that navigate to external URLs, link to files with supplemental information, launch an e-mail client, or jump to a page or section of a page within the same or even a different document. You can also verify your hyperlinks directly in InDesign with no need to export the document to a PDF or Flash (SWF) file for testing.

The Buttons panel is a centralized place to work with interactive buttons in InDesign. The Buttons panel makes it easy to create interactive buttons that perform actions when the document is exported to Flash (SWF file) or Acrobat (PDF). You can create a custom button from a selected object in an InDesign document or select a button from the built-in Samples button library. When you create an interactive button, you can add events and actions to enable navigation within a document, launch a movie, play a sound, or open a Web page.

What You'll Do

Define Hyperlink Destinations

Create Hyperlinks

Use the Hyperlinks Panel

Create Cross-References

Create Bookmarks

Add Sounds or Movies

Add Page Transitions

Use the Buttons Panel

Create Buttons

Work with Events and Actions

Work with Button States

Set Button Tab Order

Defining Hyperlink Destinations

A **hyperlink** is a text or graphic object that is linked to other parts of the document, other documents, or Web pages. A hyperlink consists of a source and a destination. The **source** is the text or graphic object that you click to jump to the hyperlink location while the **destination** is the place that InDesign sends you to. The destination can be in the same document, another document, an e-mail message, or a Web page on the Internet. You need to define a destination before you can define the source.

Create a Hyperlink Destination

1. Select the **Hyperlinks** panel.
   - ◆ Click the **Window** menu, point to **Interactive**, and then click **Hyperlinks**.

2. Click the **Options** menu, and then click **New Hyperlink Destination**.

3. Click the **Type** list arrow, and then select a hyperlink type:
   - ◆ **Page.** Creates a link to a page in the same document.
   - ◆ **Text Anchor.** Creates a link to a selected area of text.
   - ◆ **URL.** Creates a link to a Web page on the Internet.

4. Specify the options related to the hyperlink type; options vary depending on the type.
   - ◆ **For a Page.** Specify a page name, page number, and zoom setting.
   - ◆ **For a Text Anchor.** Specify a name for the anchor.
   - ◆ **For an URL.** Specify a name and address for the URL (Uniform Resource Locator).

5. Click **OK**.

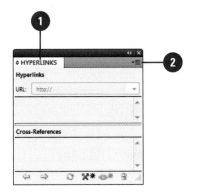

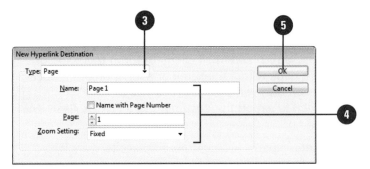

Text Anchor

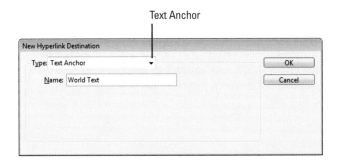

Edit or Delete a Hyperlink Destination

1. Select the **Hyperlinks** panel.

    ◆ Click the **Window** menu, point to **Interactive**, and then click **Hyperlinks**.

2. Click the **Options** menu, and then click **Hyperlink Destination Options**.

3. Click the **Destination** list arrow, and then select a destination.

4. Click **Edit** or **Delete**.

5. If editing, make the changes you want for the destination.

6. Click **OK**.

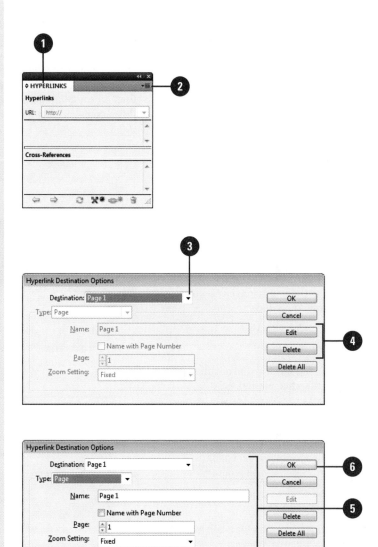

Creating Hyperlinks

ID 7.3

Before you can create a hyperlink, you need to define a hyperlink destination. After you create one or more hyperlink destinations, you can create a hyperlink source, which is a text or graphic object that you click to jump to a hyperlink destination. You can link a hyperlink to several different destination types, including URL, File, Email, Page, Text Anchor, and Shared Destination. If you need a quick hyperlink to an URL, you can create one with the New Hyperlink From URL command.

Create a Hyperlink

1. Select the text or graphic you want to use as the hyperlink.

2. Select the **Hyperlinks** panel.

   ◆ Click the **Window** menu, point to **Interactive**, and then click **Hyperlinks**.

3. Click the **Options** menu, and then click **New Hyperlink**.

4. Click the **Link To** list arrow, and then select an option:

   ◆ **URL.** Creates a link to a web page on the Internet.

   ◆ **File.** Creates a link to a document.

   ◆ **Email.** Creates an e-mail message link, which opens your default e-mail program.

   ◆ **Page.** Creates a link to a page in the same document.

   ◆ **Text Anchor.** Creates a link to a selected area of text.

   ◆ **Shared Destination.** Creates a link to the same destination from multiple sources.

5. Specify the options related to the hyperlink type; options vary depending on the type.

   ◆ **For an URL.** Specify a name and address for the URL (Uniform Resource Locator).

   ◆ **For a File.** Use the Browse button to select a file to link.

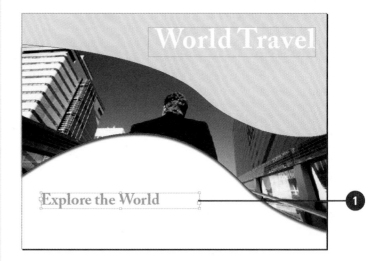

◆ **For an Email.** Specify an e-mail address and message subject line.

◆ **For a Page.** Specify a page name, page number, and zoom setting.

◆ **For a Text Anchor.** Specify a name for the anchor.

◆ **For a Shared Destination.** Specify a document name, and hyperlink destination.

6 Specify a character style for the text and appearance options for the hyperlink.

7 Click **OK**.

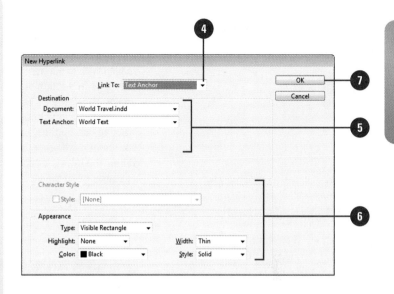

Create a Hyperlink From an URL

1 Select the text that you want to use to create a URL.

2 Select the **Hyperlinks** panel.

◆ Click the **Window** menu, point to **Interactive**, and then click **Hyperlinks**.

3 Click the **Options** menu, and then click **New Hyperlink From URL**.

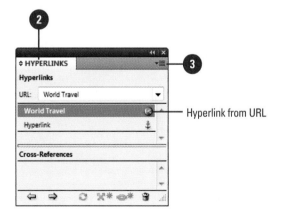

Hyperlink from URL

Using the Hyperlinks Panel

Adobe Certified Expert   ID 7.3

The Hyperlinks panel is a centralized place to work with hyperlinks and cross references in InDesign. The redesigned Hyperlinks panel (**New!**) makes it easy to create hyperlinks that navigate to external URLs, link to files with supplemental information, launch an e-mail client, or jump to a page or section of a page within the same or even a different document. You can also verify your hyperlinks directly in InDesign with no need to export the document to a PDF or Flash (SWF file) for testing. You can use buttons on the bottom of the panel to go to the hyperlink source or destination, create a new hyperlink, or delete hyperlinks. When you create or edit a hyperlink, you can change the style and appearance of the link.

Use the Hyperlinks Panel

1 Select the **Hyperlinks** panel.

◆ Click the **Window** menu, point to **Interactive**, and then click **Hyperlinks**.

2 Use any of the following buttons or commands to perform an operation:

◆ **Go to the Hyperlink Source.** Select the hyperlink, and then click the **Go to Source** button.

◆ **Go to the Hyperlink Destination.** Select the hyperlink, and then click the **Go to Destination** button.

◆ **Create a New Hyperlink.** Create a destination, and then click the **Create New Hyperlink** button.

◆ **Delete a Hyperlink.** Select the hyperlink, click the **Delete Selected Hyperlinks** button, and then click **Yes**.

◆ **Reset a Hyperlink.** Select the hyperlink, click the **Options** menu, and then click **Reset Hyperlink**.

◆ **Update a Hyperlink.** Select the hyperlink, click the **Options** menu, and then click **Update Hyperlink**.

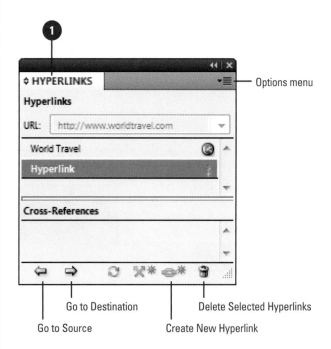

Options menu

Go to Destination

Go to Source

Delete Selected Hyperlinks

Create New Hyperlink

Edit a Hyperlink

1. Select the **Hyperlinks** panel.

2. Select the hyperlink you want to edit.

3. Click the **Options** menu, and then click **Hyperlink Options**.

   ◆ You can also double-click a hyperlink in the Hyperlinks panel.

4. Make the changes you want for the chosen hyperlink.

5. Click **OK**.

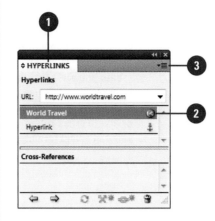

Change the Appearance of a Hyperlink

1. Select the **Hyperlinks** panel.

2. Double-click the hyperlink in the Hyperlinks panel.

3. For text, select the **Style** check box, and then select a character style.

4. Make the changes you want for the hyperlink appearance.

   ◆ **Type.** Specify a visibility setting for the hyperlink.

   ◆ **Highlight.** Specify a highlight setting for the hotspot.

   ◆ **Color.** Specify a color for the hyperlink.

   ◆ **Width.** Specify a thickness for the visible rectangle type.

   ◆ **Style.** Specify a line style for the visible rectangle type.

5. Click **OK**.

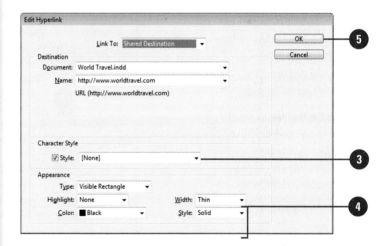

Creating Cross-References

ID 6.7, 7.3

A cross-reference refers a reader from one section of a document to another. For example, *For more information, see "Using the Hyperlinks Panel" on page 324*. The text being referred to is the destination text, while the text generated from the destination is the source cross-reference, which is editable. The Hyperlinks panel is a centralized place to create and work with hyperlinks and cross references (**New!**) in InDesign. You can use buttons on the bottom of the panel to go to the cross-reference source or destination, create a new cross-reference, or delete cross-references. When you create or edit a cross-reference, you can select format and appearance settings for the reference.

Create a Cross-Reference

1 Click to place the insertion point where you want the cross-reference.

2 Select the **Hyperlinks** panel.

◆ Click the **Window** menu, point to **Type & Tables**, and then click **Cross-References**.

3 Click the **New Cross-Reference** button on the panel.

4 Click the **Link To** list arrow, and then select a link type.

5 Click the **Document** list arrow, and then select a document location.

6 Select a paragraph in the document or a hyperlink destination for the text anchor.

7 Click the **Format** list arrow, and then select a cross-reference format.

8 Make the changes you want for the cross-reference appearance.

◆ **Type.** Specify a visibility setting.

◆ **Highlight.** Specify a highlight setting for the hotspot.

◆ **Color.** Specify a color.

◆ **Width.** Specify a thickness for the visible rectangle type.

◆ **Style.** Specify a line style for the visible rectangle type.

9 Click **OK**.

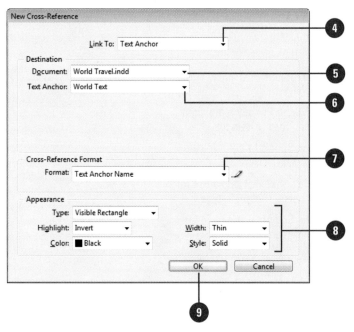

Work with Cross-References

1. Select the **Hyperlinks** panel.

   ◆ Click the **Window** menu, point to **Interactive**, and then click **Hyperlinks**.

2. Use any of the following buttons or commands to perform an operation:

   ◆ **Go to the Cross-Reference Source.** Select the reference, and then click the **Go to Source** button.

   ◆ **Go to the Cross-Reference Destination.** Select the reference, and then click the **Go to Destination** button.

   ◆ **Create a New Cross-Reference.** Select the cross-reference text, and then click the **Create New Cross-Reference** button.

   ◆ **Edit a Cross-Reference.** Double-click the cross-reference in the panel.

   ◆ **Delete a New Cross-Reference.** Select the reference, click the **Delete Selected Hyperlinks** button, and then click **Yes**.

   ◆ **Reset a New Cross-Reference.** Select the reference, click the **Options** menu, and then click **Reset Cross-Reference**.

   ◆ **Update a Cross-Reference.** Select the reference, click the **Options** menu, and then click **Update Cross-Reference**.

   ◆ **Relink a Cross-Reference.** Select the reference, click the **Options** menu, click **Relink Cross-Reference**, select the reference, and then click **OK**.

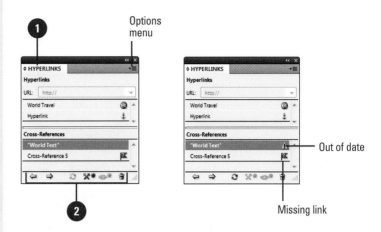

Options menu

Out of date

Missing link

Cross-reference

For Your Information

Creating or Editing Cross-Reference Formats

When you create or edit a cross-reference, you can also select a format, such as Page Number Only or Full Paragraph & Page Number. You can create new formats or edit the existing formats to customize your own. In the Cross-Reference dialog box, click the Create or Edit Cross-Reference Formats button, enter a name, click the different reference formats and add your own text to create your own definition. When you're done, click OK. You can also click the Options menu, and then click Define Cross-Reference Formats to make changes.

Creating Bookmarks

Bookmarks provide another way to navigate through a document. You can create bookmarks that will point to a place in a text frame, any selected text, a frame, or a page. You can create and work with bookmarks in the Bookmarks panel. When you create a PDF of your document, readers can use the bookmarks to navigate from one location to another by using the Bookmarks panel.

Create and Rename a Bookmark

1. Do one of the following to select a bookmark location:

   ◆ **Insertion Point.** Click to place the insertion point where you want the bookmark.

   ◆ **Text.** Select any text to specify a location.

   ◆ **Frame.** Select a text or graphic frame to specify a location.

   ◆ **Page.** Double-click a page in the Pages panel to specify a page location.

2. Select the **Bookmarks** panel.

   ◆ Click the **Window** menu, point to **Interactive**, and then click **Bookmarks**.

3. Click the **New Bookmark** button on the panel.

4. Click the bookmark to select it.

5. Click the bookmark again to make the name editable.

   ◆ You can also click the **Options** menu, click **Rename Bookmark**, enter a name, and then click **OK**.

6. Type a name for the bookmark, and then press Enter (Win) or Return (Mac).

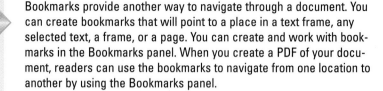

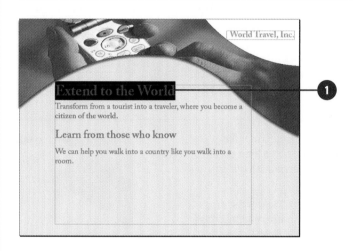

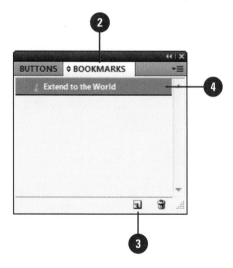

Use the Bookmarks Panel

1. Select the **Bookmarks** panel.

   ◆ Click the **Window** menu, point to **Interactive**, and then click **Bookmarks**.

2. Use any of the following buttons or commands to perform an operation:

   ◆ Create a New Bookmark. Select a location, and then click the **Create New Bookmark** button.

   ◆ Delete a Bookmark. Select the bookmark, click the **Delete Selected Bookmarks** button, and then click **OK**.

   ◆ Rename a Bookmark. Select the bookmark, click the **Options** menu, click **Rename Bookmark**, type a name, and then click **OK**.

   ◆ Go to a Selected Bookmark. Select the bookmark, click the **Options** menu, and then click **Go to Selected Bookmark**.

   ◆ Sort Bookmarks. Click the **Options** menu, and then click **Sort Bookmarks**.

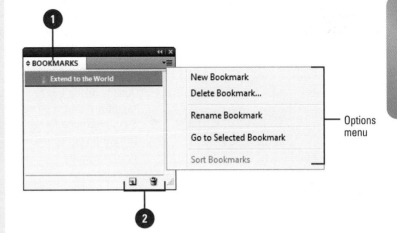

Adding Sounds or Movies

ID 7.2

You can add sounds and movies to an InDesign document just as you would add graphics. With the Place command, you can import the sound or movie clips that you want to play in your interactive document. If you're not sure what to play, you can create an empty sound or movie frame (with diagonal lines) and then import the clip later. After you import a sound or movie, you can use the Sound Options or Movie Options dialog box to set playback and other properties. When you import a sound, a poster image appears of a sound icon (named *StandardSound Poster.jpg*), which you can change or remove later. You can work with sound or movie frames like any other frame in InDesign.

Insert a Sound or Movie

1 Click the **File** menu, and then click **Place**.

2 Navigate to the location with the file you want to import.

3 Select the sound or movie file you want to place.

4 Click **Open**.

The imported sound or movie is placed in a loaded preview cursor.

5 Click or drag a rectangle frame with the loaded cursor to place the clip in a new sound or movie frame, or click in an empty sound or movie frame (designated by diagonal lines) to place it in an empty frame.

Did You Know?

You can create an empty sound or movie clip frame. If you want to create a placeholder for a sound or movie clip, you can create an empty frame and fill it later. Draw a new frame, click the Object menu, point to Interactive, and then click Sound Options or Movie Options. Enter a name, and then click OK. The frame is converted to an empty sound or movie clip frame.

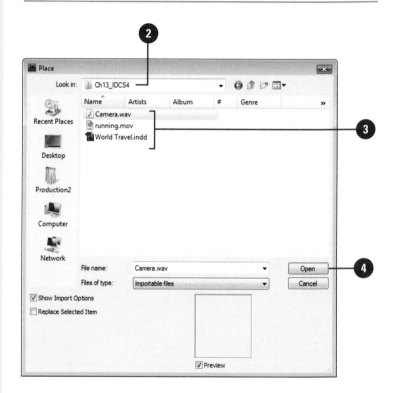

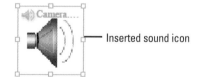
Inserted sound icon

Set Sound Options

① Double-click the sound clip.

② Enter a name for the sound clip, and then enter a description.

③ Click **Browse** (Win) or **Choose** (Mac) to add or change the sound.

④ Click the **Poster** list arrow, and then select a poster image for the sound: **None**, **Standard**, or **Choose Image as Poster**.

⑤ Select any of the following check boxes to enable the option:

   ◆ **Play on Page Turn.**

   ◆ **Do Not Print Poster.**

   ◆ **Embed Sound in PDF.**

⑥ Click **OK**.

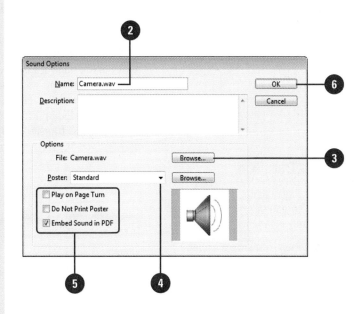

Set Movie Options

① Double-click the movie clip.

② Enter a name for the movie clip, and then enter a description.

③ Click the **Choose a File** option, and then click **Browse** (Win) or **Choose** (Mac) to add or change the movie, or click the **Specify a URL** option, and then enter an URL and click **Verify URL and Movie Size**.

④ Click the **Poster** list arrow, and then select a poster movie image.

⑤ Click the **Mode** list arrow, and then select a play option.

⑥ Select any of the following check boxes to enable the option:

   ◆ **Play on Page Turn.**

   ◆ **Show Controller During Play.**

   ◆ **Floating Window.** Specify a size and position.

⑦ Click **OK**.

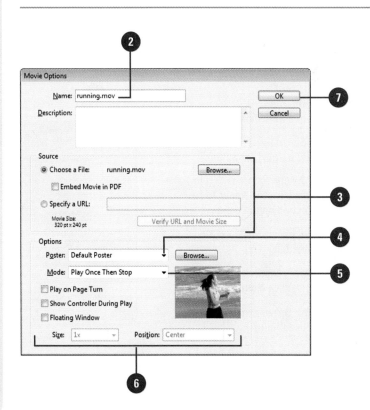

Adding Page Transitions

ID 7.4

A page transition displays a visual effect, such as a wipe or dissolve, when you turn the page in an interactive document. You can apply page transitions directly in InDesign to individual pages or to all spreads at once with a single click (**New!**). See previews of available transition types in the Page Transitions dialog box, and control the direction and speed of your transitions for export to Flash (SWF file) or PDF. When you export your document to a PDF, select the Interactive Elements option in the Export PDF dialog box to include page transitions. You can view the page transitions in Full Screen Mode in the PDF.

Apply a Page Transition

1. Select the **Pages** panel, and then select the spread to which you want to apply a page transition.

2. Select the **Page Transitions** panel.

   ◆ Click the **Window** menu, point to **Interactive**, and then click **Page Transitions**.

3. Click the **Transition** list arrow, and then select a transition.

   ◆ To select a page transition from the Page Transitions dialog box, click the **Options** menu, click **Choose**, select a transition, and then click **OK**.

4. Click the **Direction** list arrow, and then select a transition direction.

5. Click the **Speed** list arrow, and then select a transition speed.

6. To apply the current transition to all spreads, click the **Apply To All Spreads** button on the panel.

7. To clear all page transitions, do either of the following:

   ◆ Click the **Transition** list arrow, and then click **None**.

   ◆ Click the **Options** menu, and then click **Clear All**.

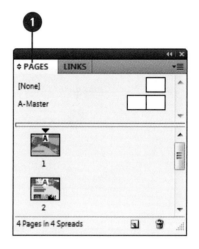

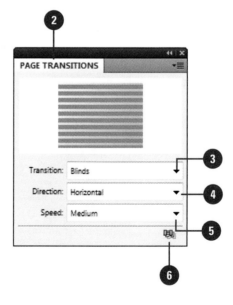

Using the Buttons Panel

The Buttons panel is a centralized place to work with interactive buttons in InDesign. The Buttons panel makes it easy to create interactive buttons that perform actions when the document is exported to Flash (SWF file) or PDF. You can use buttons on the bottom of the panel to convert an object to a button and to delete buttons. You can also use the Options menu to view sample buttons, set options to show (make visible) or hide buttons in PDFs, as well as set panel options.

Use the Buttons Panel

1. Select the **Selection** tool on the tools panel, and then select a button to view or change.

2. Select the **Buttons** panel.

   ◆ Click the **Window** menu, point to **Interactive**, and then click **Buttons**.

3. Click the **Options** menu, and then select one of the following PDF options (a check mark appears next to the selected item):

   ◆ **Visible in PDF.** Select to show and print buttons in a PDF.

   ◆ **Visible in PDF but Doesn't Print.** Select to show but not print buttons in a PDF.

   ◆ **Hidden in PDF.** Select to hide and not print buttons in a PDF.

   ◆ **Hidden in PDF but Printable.** Select to hide but print buttons in a PDF.

4. Click the **Options** menu, and then click **Panel Options**.

5. Select a thumbnail size.

6. Click **OK**.

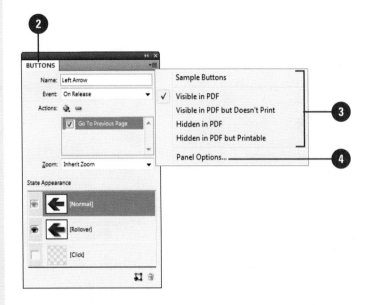

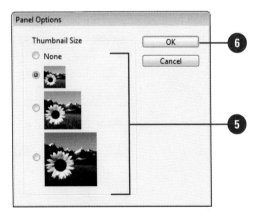

Did You Know?

You can delete a button. Select the Buttons panel, select the button, and then click the Delete button on the panel.

Creating Buttons

ID 7.2, 7.3

You can build interactive buttons to perform an action using the Buttons panel (**New!**). For example, you can create a button to navigate within a dynamic document, launch a movie, play a sound, or open a Web page. You can create a custom button from a selected object in an InDesign document or select a button from the built-in Samples button library (**New!**). The sample buttons include effects, such as adding gradient feathers and drop shadows. There are also assigned actions. For example, the arrow buttons are assigned the Go To Next Page or Go To Previous Page action.

Create a Button from a Sample

1. Select the **Buttons** panel.

   ◆ Click the **Window** menu, point to **Interactive**, and then click **Buttons**.

2. Click the **Options** menu, and then click **Sample Buttons**.

   The Sample Buttons panel appears.

3. Drag a button from the Sample Buttons panel to the document.

4. Click the **Close** button on the Sample Buttons panel.

5. Select the button using the **Selection** tool on the Tools panel.

   ◆ You can drag a resize handle to change the size of the button, and then move it to where you want.

6. Enter a name and make changes to the button settings in the Buttons panel.

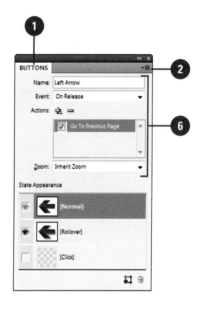

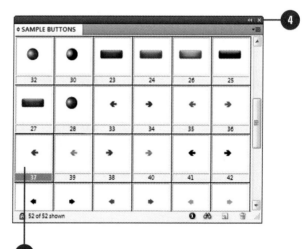

Convert an Object to a Button

1. Create and select an object that you want to convert to a button.

   IMPORTANT *You can convert any object to a button except a sound, movie, or poster.*

2. Select the **Buttons** panel.

   ◆ Click the **Window** menu, point to **Interactive**, and then click **Buttons**.

3. Click the **Convert Object to Button** button on the panel.

4. Type a name for the button.

5. Click the **Event** list arrow, and then select an event type.

   ◆ The options include On Release, On Click, On Roll Over, On Roll Off, On Focus, and On Blur.

6. Click the **Add New Action** button, and then select an action to perform for the button.

   ◆ The options include Close, Exit, Go To First Page, Go To URL, Movie, Sound, and Open File, among others.

7. Specify the various options for the selected action type (options vary).

Did You Know?

You can convert a button to an object. Select the button, select the Buttons panel, click the Convert Button To An Object button, and then click OK.

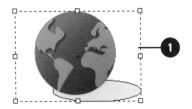

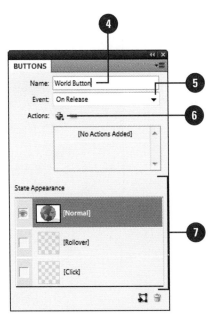

Working with Events and Actions

ID 7.2, 7.3

An event determines when to trigger an action that will execute a button operation. For example, the On Release event triggers an action when the mouse button is released after a button click. An action is associated with an event. You can assign an action type to a button to perform an action. For example, the Go To URL action type opens a web page in your default browser from the PDF document with the interactive button. You can create actions to navigate to anchor text or bookmarks, document pages and views, to launch a movie, play a sound, or open a web page (**New!**). You can work with events and actions for a selected button in the Buttons panel (**New!**).

Select Events for a Button

1. Select the **Selection** tool on the tools panel, and then select a button to change.

2. Select the **Buttons** panel.

   ◆ Click the **Window** menu, point to **Interactive**, and then click **Buttons**.

3. Click the **Event** list arrow, and then select an event type.

   ◆ **On Release.** Event occurs when the mouse button is released after a click.

   ◆ **On Click.** Event occurs when the mouse button is clicked.

   ◆ **On Roll Over.** Event occurs when the mouse pointer enters the button.

   ◆ **On Roll Off.** Event occurs when the mouse pointer moves off the button.

   ◆ **On Focus.** Event occurs when the button gets the focus using the Tab key.

   ◆ **On Blur.** Event occurs when the focus moves to another button or form field using the Tab key or mouse click.

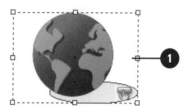

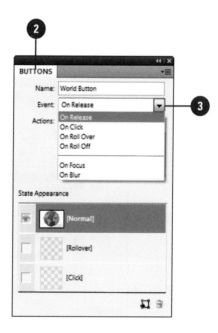

Add or Edit Actions for a Button

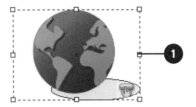

1. Select the **Selection** tool on the tools panel, and then select a button to change.

2. Select the **Buttons** panel.

   ◆ Click the **Window** menu, point to **Interactive**, and then click **Buttons**.

3. Click the **Event** list arrow, and then select an event type.

4. Click the **Add New Action** button, and then select an action to perform for the button.

   ◆ Close (PDF).
   ◆ Exit (PDF).
   ◆ Go To Anchor.
   ◆ Go To First/Last/Next/ Previous Page.
   ◆ Go To Previous/Next View (PDF).
   ◆ Go To Page (SWF Only).
   ◆ Go To URL.
   ◆ Movie (PDF).
   ◆ Open File (PDF).
   ◆ Show/Hide Buttons.
   ◆ Sound (PDF).
   ◆ View Zoom (PDF).

5. Specify the various options for the selected action type (options vary).

6. To enable or disable an action, select or deselect the check box next to the action name.

7. To delete an action, select the action, click the **Delete Selected Action** button, and then click **OK**.

8. To change an action order, drag an action to a new position.

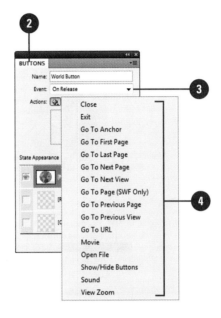

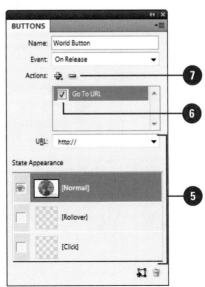

Working with Button States

ID 7.2, 7.3

A button consists of a group of individual objects. When you view a button, an object appears. When you point to or click on a button, another object appears. Each object represents a button state. Each button can have up to three states: Normal, Rollover, and Click. The button is in Normal state when you don't point to or click on the button, Rollover occurs when you point to the button, and Click occurs when you click the button. You can work with button states for a selected button in the Buttons panel (**New!**). When you activate a state in the Buttons panel, the Normal state (default) is copied to it. After it's copied, you can change the appearance of the button using InDesign color, text, and image tools.

Work with Button States

1. Use the **Selection** tool to select a button or use the **Direct Selection** tool to select a button as an individual object (state).

2. Select the **Buttons** panel.

   ◆ Click the **Window** menu, point to **Interactive**, and then click **Buttons**.

3. Click the **[Rollover]** or **[Click]** state to activate it.

4. Use any of the following to change the state appearance in the layout view.

   ◆ Change Color. Use the **Color** and **Swatches** panel to select a color.

   ◆ Add Text. Select the **Type** tool, click a button, and then type.

   ◆ Insert Graphic. Click the **File** menu, click **Place**, and then double-click a graphic file.

5. To disable/enable a state, click the **Eye** icon next to the state. Disabled states (no Eye icon) are not exported to the SWF or PDF.

6. To delete a state, select the **[Rollover]** or **[Click]** state, and then click the **Delete** button on the panel (you can't delete Normal).

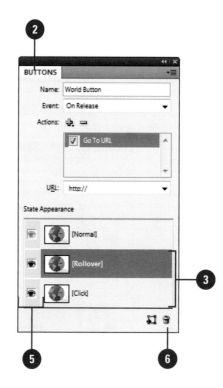

Setting Button Tab Order

The tab order determines when a button receives focus as you press the Tab key in a SWF or PDF document. When a button receives focus, you can press Enter (Win) or Return (Mac) to execute the button. You can also use the On Focus event to trigger an action when a button gets the focus. In the Tab Order dialog box, you can change the tab order for optimal use. The tab order includes buttons on hidden layers, but not buttons on master pages.

Set the Button Tab Order

1. Select the **Pages** panel, and then double-click the page containing the buttons you want to set the tab order for.

2. Click the **Object** menu, point to **Interactive**, and then click **Set Tab Order**.

   ◆ The tab order includes buttons on hidden layers, but not buttons on master pages.

3. Select the button you want to move.

4. Click the **Move Up** or **Move Down** buttons to adjust the order.

5. Click **OK**.

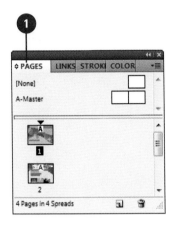

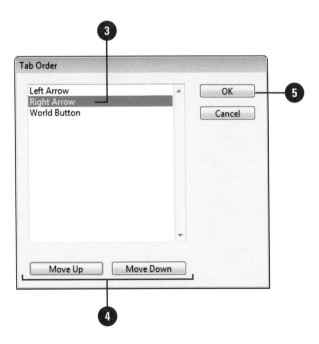

Automating the Way You Work

14

Introduction

A library stores InDesign items, such as text frames, graphics frames, shapes, buttons, sounds, and movies so you can use them in other documents. A library is not an InDesign document; it's a separate file (INDL). After you add items to a library, you can use them in any InDesign document. A snippet is an item from an InDesign document that you can save as an external InDesign Snippet file (IDMS) for use later. Snippets and libraries are similar. However, there are a few differences. Libraries are composed of a group of items, while snippets as individual items. You can store hundreds of items in a library. You may not want to do that, but you can if you want. When a library contains a lot of items, it can be hard to find the one you want. You can use the Show Subset dialog box to search for any item in a library. The powerful search features allow you to specify one or more levels of search criteria to find exactly what you want.

Conditional text allows you to create different versions of the same document. If you want to create two versions of the same document without having to create two separate files, you can create conditions for different text, and then show and hide conditions to create multiple versions. You can also merge data between documents. With the Data Merge panel, you can create a form letter, envelopes, or mailing labels by merging data from a source file with an InDesign target document.

A script is external code that allows you to extend the functionality of InDesign. InDesign comes with a set of sample scripts that you can run at any time. If you know how to write code for a script, you can create your own. XML (Extensible Markup Language) provides a way to reuse data from one file in another file. If you have some experience with XML, it's a good way to reuse information and automate the way you work with content.

What You'll Do

Create a Library

Use and Update a Library

Change Library Item Information

Search and Sort Libraries

Create and Use Snippets

Create Conditional Text

Use and Run Scripts

Use Data Merge

Work with XML

Export XML or IDML

Creating a Library

A library stores InDesign items, such as text frames, graphics frames, shapes, buttons, sounds, and movies so you can use them in other documents. A library is not an InDesign document; it's a separate file (INDL). When you create a new library or open an existing library, the Library panel appears, displaying the library name in the title tab. In the Library panel, you can add, remove, or update items. You can add items to the library one at a time, all items from a page, or as a whole page.

Create a New Library

1. Click the **File** menu, point to **New**, and then click **Library**.

2. Enter a name for the library file.

3. Navigate to the drive or folder location where you want to save the library.

4. Click **Save**.

   The tab for the Library panel displays the name of the library.

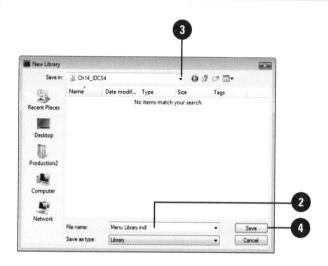

Open an Existing Library

1. Click the **File** menu, and then click **Open**.

2. Navigate to the drive or folder location where the library you want to open is stored.

3. Select the library file you want to open.

4. Click **Open**.

   The Library panel opens.

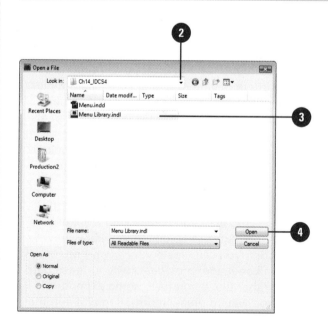

Add or Delete Items in a Library

1. Open the library you want to edit.

2. Do any of the following:

   ◆ **Add an Item.** Select the item in layout view, and then click the **New Library Item** button on the panel.

   ◆ **Add a Page.** Display the page in layout view, click the **Options** menu, and then click **Add Items on "Page."**

   ◆ **Add All Items on a Page as Separate Objects.** Display the page in layout view, click the **Options** menu, and then click **Add Items on "Page" as Separate Objects**.

   ◆ **Delete Items.** Select the items in the Library panel, click the **Delete Library Item** button on the panel, and then click **Yes**.

      ◆ Press Ctrl (Win) or ⌘⌥ (Mac) to select multiple non-contiguous items or press Shift to select multiple contiguous items.

      ◆ Press Alt (Win) or Option (Mac) to bypass the confirmation dialog box.

3. Click the **Close** button to exit the library.

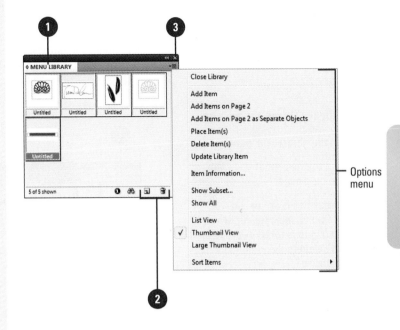

Options menu

For Your Information

Using Libraries from Adobe Bridge

A library file (INDL) appears in Adobe Bridge like any other file. However, the files appears as icons, not as preview documents. You can open a library from Bridge as you would any InDesign file.

Using and Updating a Library

After you add items to a library, you can use them in any InDesign document. You can add library items to a page by dragging them individually, dragging a selection, or by using the Place Item(s) command on the Options menu. If you change a library item in your document, you can use the Update Library Item on the Options menu to replace the existing item in the library with the updated one.

Place Library Items on a Page

1. Open the library you want to use.

2. Select the items that you want to place on a page.

   ◆ Press Ctrl (Win) or ⌘ (Mac) to select multiple non-contiguous items or press Shift to select multiple contiguous items.

3. Drag the selection from the Library panel onto the page.

Update a Library Item in the Library

1. Select and modify the library item that you want to update in the Library panel.

2. Open the library you want to use.

3. Click the **Options** menu, and then click **Update Library Item**.

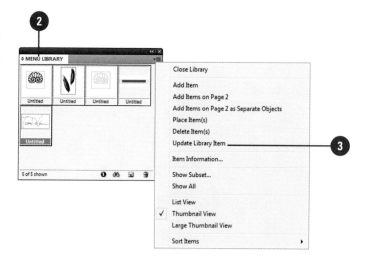

Changing Library Item Information

When you add items to a library, the item appears as an untitled element. You'll want to name the items for searching and sorting purposes. InDesign tries to assign an object type to the item, but it may not always be what you want. If an item contains multiple objects, such as a shape with text or a button with text, you may want to change the object type. You can change the item name and object type, as well as add a short description in the Item Information dialog box.

Change Library Item Information

1. Open the library you want to use.

2. Select the item that you want to change.

3. Click the **Library Item Information** button on the panel.

   ◆ You can also double-click a library item.

4. Enter a name for the item.

5. Click the **Object Type** list arrow, and then select an object type:

   ◆ **Image.** Specifies a raster graphic.

   ◆ **EPS.** Specifies an EPS file.

   ◆ **PDF.** Specifies a PDF file.

   ◆ **Geometry.** Specifies frames and rules that don't contain graphics or text.

   ◆ **Page.** Specifies an entire page.

   ◆ **Text.** Specifies a text frame.

   ◆ **Structure.** Specifies an XML element.

   ◆ **InDesign File.** Specifies an InDesign file.

6. Enter a short description for the item.

7. Click **OK**.

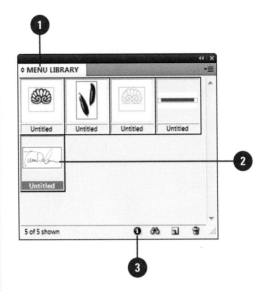

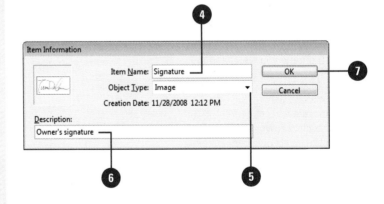

Searching and Sorting Libraries

You can store hundreds of items in a library. You may not want to do that, but you can if you want. When a library contains a lot of items, it can be hard to find the one you want. You can use the Show Subset dialog box to search for any item in a library. The powerful search features allow you to specify one or more levels of search criteria to find what you want. In addition to searching for items, you can also sort items in a library by name, newest, oldest, and type. A library panel displays items as thumbnails by default. If your prefer using a list to help you find what you want, you can change the library display.

Search in a Library

① Open the library you want to use.

② Click the **Show Library Subset** button on the panel.

③ Click the **Search Entire Library** option to search all items in the library or click the **Search Currently Shown Items** option to search only those items currently displayed in the library.

④ Use the list arrows under Parameters to specify the search criteria you want.

⑤ If you want to add multiple levels of search criteria, click **More Choices**.

⑥ With More Choices, use the list arrows to specify the next level of search criteria you want, and then click the **Match All** or **Match Any One** option.

⑦ To remove a level of search criteria, click **Fewer Choices**. To add more levels of criteria, click More Choices again.

⑧ Click **OK**.

All the items that match the search criteria appear in the library.

⑨ To show all library items, click the **Options** menu, and then click **Show All**.

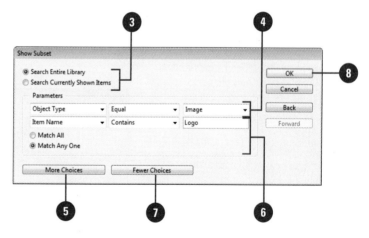

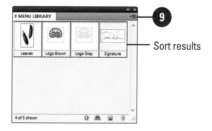

Sort results

Sort Library Items

1. Open the library you want to use.

2. Click the **Options** menu, point to **Sort Items**, and then select a sort command:

   ◆ **by Name.** Sorts library items by name.

   ◆ **by Newest.** Sorts library items from newest to oldest.

   ◆ **by Oldest.** Sorts library items from oldest to newest.

   ◆ **by Type.** Sorts library items into groups by object type.

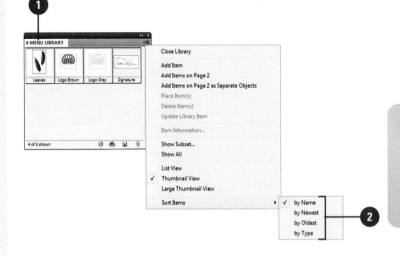

Change the Library Display

1. Open the library you want to use.

2. Click the **Options** menu, and then select a display command:

   ◆ **List View.** Displays library items with a name and an icon that indicates the item type.

   ◆ **Thumbnail View.** Displays library items with a name and image preview.

   ◆ **Large Thumbnail View.** Displays library items with a name and large image preview.

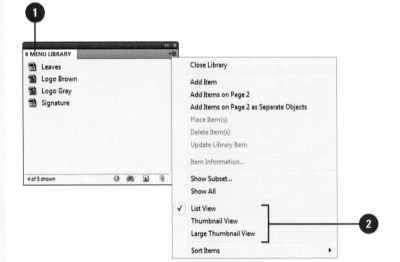

Creating and Using Snippets

ID 1.5

A snippet is an item from an InDesign document, such as a text frame, graphics frame, shape, button, sound, or movie, that you can save as an external InDesign Snippet file (IDMS) for use later. You can't use a text selection as a snippet, but you can use a text frame. Snippets and libraries are similar. However, there are a few differences. Libraries are composed of a group of items, while snippets individual items. You can drag individual snippets from a folder, desktop, or the Adobe Bridge into an InDesign document, which you can't do with library items. Since snippets are individual items, you can preview them (unlike library items). Snippets also typically have a smaller file size than a library file.

Create a Snippet

1. Select the items on the page that you want to use to create a snippet.

2. Click the **File** menu, and then click **Export**.

3. Enter a name for the file.

4. Click the **Save as Type** list arrow (Win) or **Format** popup (Mac), and then click **InDesign Snippet**.

5. Navigate to the drive or folder location where you want to save the snippet.

6. Click **Save**.

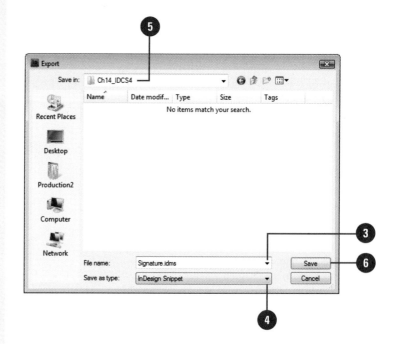

Create a Snippet by Dragging

① Select the items on the page that you want to use to create a snippet.

② Drag the items into a folder or onto the desktop.

The snippet appears with a file name assigned by InDesign, and a file extension of .idms.

③ Click the icon name, type a new name, and then press Enter (Win) or Return (Mac).

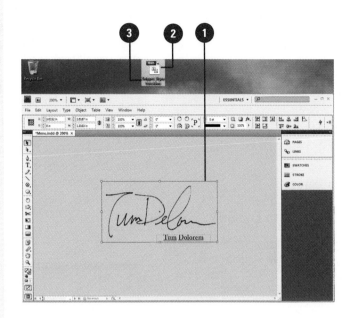

Use a Snippet

① Select the snippet in a folder, on the desktop, or from Adobe Bridge.

② Drag the snippet icon onto the InDesign document page.

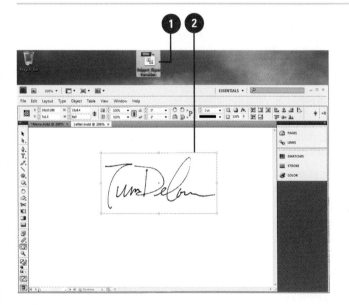

Creating Conditional Text

ID 6.6

Conditional text (**New!**) allows you to create different versions of the same document. If you want to create two versions of the same document without having to create two separate files, you can create conditions for different text, and then show and hide different conditions to create multiple versions. For example, if you're creating a computer book for the Macintosh and Windows operating systems, like the one you're reading, you can create text conditions for each Macintosh and Windows step instead of creating two separate files. You can apply conditions to text in a frame or table. A condition includes formatting indicators to make each condition easy to see in a document. To display different versions quickly, you can create condition sets. A condition set saves the visibility settings (the Eye icon) for all conditions.

Create and Apply a Condition

1. To create a condition for all new documents, close all documents. Otherwise any new conditions are saved only with the current document.

2. Select the **Conditional Text** panel.

   ◆ Click the **Window** menu, point to **Type & Tables**, and then click **Conditional Text**.

3. Click the **New Condition** button on the panel.

4. Enter a name for the condition.

5. Specify the following condition indicator options:

   ◆ **Method.** Highlights or underlines the conditional text.

   ◆ **Appearance.** Displays an underline style for the conditional text.

   ◆ **Color.** Displays a color for highlighted conditional text or for the underline indicator.

6. Click **OK**.

7. To apply a condition, select the text you want, and then click the condition name on the panel.

   ◆ To remove a condition, deselect the check box next to the condition name on the panel.

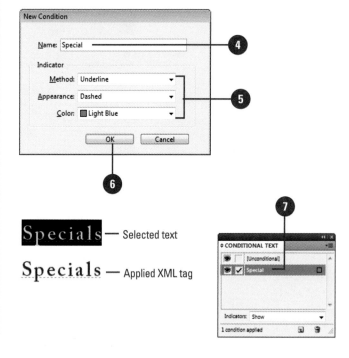

Specials — Selected text

Specials — Applied XML tag

Use the Conditional Text Panel

1. Select the **Conditional Text** panel.
   - Click the **Window** menu, point to **Type & Tables**, and then click **Conditional Text**.

2. Use any of the following buttons or commands:
   - Apply a Condition. Select text, and then click a condition.
   - Show or Hide Conditions. Click the **Eye** icon to toggle on/off.
   - Delete a Condition. Select a condition, and then click the **Delete Condition** button.
   - Edit a Condition. Double-click a condition and make changes.
   - Condition Indicators. Specify an option: **Show**, **Show and Print**, or **Hide**.

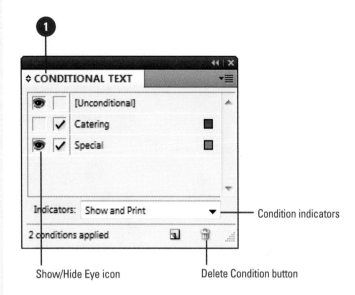

Condition indicators

Show/Hide Eye icon   Delete Condition button

Create a Condition Set

1. Apply conditions to text.

2. Select the **Conditional Text** panel.

3. Click the **Set** list arrow, and then click **Create New Set**.
   - If the Set menu doesn't appear, click the **Options** menu, and then click **Show Options**.

4. Enter a name for the condition set.

5. Click **OK**.

6. To use a condition set, click the **Set** list arrow, and then select a sort command:
   - **Set Name.** Applies the condition set to the document.
   - **Delete Set.** Deletes the condition set.
   - **Rename/Redefine.** Renames or redefines the condition set.

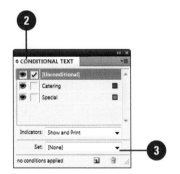

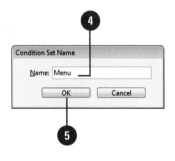

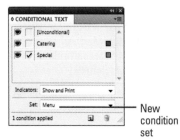

New condition set

Using and Running Scripts

A script is external code that allows you to extend the functionality of InDesign. InDesign comes with a set of sample scripts that you can run at any time. If you know how to write code for a script, you can create your own. InDesign works with AppleScripts on the Macintosh and Visual Basic scripts in Windows. If you want to use the same scripts on both platforms, you can use JavaScript. The Scripts panel displays all the available scripts in InDesign. The sample scripts are located in the Samples folder within the InDesign application folder.

Use the Scripts Panel

1. To display your own scripts in the Scripts panel, put the script file in the following folder:

   - **Windows.** C:\User*name*\AppData\Roaming\Adobe\InDesign\Version 6.0\en_US\Scripts\Scripts Panel

   - **Macintosh.** Hard Disk\Users*name*\Library\Preferences\Adobe InDesign\Version 6.0\en_US\Scripts\Scripts Panel

2. Select the **Scripts** panel.

   - Click the **Window** menu, point to **Automation**, and then click **Scripts**.

3. Click the triangle to expand folders in the Scripts panel to locate a script.

4. Select a script.

5. Click the **Options** menu, and then select any of the following commands:

   - **Run Script.** Runs the selected script file.

   - **Edit Script.** Opens the selected script file in a code editor.

   - **Reveal in Explorer (Win)** or **Finder (Mac).** Displays the script file in Windows Explorer or Macintosh Finder.

   - **Delete Script File.** Deletes the selected script file.

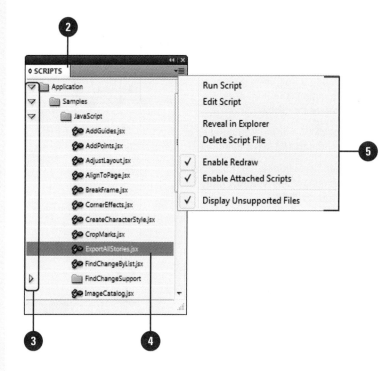

Run a Script

① If a specific script requires it, select an object or text.

② Select the **Scripts** panel.

◆ Click the **Window** menu, point to **Automation**, and then click **Scripts**.

③ Click the triangle to expand folders in the Scripts panel to locate a script.

④ Double-click the script name.

◆ You can also click the **Options** menu, and then click **Run Script**.

The script runs.

See Also

See "Defining Shortcut Keys" on page 427 for more information on assigning keyboard shortcuts to scripts.

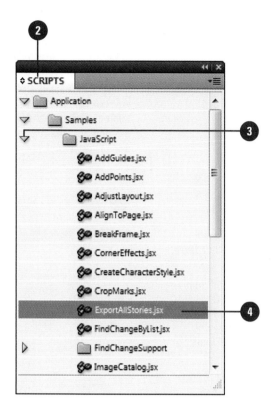

Using Data Merge

ID 1.4

With the Data Merge panel, you can create a form letter, envelopes, or mailing labels by merging data from a source file with an InDesign target document. The source file, such as a Microsoft Excel spreadsheet, in CSV (comma-delimited) or TXT (tab-delimited) contains data **fields** (columns) and **records** (rows). Each column of data is a field, such as Name, Address, and so on, while each row of data is a record. If you want to add images to the source file, type an @ before the field name, such as @Photo, and enter the path to the image for each record. The merged document is the result of the data merge between the source and target, which is then exported to a PDF document (**New!**).

Create a Data Merge

1. Select the **Data Merge** panel.

   ◆ Click the **Window** menu, point to **Automation**, and then click **Data Merge**.

2. Click the **Options** menu, and then click **Select Data Source**.

3. Navigate to the folder location, select the source file (CSV or TXT), and then click **Open**.

   ◆ Select the **Show Import Options** check box to change options. Specify import options, and then click **OK**.

4. Click to place the insertion point in the text frame (document or master page) where you want data field.

5. Click a field in the Data Merge panel list.

   ◆ For image data, drag the image field onto an empty frame or existing graphics frame.

   Text fields appear with double angled brackets, such as <<Name>>.

6. Select the **Preview** check box on the panel to preview data in the target document.

7. Click the **Preview First Record**, **Preview Previous Record**, **Preview Next Record**, or **Preview Last Record** button on the panel to view the record data in the target document.

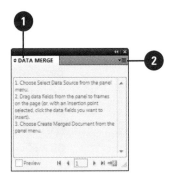

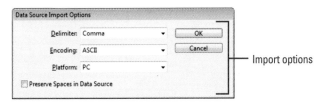

Import options

8 To work with the data source, do any of the following:

- ◆ Update. Edit the data source file in the source program, click the **Options** menu, and then click **Update Data Source**.

- ◆ Remove Connection. Click the **Options** menu, and then click **Remove Data Source**.

- ◆ Replace. Click the **Options** menu, click **Select Data Source**, select a new file, and then click **Open**.

- ◆ Image Placement. Click the **Options** menu, click **Content Placement Options**, select options, and then click **OK**.

9 Click the **Create Merged Document** button on the panel.

10 Specify the following options on the Records tab:

- ◆ Records To Merge. Specify the records you want to merge.

- ◆ Records Per Document Page. Select **Single Record** to start each record at the top of the next page, or select **Multiple Records** to create more than one record per page.

11 If you select Multiple Records, click the **Multiple Record Layout** tab, and then specify settings for margins, and the column and row record layout.

- ◆ Select the **Preview Multiple Record Layout** check box to preview the data.

12 Click **OK**.

13 Specify options to export the merged document to a PDF (see Chapter 15 for details), and then click **Export**.

14 Enter a name, specify a location, and then click **Save**.

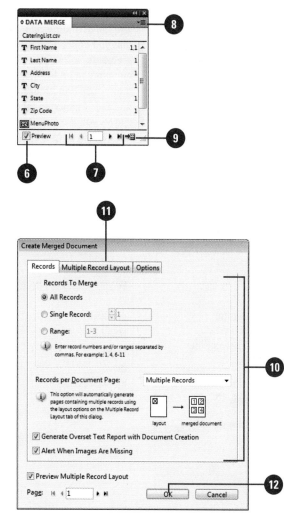

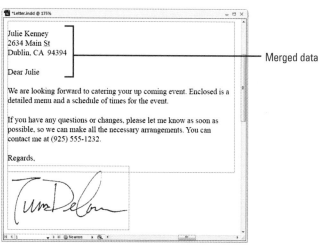

Merged data

Working with XML

ID 7.6, 7.7

XML (Extensible Markup Language) provides a way to reuse data from one file in another file. XML uses tags to describe data in the XML file that you can export into a different file. Tagged data are called **elements**. InDesign can create and use XML data. You can tag data as elements in an InDesign document, save and export data as XML, and then reuse it in other documents. InDesign provides the Structure pane and the Tags panel for working with XML data. The Structure pane shows you the hierarchy and structure of XML data and text snippets for viewing purposes, while the Tags panel lists tags for elements and provides tools to import, export, add, delete, and rename tags.

Create an XML Tag

1. Select the **Tags** panel.

   ◆ Click the **Window** menu, and then click **Tags**.

2. Click the **New Tag** button on the panel.

3. Type a name for the tag (no spaces or non-standard characters), and then press Enter (Win) or Return (Mac).

4. Double-click the tag, select a color, and then click **OK**.

   The color appears when you apply the tag to a frame or text.

Did You Know?

You can delete a tag. Select the Tags panel, select the tag, and then click the Delete Tag button on the panel.

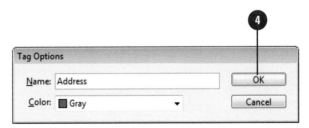

Place XML Tags in a Document

1. Click the **View** menu, point to **Structure**, and then click **Show Structure**.

2. Select the **Tags** panel.

   ◆ Click the **Window** menu, and then click **Tags**.

3. Select the text frame or individual text.

4. Click a tag in the Tags panel.

   ◆ To untag an item, select the element in the Structure pane, and then click **Untag** in the Tags panel.

5. To show tagged frames or text or frames, click the **View** menu, point to **Structure**, and then click **Show Tag Markers** or **Show Tagged Frames**.

6. To map XML tags to styles in your document for formatting, click the **Options** menu, click **Map Tags To Styles**, select a style for each tag, and then click **OK**.

Did You Know?

You can import XML data. Create a placeholder frame, click the File menu, click Import XML, select the Show XML Import Options check box, click the Merge Content or Append Content option, select the XML file, click Open, select the options you want, and then click OK.

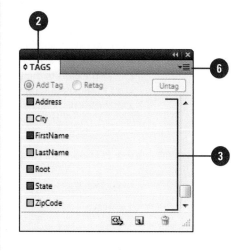

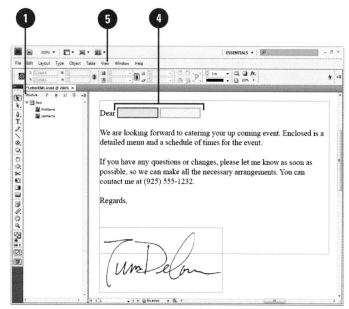

Exporting XML or IDML

After you finish creating or loading element tags, applying them to items on the page in your document, and making any final adjustments in the hierarchy of the tagged elements in the Structure pane, you're ready to export your document to XML for use in other documents. The export process is similar to saving a file. In addition to XML files, you can also export to the InDesign Markup Language (IDML) format, which is an XML-based format. This allows you to create (export) and open XML InDesign documents using standard XML tools (**New!**).

Export XML or IDML

1. Click the **File** menu, and then click **Export**.

2. Enter a name for the file.

3. Click the **Save as Type** list arrow (Win) or **Format** popup (Mac), and then click **XML** or **InDesign Markup (IDML)**.

4. Navigate to the drive or folder location where you want to save the XML document.

5. Click **Save**.

6. For XML, specify any of the following options on the General tab:

   ◆ **Include DTD Declaration.** Uses the DTD along with the XML.

   ◆ **View XML Using.** Open the exported file in a browser.

   ◆ **Export From Selected Element.** Starts the export from the selected element in the Structure pane.

   ◆ **Export Untagged Tables as CALS XML.** Exports untagged tables in the CALS XML format.

   ◆ **Remap Break, Whitespace, and Special Characters.** Exports items as decimal characters.

   ◆ **Apply XSLT.** Applies a stylesheet (XSLT) to define the transformed, exported XML.

   ◆ **Encoding.** Specifies an encoding method.

7. Click **Export**.

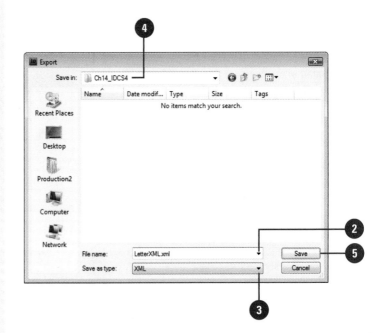

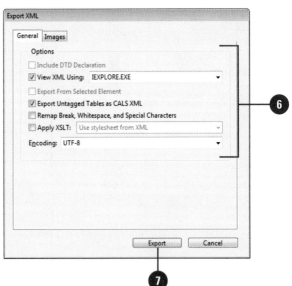

Exporting a Document

15

Introduction

After you finish creating your document in InDesign, you can export your work in another file format for use in other programs. There are eight main file formats to which you can export your document, which include Adobe Flash CS Pro XFL, Adobe PDF (Portable Document Format), EPS (Encapsulated PostScript), JPEG, Flash SWF (ShockWave Flash), and XML (Extensible Markup Language). In addition to these file formats, you can also export text in the Adobe InDesign Tagged Text, Rich Text Format, and Text Only file formats. When you export from InDesign, your content can be altered using the Options dialog box for the specific file format.

If a co-worker or client doesn't have InDesign, you can create an Adobe PDF of a document for them to review your work. Adobe PDF is a useful file format for document sharing, viewing, and proofing with Adobe Acrobat Reader or Adobe Acrobat Professional, which can be used to add comments and annotations. If you frequently use custom settings to export an InDesign document to an Adobe PDF file, you can save time by creating a preset.

If you use Adobe Flash CS4 Professional to create vector-based animation and interactivity, you can export content from InDesign to the XFL format for use in Flash. You can open XFL files in Flash and then use the authoring environment to add video, audio, animation, and complex interactivity. If you want to use InDesign content on the Web, you can export your document as a Digital Editions eBook file or an Adobe Dreamweaver HTML file. A digital edition is a XHTML-based ebook (EPUB) that is compatible with the Adobe Digital Editions reader software. Dreamweaver is a HTML editor that allows you to create and manage Web sites and pages.

What You'll Do

Export a Document

Understand Export File Formats

Export PDF Files

Set PDF General Options

Set PDF Compression Options

Set PDF Marks and Bleeds Options

Set PDF Output Options

Set PDF Advanced Options

Set PDF Security Options

Export with PDF Presets

Export as an EPS

Export as a Flash Movie

Export as an XFL for Flash

Export Cross-Media Files

Export as a JPEG

Exporting a Document

After you finish creating your document in InDesign, you can export it for use in other programs. If you have a document that is composed primarily of text, you can export the file as a text document, which you can open in a word processing program. If you have a document composed mostly of artwork, you can export it as a JPEG file (for use on the web). If you want to use content from an InDesign document in Adobe Flash CS4 Pro, you can export it as a XFL file (**New!**). In addition, you can export a document as a SWF movie (**New!**) for use in the Flash Player. See the list on the next page for more information about all the file formats.

Export a Document

1. Click the **File** menu, and then click **Export**.

2. Enter a name for the file in the File Name (Win) or Save As (Mac) box.

3. Click the **Save as Type** list arrow (Win) or **Format** popup (Mac), and then select a file format.

   ◆ All the formats don't display unless you place the insertion point in a text frame.

   ◆ InDesign also remembers your last export format for next time.

   See the list on the next page for more information about all the file formats.

4. Navigate to the drive or folder location where you want to save the document.

5. Click **Save**.

   For some formats, an Options dialog box appears, prompting you for additional settings.

6. If prompted, specify the options that you want, and then click **Export**.

   ◆ For help, point to an option to display a description at the bottom of the Options dialog box.

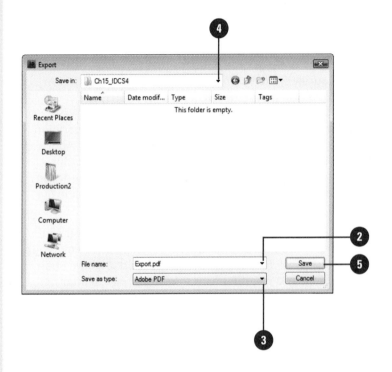

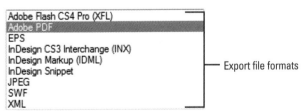

Export file formats

Understanding Export File Formats

Export File Formats

Format	Usage
Adobe Flash Pro (XFL)	Creates a file in the XFL format for use in Adobe Flash Professional CS4.
Adobe InDesign Tagged Text	Creates a text file formatted with text codes.
Adobe PDF	Creates a file in the PDF (Portable Document Format) for use on the Web and in other documents.
EPS	Creates a file in the EPS (Encapsulated PostScript) format for use as a graphic document.
InCopy CS3 Interchange	Creates a file in a special format for converting InDesign CS4 documents to InCopy CS3 documents.
InCopy Document	Creates a file for use in InCopy.
InDesign CS3 Interchange (INX)	Creates a file in a special format for converting InDesign CS4 documents to InDesign CS3 documents.
InDesign Markup (IDML)	Creates a file in the IDML (InDesign Markup Language) format, an XML-based format for use with documents that will be created and modified outside of InDesign. This format is also useful for saving QuarkXPress or PageMaker files opened in InDesign with compatibility problems.
JPEG	Creates a file in the JPG or JPEG (Joint Photographic Experts Group) format for use as a compression method to reduce the size of image files primarily for the Web.
Rich Text Format	Creates a file in the RTF (Rich Text Format) format for use as formatted text.
SWF	Creates a file in the SWF (ShockWave Flash) movie format for use on the Web using the Flash player.
Text Only	Creates a file in the TXT format for use as a plain text document.
XML	Creates a file in the XML (Extensible Markup Language) format for use as a reusable document with customized definitions and tags.

Exporting PDF Files

ID 7.3, 8.5

If a co-worker or client doesn't have InDesign, you can create an Adobe PDF of a document for them to review your work. Adobe PDF (Portable Document Format) is a useful file format for document sharing, viewing, and proofing with Adobe Acrobat Reader, which is free for download on the web at *www.adobe.com*.

Export to a PDF File

1. Click the **File** menu, and then click **Export**.

2. Enter a name for the file in the File Name (Win) or Save As (Mac) box.

3. Click the **Save as Type** list arrow (Win) or **Format** popup (Mac), and then click **Adobe PDF.**

4. Navigate to the drive or folder location where you want to save the document.

5. Click **Save**.

6. Click the **Adobe PDF Preset** list arrow, and then select a preset option, or specify your own options to create a custom preset.

   ◆ To create a preset that you can use later, set your options, click **Save Preset**, enter a name, and then click **OK**.

7. Select each category on the left and then select the options you want.

   See topics on the following pages that describe the available options in detail.

   ◆ To reset options to the defaults, hold down Alt (Win) or Option (Mac), and then click **Reset**.

8. Click **Export**.

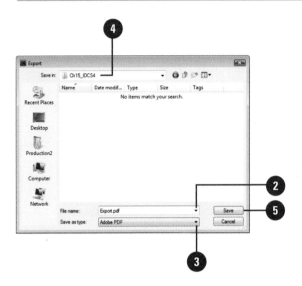

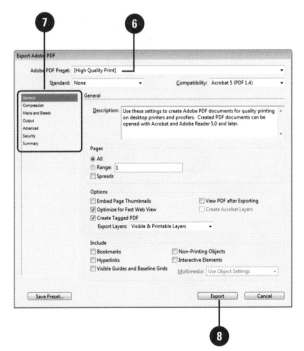

Use Adobe PDF Preset Options

1 Follow steps 1 through 5 on the previous page.

2 Click the **Adobe PDF Preset** list arrow, and then select one of the following presets:

◆ **High Quality Print.** Creates PDFs for quality printing on desktop printers and proofing devices.

◆ **PDF/X-1a: 2001/2003.** Creates PDFs that meet printing standards for Acrobat Reader 4.0 or later. Useful for a CMYK workflow.

◆ **PDF/X-3: 2002/2003.** Creates PDFs that meet printing standards for Acrobat Reader 7.0 or later. Useful for a color-managed workflow.

◆ **PDF/X-4.** Creates PDFs that meet printing standards for Acrobat Reader 7.0 or later. Useful for a color-managed workflow with added support for preserving transparency.

◆ **Press Quality.** Creates PDFs for high quality print production (digital printing or separations).

◆ **Smallest File Size.** Creates compressed PDFs for use on the Web or e-mail distribution.

3 Click **Export**.

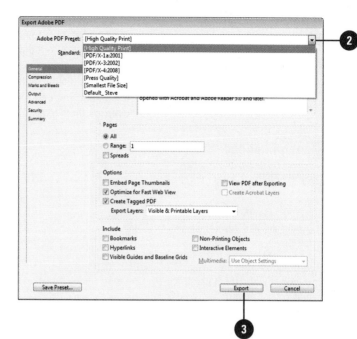

Setting PDF General Options

 ID 8.5

The General PDF options allow you to specify PDF compatibility, a page range, conversion options, and to choose what elements to include in the PDF file. The important options to consider here are the page range, Export Layers, and the elements you want to include in the PDF file. Some of the important options include Bookmarks, Hyperlinks, and Interactive Elements (**New!**). If you have sounds and movies in your document, you can specify options to use current media settings or override them to link or embed all of them in the PDF document.

Set PDF General Options

1. Click the **File** menu, and then click **Export**.

2. Enter a name, specify a location, select the **Adobe PDF** format, and then click **Save**.

3. Click the **Compatibility** list arrow, and then select with which version of Acrobat you want your file to be compatible.

4. Click the **Standard** list arrow, and then select a PDF/x option.

   The PDF/x options use ISO international standards for compatibility. See page 363 for details about the available options.

5. Click the **General** category.

6. Specify any of the following General options:

   ◆ **Pages.** Select the All or Range option, and specify a range.

   ◆ **Spreads.** Select to keep pages within spreads together.

   ◆ **Embed Page Thumbnails.** Select to add a thumbnail image for each page; only necessary for Acrobat 5 or earlier.

   ◆ **Optimize for Fast Web View.** Select to optimize the document for downloading from web servers.

   ◆ **Create Tagged PDF.** Select to add tags for use with screen readers.

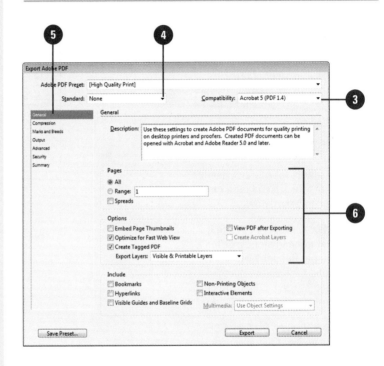

- ◆ **View PDF after Exporting.**
  Select to open the PDF file in
  Adobe Reader or Acrobat Pro.

- ◆ **Create Acrobat Layers.** Select
  to convert InDesign layers into
  Acrobat layers.

- ◆ **Export Layers.** Select the option
  to export layers.

7. Specify any of the following
   Include options:

- ◆ **Bookmarks.** Select to create
  bookmarks for entries in a table
  of contents.

- ◆ **Hyperlinks.** Select to convert
  InDesign hyperlinks, tables of
  contents, and index entries into
  Acrobat hyperlinks.

- ◆ **Visible Guides and Baseline
  Grids.** Select to use current
  guides and grids in the PDF
  document.

- ◆ **Non-Printing Objects.** Select to
  export objects with the non-
  printing option.

- ◆ **Interactive Elements.** Select to
  export buttons and other
  multimedia elements as
  interactive PDF elements
  (**New!**).

- ◆ **Multimedia.** Select from the
  following options:

  - ◆ **Use Object Settings.** Uses
    media option settings.

  - ◆ **Link All.** Overrides media
    options and links all media.

  - ◆ **Embed All.** Overrides media
    options and embeds all
    media.

8. Click **Export**.

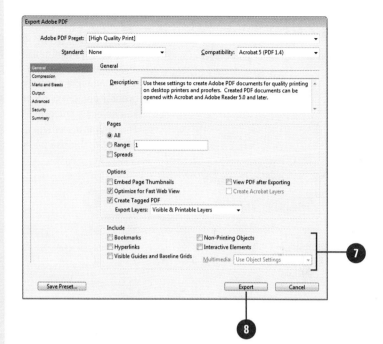

Setting PDF Compression Options

 ID 8.5

The Compression PDF options allow you to specify compression settings for color, grayscale, and monochrome (black and white) images. The important settings to consider are sampling, compression method, and image quality. The sampling option allows you to select how much downsampling of pixels takes place. The greater the downsampling, the greater compression and lower the quality. The compression option lets you select a compression method. Automatic (JPEG) is recommended. The higher the image quality level, the lower the compression and vice versa. So, choose an image quality level that best suits your needs.

Set PDF Compression Options

1. Click the **File** menu, and then click **Export**.

2. Enter a name, specify a location, select the **Adobe PDF** format, and then click **Save**.

3. Click the **Compression** category.

4. Specify the following options for Color, Grayscale, and Monochrome Images:

   ◆ **Sampling.** Select from the following options:

      ◆ **Do Not Downsample.** Retains all pixels.

      ◆ **Average Downsampling to.** Averages pixels in an area.

      ◆ **Subsampling to.** Fastest results with low quality.

      ◆ **Bicubic downsampling to.** Slowest results with high quality.

   ◆ **Compression.** Select a compression method.

   ◆ **Image Quality.** Select an image quality level.

   ◆ **Resolution.** Enter resolution settings for all the options.

   ◆ **Compress Text and Line Art.** Select to compress text or line art.

   ◆ **Crop Image Data to Frames.** Select to crop and reduce size.

5. Click **Export**.

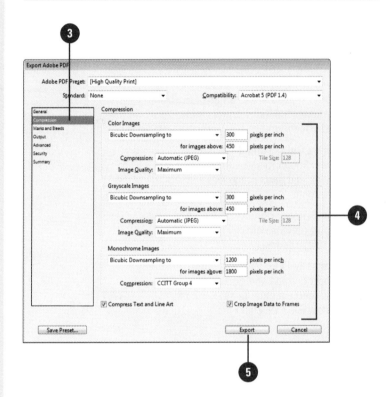

Setting PDF Marks and Bleeds Options

 ID 8.5

The Marks and Bleeds PDF options allow you to specify what printer's marks—crop marks, bleed marks, registration marks, color bars, and page numbers—you want to include in the PDF file. Printer's marks appear outside of the page boundary for commercial printing purposes. They don't affect the visual display of the page. You can also set options for the bleed and slug. The bleed is an area outside the trim of the page where objects still print, while the slug is an area outside the page trim that may or may not print. The slug is typically used to add non-printing information to a document.

Set PDF Marks and Bleeds Options

1. Click the **File** menu, and then click **Export**.

2. Enter a name, specify a location, select the **Adobe PDF** format, and then click **Save**.

3. Click the **Marks and Bleeds** category.

4. Select the **All Printer's Marks** check box to display the available printer's marks options.

5. Select the check boxes for the printer's marks you want to include in the PDF document.

6. Select the bleed and slug options you want:

   ◆ **Use Document Bleed Settings.** Select to use document settings for the bleed.

   ◆ **Bleed.** Specify the bleed values for top, bottom, inside and outside.

   ◆ **Make All Settings the Same.** Click the chain icon to make all settings the same.

   ◆ **Include Slug Area.** Select to include the slug area in the export.

7. Click **Export**.

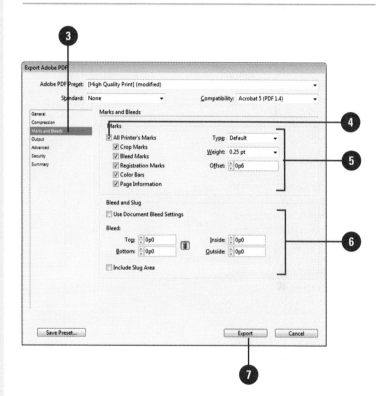

Setting PDF Output Options

 ID 8.2, 8.5

The Output PDF options allow you to specify color options and PDF/X compatibility settings. The important options to consider here are color conversion, destination, and profile inclusion policy. The color conversion option allows you to select whether to use the current color profile in the destination PDF document. The destination option lets you choose a profile for the destination PDF document, while the profile include policy lets you choose how it's used. You can also set PDF/X options, if you need to.

Set PDF Output Options

1. Click the **File** menu, and then click **Export**.

2. Enter a name, specify a location, select the **Adobe PDF** format, and then click **Save**.

3. Click the **Output** category.

4. Specify the following Color options:

   ◆ **Color Conversion.** Select an option: No Color Conversion, Convert to Destination, or Convert to Destination (Preserve Numbers), which converts to the destination only if the embedded profile is different.

   ◆ **Destination.** Select a color profile.

   ◆ **Profile Inclusion Policy.** Select an option: Don't Include Profiles, Include All Profiles, Include Tagged Source Profiles (for output calibrated output devices), or Include All RGB and Tagged Source CMYK Profiles (for output calibrated RGB and CMYK files).

5. Select the **Simulate Overprint** check box to simulate overprinting on the screen.

6. To control ink type, density, and sequence for process and spot colors, click **Ink Manager**.

7. Click **Export**.

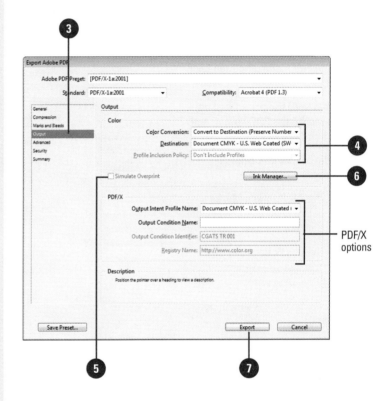

Setting PDF Advanced Options

 ID 8.5

The Advanced PDF options allow you to specify when all characters of the font are embedded, whether to use OPI (Open Prepress Interface) with document graphics, and what resolution to use for transparency flattening. OPI options are used when you send files to Scitex and Kodak prepress systems. OPI uses low-resolution images for layout and high-resolution images for printing. When you use transparency in a document, you need to specify a resolution setting to flatten, or convert, the effect into vector and raster images.

Set PDF Advanced Options

1 Click the **File** menu, and then click **Export**.

2 Enter a name, specify a location, select the **Adobe PDF** format, and then click **Save**.

3 Click the **Advanced** category.

4 Specify the following Advanced options:

- ◆ **Fonts.** Enter a percentage amount for the threshold when all characters of the font are embedded.

- ◆ **OPI.** OPI uses low-resolution images for layout and uses high-resolution images for printing. Select the check boxes for the image types to which you want to apply the OPI setting.

- ◆ **Transparency Flattener Preset.** Select a resolution to convert transparency into rasterized images.

- ◆ **Ignore Spread Overrides.** Select if you flatten individual spreads using the Pages panel.

5 Select the **Create JDF File Using Acrobat** check box to add job definition format information to the PDF document.

- ◆ You need Acrobat 7 Pro or later installed for this option.

6 Click **Export**.

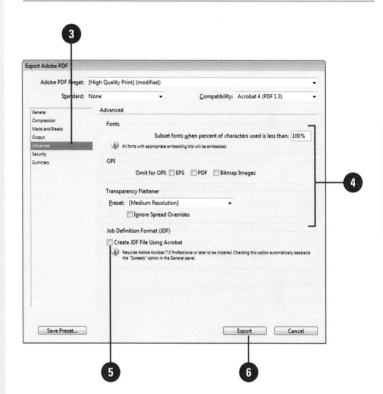

Setting PDF Security Options

 ID 8.5

If you only want certain users to open the exported PDF file, you can require a password. If you don't want to restrict complete access to the PDF file, yet you still want to have some restrictions in place, you can require a password for printing, editing, and other tasks. You can specify what a user can print and change. The password to open the document needs to different than the one to required to print, edit, or perform other tasks. Passwords are case-sensitive, so you can use upper and lowercase letter as well as numbers to create a secure password.

Set PDF Security Options

1. Click the **File** menu, and then click **Export**.

2. Enter a name, specify a location, select the **Adobe PDF** format, and then click **Save**.

3. Click the **Security** category.

4. To require a password, select the **Require a password to open the document** check box, and then enter a password in the box.

5. To require a password for certain tasks, select the **Use a password to restrict printing, editing and other tasks** check box, and then enter a password in the box.

   ◆ **Printing Allowed.** Select an option: None, Low Resolution (150 dpi), or High Resolution.

   ◆ **Changes Allowed.** Select an option:

     ◆ None.

     ◆ Inserting, deleting and rotating pages.

     ◆ Filling in form fields and signing.

     ◆ Commenting, filling in form fields, and signing.

     ◆ Any except extracting pages.

   ◆ **Enable copying of content and access for the visually impaired.**

6. Click **Export**.

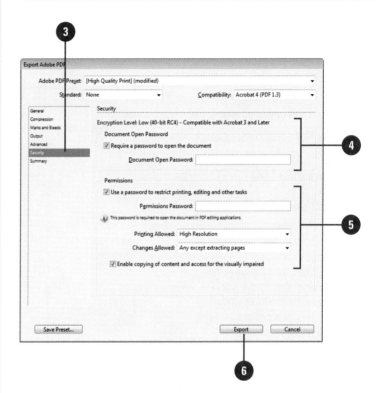

Exporting with PDF Presets

 ID 8.5

If you frequently use custom settings to export an InDesign document to an Adobe PDF file, you can save time by creating a preset. Adobe Creative Suite programs, including InDesign, Illustrator, Photoshop, and Acrobat, provide built-in presets that you can use in any of the programs. When you create your own preset, you can also use it in other Adobe CS programs. The process for creating a preset for an Adobe PDF is similar to creating a preset in other Adobe CS programs.

Create a Preset for an Adobe PDF

1. Click the **File** menu, point to **Adobe PDF Presets**, and then click **Define**.

2. Perform any of the following:

   ◆ New. Click **New**, specify the options that you want, and then click **OK**.

   ◆ Edit. Select a custom preset (not a predefined one), click **Edit**, change the options, and then click **OK**.

   ◆ Delete. Select a custom preset (not a predefined one), and then click **Delete**.

   ◆ Import. Click **Load**, navigate to the preset file, select it, and then click **Open**.

   ◆ Export. Select a preset, click **Save As**, specify a location and name, and then click **Save**.

   For PDF files, the preset is saved with the *.joboptions* extension.

3. Click **Done**.

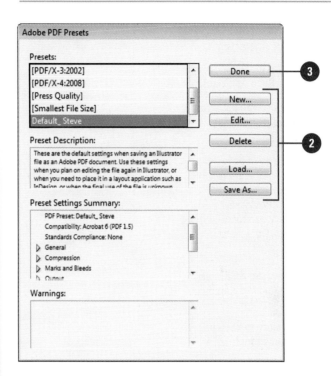

Exporting as an EPS

EPS (Encapsulated PostScript) is a commonly used file format that you can import into graphics, word processing, and page layout programs. An EPS file can contain vector and bitmap graphics, so it makes the format more versatile for use in other programs. EPS does a good job of preserving graphic objects in an InDesign document.

Export a Document as an EPS File

1. Click the **File** menu, and then click **Export**.

2. Enter a name for the file in the File Name (Win) or Save As (Mac) box.

3. Click the **Save as Type** list arrow (Win) or **Format** popup (Mac), and then click **EPS**.

4. Navigate to the drive or folder location where you want to save the document.

5. Click **Save**.

6. Specify any of the following General options:

   ◆ **Pages.** Select the All Pages or Ranges option, and specify a range, if necessary.

   ◆ **Spreads.** Select to keep pages within spreads together.

   ◆ **PostScript.** Select Level 2 for older printers or Level 3 for newer printers. Check your specific printer for capabilities.

   ◆ **Color.** Select from the following options or select **Leave Unchanged**:

      ◆ **CMYK** Uses CMYK. Useful for separations.

      ◆ **Gray.** Converts to grayscale. Useful for black and white.

      ◆ **RGB.** Converts to RGB. Useful for onscreen images.

      ◆ **PostScript Color Management.** Uses the PostScript printer to control the color separations.

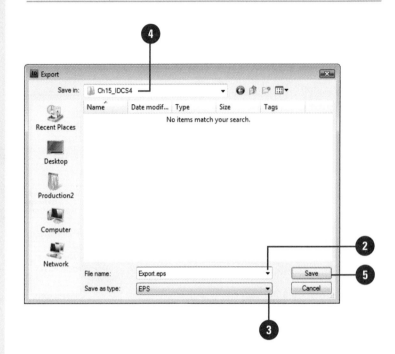

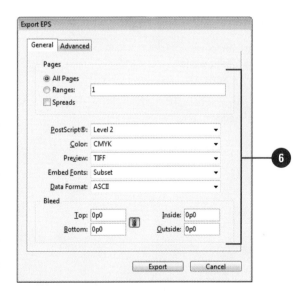

- ◆ **Preview.** Select None for no preview, TIFF for an image preview (Mac and Win), or PICT for an image preview (Mac only).

- ◆ **Embed Fonts.** Select None to not embed, Complete to embed all characters in fonts, or Subset to embed only the characters used in the file.

- ◆ **Data Format.** Select Binary for universal use or ASCII for use on PC computers.

- ◆ **Bleed.** Specify the bleed values for top, bottom, inside and outside.

7 Click the **Advanced** tab.

8 Specify the following Advanced options:

- ◆ **Send Data.** Sends All image data in high resolution or Proxy in low resolution.

- ◆ **OPI.** OPI uses low-resolution images for layout and high-resolution images for printing. Select the check boxes for the image types you want to apply the OPI setting.

- ◆ **Transparency Flattener Preset.** Select a resolution to convert transparency into rasterized images.

- ◆ **Ignore Spread Overrides.** Select if you flatten individual spreads using the Pages panel.

9 To control ink type, density, and sequence for process and spot colors, click **Ink Manager**.

10 Click **Export**.

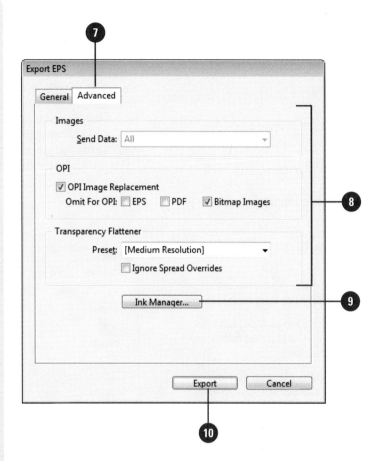

Exporting as a Flash Movie

 ID 7.3

The SWF file format delivers vector graphics, text, video, and sound to the Web using Adobe Flash player or Adobe AIR software. Adobe Flash Pro produces SWF (ShockWave Flash) movie files as a native format. However, you can also create SWF files directly from InDesign by using the Export command. The Export command gives you options to specify how you want to create a SWF movie. When you export SWF files from within InDesign, you can include page transitions, interactive buttons, rollovers, and hyperlinks (**New!**). When InDesign finishes the export, you can have your browser automatically open and display the SWF file using the Adobe Flash Player (**New!**).

Export a Document as a Flash Movie

1. Click the **File** menu, and then click **Export**.

2. Enter a name for the file in the File Name (Win) or Save As (Mac) box.

3. Click the **Save as Type** list arrow (Win) or **Format** popup (Mac), and then click **SWF**.

4. Navigate to the drive or folder location where you want to save the document.

5. Click **Save**.

6. Select a Size option:

   ◆ **Scale.** Increases or decreases the size of the original by a percentage.

   ◆ **Fit To.** Changes the size to fit a certain screen size.

   ◆ **Width and Height.** Changes the size to exact width and height settings.

7. Specify any of the following Pages options:

   ◆ **Pages.** Select the All or Range option, and specify a range, if necessary.

   ◆ **Spreads.** Select to keep pages within spreads together.

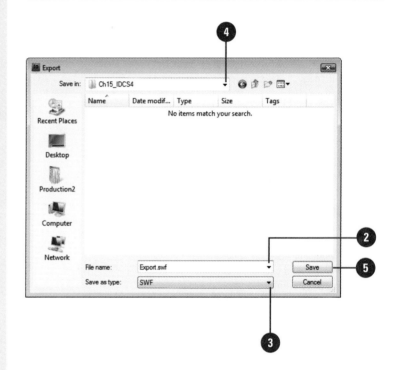

- ◆ **Rasterize Pages.** Select to create pages as bitmap images.

- ◆ **Generate HTML File.** Select to create a HTML file that plays back the SWF.

- ◆ **View SWF after Exporting.** Select to automatically open the SWF file in your browser after exporting.

8 Click the **Text** list arrow, and then select an option to convert text to **Flash Text**, **Vector Paths**, or **Raster Image**.

9 Specify any of the following Interactivity options:

- ◆ **Include Buttons.** Select to include interactive buttons.

- ◆ **Include Hyperlinks.** Select to include hyperlinks.

- ◆ **Include Page Transitions.** Select to include page transitions.

- ◆ **Include Interactive Page Curl.** Select to enable users to drag a corner of the page to turn it.

10 Specify any of the following additional options:

- ◆ **Image Compression.** Select Auto to let InDesign handle the compression, JPEG for use with grayscale and color images, or Lossless (Do Nothing) to not compress.

- ◆ **JPEG Quality.** Select a quality level. The higher the quality, the higher the file size and slower the display.

- ◆ **Curve Quality.** Select a quality level for vector-based Bezier curves.

11 Click **OK**.

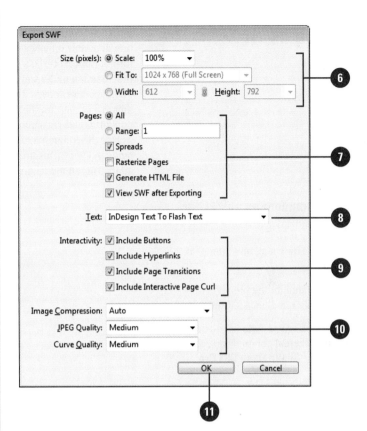

Exporting as an XFL for Flash

 ID 7.1

If you use Adobe Flash CS4 Professional to create vector-based animation and interactivity, you can export content from InDesign to the XFL format (**New!**) for use in Flash. You can open XFL files in Flash and then use the authoring environment to add video, audio, animation, and complex interactivity. InDesign text exported as XFL remains fully editable when the XFL file is opened in Flash. InDesign automatically converts high-resolution print assets (CMYK) to low-resolution web assets (RGB) upon export as an XFL file. An image placed multiple times in your InDesign document is saved as a single image asset with shared locations when exported as an XFL file.

Export a Document as an XFL for Flash

1. Click the **File** menu, and then click **Export**.

2. Enter a name for the file in the File Name (Win) or Save As (Mac) box.

3. Click the **Save as Type** list arrow (Win) or **Format** popup (Mac), and then click **Adobe Flash CS4 Pro (XFL)**.

4. Navigate to the drive or folder location where you want to save the document.

5. Click **Save**.

6. Select a Size option:

   ◆ **Scale.** Increases or decreases the size of the original by a percentage.

   ◆ **Fit To.** Changes the size to fit a certain screen size.

   ◆ **Width and Height.** Changes the size to exact width and height settings.

7. Specify any of the following Pages options:

   ◆ **Pages.** Select the All or Range option, and specify a range, if necessary.

   ◆ **Spreads.** Select to keep pages within spreads together.

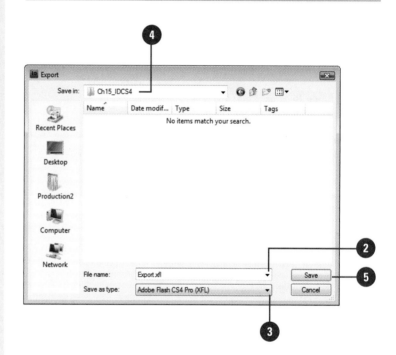

- ◆ **Rasterize Pages.** Select to create pages as bitmap images.

- ◆ **Flatten Transparency.** Select to flatten all objects with transparency.

8. Click the **Text** list arrow, and then select an option to convert text to **Flash Text**, **Vector Paths**, or **Raster Image**.

9. Click **OK**.

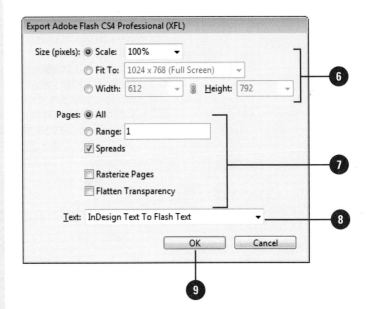

Exporting Cross-Media Files

ID 7.5

If you want to use content from your InDesign document on the Web, you can export your document as a Digital Editions eBook file or an Adobe Dreamweaver HTML file. A digital edition is an XHTML-based ebook (EPUB) document that is compatible with the Adobe Digital Editions reader software. Dreamweaver is an HTML editor that allows you to create and manage web sites and pages. InDesign uses XHTML for compatibility. However, the export options for a digital edition file and a Dreamweaver file are different.

Export a Document for Digital Editions

1. Click the **File** menu, and then click **Export for Digital Editions**.

2. Enter a name, specify a location, and then click **Save**.

3. Specify any of the following General options:

   ◆ **eBook.** Specify options to include metadata and add publisher information.

   ◆ **Base for CSS Styles.** Specify an option to determine which styles to use in the eBook.

   ◆ **Bullets and Numbers.** Select conversion options for bullets and numbers.

   ◆ **Include Embeddable Fonts.** Select to embed fonts in the eBook.

   ◆ **View eBook after Exporting.** Select to automatically open the eBook after exporting.

4. Click the **Images** category, click the **Copy Images** list arrow, and then click **Original** or **Optimized**. If you select Optimized, select conversion options for GIF and JPEG.

5. Click the **Contents** category, and then select the EPUB format (XHTML or DTBook) and whether or not to create a table of contents.

6. Click **Export**.

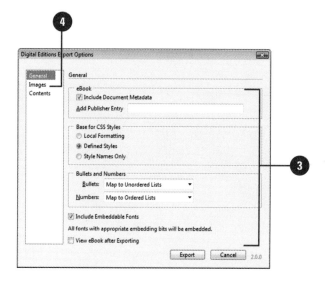

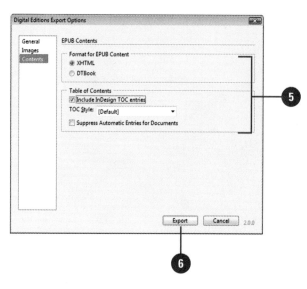

Export a Document for Adobe Dreamweaver

1. Click the **File** menu, and then click **Export for Dreamweaver**.

2. Enter a name, specify a location, and then click **Save**.

3. Specify any of the following General options:

   - ◆ **Export.** Specify an option to export the current selection or entire document.

   - ◆ **Bullets and Numbers.** Select conversion options for bullets and numbers.

4. Click the **Images** category.

5. Click the **Copy Images** list arrow, and then click **Original** or **Optimized**, or **Link to Server Path**.

   - ◆ **For Optimized.** Specify conversion options for GIF and JPEG.

   - ◆ **For Link to Server Path.** Allows you to export to a server. Enter a path to the server and the file extension.

6. Click the **Advanced** category, and then specify any of the following options:

   - ◆ **CSS Options.** CSS (Cascading Style Sheets) are a collection of formatting rules that control page appearance. Select an option: **Empty CSS Declarations** (creates style without attributes), **No CSS**, or **External CSS**, and specify a path, if necessary.

   - ◆ **Link to External JavaScript.** Select to run a JavaScript when the HTML page opens.

7. Click **Export**.

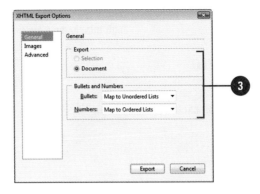

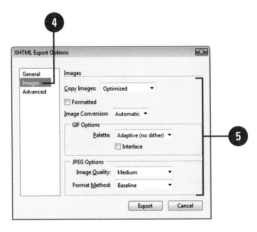

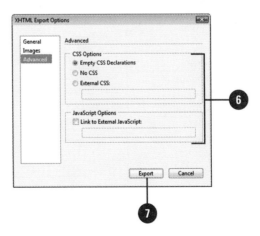

Exporting as a JPEG

If you have a document that you want to post on the Web, you can export it as a JPEG file. JPEG is a compressed format with relatively high quality, so it's a common file format for the Web.

Export a Document as a JPEG File

1. Click the **File** menu, and then click **Export**.

2. Enter a name for the file in the File Name (Win) or Save As (Mac) box.

3. Click the **Save as Type** list arrow (Win) or **Format** popup (Mac), and then click **JPEG**.

4. Navigate to the drive or folder location where you want to save the document.

5. Click **Save**.

6. Specify any of the following General options:

   ◆ **Pages.** Select the Selection, Range, or All option, and specify a range, if necessary.

   ◆ **Spreads.** Select to keep pages within spreads together.

   ◆ **Quality.** Select a quality level. The higher the quality, the higher the file size and slower the display.

   ◆ **Format Method.** Select Progressive to create an image that appears gradually on the page, or select Baseline to create an image that appears all at once, which is slower.

   ◆ **Resolution (ppi).** Specify a resolution. 72 ppi is common for the Web.

7. Click **Export**.

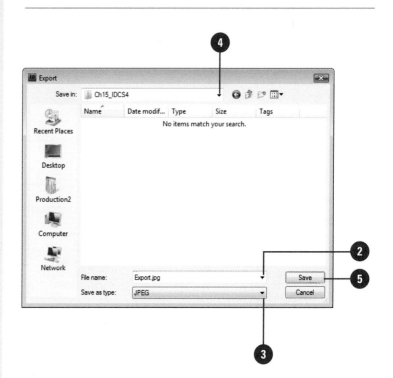

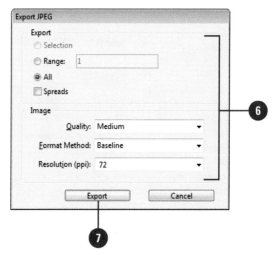

Printing and Outputting a Document

16

Introduction

The Print command is probably the most used of all InDesign's print options. The Print command is a portal to other menus that let you control specific printing functions, such as crop marks and bleeds, output ink, graphics, and color management. Color separations divide artwork into four plates by color, known as process colors. Each plate represents a CMYK (Cyan, Magenta, Yellow, and Black) color. The Separations Preview panel allows you to preview color separations on your screen. If you frequently use custom settings to send an InDesign document to a local printer or commercial printer for printing, you can save time by creating a preset. Before you print your document, it's important to check the Summary category in the Print dialog box. The summary information is good to check if you're having problems printing your job at a commercial printer.

When you print a document with spreads (for example, as a booklet), the pages need to be arranged as imposing pages, also known as printer's spreads. For example, page one of a 4 page project is paired with page four while page two and page three are paired together. You can arrange your document into imposing pages by using the Print Booklet command on the File menu.

Before you print or send your document to a commercial printer or service provider, you can should check your document for errors. Catching errors before you send out a print job can save you time and lower production costs. You can use live preflighting in the Preflight panel to catch errors, such as missing files or fonts, low-resolution images, and overset text. When you're ready to send a document, you can create a package file, which gathers together all the files related to your document, including linked graphics and fonts, to make it easy to deliver.

What You'll Do

Print a Document

Print with Presets

Set General and Setup Print Options

Set Marks and Bleed Options

Set Graphics Options

Preview Color Separations

Set Output Options

Set Trapping Options

Set Advanced Options

Set Color Management Options

Create a Print Summary

Print Spreads in a Booklet

Use Live Preflight

Insert File Information

Create a Package

Printing a Document

ID 8.4

The Print command is probably the most used of all InDesign's print options. The Print command is a portal to other menus that let you control specific printing functions, such as crop marks and bleeds, output ink, graphics, and color management. Understand that the options available for the Print command will be partially determined by your default printer. For example, if your default printer uses more than one paper tray, you will see options for selecting a specific tray for the current print job. In spite of the differences, there are some universal options for all print jobs, and these are covered here.

Print a Document

1. Click the **File** menu, and then click **Print**.

   TIMESAVER *Ctrl+P or* ⌘+*P.*

2. Click the **Print Preset** list arrow, and then select a preset.

3. Click the **Printer** list arrow, and then select an available printer.

4. Click the **PPD** list arrow, and then select a PPD (if available).

   ◆ A PPD (PostScript Printer Description) is a printer driver, a specific file used by commercial and specialty printers to define an output device.

5. Select a print category (**General, Setup, Marks and Bleed, Output, Graphics, Color Management, Advanced**) with your desired settings.

6. Select the options that you want; see other pages in this chapter for option specifics.

7. Click the Preview to display information about the document.

8. When you're finished, click **Print**.

   ◆ If you select a PostScript printer, click **Save**, specify a name and location, and then click **Save**.

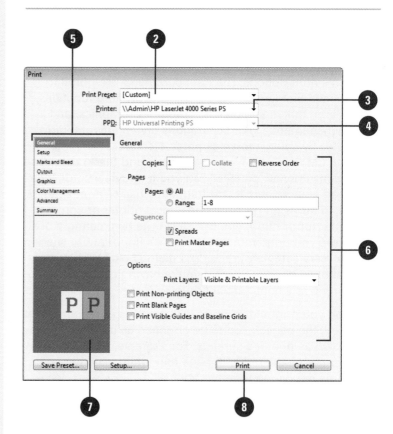

Printing with Presets

If you frequently use custom settings to send an InDesign document to a local printer or commercial printer for printing, you can save time by creating a preset. Adobe Creative Suite programs, including InDesign, Illustrator, Photoshop, and Acrobat, provide built-in presets that you can use in any of the other programs. When you create your own preset, you can also use it in other CS programs.

Create a Preset for Printing

1 Click the **File** menu, point to **Print Presets**, and then click **Define**.

2 Perform any of the following:

◆ New. Click **New**, specify the options that you want, and then click **OK**.

◆ Edit. Select a custom preset (not a predefined one), click **Edit**, change the options, and then click **OK**.

◆ Delete. Select a custom preset (not a predefined one), and then click **Delete**.

◆ Import. Click **Load**, navigate to the preset file, select it, and then click **Open**.

◆ Export. Select a preset, click **Save**, specify a location and name, and then click **Save**.

3 Click **OK**.

Print preset

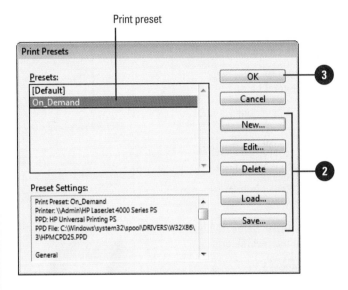

Setting General and Setup Print Options

 ID 8.4

The General and Setup categories in the Print dialog box allow you to set the page size and orientation (Portrait Up, Portrait Down, Landscape Left, Landscape Right), number of pages to print, and page scaling and tiling options. You can also ignore blank pages for printing. In addition, you can specify which layers you want to print: Visible & Printable Layers, Visible Layers, or All Layers.

Set General and Setup Print Options

1. Click the **File** menu, and then click **Print**.

2. Click the **General** category.

3. Select from the various General options:

   ◆ **Copies.** Enter the number of copies you want to print.

   ◆ **Collate.** Select to print pages in collated order.

   ◆ **Reverse Order.** Select to print pages in the reverse order.

   ◆ **All or Range.** Select an option to print all pages or only even or odd pages.

   ◆ **Sequence.** Select an option to print all or a range of pages.

   ◆ **Spreads.** Select to keep spreads together.

   ◆ **Print Master Pages.** Select to print master pages.

   ◆ **Print Layers.** Select an option to print layers: Visible & Printable Layers, Visible Layers, or All Layers.

   ◆ **Print Non-printing Objects.** Select to print nonprinting objects.

   ◆ **Print Blank Pages.** Select to print blank pages.

   ◆ **Print Visible Guides and Baseline Grids.** Select to print guides and baseline grids.

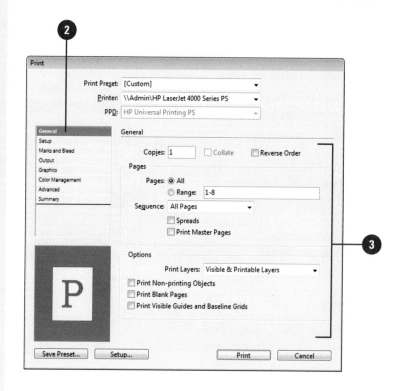

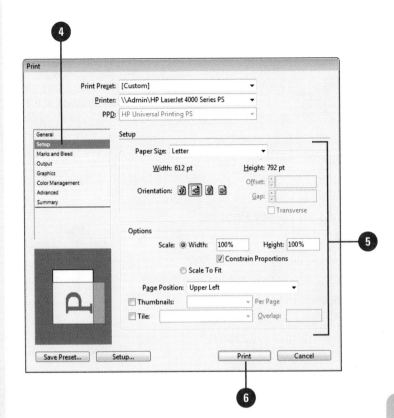

④ Click the **Setup** category.

⑤ Select from the various Setup options:

◆ **Page Size.** Select a page size, such as Letter, Legal, 11x17, A3, A4, and Envelope #10.

For Custom, specify **Width** and **Height** values.

◆ **Orientation.** Click an icon to select a page orientation.

◆ **Transverse.** Select to rotate the printed document 90 degrees.

◆ **Scale.** Select an option: Width to enter width and height percentages or Scale To Fit to scale to fit the page.

◆ **Page Position.** Select to position the page during printing (Upper Left, Centered, etc.).

◆ **Thumbnails.** Select to print small versions of the pages on a page, and then specify a number per page.

◆ **Tile.** Select to print pages that are larger than the page on multiple pages, and then specify a tiling option, and overlap settings.

Select **Auto** to tile automatically on the page, **Auto Justified** to tile automatically to the right edge of the page, or **Manual** to set the tile position in the document yourself. View the preview to see results.

⑥ When you're finished, click **Print**.

Setting Marks and Bleed Options

 ID 8.4

The Marks and Bleed category in the Print dialog box allows you to select printer's marks and create a bleed. Printer's marks appear at the edge of the printable page. Commercial printers use printer's marks to trim the paper, registration marks to align printing plates, and color bars to print colors properly. Bleed is the amount of the document that appears outside of the printing area, which includes the bounding box and trim marks. The bleed is useful to give you a margin of error. Having a bleed ensures that ink is printed all the way to the edge of the page so there are no gaps between the page and the edge of the trimmed document page. Your commercial printer can advise you on the best bleed settings based on your print job.

Set Marks and Bleed Print Options

1. Click the **File** menu, and then click **Print**.

2. Click the **Marks and Bleed** category.

3. Select from the various Marks options:

   ◆ **All Printer's Marks.** Select to enable the following check boxes: Crop Marks, Bleed Marks, Registration Marks, Color Bars, and Page Information.

   ◆ **Crop Marks.** Select to add crop marks where the page is trimmed.

   ◆ **Bleed Marks.** Select to show bleed marks outside the crop marks for the printer.

   ◆ **Registration Marks.** Select to add small targets for aligning color separations.

   ◆ **Color Bars.** Select to add small color squares with color information for the printer.

   ◆ **Page Information.** Select to add labels with document information such as: name, page number, time and date, plate color, and screen angle.

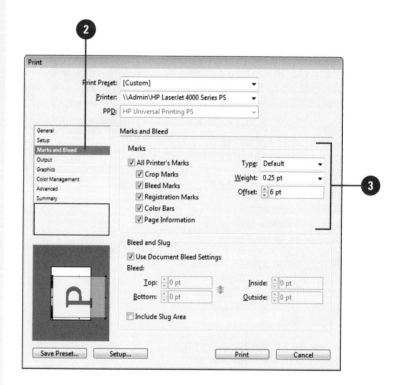

- **Type.** Specify a set of marks for custom use, such as for Japanese printing.

- **Weight.** Enter an amount for the thickness of the crop marks.

- **Offset.** Specify an offset value (0-72 points) for the distance between trim marks and the bounding box.

  Enter an offset value to make sure that any printer's marks will not be overlapped by the bleed.

④ Select from the various Bleed and Slug options:

- **Use Document Bleed Settings.** Select to use bleed settings defined in the New Document dialog box.

- **Top, Bottom, Inside and Outside.** Enter values to define the bleed area.

  Your commercial printer can advise you on the best bleed settings based on your print job.

- **Include Slug Area.** Select to include the slug area in the printed file.

⑤ When you're finished, click **Print**.

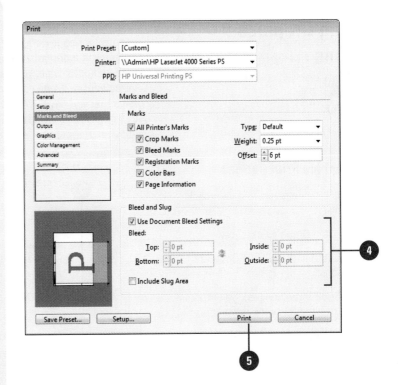

Setting Graphics Options

 ID 8.4

The Graphics category in the Print dialog box allows you to set printing options for image data, fonts, and PostScript files. When you send graphics to a printer, you can control how much information gets sent to the output device. You can include all image information or an optimized subset. When you include typeface fonts in your document, the fonts that you have used need to be downloaded to your printer. You can choose to download all or a subset of the characters used in your document.

Set Graphics Print Options

1. Click the **File** menu, and then click **Print**.

2. Click the **Graphics** category.

3. Select from the various Graphics options:

   ◆ **Send Data (Images).** Select from the following options:

     ◆ **All.** Sends all image data (slowest option).

     ◆ **Optimized Subsampling.** Sends only the image data needed by the output device.

     ◆ **Proxy.** Sends only a 72-ppi version of the image.

     ◆ **None.** Replaces the image with crosshairs. Useful for proofing text.

   ◆ **Download (Fonts).** Select a download option: None, Subset (only characters, or glyphs, used), or Complete (all fonts used). Select the **Download PPD Fonts** check box to send all fonts to the printer.

   ◆ **PostScript.** Choose from Language Level 2 or Language Level 3. Level 3 delivers the best speed and quality if you are printing to a PostScript 3 device (for PostScript printer).

   ◆ **Data Format.** Choose ASCII or Binary to determine how the data is sent to the printer.

4. When you're finished, click **Print**.

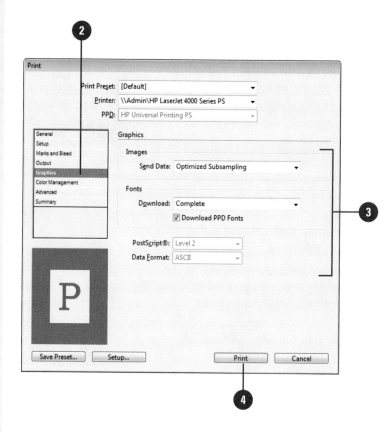

Previewing Color Separations

ID 8.2

Color separations divide content into four plates by color, known as process colors. Each plate represents a CMYK (Cyan, Magenta, Yellow, and Black) color. The Separations Preview panel allows you to preview color separations on your screen. As you move your cursor around the page, the panel displays an ink percentage usage for the item next to each plate. In the panel, you can use the Visibility column to show and hide different separation color inks to preview your content on the page. Printers have ink limits, typically 300%. You can use the panel to check ink limits to make sure you have not exceeded them.

Preview Color Separations with the Separations Preview Panel

1. Select the **Separations Preview** panel.

   ◆ Click the **Window** menu, point to **Output**, and then click **Separations Preview**.

2. Click the **View** list arrow, and then click **Separations**.

3. Do any of the following:

   ◆ **View Ink Amounts.** Move the cursor around the page to display ink percentages on the panel.

   ◆ **Hide/Show Separation Ink.** Click the eye icon for each ink you want to hide. Click the eye icon again to make the effects of the ink visible.

   ◆ **View All Inks.** Click the CMYK eye icon.

4. To make sure inks don't exceed printer limits, click the **View** list arrow, and then click **Ink Limit**.

   In Ink Limit view, the document preview changes to a grayscale image. Any areas over the limit appear in red.

5. To turn separations view off, click the **View** list arrow, and then click **Off**.

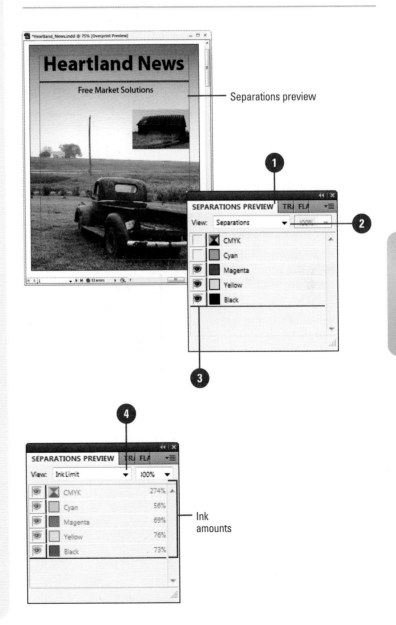

Separations preview

Ink amounts

Setting Output Options

ID 8.2, 8.4

The Output category in the Print dialog box allows you to create and print color composites and separations. A composite prints all colors together on a page, while separations prints each color on a separate page. When you choose to create color separations, you also have the option of selecting which color plates that you want to print. The Inks area allows you to control how inks are separated and printed. If you have spot colors, you can use the Ink Manager to convert them to process inks or map one color to another. Since options vary from job to job, check with your commercial printer for help with specific values for your print job.

Set Output Print Options

1. Click the **File** menu, and then click **Print**.

2. Click the **Output** category.

   Check with your commercial printer for help with specific values for your print job.

3. Click the **Color** list arrow, and then select an option:

   - **Composite Leave Unchanged.** Use current composite settings.

   - **Composite Gray, RGB, or CMYK.** Use to print with no separations using Gray, RGB, or CMYK

   - **Separations.** Use to create separations.

   - **In-RIP Separations.** Use to have InDesign create a PostScript file that creates the separations in RIP (Raster Image Processing).

4. Select from the various options:

   - **Text as Black.** Select to print colored text as black.

   - **Trapping.** For separations, select an option to compensate for the misregistration of printing plates.

   - **Negative.** Select to create a negative. Useful for creating film separations.

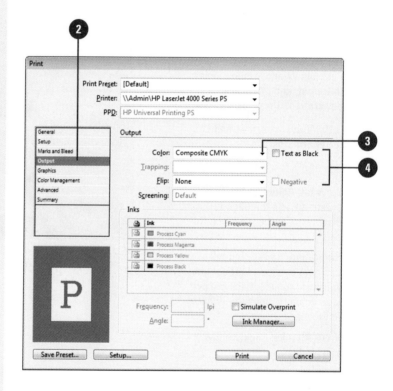

- **Flip.** Select an option to flip the orientation of the page.

5 For separations, click the **Screening** list arrow, and then select a frequency and angle.

- In the Inks area, select a color, and then enter values for **Frequency** and **Angle**.

    Check with your commercial printer for these settings.

6 Select the **Simulate Overprint** check box to simulate overprinting on the screen.

7 To control ink type, density, and sequence for process and spot colors, click **Ink Manager**.

8 When you're finished, click **Print**.

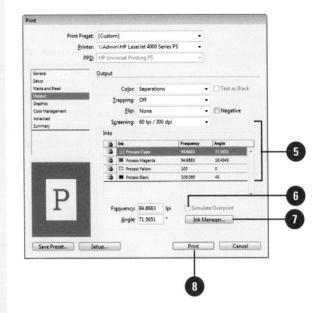

Use the Ink Manager

1 Click the **File** menu, and then click **Print**.

2 Click the **Output** category.

3 Click **Ink Manager**.

4 To convert spot color to process inks, do any of the following:

- **Individual.** Click the color icon next to the name to toggle between CMYK or spot color.

- **All.** Select the **All Spots to Process** check box.

- **Use Standard Lab Values for Spots.** Select to use built-in values.

5 To change ink density, select a color, and then enter an ink value.

6 To map a color to another color, select a color you want to map, click the **Ink Alias** list arrow, and then click a color.

7 Click **OK**.

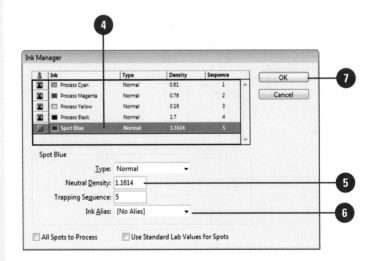

Setting Trapping Options

In the Output section of the Print dialog box, you can set a trapping option to correct for misregistration of printing plates. Trapping slightly expands one object so it overlaps with another to prevent color gaps. Trapping requires inks to overprint each other to prevent knockouts. You can use Adobe InDesign CS4 built-in trapping or Adobe In-RIP Trapping to trap text and graphics in your document. Both work well. You can also apply trapping settings to a page or page range by using trap presets in the Trap Presets panel. Since options vary from job to job, check with your commercial printer for help with specific values for your print job.

Create a Trap Preset

1. Select the **Trap Presets** panel.
   - Click the **Window** menu, point to **Output**, and then click **Trap Presets**.
2. Click the **Create New Trap Preset** button on the panel.
3. Double-click the new trap preset.
4. Enter a name for the preset.
5. Specify the trap settings you want for your document.

   Since options vary from job to job, check with your commercial printer for help with specific values for your print job.
6. Click **OK**.

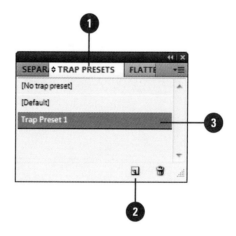

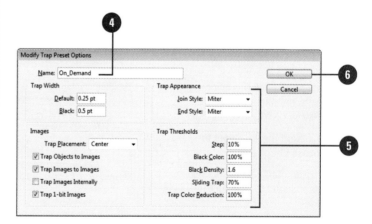

Did You Know?

You can delete a trap preset. Select the Trap Presets panel, select the trap preset, click the Delete Selected Preset button on the panel, and then click Yes.

Assign a Trap Preset to Pages

1. Select the **Trap Presets** panel.

   ◆ Click the **Window** menu, point to **Output**, and then click **Trap Presets**.

2. Click the **Options** menu, and then click **Assign Trap Preset**.

3. Click the **Trap Preset** list arrow, and then select a preset.

4. Click the **All** or **Range** option, and then specify a range as needed.

5. Click **Assign**.

6. Click **Done**.

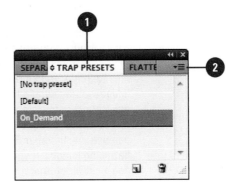

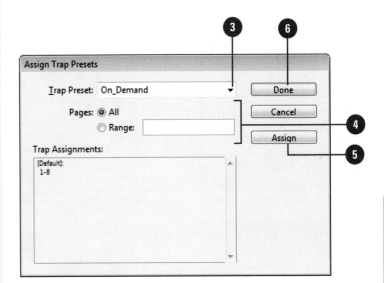

Setting Advanced Options

ID 8.3, 8.4

The Advanced category in the Print dialog box allows you to specify when all characters of the font are embedded, whether to use OPI (Open Prepress Interface) with document graphics, and what resolution to use for transparency flattening. OPI options are used when you send files to Scitex and Kodak prepress systems. OPI uses low-resolution images for layout and high-resolution images for printing. When you use transparency in a document, you need to specify a resolution setting to flatten, or convert, the effects into vector and raster images. You can use the Flattener Preview panel to highlight the areas affected by flattening images. If you have problems printing vector objects to a non-PostScript printer, select the Print as Bitmap option to convert vector objects to bitmap raster images for print purposes.

Set Advanced Print Options

1. Click the **File** menu, and then click **Print**.

2. Click the **Advanced** category.

3. Select from the various Advanced options:

   ◆ **Print as Bitmap.** Select if you have problems printing vector objects to a non-PostScript printer.

   ◆ **OPI.** OPI uses low-resolution images for layout and high-resolution images for printing. Select the check boxes for the image types to which you want to apply OPI.

   ◆ **Transparency Flatter Preset.** Select a resolution to convert transparency into rasterized images.

   ◆ **Ignore Spread Overrides.** Select if you flatten individual spreads using the Pages panel.

4. When you're finished, click **Print**.

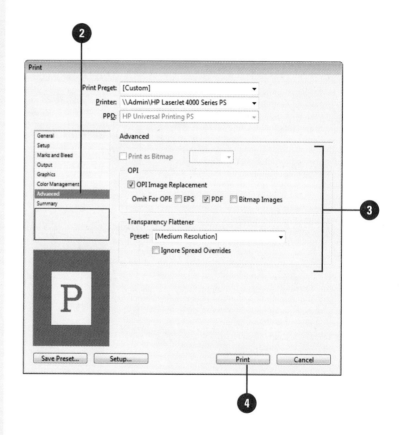

Preview Flattened Artwork

1. Click the **Window** menu, point to **Output**, and then click **Flattener Preview**.

2. Click the **Highlight** list arrow, and then select a highlight option.

3. Click the **Preset** list arrow, and then select a flattener preset.

4. Select the **Auto Refresh Highlight** check box or click **Refresh** to display a fresh preview.

5. Select the **Ignore Spread Overrides** check box to use for the setting in the Preset menu.

6. Click **Apply Settings to Print** to apply settings to Advanced options in the Print dialog box.

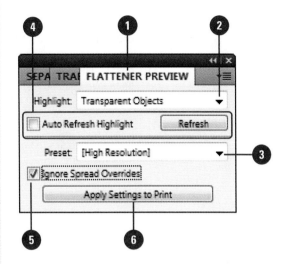

Create a Preset for Transparency Flattener

1. Click the **Edit** menu, and then click **Transparency Flattener Presets**.

2. Perform any of the following:

   ◆ New. Click **New**, specify the options that you want, and then click **OK**.

   ◆ Edit. Select a custom preset (not a predefined one), click **Edit**, change the options, and then click **OK**.

   ◆ Delete. Select a custom preset (not a predefined one), and then click **Delete**.

   ◆ Import. Click **Import**, navigate to the preset file, select it, and then click **Open**.

   ◆ Export. Select a preset, click **Export**, specify a location and name, and then click **Save**.

3. Click **OK**.

Transparency Flattener preset

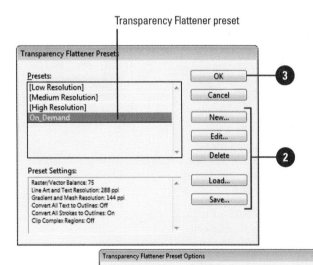

Setting Color Management Options

The Color Management category in the Print dialog box allows you to select a document profile for printing and a printer profile. A document profile and an output profile for a device can be different, so you can select color management options for the best results. In most cases, it's best to use the default options for Color Management unless you've been give specific instructions from a printer to change them.

Set Color Management Print Options

1. Click the **File** menu, and then click **Print**.

2. Click the **Color Management** category.

3. Select from the various Color Management options:

   ◆ **Print Profile.** Select an option: **Document** to use the current Document profile or **Proof** to emulate the profile for the device.

   ◆ **Color Handling.** Select a color option: **Let InDesign Determine Colors** or **Let PostScript Printer Determine Colors**.

   ◆ **Printer Profile.** Select the profile for your output device.

   ◆ **Preserve Color Numbers.** Select to preserve the color mode when a color profile is not available. Deselect to have InDesign convert colors for use on the output device.

   ◆ **Simulate Paper Color.** Select to simulate how colors look on paper for the output device.

4. When you're finished, click **Print**.

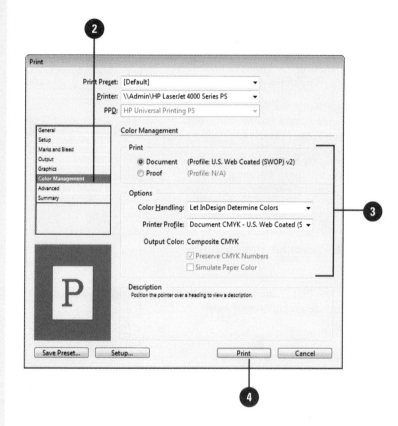

Creating a Print Summary

Before you print your document, it's important to check the Summary category in the Print dialog box. The summary information is good to check if you're having problems printing your job at a commercial printer. You can save the information and send it to the printer to help diagnose the problem.

View and Save Summary Print Options

1. Click the **File** menu, and then click **Print**.

2. Click the **Summary** category.

3. Scroll through the print summary to review your print settings.

4. To print the summary information to a file, click **Save Summary**, enter a name, specify a location, and then click **Save**.

5. When you're finished, click **Print**.

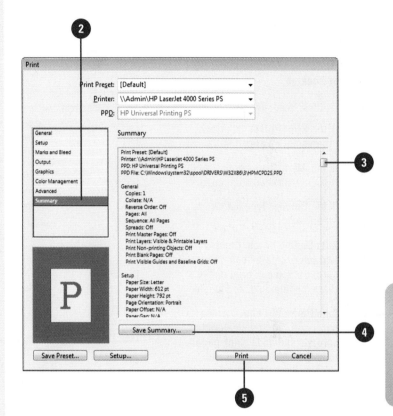

Printing Spreads in a Booklet

When you work on page spreads in a document, two pages appear side by side. However, when you print a document with spreads, the pages need to be arranged as imposing pages, also known as printer's spreads. For example, page one of a four-page project is paired with page four while page two and page three are paired together. You can arrange your document into imposing pages by using the Print Booklet command on the File menu.

Print Spreads in a Booklet

1. Click the **File** menu, and then click **Print Booklet**.

2. Click the **Setup** category.

3. Click the **Print Preset** list arrow, and then select a preset.

4. Click the **All** or **Range** option, and then specify a range as needed.

5. Click the **Booklet Type** list arrow, and then select an option:

    ◆ **2-up Saddle Stitch.** Creates two-page, side-by-side printer spreads. You can print on both sides, collate, fold, and staple.

    ◆ **2-up Perfect Bound.** Creates two-page, side-by-side printer spreads and adds blank pages to fit the signature. You can print on both sides, cut, and bind to a cover.

    ◆ **Consecutive.** Creates two-, three-, or four-page panels for a foldout booklet or brochure.

6. Specify the following values (options vary depending on the Booklet type):

    ◆ **Space Between Pages.** Specify the amount of space between pages.

    ◆ **Bleed Between Pages.** Specify the amount of space added around pages.

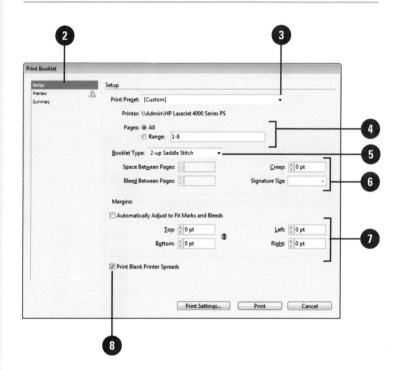

◆ **Creep.** Specify the amount of space for the thickness of folded pages.

◆ **Signature Size.** Specify the number of pages bound together.

7 Select the **Automatically Adjust to Fit Marks and Bleeds** check box to automatically fit printer's marks and bleeds. Deselect to enter your own values.

8 Select the **Print Blank Printer Spreads** check box to print empty page spreads.

9 Click the **Preview** category.

10 Scroll through the pages to preview the imposed pages.

11 Check the Messages and Warning boxes for information or problems that you should know about or fix before you print.

12 Click the **Summary** category.

13 Scroll through the print summary to review your print settings.

14 To print the summary information to a file, click **Save Summary**, enter a name, specify a location, and then click **Save**.

15 When you're finished, click **Print**.

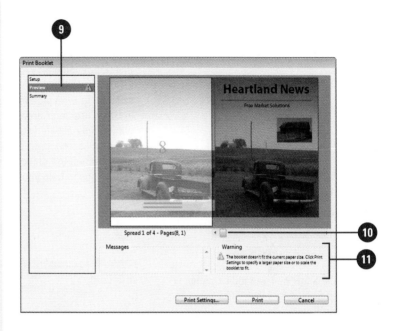

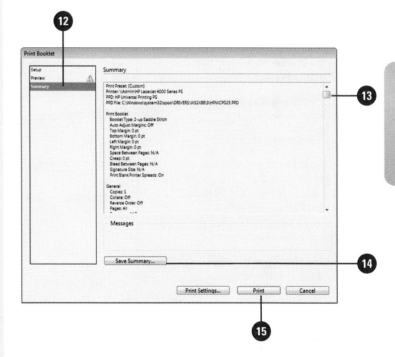

Using Live Preflight

ID 8.1

Before you print or send your document to a service provider, you should check your document for errors. Catching errors before you send out a print job can save you time and lower production costs. Instead of using an external program, you can use live preflighting in InDesign's Preflight panel (**New!**) to catch errors, such as missing files or fonts, low-resolution images, and overset text. You can use the built-in Basic profile or create one of your own to catch the type errors you want. If you create your own, you can embed the profile into your document for use on other computers. The Preflight panel lets you navigate to and select the objects that are triggering preflight errors. View contextual tips to help you correct errors directly in layout.

Create and Embed a Preflight Profile

1. Select the **Preflight** panel.

   ◆ Click the **Window** menu, point to **Output**, and then click **Preflight**.

   TIMESAVER *Double-click the Preflight icon on the bottom of the document window.*

2. Click the **Options** menu, and then click **Define Profiles**.

3. Click the **New Preflight Profile** button.

4. Enter a name for the profile.

5. Click the triangles to expand settings for each of the categories (**Links, Color, Images and Objects, Text,** and **Document**), and then select the options you want and deselect the ones you don't.

   A shaded check box indicates some items are selected.

6. Click **OK**.

7. Click the **Profile** list arrow, and then select a custom profile.

8. Click the **Embed** button on the panel.

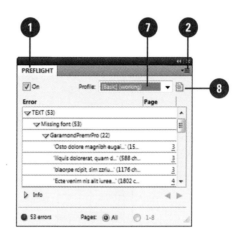

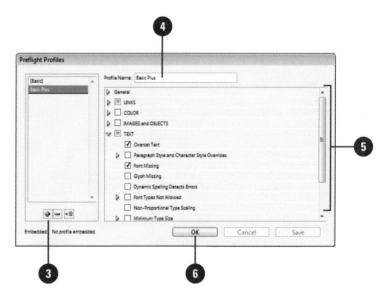

Use the Preflight Panel

1. Select the **Preflight** panel.
   - Click the **Window** menu, point to **Output**, and then click **Preflight**.

2. Use any of the following buttons or commands to perform an operation:
   - **Enable/Disable Live Preflight.** Select or deselect the **On** check box on the panel.
   - **Resolve Errors.** Double-click a row or page number, click the Info arrow to view information about the problem and suggestions for resolving it.
   - **Limit Number of Rows Per Error.** Click the **Options** menu, point to **Limit Number of Rows Per Error**, and then select a number or **No Limit**.
   - **Specify Pages.** Specify a page range or use **All** on the panel.
   - **Set Preflight Options.** Click the **Options** menu, click **Preflight Options**, select a profile, specify options for profile use, including layers, and other objects, and then click **OK**.
   - **Create a PDF Report.** Click the **Options** menu, click **Save Report**, specify a name and location, and then click **Save**.
   - **Delete a Profile.** Click the **Options** menu, click **Define Profiles**, select a profile, click the **Delete Preflight Profile** button, and then click **OK**.
   - **Unembed a Profile.** Click the **Options** menu, click **Define Profiles**, select a profile, click the **Preflight Profile** menu, and then click **Unembed Profile**.

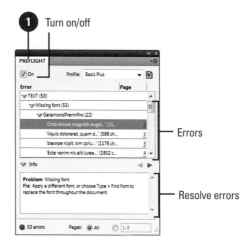

Turn on/off

Errors

Resolve errors

Preflight options

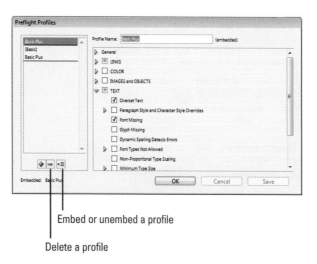

Embed or unembed a profile

Delete a profile

Inserting File Information

When you save a document, you have the ability to save more than just InDesign information. You can save copyright, camera, and even image category information. This data is saved with the file as metadata in the XMP format (Extensible Metadata Platform) in InDesign files, and can be recognized and accessed by any application, such as Adobe Bridge, that reads XMP metadata. In addition, if an image is a photograph, you can save data specifying the type of image, where it was shot, or the camera used. You can even get information on shutter speed and f-stop. You can do the same with video and audio data. That information will not only protect your intellectual property, but will supply you with vital statistics on exactly how you created that one-of-a-kind document.

Insert File Information into a Document

1. Open a document.

2. Click the **File** menu, and then click **File Info**.

3. Click the **Description** tab, and then enter information concerning the document title, description of file, author and any copyright information.

4. Click the **IPTC** tab to enter information concerning the image's creator, description and keywords, location where photograph was taken, date created, copyright, and usage terms.

5. Click the **Camera Data** tab, which reveals information about the camera that took the image.

6. Click the **Video Data** tab or **Audio Data** tab to reveal information about video and audio data, and then enter any custom video and audio data.

7. Click the **Mobile SWF** tab, and then enter the file information for a mobile SWF document.

8. Click the **Categories** tab, and then enter category keywords for search purposes.

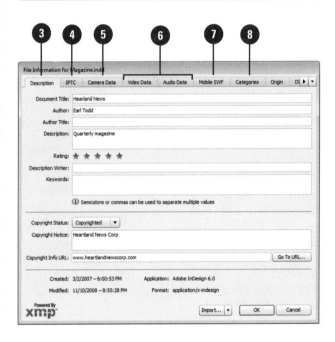

9 Click the **Origin** tab, and then enter data pertaining to the origin of the image.

10 Click the **DICOM** tab, and then enter data pertaining to the Digital Imaging and Communications in Medicine options (patient name, ID, etc.).

11 Click the **History** tab to view historical information about the active document, such as dates last opened and saved, and a list of image adjustments.

12 Click the **Illustrator** tab, and then select an Illustrator document profile.

13 Click the **Advanced** tab to view additional information on the active document, such as EXIF, and PDF document properties.

14 Click the **Raw Data** tab to view raw RDF/XML information.

15 Click **OK**.

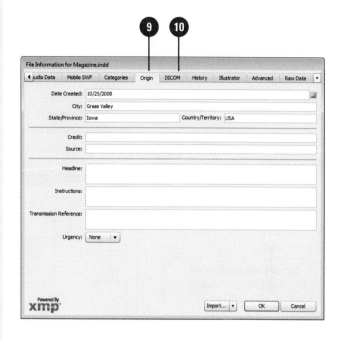

Did You Know?

You can add metadata to files saved in the PSD, PDF, EPS, PNG, GIF, JPEG, and TIFF formats. The information is embedded in the file using XMP (Extensible Metadata Platform). This allows metadata to be exchanged between Adobe applications and across operating systems.

You can use the XMP Software Development Kit to customize the creation, processing, and interchange of metadata. You can also use the XMP kit to add fields to the File Info dialog box. For information on XMP and the XMP SDK, check the Adobe Solutions Network.

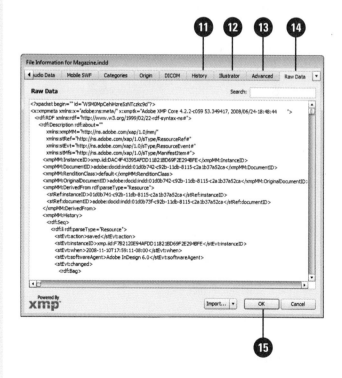

Creating a Package

A package file gathers all the files related to your document, including linked graphics and fonts, to make it easy to deliver to a printer or service provider. During the packaging process, you can display any problems, so you can fix them before you continue. When you create a package, you create a folder that contains your document, linked graphics, text files, any fonts, and a customized report. The report includes information about all the files in the package and any printer instructions required to print your document.

Create a Package

1. Click the **File** menu, and then click **Package**.

2. Review the summary information for your document.

3. Select the **Show Data For Hidden and Non-Printing Layers** check box to show the data and layers in the Package.

4. Select the **Fonts** category.

5. Select the **Show Problems Only** check box to view any problems with fonts.

   ◆ If there are any problems, select the font, and then click **Find Font** to locate and fix the problem.

6. Select the **Links and Images** category.

7. Select the **Show Problems Only** check box to view any problems with links and images.

   ◆ If there are any problems, select it, and then click **Update** to locate and fix the problem or click **Repair All**.

8. Select the **Colors and Inks**, **Print Settings**, and **External Plug-ins** categories, and then view the current settings.

9. To create a report, click **Report**, enter a name, specify a location, and then click **Save**.

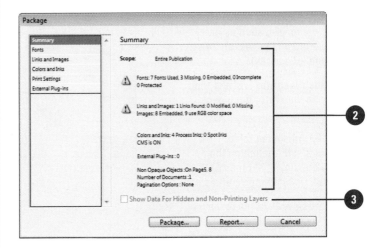

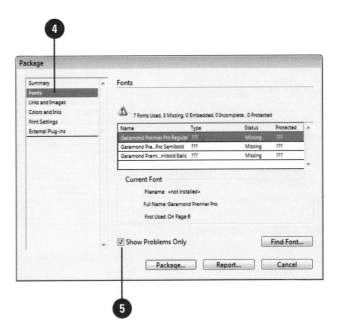

10 Click **Package**.

◆ If prompted, click **Save** to save your document.

11 Enter contact information in the Printing Instructions dialog box, and then click **Continue**.

12 Enter a name for the package, and then specify a location.

13 Select/Deselect any of the following check boxes:

◆ **Copy Fonts (Except CJK).** Copies all fonts used in your document, except double-byte fonts, such as Japanese.

◆ **Copy Linked Graphics.** Copies linked images. Embedded images stay with the document.

◆ **Update Graphic Links In Package.** Updates any modified linked graphics.

◆ **Use Document Hyphenation Exceptions Only.** Uses only the hyphenation exceptions from the document.

◆ **Include Fonts and Links From Hidden and Non-Printing Content.** Includes fonts and graphic links from hidden and non-printing items.

◆ **View Report.** Opens a text editor and the package report.

14 Click **Package**.

◆ If a warning alert appears, click **OK**.

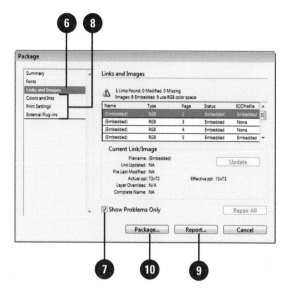

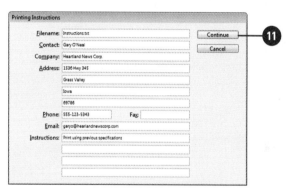

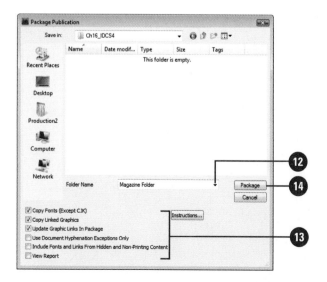

Customizing the Way You Work

17

Introduction

No description of Adobe InDesign would be complete without that well-known, but little utilized area called Preferences. InDesign preferences serve several purposes. They help customize the program to your particular designing style, and they help you utilize available computer resources to increase the overall performance of the program.

As you use InDesign, you'll come to realize the importance of working with units and rulers. Precision is the name of the game when you are working with graphic designs and text. What about the color of your guides and grids? No big deal, you say. Well, if you've ever tried viewing a blue guide against predominantly blue artwork, you know exactly why guide color is important. By setting your own preferences, such as Display Performance, you can increase speed by up to 20%.

In addition, customizing the program helps make you more comfortable, and studies show that the more comfortable you are as a designer, the better your designs. Plus, being comfortable allows you to work faster, and that means you'll accomplish more in the same amount of time. What does setting up preferences do for you? They make InDesign run faster, you work more efficiently, and your designs are better. That's a pretty good combination. InDesign doesn't give you Preferences to confuse you, but to give you choices, and those choices give you control.

Setting General Preferences

InDesign's General preferences help you configure some of the more general features of the program. Some of the options include how to implement page numbering, font downloading and embedding, and text scaling. You can also enable or disable the use of JavaScript in your document. Disabling JavaScript can protect your computer from harmful security threats. Enable it only when you know the script is safe. You can also click the Reset All Warning Dialogs to allow warnings for which you previously selected the Don't Show Again check box.

Set General Preferences

1. Click the **Edit** (Win) or **InDesign** (Mac) menu, and then point to **Preferences**.

2. Click **General**.

   TIMESAVER *Ctrl+K (Win) or* ⌘+K *(Mac).*

3. Select the various options you want to use:

   ◆ **Page Numbering View.** Select **Absolute Number** to use the physical placement number of the page or **Section Numbering** to use section numbers.

   ◆ **Font Downloading and Embedding.** Enter a minimum number of glyphs to activate the use subset of fonts.

   ◆ **When Scaling.** Select **Apply to Content** to scale text with point size changes or **Adjust Scaling Percentage** to scale text with point size changes, but still display new and old scale.

   ◆ **Scripting.** Select to use scripts. Deselect to prevent scripts from being executed.

   ◆ **Reset All Warning Dialogs.** Click to allow warnings for which you previously selected the Don't Show Again check box.

4. Click **OK**.

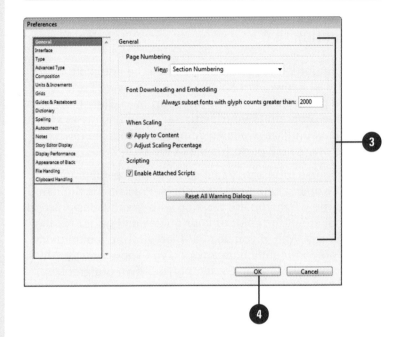

Setting Interface Preferences

Interface preferences give you control over some user interface features. When you place text or graphics or transform objects, the cursor changes to display information. If you prefer not to see the information, you can deselect cursor options. In addition, you can also set options to automatically collapse icon panels or show hidden panels when you click away from them, and instruct InDesign to allow you to open documents as tabs instead of individual document windows.

Set Interface Preferences

1 Click the **Edit** (Win) or **InDesign** (Mac) menu, and then point to **Preferences**.

2 Click **Interface**.

3 Select the various options you want to use:

◆ **Tool Tips.** Specify an option for showing tips when you point to an onscreen element, such as a button. Select Normal, None, or Fast.

◆ **Show Thumbnails on Place.** Select to show the text or graphic preview with the loaded cursor when you place an item.

◆ **Show Transformation Values.** Select to show transformation values in a gray tag as you size, rotate, or create an object (**New!**).

◆ **Floating Tools Panel.** Specify an option for displaying the Tools panel.

◆ **Auto-Collapse Icon Panels.** Select to have an expanded panel icon automatically collapse when you click away.

◆ **Auto-Show Hidden Panels.** Select to have a hidden panel icon automatically revealed when you click away (**New!**).

◆ **Open Documents as Tabs.** Select to open documents in tabbed windows. Deselect to open as floating windows.

4 Click **OK**.

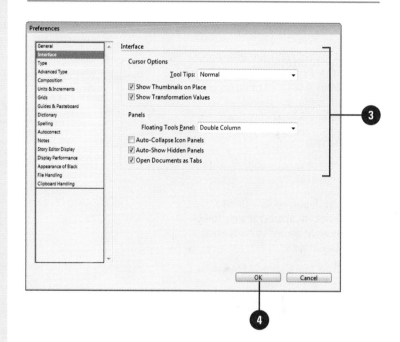

Setting Type Preferences

InDesign is by definition a typesetting application, so it contains some very powerful type features. For example, Adobe InDesign allows you to set options to customize the way you display, select, and drag-and-drop text. In addition, InDesign's type menu lets you see fonts exactly as they will print or display. For designers who use a lot of fonts, this WYSIWYG (What You See Is What You Get) font menu is a timesaver. Instead of manually threading text from text frame to text frame, you can let InDesign add or remove pages automatically when you type text or change your text flow (**New!**). You can use Type preferences to help you select the type and font options you want to use.

Set Type Preferences

1. Click the **Edit** (Win) or **InDesign** (Mac) menu, and then point to **Preferences**.

2. Click **Type**.

3. Select the various options you want to use:

   ◆ **Use Typographer's Quotes.** Select to automatically change straight quotes to curly quotes as you type.

   ◆ **Type Tool Converts Frames to Text Frames.** Select to be able to double-click a frame to change from one of the Selection tools to the Type tool.

   ◆ **Automatically Use Correct Optical Size.** Select to automatically set the correct value for the optical size of multiple master fonts.

   ◆ **Triple Click to Select a Line.** Select to use triple-click to select a line. Deselect to use triple-click to select a paragraph.

   ◆ **Apply Leading to Entire Paragraphs.** Select to apply leading to an entire paragraph.

   ◆ **Adjust Spacing Automatically When Cutting and Pasting.** Select to prevent from adding two spaces when pasting text from one location to another.

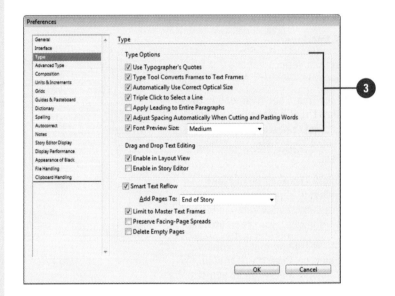

- ◆ **Font Preview Size.** Select to enable font preview on the Type menu, and then specify the size of the preview fonts (Medium is default). The Large option takes longer to display.

4 Select the Drag and Drop Text Editing options you want to use:

- ◆ **Enable in Layout View.** Select to enable drag-and-drop text within frames.

- ◆ **Enable in Story Editor.** Select to enable drag-and-drop text within the Story Editor.

5 Select the Smart Text Reflow options (**New!**) you want to use:

- ◆ **Smart Text Reflow.** Select to enable Smart Text Reflow.

- ◆ **Limit to Master Text Frames.** Select to limit the use of reflowed text to master text frames.

- ◆ **Preserve Facing-Page Spreads.** Select to preserve facing-page spreads during a reflow of text to new pages.

- ◆ **Delete Empty Pages.** Select to delete empty pages when text is removed during a reflow.

6 Click **OK**.

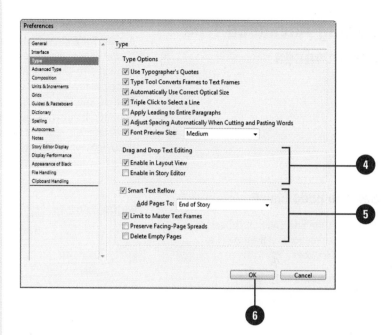

Did You Know?

You can set text to be greeked. Greeked text describes text that appears as a gray band when it's too small to display individual characters. Click the Edit (Win) or InDesign (Mac) menu, point to Preferences, click Display Performance, enter a minimum greek level, and then click OK.

Setting Advanced Type Preferences

Advanced Type preferences allow you to control text character setting options for superscript, subscript and small caps, and specify the language you want to use. For superscript, subscript and small caps, you can set size and position values to control the size and position above or below the baseline of characters. Latin typefaces, such as English, French, and Spanish, use a different character structure than other non-latin languages, such as Japanese, Korean, and Chinese. If you want to use a non-Latin language, you need to enable an option to use the Windows or Macintosh operating system controls for language input.

Set Advanced Type Preferences

1. Click the **Edit** (Win) or **InDesign** (Mac) menu, and then point to **Preferences**.

2. Click **Advanced Type**.

3. Select the following options for the size and position of text for **Superscript**, **Subscript**, and **Small Cap** text:

   ◆ **Character Settings for Size.** Enter Size values to control the size of characters.

   ◆ **Character Settings for Position.** Enter Position values to control text position above or below the baseline.

4. Select the **Use Inline Input for Non-Latin Text** check box to use non-latin text, such as Japanese, Korean, and Chinese, for the Windows and Macintosh operating systems.

5. Click **OK**.

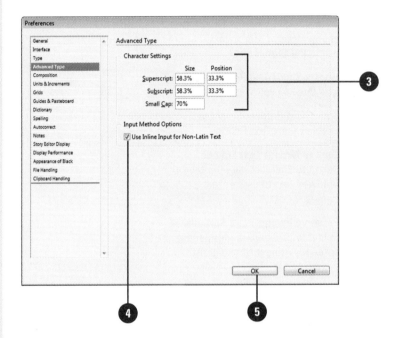

Setting Composition Preferences

Composition preferences enable the program to highlight text when composition or typographic violations and substitutions are made by InDesign based on other settings, and control how text wraps around an object. For example, you can highlight text with tracking or kerning applied or substituted fonts or Open Type characters with glyphs. When you wrap text around an object, you can set options to justify text, and adjust leading, change text position.

Set Composition Preferences

1. Click the **Edit** (Win) or **InDesign** (Mac) menu, and then point to **Preferences**.

2. Click **Composition**.

3. Select the various options you want to use:

   ◆ **Keep Violations.** Select to display lines that violate Keep With settings.

   ◆ **H&J Violations.** Select to highlight text that violate hyphenation or justification settings.

   ◆ **Custom Tracking/Kerning.** Select to highlight text with tracking or kerning applied.

   ◆ **Substituted Fonts.** Select to highlight substituted fonts.

   ◆ **Substituted Glyphs.** Select to highlight substituted Open Type characters with glyphs.

   ◆ **Justify Text Next to an Object.** Select to justify text that is wrapped around an object.

   ◆ **Skip by Leading.** Select to adjust text to the next leading increment that is wrapped around an object.

   ◆ **Text Wrap Only Affects Text Beneath.** Select to wrap text around an object only below the object.

4. Click **OK**.

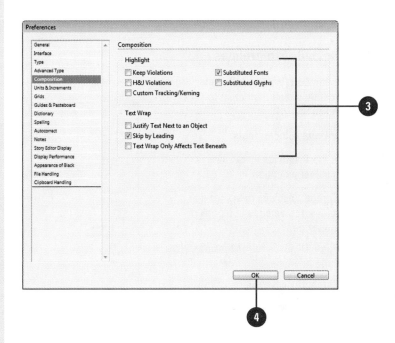

Setting Units & Increments Preferences

Units & Increments preferences allow you to set ruler measurement units, the number of points per inch, and the amount that keyboard shortcuts change text. When you use a ruler in a document, InDesign uses the settings in the Ruler Units section to display the ruler with the measurement system and origin you want. You can also set the number of points per inch. Typically this is set to PostScript (72 pts/inch). This is the recommended setting unless a commercial printer asks you to change it. When you change text, such as size/leading, baseline shift, or kerning/tracking using keyboard shortcuts, you can specify the amounts you want to apply for each keystroke.

Set Ruler Units Preferences

1. Click the **Edit** (Win) or **InDesign** (Mac) menu, and then point to **Preferences**.

2. Click **Units & Increments**.

3. Click the **Origin** list arrow, and then select an option:

   ◆ **Spread.** Displays rulers for two pages at a time, as in a book or magazine.

   ◆ **Page.** Displays rulers for one page at a time.

   ◆ **Spine.** Displays rulers for the area where two page spreads are bound together.

4. Click the **Horizontal** and **Vertical** list arrows, and then select a measurement from the available options.

   ◆ If you selected **Custom**, enter the number of points for each unit on the ruler.

5. To set an exact number for points per inch, click the **Points/Inch** list arrow, and then select an option.

6. Click **OK**.

   IMPORTANT *If the Rulers are not visible in the active document, click the View menu, and then click Show Rulers.*

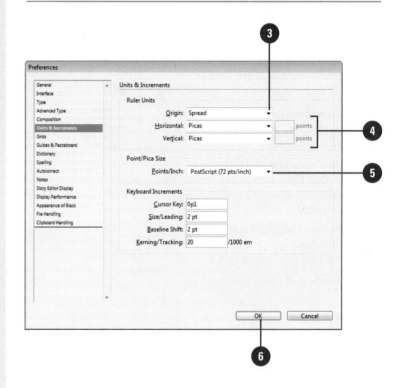

Set Keyboard Increments Preferences

1. Click the **Edit** (Win) or **InDesign** (Mac) menu, and then point to **Preferences**.

2. Click **Units & Increments**.

3. Enter the Keyboard Increment values you want to use:

   ◆ **Cursor Key.** Enter a value to move objects with the arrows keys.

   ◆ **Size/Leading.** Enter a default value to control type size and leading.

   ◆ **Baseline Shift.** Enter a default value to control text baseline shift.

   ◆ **Kerning/Tracking.** Enter a default value to control text kerning and tracking.

4. Click **OK**.

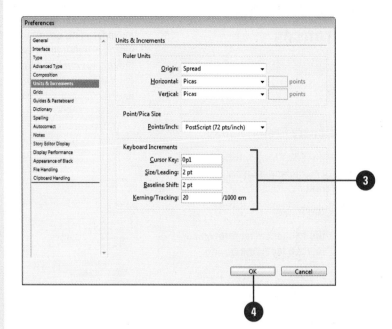

Setting Dictionary Preferences

Dictionary preferences allow you to specify and use different languages and dictionaries for text in your documents and set options to avoid flagging correctly spelled words as unrecognized words. Many words are flagged as misspelled because of hyphenation. You can set options for hyphenation exceptions to reduce the annoyance. If you work with a unique set of words for your profession, you can create a new dictionary, which you can share with others.

Set Dictionary Preferences

1. Click the **Edit** (Win) or **InDesign** (Mac) menu, and then point to **Preferences**.

2. Click **Dictionary**.

3. Click the **Language** list arrow, and then select a language for the dictionary.

4. Use any of the following to work with User Dictionaries:

   - **Relink User Dictionary.** Relinks an existing dictionary that has been moved to another folder.

   - **New User Dictionary.** Creates a new user dictionary.

   - **Add User Dictionary.** Adds an existing user dictionary for use in your documents.

   - **Remove User Dictionary.** Removes a user dictionary from the list. The default dictionary cannot be deleted.

5. Select the various options you want to use:

   - **Hyphenation.** For installed special hyphenation preferences, select a preference option.

   - **Spelling.** For installed special spelling preferences, select a preference option.

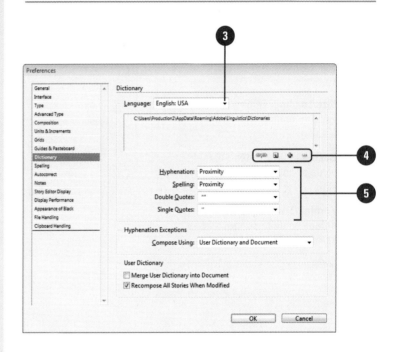

416

◆ **Double Quotes.** Specify a default style for double quotation marks.

◆ **Single Quotes.** Specify a default style for single quotation marks.

6 Click the **Compose Using** list arrow, and then select an option to apply hyphenation exceptions:

◆ **User Dictionary.** Uses only the hyphenation exceptions set by editing the dictionary.

◆ **Document.** Uses the hyphenation exceptions list in the document.

◆ **User Dictionary and Document.** Merges the hyphenation exceptions in the user dictionary and document.

7 Select the User Dictionary options you want to use:

◆ **Merge User Dictionary into Document.** Select to merge the hyphenation exceptions in the document with the user dictionary.

◆ **Recompose All Stories When Modified.** Select to apply the new hyphenation exceptions in the user dictionary or any added or deleted dictionary words to all stories in the document.

8 Click **OK**.

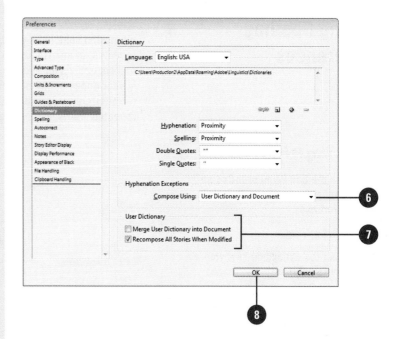

Setting Spelling Preferences

Spelling preferences allow you to set options to control what types of words and sentences get flagged as unrecognized, misspelled, repeated, or incorrectly capitalized in the spelling checker, and enable and set options for dynamic spelling. Dynamic spelling highlights errors in your document as they happen. You can specify underline colors for the different types of errors that appear, such as misspelled words, repeated words, and uncapitalized word or sentences.

Set Spelling Preferences

1. Click the **Edit** (Win) or **InDesign** (Mac) menu, and then point to **Preferences**.

2. Click **Spelling**.

3. Select the various options you want to use:

   ◆ **Misspelled Words.** Select to find and flag unrecognized words in the spelling dictionary.

   ◆ **Repeated Words.** Select to find and flag repeated words next to each other in a document. For example, "The the Spelling preferences dialog box ..."

   ◆ **Uncapitalized Words.** Select to find and flag uncapitalized proper nouns in the spelling dictionary (for example, proper name, such as "Steve").

   ◆ **Uncapitalized Sentences.** Select to find and flag uncapitalized words in the spelling dictionary that begin sentences.

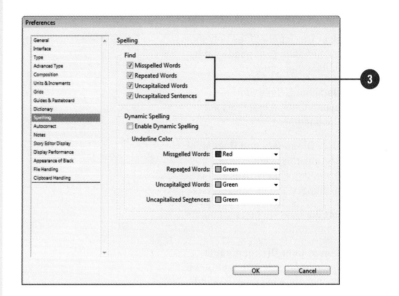

4 Select the Dynamic Spelling options you want to use:

◆ **Enable Dynamic Spelling.** Select to enable dynamic spelling, which highlights errors in your document as they occur.

◆ **Misspelled Words.** Select a color to highlight unrecognized words in the spelling dictionary.

◆ **Repeated Words.** Select a color to highlight repeated words next to each other in a document. For example, "The the Spelling preferences dialog box ..."

◆ **Uncapitalized Words.** Select a color to highlight uncapitalized proper words in the spelling dictionary (for example, proper name, such as "Steve").

◆ **Uncapitalized Sentences.** Select a color to highlight uncapitalized words in the spelling dictionary that begin sentences.

5 Click **OK**.

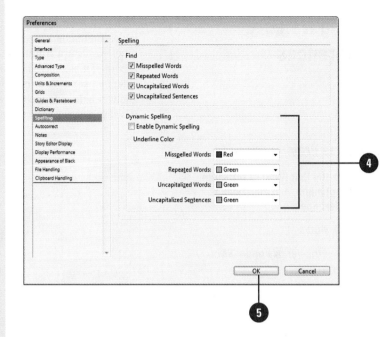

Setting Notes Preferences

When you work with more than one person on the same document, it's important to communicate changes and other information with each other. Notes are a great way to communicate with others and keep a record of it along with the document. Notes preferences allow you to select a user note color to make it easier to identify who wrote notes, show or hide note tooltips, and specify whether to include Notes text when you check spelling or use the Find/Change command.

Set Notes Preferences

1. Click the **Edit** (Win) or **InDesign** (Mac) menu, and then point to **Preferences**.

2. Click **Notes**.

3. Select the various options you want to use:

   ◆ **Note Color.** Specify a color for user notes.

   ◆ **Show Note Tooltips.** Select to display the text for a note when you point to it.

   ◆ **Include Note Content When Checking Spelling.** Select to check spelling for text in notes.

   ◆ **Include Note Content in Find/Change Operations.** Select to include text from notes in the Find/Change command on the Edit menu.

   ◆ **Inline Background Color.** Specify a background color for notes in the Story Editor.

4. Click **OK**.

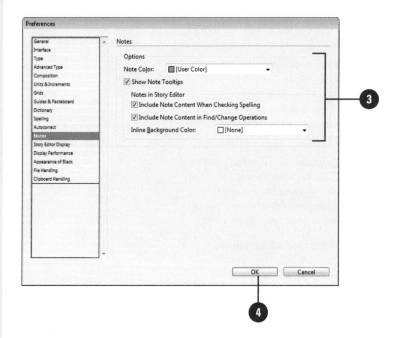

Working with Appearance of Black Preferences

If a printer uses a combination of CMYK inks instead of the actual 100K black tone to create a rich black look, you can set options in the Appearance of Black preferences to specify how you want to create the appearance of black in your documents. There are two available options to determine the appearance of black in your document: one for On Screen and another one for Printing/Exporting. Each of the options allows you to specify how you want to work with the appearance of black (true black or rich black) in your documents.

Work with Appearance of Black Preferences

1 Click the **Edit** (Win) or **InDesign** (Mac) menu, and then point to **Preferences**.

2 Click **Appearance of Black**.

3 Select from the following Appearance of Black options:

◆ **On Screen.** Select **Display All Blacks Accurately** to display blacks based on actual CMYK color values or select **Display All Blacks as Rich Black** to display all blacks as rich blacks (a mix of CMYK values).

◆ **Printing / Exporting.** Select **Output All Blacks Accurately** to print blacks using actual CMYK color values on RGB and grayscale devices, or select **Output All Blacks as Rich Black** to print blacks as rich blacks (a mix of CMYK values) on RGB devices.

4 Select the **Overprint [Black] Swatch at 100%** check box to improve printing or saving separations for objects that use the [Black] (100K) swatch. This applies to PostScript and PDF output. Deselect to knock out objects below.

5 Click **OK**.

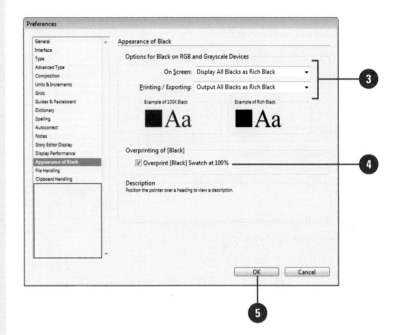

Setting Story Editor Display Preferences

The Story Editor is a separate window that only displays the text in your document. This is helpful when you want to focus just on the text and not on any of the other elements in your document. Story Editor Display preferences allow you to set text and background display options for the Story Editor window. You can specify the display font, font size, line spacing, text color, background or theme, and cursor or insertion point, style. A theme is a preset background and text color. If you want to display smoother text, you can enable the anti-aliasing option and select the type of anti-aliasing that best works for you. If the insertion point cursor is hard to see in the Story Editor, you can select cursor options to make it easier to see.

Set Story Editor Display Preferences

1 Click the **Edit** (Win) or **InDesign** (Mac) menu, and then point to **Preferences**.

2 Click **Story Editor Display**.

3 Select the Text Display options you want to use:

◆ **Font.** Specify a font typeface.

◆ **Font Size.** Specify a font size.

◆ **Line Spacing.** Specify a line spacing option: Singlespace, 150% space, Doublespace, or Triplespace.

◆ **Text Color.** Specify a text color.

◆ **Background.** Specify a background color.

◆ **Theme.** Specify a preset font color and background: Ink on Paper, Amber Monochrome, Classic System, or Terminal.

4 Select the **Enable Anti-aliasing** check box to soften the edges of text.

5 If you selected the Enable Anti-aliasing check box, click the **Type** list arrow, and then select one of the following options:

◆ **Default.** Uses normal anti-aliasing.

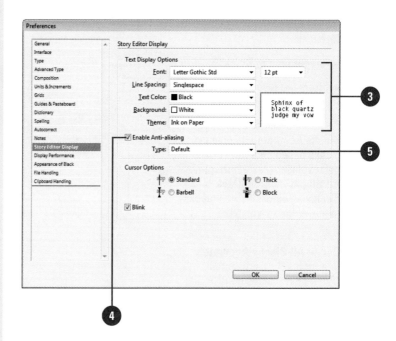

- **LCD Optimized.** Optimizes the display for light colored backgrounds with black text.

- **Soft.** Creates a softer look than the default setting.

6 Select the Cursor options you want to use:

- **Cursor.** Select a cursor display type: Standard (default), Barbell, Thick, or Block.

- **Blink.** Select to have the cursor blink on and off within the text.

7 Click **OK**.

Did You Know?

You can select or deselect anti-aliasing for display performance. Click the Edit (Win) or InDesign (Mac) menu, point to Preferences, click Display Performance, select the Enable Anti-aliasing check box, and then click OK.

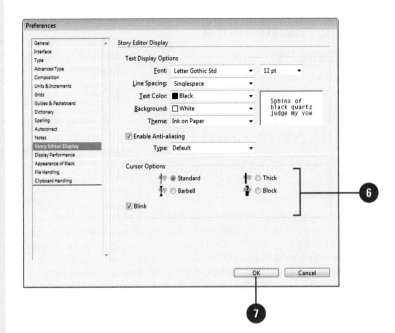

Setting File Handling Preferences

File Handling preferences allow you to specify a document recovery data folder, create a preview thumbnail with saved documents, control the location of imported snippets when you drag them into a document, and control how graphic links are maintained and updated. You can also specify the number of files you want to display in the Recent Items list on the Welcome Screen or the Open Recent submenu on the File menu.

Set File Handling Preferences

1. Click the **Edit** (Win) or **InDesign** (Mac) menu, and then point to **Preferences**.

2. Click **File Handling**.

3. To specify a document recovery data folder, click **Browse** (Win) or **Choose** (Mac), navigate to the folder, and then click **Select**.

4. Select the Saving InDesign Files options you want to use:

   ◆ **Number of Recent Items to Display.** Specify the number of files you want to display in the Recent Items list on the Welcome Screen or on the Open Recent submenu on the File menu.

   ◆ **Always Save Preview Images with Documents.** Select to save a preview image of the InDesign document along with the document for preview purposes in Open dialog boxes and other thumbnails.

   Click the **Preview Size** list arrow, and then select a thumbnail size.

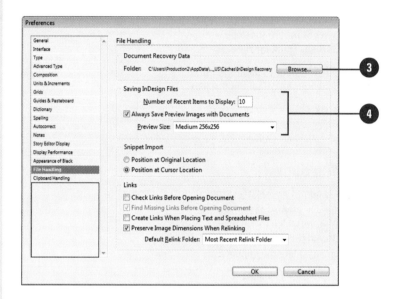

5 Select the Snippet Import option you want to use when you drag a snippet onto a page:

◆ **Position at Original Location.** Places the snippet at its original location.

◆ **Position at Cursor Location.** Places the snippet at the current cursor location instead of the original location.

6 Select the Links options you want to use:

◆ **Check Links Before Opening Document.** Select to check graphic links before opening a document (**New!**).

◆ **Find Missing Links Before Opening Document.** Select to prompt you to locate missing linked graphics before opening a document (**New!**).

◆ **Create Links When Placing Text and Spreadsheet Files.** Select to create links to styles from original text and spreadsheet files to your new document.

◆ **Preserve Image Dimensions When Relinking.** Select to maintain graphic size when relinking the file (**New!**).

7 Click **OK**.

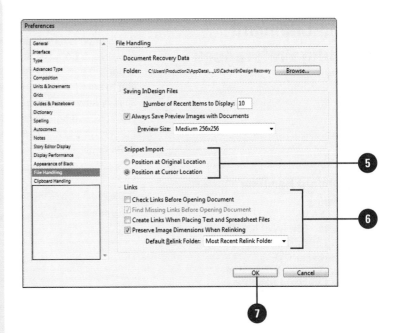

Did You Know?

You can restore preferences and default settings. Sometimes the file that stores all of your preferences and default settings gets corrupted. If so, you can restore it. As you start InDesign, press Ctrl+Alt+Shift (Win) or ⌘+Option+Shift+Control (Mac).

Setting Clipboard Handling Preferences

When you copy and paste information into an InDesign document, the information is temporarily stored on the Clipboard until something else replaces it. Copying and pasting information from other programs is an important part of creating an InDesign document, so InDesign allows you to set Clipboard preferences. Clipboard preferences allow you to specify how you want information to be pasted into a document. For example, you can have graphics or data pasted into a document as a PDF file, or paste text and tables from other programs with or without formatting.

Set Clipboard Handling Preferences

1. Click the **Edit** (Win) or **InDesign** (Mac) menu, and then point to **Preferences**.

2. Click **Clipboard Handling**.

3. Select the Clipboard options you want to use:

   ◆ **Prefer PDF When Pasting.** Select to paste graphics as independent PDF files.

   ◆ **Copy PDF to Clipboard.** Select to copy data as PDF files.

   ◆ **Preserve PDF Data at Quit.** Select to maintain copied PDF information on the Clipboard when you exit InDesign.

4. Click the **All Information or Text Only** option to either maintain formatting for all imported information or remove formatting for imported plain text.

5. Click **OK**.

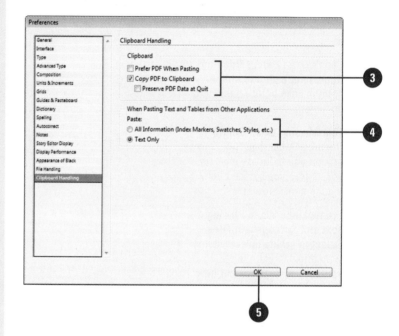

Defining Shortcut Keys

A wise man once wrote "time is money," and InDesign is a program that can consume a lot of time. That's why the InDesign application uses keyboard shortcuts. **Keyboard Shortcuts**, as their name implies, let you perform tasks in a shorter period of time. For example, if you want to open a new document in InDesign, you can click the File menu, and then click New, or you can abandon the mouse and press Ctrl+N (Win) or ⌘+N (Mac) to use shortcut keys. Using shortcut keys reduces the use of the mouse and speeds up operations. InDesign raises the bar by not only giving you hundreds of possible shortcut keys, but also actually allowing you to define your own shortcuts. In fact, you can select options to create shortcuts for menus, panels, tools, and object editing (**New!**), such as scaling and sizing objects. In addition to adding shortcuts, you can delete any of them you don't want and even print out a summary of shortcuts defined in InDesign.

Create or Edit a Keyboard Shortcut

1. Click the **Edit** menu, and then click **Keyboard Shortcuts**.

2. Click the **Set** list arrow, and then select a set.

3. Click the **Product Area** list arrow, and then select the area that contains the command for which you want to create or edit a shortcut.

4. Select an item from the Commands list.

5. Use the keyboard to create or change the shortcut. For example, press Ctrl+N (Win) or ⌘+N (Mac), and then click **Assign**.

6. Click **OK**.

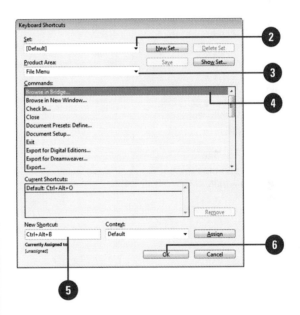

Did You Know?

You can print out a list of keyboard shortcuts. Click the Edit menu, click Keyboard Shortcuts, select a set, click Show Set to display the shortcuts in Notepad (Win) or TextEdit (Mac), and then print the text file.

For Your Information

Working with Keyboard Shortcuts Sets

A set is a collection of keyboard shortcuts, such as Shortcuts for PageMaker 7.0 and Shortcuts for QuarkXPress 4.0. You can create your own set or modify an existing one. Click the Edit menu, click Keyboard Shortcuts, and then use the appropriate buttons, such as Save (Shortcut Set), Delete Set (Shortcut Set), Remove (remove shortcut), or New Set (create Shortcut Set) to perform the tasks you want.

Customizing Menus

InDesign's pull-down menus actually contain hundreds of options (yes, I did say hundreds). If you find navigating through menus a hassle, then Adobe has the answer to your problem with a customizable user interface. In InDesign, you have the ability to choose what menu items appear on the pull-down menus and you can even colorize certain menu items for easier visibility.

Customize Menus

1. Click the **Edit** menu, and then click **Menus**.

2. Click the **Set** list arrow, and then select a listing of modified User Interfaces (if available) or customize the InDesign Defaults set to make your own.

3. To create a new set based on the current active set, click **Save As**, enter a name, and then click **Save**.

4. Click the **Category** list arrow, and then click **Application Menus** or **Context & Panel Menus** with the items you want to modify.

5. Click an arrow (left column) to expand the menu that contains the command you want to modify.

6. Click the **Visibility** icon associated with a command to show or hide the command.

7. Click the **Color** list arrow, and select a color for the selected command.

8. Click **Save** to save the new customized User Interface.

9. Click **OK**.

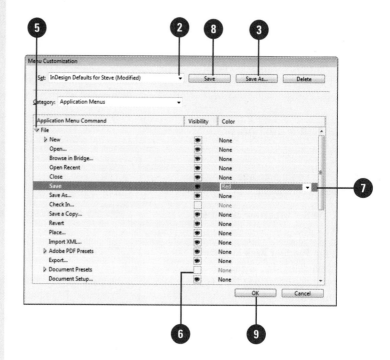

Configuring Plug-Ins

Plug-ins are external programs that provide additional functionality for the program. InDesign uses plug-ins to perform standard operations in the program. If you want to add more functionality, you can import a plug-in. Check the Adobe web site at *www.adobe.com* for information on the different plug-ins that are available for InDesign. The Configure Plug-ins dialog box gives you the ability to work with InDesign plug-ins. Typical plug-in options include enabling, disabling, deleting, and importing plug-ins.

Configure Plug-Ins

1. Click the **Help** (Win) or **InDesign** (Mac) menu, and then click Configure Plug-ins.

2. Click the **Set** list arrow, and then select a set, such as **All Plug-ins**, **Adobe Plug-ins**, or **Required Plug-ins**.

3. Select the plug-in you want to change.

4. Select check box options for **Enabled**, **Disabled**, **Adobe**, **Third Party**, **Required**, or **Optional**.

5. Use any of the following buttons to perform an operation:

   ◆ **Duplicate.** Click to duplicate the selected plug-in.

   ◆ **Rename.** Click to rename the selected plug-in.

   ◆ **Delete.** Click to remove the selected plug-in.

   ◆ **Import.** Click to import a plug-in.

   ◆ **Export.** Click to export a plug-in.

   ◆ **Show Info.** Click to display information about the selected plug-in.

6. Click **OK**.

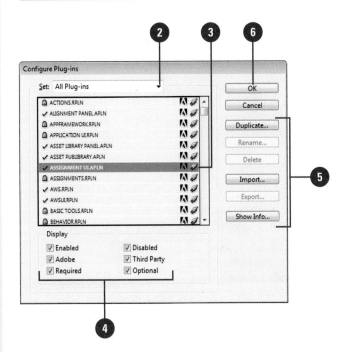

Customizing the Control Panel

The Control panel appears at the top of the document window. The Control panel displays the options for the currently selected tool. However, if you want to display additional tools, you can use the Customize Control Panel dialog box to select the tools you want or remove the ones you don't. If you prefer the Control panel in a different location, you can select options on the Control Panel menu (located on the far right-side of the panel).

Customize the Control Panel

1 Click the **Control Panel** menu, and then click **Customize**.

2 Click the triangle to expand the settings category.

3 Select or deselect the check boxes with the options you want and don't want on the Control panel.

4 Click **OK**.

5 To change the position of the Control panel, click the **Control Panel** menu, and then select one of the following:

- ◆ **Dock at Top.** Docks the Control panel at the top of the document window.

- ◆ **Dock at Bottom.** Docks the Control panel at the bottom of the document window.

- ◆ **Float.** Undocks the Control panel into a floating window.

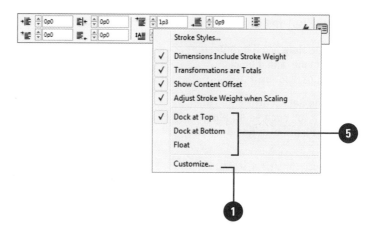

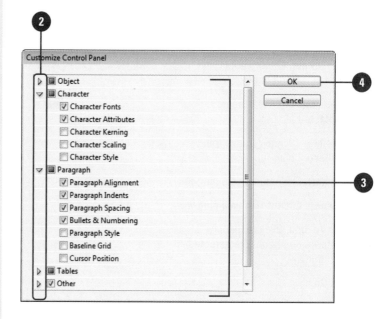

Collaborating with Others

18

Introduction

Adobe InCopy is a stand-alone writing and editing program that allows you to work seamlessly with Adobe InDesign. The integration with InCopy allows InDesign users to select text and graphics in a document, and then assign the content to InCopy users for writing and editing.

Exporting content from InDesign allows you to make content available to InCopy users to check out and change while still maintaining a link back to the original document. After you export content to InCopy, the file is called a managed file. Icons appear at the top left of the exported frame in InDesign and InCopy, and in the Assignments panel to indicate the content is currently assigned to another user for changes.

The Assignments panel is a centralized place to work with content assignment in InDesign. The panel displays the content files exported from the current document and an icon indicating the status of the content. You can use buttons on the bottom of the panel to quickly identify the assigned user, update content, check out content, create new assignments, and delete assignments.

Before you can open and edit an assignment file, the content needs to be checked out. This prevents two users from accidentally editing the same file at the same time. When content is updated in InCopy or InDesign by the assigned user, an out-of-date icon appears in the Assignments and Links panel. In the Assignments panel, you can update the content in the original document by choosing update commands on the Options menu for selected, out-of-date, or all content.

What You'll Do

Share Content with Adobe InCopy

Set Up User Identification

Export Content from InDesign

Use the Assignments Panel

Create an Assignment

Check Content Out and In

Update Content

Work with InCopy

Sharing Content with Adobe InCopy

Adobe InCopy is a stand-alone writing and editing program that allows you to work seamlessly with Adobe InDesign. The integration with InCopy allows InDesign users to select text and graphics in a document, and then assign the content to InCopy users for writing and editing. Content designates either a body of text that flows through one or more frames or an imported graphic.

InCopy users can open an assignment file with only the material assigned to them and then make changes to it. An assignment file is a container that stores a piece of content from an InDesign document and other related file-locking and notification tools. You can share assignment files on a server for easy access or through assignment packages.

InCopy uses live layout view to display how the content changes affect the InDesign document. Multiple InCopy or InDesign users can open the same content file at the same time as a read-only file. However, only one user can check out the content file to make changes. You can open a content file by opening an assignment file, assignment package, linked InCopy file, or InDesign file with linked content. An assignment package is a compressed version of an assignment file. If users don't have access to a common network server, you can can create assignment packages and then send them to the assigned user as an e-mail attachment. The assigned user can open the assignment package, make changes, and then return it. If an assigned user is done with the update or you no longer want the user to make changes, you can unlink or cancel the assignment.

Working Together on a Local Server

1. In InDesign, create assignments and add content to them.

2. Save the assignment files for InCopy users on a local server.

3. In InCopy, open the assignment file, and check out and edit the content. When you finish, check in the content.

4. In Design, while the content is checked out, you can still make changes to the rest of the InDesign document. When the content file is checked back in, you can make changes to the content.

5. In InCopy, open the assignment file, check out, and edit a story or graphic.

Exporting content from InDesign allows you to make content available to InCopy users to check out and change while still maintaining a link back to the original document. You can export content from an InDesign document to InCopy by creating an assignment file, or by exporting text and graphics frames separately as files. After you export content to InCopy, the file is called a **managed file**. Icons appear at the top left of the exported frames in InDesign and InCopy, and in the Assignments panel to indicate the content is currently assigned to another person. A link to the exported file also appears in the Links panel.

Setting Up User Identification

When you work with InCopy, all users who want to check files in and out need to have a unique identification name. You can specify or change a unique user Identification name and select a linked color by using the User command on the File menu or the Assignments panel. If you want to change a user identification name, make sure you don't have any files checked out.

Set Up User Identification

1. Click the **File** menu, and then click **User**.

2. Type a unique name.

3. Click the **Color** list arrow, and then select a color.

4. Click **OK**.

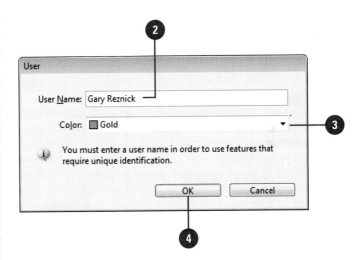

Did You Know?

You can add notes and track changes.
When you add notes to managed files, the information in the notes is pasted along with content for viewing and changing in InCopy. Use commands on the Notes submenu on the Type menu to create and manage notes.

Exporting Content from InDesign

Exporting content from InDesign allows you to make content available to InCopy users to check out and change while still maintaining a link back to the original document. You can export content from an InDesign document to InCopy by creating an assignment file (ICMA for CS4 and INCA for CS3), or by exporting text and graphics frames separately as files (ICML for CS4 and INCX for CS3) using one of the Export commands for InCopy. When you use one of the Export commands, the managed file is unassigned, which you can change later. Icons appear at the top left of the exported frame in InDesign and InCopy, and in the Assignments panel to indicate the content is currently assigned to another person for changes. A link to the exported file also appears in the Links panel.

Export Content from InDesign

1. Select the text or graphics frames that you want to export.

2. Click the **Edit** menu, point to **InCopy**, and then point to **Export**.

3. Click one of the following commands:

   ◆ **Selection.** Use to export all selected text or graphics frames.

   ◆ **Layer.** Use to export all content on the selected layer.

   ◆ **All Stories.** Use to export all text in stories that have not been exported already.

   ◆ **All Graphics.** Use to export all graphics that has not been exported already.

   ◆ **All Graphics and Stories.** Use to export all graphics and text in stories that have not been exported already.

4. Enter a name for the file.

5. Navigate to the location where you want to save the content file.

6. To make the file compatible with CS3, click the **Save as Type** list arrow (Win) or **Format** popup (Mac), and then click **InCopy CS3 Interchange**.

7. Click **Save**.

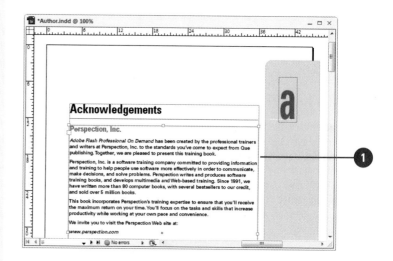

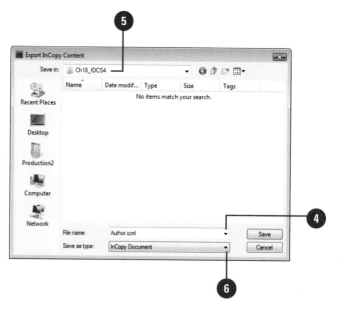

Using the Assignments Panel

The Assignments panel is a centralized place to work with content assignment in InDesign. The panel displays the content files exported from the current document and an icon indicating the status of the content. You can use buttons on the bottom of the panel to quickly identify the assigned user, update content, check out content, create new assignments, and delete assignments. You can also use the Options menu to select these and other commands. For example, you can select commands to update assignments for selected, out-of-date, or all content (**New!**). Before you can make an assignment, you need to save your InDesign document. If you have not yet saved the file, InDesign will prompt you to save it (**New!**).

Use the Assignments Panel

1. Select the **Assignments** panel.

   ◆ Click the **Window** menu, and then click **Assignments**.

2. Use any of the following buttons to perform an operation:

   ◆ **Update Content.** Select the assignment, and then click the **Update Content** button.

   ◆ **Check Out/Check In Content.** Select the assignment, and then click the **Check Out/Check In Selection** button.

   ◆ **Create New Assignment.** Click the **New Assignment** button, enter information, select options, and then click **OK**.

   ◆ **Delete Assignment.** Select the assignment, and then click the **Delete** button.

3. To locate and select the text and graphics associated with an assignment, double-click the assignment name in the panel.

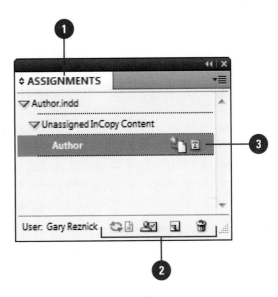

Creating an Assignment

You can create an assignment file several ways. One is to create an empty assignment file and add content to it later. Another is to create an assignment and add content at the same time. The last way is to add content to an existing assignment. When you create an assignment, a folder is created in the same location as the InDesign document file in order to store the assignment files (ICMA) and any exported InCopy story files (ICML). After you create an assignment, you can move the folder into a location where all users have access to it or create and distribute an assignment package.

Create an Assignment and Add Content

1. Select the **Assignments** panel.

   ◆ Click the **Window** menu, and then click **Assignments**.

2. Click the **New Assignment** button on the panel.

3. Specify the following New Assignment options:

   ◆ **Assignment Name.** Enter a unique name for the assignment.

   ◆ **Compatibility.** Select to optimize for CS4 or make the file compatible with CS3.

   ◆ **Assigned To.** Enter a name to associate with the assignment.

   ◆ **Color.** Select a color to associate with the assignment.

   ◆ **Change.** Click to specify a new location for the assignment file.

   ◆ **Include.** Select an option to include placeholder frames, assigned spreads, or all spreads.

   ◆ **Linked Image Files when Packaging.** Select to include linked image files when packaging. This keeps all the content together, so you can send everything in one file.

4. Click **OK**.

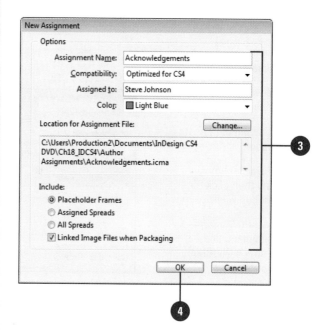

Create an Assignment and Add Content at the Same Time

1. Select the text and graphics frames you want to include in a new assignment file.

2. Click the **Edit** menu, point to **InCopy**, and then point to one of the following commands:

   - ◆ **Add Selection to Assignment.**
   - ◆ **Add Layer to Assignment.**
   - ◆ **Add All Stories to Assignment.**
   - ◆ **Add All Graphics to Assignment.**

3. Click **New** on the submenu.

4. Specify the new assignment options; see the previous page for details.

5. Click **OK**.

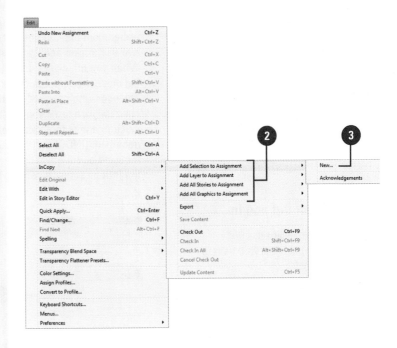

Add to an Existing Assignment

1. Select the text and graphics frames you want to include in an existing assignment file.

2. Click the **Edit** menu, point to **InCopy**, and then point to one of the following commands:

   - ◆ **Add Selection to Assignment.**
   - ◆ **Add Layer to Assignment.**
   - ◆ **Add All Stories to Assignment.**
   - ◆ **Add All Graphics to Assignment.**

3. Select an assignment name on the submenu.

4. Click the **Options** menu, and then click **Update All Assignments**.

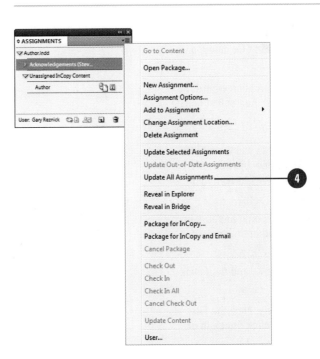

Checking Content Out and In

Anyone can open an assignment file for review. However, only one user at a time can open and edit the file. Before you can open and edit an assignment file, the content needs to be checked out. This prevents two users from accidentally editing the same file at the same time. When you check out a file, a hidden lock file (IDLK) is attached to the file on your computer. Once the file is locked, no one else can access it. The user who checked out the file has exclusive use of it until the file is checked in, even if you exit the program and come back later. You can make changes to an assignment file (INCA) in InCopy or in the InDesign document (INDD) that contains the assigned content. In this case, I'm focusing on InCopy. The same commands are available in InDesign on the InCopy submenu on the Edit menu.

Check Content Out and In

1. In InDesign, select the text or graphic frames that you want to check out.

2. Click the **Check Out** button on the Assignments panel.

   ◆ You can also click the **Edit** menu, point to **InCopy**, and then click **Check Out**.

   A pencil icon appears on the InDesign frame indicating the content is checked out.

3. In InCopy, click the **File** menu, and then click **Open**.

4. Navigate to the location where the file is stored, and then select it.

5. Click **Open**.

6. Make the changes you want to the content. Story view provides a quick and easy way to write and edit text.

   A pencil with line icon appears on the frame indicating the content is [in] use.

   [Clic]k the **File** menu, and then click [Sav]e Content.

   [Whe]n you're done, click the **File** [menu,] and then click **Check In** or [Check] **In All**.

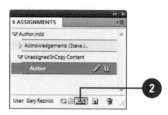

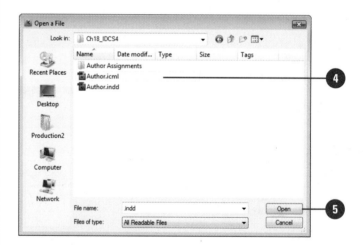

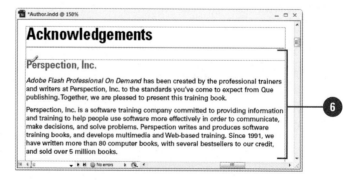

Updating Content

When content is updated in InCopy or InDesign by the assigned user, an out-of-date icon appears in the Assignments and Links panel. In the Assignments panel, you can update the content in the original document by choosing update commands on the Options menu for selected, out-of-date, or all content (**New!**). If an assignment file was moved during the editing process, the original document is not going to know where the file is located. You can also use the same update commands to help you locate and relink the file.

Update or Relink Content

1. In InDesign, open the document with the content you want to update.

2. Select the **Assignments** panel.

   ◆ Click the **Window** menu, and then click **Assignments**.

3. Select the assignment you want to update.

4. Click the **Options** menu, and then select any of the following:

   ◆ **Update Selected Assignments.**

   ◆ **Update Out-of-Date Assignments.**

   ◆ **Update All Assignments.**

5. To update content from the document window, select the text or graphics frames, click the **Edit** menu, point to **InCopy**, and then click **Update Content**.

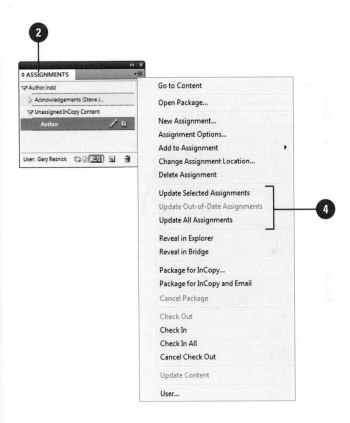

Did You Know?

You can override locked files. If you need access to a locked file, you can take back ownership. In InDesign, select the Assignments panel, select the assignment file you want back, click the Options menu, and then click Unlink Content.

Working with InCopy

When you start InCopy, the program window displays several windows of varying types you can use to work with documents.

A **menu** is a list of commands that you use to accomplish specific tasks. A **command** is a directive that accesses a feature of a program. InCopy has its own set of menus. The **Application bar** (**New!**) provides easy access to commonly used features, such as choosing zoom levels, view options, screen mode, document arrangement, workspaces, and InCopy's community online Help.

The **Tools panel** contains a set of tools you can use to work with text, create notes, and change the display view. Additional options and tools are available on the **Command Bar**.

The **Document window** displays open InCopy documents. InCopy includes tabs to make it easier to switch back and forth between documents and a close button to quickly close a document (**New!**). In InCopy, a collection of panels are available to help you work with documents. A **panel** is a window you can collapse, expand, and group with other panels, known as a **panel group**, to improve accessibility and workflow. A panel group consists of either individual panels stacked one on top of the other or related panels organized together with tabs to navigate from one panel to another. InCopy displays the following panels by default: Command Bar, Tools, Copyfit Info, Gallery & Story Appearance, Character, and Paragraph.

Command bar
Displays buttons for file-related commands.

Application bar
Displays buttons and menus to change the document layout.

Document window
Displays open InCopy documents.

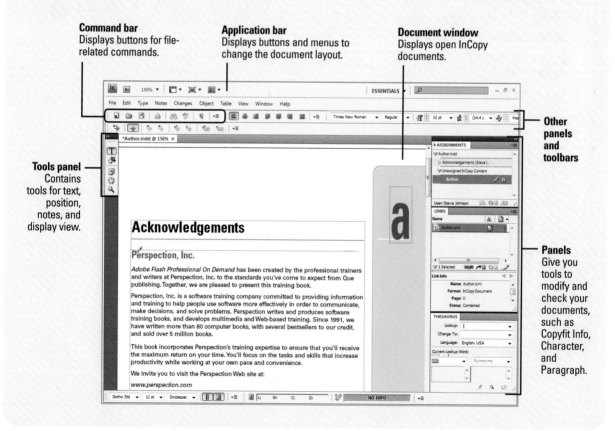

Tools panel
Contains tools for text, position, notes, and display view.

Other panels and toolbars

Panels
Give you tools to modify and check your documents, such as Copyfit Info, Character, and Paragraph.

Working Together with Adobe Programs

19

Introduction

Adobe programs are designed to work together so you can focus on what you need to do, rather than on how to do it. In fact, the Adobe programs share tools and features for your most common tasks so you can work uninterrupted and move seamlessly from one program to another. Adobe Creative Suite is an integrated collection of programs that work together to help you create designs in print, on the Web, or on mobile devices. When you install Adobe Creative Suite or a stand-alone Adobe program, you also get additional Adobe programs—Bridge, Version Cue, Drive, ConnectNow, Device Central, and Extension Manager—to help you perform specific jobs, such as locating, downloading, and modifying images for projects, managing files and program extensions and testing files for different mobile devices.

Adobe Bridge is a program that lets you view, open, modify, and manage images located on your computer from any Adobe Creative Suite program. Adobe Bridge is literally the glue that binds Adobe Creative Suite programs together into one cohesive unit with shared tools. Bridge allows you to search, sort, filter, manage, and process image files one at a time or in batches. You can also use Bridge to do the following: create new folders; rename, move, delete and group files; edit metadata; rotate images; create web galleries and contact sheets; and run batch commands. You can also import files from your digital camera and view file information and metadata.

What You'll Do

Explore Adobe Programs

Explore Adobe Bridge

Get Started with Adobe Bridge

Get Photos from a Digital Camera

Work with Raw Images from a Digital Camera

Work with Images Using Adobe Bridge

Apply Image Adjustments

Create a Web Photo Gallery

Automate Tasks in Adobe Bridge

Share My Screen

Manage Files Using Adobe Version Cue

Work with Adobe Drive

Explore Adobe Device Central

Check Content Using Adobe Device Central

Use Adobe Extension Manager

Exploring Adobe Programs

Adobe Creative Suite 4

Adobe Creative Suite 4 is an integrated collection of programs that work together to help you create designs in print, on the Web, or on mobile devices. Adobe's Creative Suite 4 comes in different editions with different combinations of Adobe programs. The main programs for print design include InDesign and Acrobat Professional; for graphic design the programs include Photoshop, Illustrator, and Fireworks; for video and sound design the programs include Premiere, After Effects Professional, Encore, and Soundbooth; and for web design the programs include Flash Professional, Dreamweaver, Fireworks, and Contribute.

Working Together with Adobe Programs

When you install Adobe Creative Suite 4 or a stand-alone Adobe program, you also get additional Adobe programs—Bridge, Version Cue, Drive, ConnectNow, Device Central, and Extension Manager—to help you perform specific jobs such as managing files and program extensions and testing files for mobile devices.

Adobe Bridge

Adobe Bridge CS4 is a file management/batching program that manages and processes images while you work in your other Adobe programs. To use Bridge, click Browse in Bridge on the File menu within an Adobe product, such as Flash, or from the desktop use the Start menu (Win) or go to the Applications folder (Mac).

Adobe Version Cue

Adobe Version Cue is a file tracking management program you can use to keep track of changes to a file as you work on it or if you work collaboratively on the same files with colleagues. You use Adobe Bridge as a central location from which to use Version Cue. You can track Adobe and non-Adobe program files.

Adobe Drive

Adobe Drive (**New!**) allows you to connect to and use Version Cue servers as if they were a local hard drive or mapped network drive. After you set up a connection, you can work with Version Cue files by using the Open, Import, Export, Place, Save, or Save As dialog boxes, and Explorer (Win) or Finder (Mac).

Adobe ConnectNow

The Share My Screen command (**New!**) on the File menu allows you to connect to Adobe ConnectNow, which is a secure Web site where you can start an online meeting. You can share and annotate your computer screen or take control of an attendee's computer. During the meeting, you can communicate by sending chat messages, using live audio, or broadcasting live video.

Adobe Device Central

Adobe Device Central CS4 allows you to test your content to see how it would look on a variety of mobile devices. You can interact with the emulated device in a way that allows you to test your content in real-world situations. Device Central provides a library of devices and each device includes a profile with information about the device, including media and content support types.

Adobe Extension Manager

Adobe Extension Manager CS4 allows you to install and delete added program functionality, known as extensions, to many Adobe programs.

Exploring Adobe Bridge

Inspector panel
Displays or hides
Version Cue panels.

Folders panel
Displays the folders
on your computer in
a tree structure.

Workspaces (New!)
Choose from common
workspaces.

Quick Search (New!)
Search for file names,
keywords, folder names.

Preview panel
Displays a preview of
the selected image.

**File path
(New!)**
To trace file
back to its
folder.

Favorites panel
Displays links
to common
features and
favorite places.

Filter panel
Displays files
based on filter
criteria.

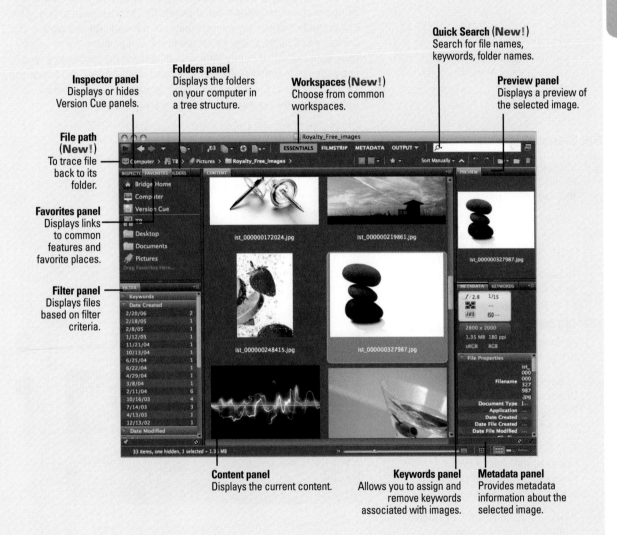

Content panel
Displays the current content.

Keywords panel
Allows you to assign and
remove keywords
associated with images.

Metadata panel
Provides metadata
information about the
selected image.

Getting Started with Adobe Bridge

Adobe Bridge CS4 is a stand-alone program that lets you view, open, and manage images located on your computer from any Adobe Creative Suite 4 program. Adobe Bridge is literally the glue that binds Adobe Creative Suite 4 programs and shared tools together into one cohesive unit. Adobe Bridge integrates with shared tools including Adobe Version Cue, a file tracking project management program. The Bridge program provides a set of panels that make it easy to find, view, and manage the files on your computer or network. As you work with Bridge, you'll open, close, and move (dock and undock) the panels to meet your individual needs. After you customize the workspace, you can save the location of the panels as a custom workspace, which you can display using the Workspace command on the Window menu. Bridge also provides some predefined workspaces.

Get Started with Adobe Bridge

1. Launch your Adobe product, click the **File** menu, and then click **Browse in Bridge**.

   ◆ You can also start Adobe Bridge CS4 from the Start menu (Win) or the Applications folder (Mac).

2. To open and close a panel, click the **Window** menu, and then click the panel name you want.

3. To move a panel, drag the panel tab you want to another location in the Bridge window.

4. To save a workspace, click the **Window** menu, point to **Workspace**, click **New Workspace**, type a name, and then click **OK**.

5. To display a workspace, click the **Window** menu, point to **Workspace**, and then click the workspace you want.

6. When you're done, click the **Close** button in the Bridge window.

The Launch Bridge button on the Application bar in Photoshop

Getting Photos from a Digital Camera

If you have raw or other images from your digital camera, you can use the Get Photos from Camera command in Adobe Bridge to retrieve and copy them to your computer. This allows you to specify where you want to store the files, rename them if you want, preserve metadata, or convert them to the DNG format. When you convert raw files to the DNG format, you specify preview size, compression, and whether to preserve the raw image data or embed the original raw file.

Import Raw and Other Files from a Camera

1 In Adobe Bridge, click the **File** menu, and then click **Get Photos from Camera** or click the camera icon on the Application bar. (**New!**)

2 Click the **Get Photos From** popup, and then select the source camera or memory card.

3 Create a new subfolder to store the images (optional).

4 To rename the files, select a method, and then enter file name text.

5 Select the options you want:

◆ **Preserve Current Filename in XMP.** Select to save the current filename as image metadata.

◆ **Open Adobe Bridge.** Select to open and display the files in Adobe Bridge.

◆ **Convert To DNG.** Select to convert Camera Raw files to DNG. Click Settings to set DNG conversion options.

◆ **Delete Original Files. (New!)** Select to delete original files from camera or memory card.

◆ **Save Copies To.** Select to save copies to another folder for backup.

6 To apply metadata to the files, click **Advanced Dialog**.

7 Click **Get Photos**.

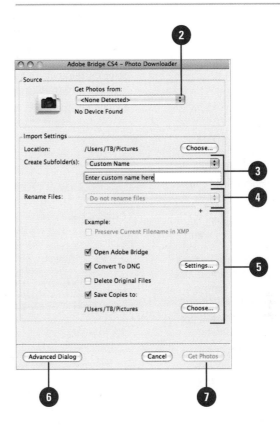

Working with Raw Images from a Digital Camera

Raw image file formats are created by most mid- to high-end digital cameras and contain information about how the image was taken. The raw format turns off all camera adjustments, and simply saves the image information. Using the raw format is as close to using traditional film as a digital camera can get. Raw images are larger; however, the increase in file size gives you more information that can be used by Camera Raw to adjust the image. From Adobe Bridge, you can use Camera Raw to open raw files, JPEG, and TIFF files to make image enhancements. If you're not sure what to do, you can click Auto to have Camera Raw do it or drag color sliders to adjust options manually. Raw images can be converted into 16-bit images. When you use a 16-bit image, you have more control over adjustments such as tonal and color corrections. Once processed, raw images can be saved in the DNG, TIFF, PSD, PSB, or JPEG formats. After you make Camera Raw adjustments, you can save the settings so you can use them later.

Set Camera Raw Preferences

1. In Adobe Bridge, click the **Edit** (Win) or **Adobe Bridge** (Mac) menu, and then click **Camera Raw Preferences**.

2. Select the preferences you want:

   ◆ **General.** Specify where Camera Raw file settings are stored. Use Sidecar XMP files to store settings separately, or Camera Raw Database to store settings in a searchable database.

   ◆ **Default Image Settings.** Select options to automatically apply settings or set defaults.

   ◆ **Camera Raw Cache.** Set a cache size to shorten loading time for thumbnails and previews.

   ◆ **DNG File Handling.** Select options to ignore XMP files or update embedded content.

   ◆ **JPEG and TIFF Handling.** (**New!**) Automatically open JPEGs and/or TIFFs in Camera Raw.

3. Click **OK**.

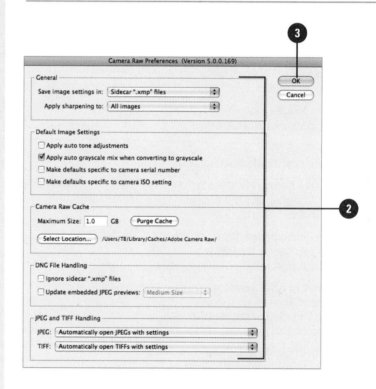

Modify a File in Camera Raw

1 Right-click the image, and then click **Open in Camera Raw**.

2 Use the **Zoom**, **Hand**, **Rotate**, **Crop**, and **Straighten** tools to change the size, orientation, and position of the image, or use the **White Balance** tool to set the white balance or the **Color Sampler** tool to sample a color, or use the **Retouch** and **Red Eye Removal** tools to correct the image. Use the **Adjustment Brush** and **Graduated Filter** for local adjustments (**New!**).

3 Select from the available image view options:

- ◆ **Image Preview.** Displays the active image.
- ◆ **Zoom Level.** Changes the view of the active image.
- ◆ **Histogram.** Displays information on the colors and brightness levels in the active image.

4 Click the **Basic**, **Tone Curve**, **Detail**, **Lens**, **HSL/ Grayscale**, **Split Toning**, **Lens Corrections**, or **Camera Calibration** tabs, and then click **Auto** (Basic tab) or drag sliders to modify the color and tonal values of the image.

5 Click **Save Image** to specify a folder destination, file name, and format for the processed images.

6 Select the images you want to synchronize (apply settings) in the Filmstrip (if desired, click Select All), and then click **Synchronize**.

7 Click the **Camera Raw Menu** button to **Load**, **Save**, or **Delete** a specific set of Raw settings, or to modify dialog box settings.

8 Click **Done** to process the file, but not open it, or click **Open Image** to process and open it in Photoshop. Hold Alt (Win) or Option (Mac) to use **Open Copy** or **Reset**.

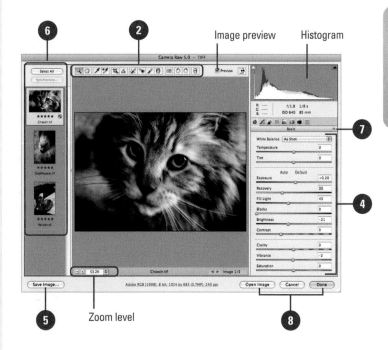

Image preview   Histogram

Zoom level

For Your Information

What is the DNG File Format?

The DNG, or Digital Negative, format is an openly published raw file format from Adobe that stores "raw" pixel data captured by digital cameras before it has been converted to another format, such as TIFF or JPEG. In addition, it captures standard 'EXIF' metadata, such as date, time, camera used, and camera settings. Saving raw files in the DNG format provides several advantages. DNG files are smaller than uncompressed TIFFs, and they do not have the artifacts of compressed JPEGs. Many key camera parameters, such as white balance, can be modified even after the image is captured. You have access to 16-bit data for greater detail and fidelity, and the added flexibility of converting a single file using multiple conversion settings. When you convert raw images into the DNG format, you are using a format that is openly published by Adobe and usable by other software and hardware vendors, which makes it a safe format for the long-term storage and archiving of digital images. The raw format used by digital cameras is proprietary to the specific camera (e.g., NEF for Nikon, CR2 for Canon, RAF for Fuji), so the format might not be supported once that camera and its proprietary software is obsolete, which means at some point in the future, you might not be able to open any of your archived raw images. The DNG format solves that problem. To get a free copy of the DNG converter, go to *www.adobe.com* and then search for DNG converter.

Working with Images Using Adobe Bridge

With Adobe Bridge, you can drag assets into your layouts as needed, preview them, and add metadata to them. Bridge allows you to search, sort, filter, manage, and process image files one at a time or in batches. You can also use Bridge to create new folders; rename, move, delete and group files (known as stacking); edit metadata; rotate images; and run batch commands. You can also view information about files and data imported from your digital camera.

Work with Images Using Bridge

1. Launch your Adobe product, click the **File** menu, and then click **Browse in Bridge**, or click the **Launch Bridge** button (if available).

2. Click the **Folder** path, and then select a folder.

3. Click the **Folders** tab and choose a folder from the scrolling list.

4. Click the **Favorites** tab to choose from a listing of user-defined items, such as Pictures or Version Cue.

5. Click an image within the preview window to select it.

6. Click the **Metadata** tab to view image information, including date and time the image was shot, and aperture, shutter speed, and f-stop.

7. Click the **IPTC Core** arrow to add user-defined metadata, such as creator and copyright information, or captions.

8. Click the **Preview** tab to view a larger thumbnail of the selected image. Multiple images appear when you select them.

   ◆ Click the image in the Preview tab to display a Loupe tool for zooming. Drag magnified box to change positions. Click it to deactivate the tool.

9. Drag the **Zoom** slider to increase or decrease the thumbnail views.

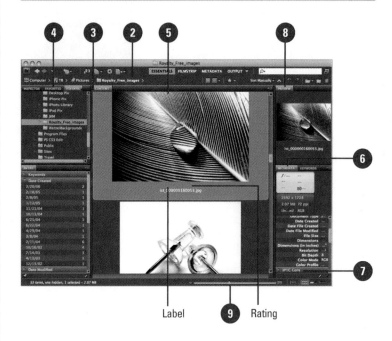

Label   9   Rating

10 Click the preview buttons to select a different view of the workspace you have chosen. If you want to view your images in filmstrip or metadata focus mode, choose that workspace from the Window menu.

◆ **View Content as Thumbnails.** Default view. Displays the images as thumbnails with the file name underneath.

◆ **View Content as Details.** Displays a thumbnail of each image with selected details about the image such as date created, document type, resolution.

◆ **View Content as List.** Displays a small thumbnail of each image with metadata information details, such as date created and file size.

11 Use the file management buttons to rotate or delete images, or create a new folder.

12 To narrow down the list of images using a filter, click the criteria you want to use in the Filter panel.

13 To add a label or rating to images, select the ones you want, click the **Label** menu, and then select the label or rating you want.

14 To group related images as a stacked group, select the images, click the **Stacks** menu, and then click **Group as Stack**.

◆ Use the Stacks menu to ungroup, open, expand, or collapse stacks.

15 Double-click on a thumbnail to open it in the default program, or drag the thumbnail from the Bridge into an open Adobe application.

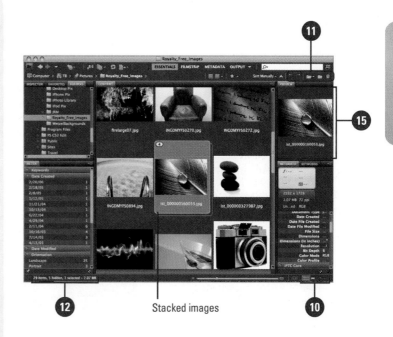

Stacked images

For Your Information

What is Metadata?

Metadata is information about an image file, such as its author, copyright, creation date, size, version, color space, resolution, and searchable keywords. This data is stored in the file or in a separate file known as a **sidecar file**, using a standard format called **Extensible Metadata Platform (XMP)**. Bridge and Version Cue use XMP files to help you organize and search for files on your computer. Metadata is also stored in other formats, such as EXIF (digital camera data), IPTC (photographer and image data), GPS (global positioning system data), and TIFF, which are all synchronized with XMP.

Applying Image Adjustments

Adobe Bridge makes it easy to make adjustments to one image in Camera Raw and then apply those adjustments to other images directly from Bridge without going back into Camera Raw. For instance, you may be correcting the white balance for an image and have many other images that were shot at the same time, under the same lighting conditions. You can use the initial settings to correct the rest of your images right from Bridge. You can also make a preset from your favorite adjustments, which will then be available as a develop setting within Bridge.

Modify Images in Adobe Bridge

① In Adobe Bridge, display and select the images that you want to adjust.

② Use any of the following methods to modify an image:

◆ **Apply a Preset Adjustment.** Click the **Edit** menu, point to **Develop Settings**, and then select a preset adjustment.

◆ **Copy and Paste Settings.** Click the **Edit** menu, point to **Develop Settings**, and then click **Copy Settings**. Select the image(s) to which you want to apply the settings. Click the **Edit** menu, point to **Develop Settings**, and then click **Paste Settings**. Select the options to apply, and then click **OK**.

◆ **Apply the Most Recent Adjustment.** Click the **Edit** menu, point to **Develop Settings**, and then click **Previous Conversion**.

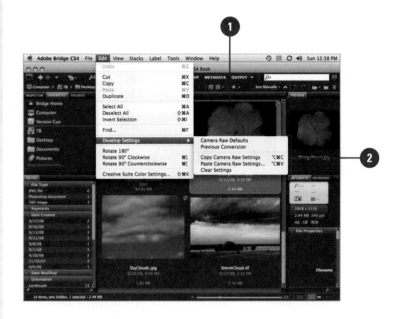

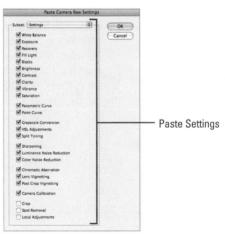

Paste Settings

Did You Know?

You can use Photoshop automation commands in Adobe Bridge. You can use the Batch or Image Processor commands on the Tools menu under Photoshop In Bridge to automate the processing of your camera's raw files.

Creating a Web Photo Gallery

Adobe Bridge takes the drudgery out of creating a Web Photo Gallery (**New!**) (thumbnail images on web pages). The pages generated with this command display small thumbnails of a group of images—when you click on an image, a larger version is displayed within another window or section of the page. If your goal is to show the world your photographs, but you don't want to write all the HTML code involved in making that happen, then the Web Photo Gallery is just what you need.

Create a Web Photo Gallery in Adobe Bridge

1. In Adobe Bridge, select a folder with the images that you want to use for the photo gallery.

2. Click the **Workspace** menu, and then click **Output**.

3. Click the **Web Gallery** button.

4. Click the **Template** list arrow, and then select a template.

   ◆ Click the **Refresh Preview** button to view your template choices or click the **Preview in Browser** button to see how it would look on the Web.

5. Use the following panels to customize the Web gallery:

   ◆ **Site Info.** Provide descriptive information about the Web Photo gallery.

   ◆ **Color Palette.** Select custom colors for screen elements.

   ◆ **Appearance.** Specify options to show file names, a preview and thumbnail size, slide duration, and a transition effect.

6. In the Create Gallery panel, enter a gallery name, and then select a creation option:

   ◆ **Save to Disk.** Click **Browse** to specify a location, and then click **Save**.

   ◆ **Upload.** Specify the FTP server location, user name, password, a folder, and then click **Upload**.

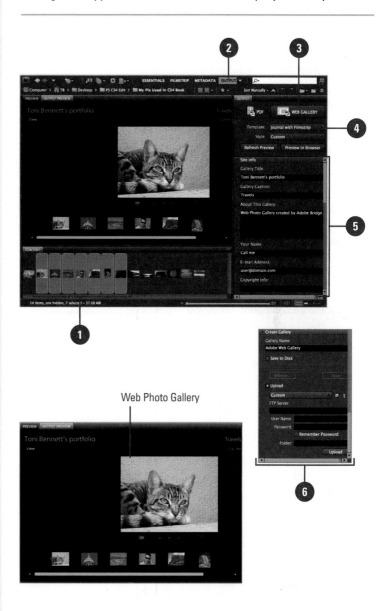

Web Photo Gallery

Automating Tasks in Adobe Bridge

The Tools menu provides commands you can use to automate tasks in Bridge. For example, you can automate the process of renaming a group of files using the Batch Rename command. If you use Photoshop, InDesign, or Version Cue, you can use commands on submenus to run automated tasks, such as adding and synchronizing files with Version Cue or processing raw images with Photoshop, or you can create a contact sheet of images in InDesign. You can also use the Tools menu to start other Adobe programs, such as Device Central and Acrobat Connect (Start Meeting) as well as create and edit Metadata templates, which you can use to append or replace metadata in Adobe InDesign or other XMP-enabled programs.

Rename Files Automatically in Adobe Bridge

1. In Adobe Bridge, select the files or folders you want to use.

2. Click the **Tools** menu, and then click **Batch Rename**.

3. Select the Destination Folder option you want: **Rename in same folder**, **Move to other folder**, or **Copy to other folder**, and then click **Browse** to specify a new folder location.

4. Click the **Element** drop-down, and then select options to specify how you want to name the files:

   ◆ Text, New Extension, Current Filename, Preserved Filename, Sequence Number, Sequence Letter, Date/Time, Metadata, or Folder Name.

5. Enter the text you want to use in conjunction with the Element selection to name the files.

6. Select the **Preserve Current File Name In XMP Metadata** check box to retain the original filename in the metadata.

7. Select the check boxes for the operating systems with which you want the renamed files to be compatible.

8. Click **Rename**.

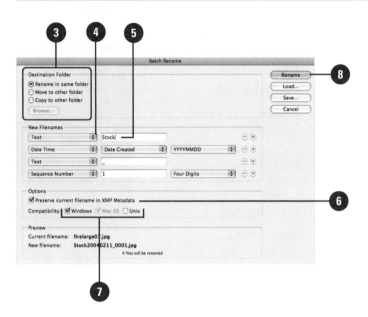

Sharing My Screen

The Share My Screen command (**New!**) on the File menu allows you to connect to Adobe ConnectNow, which is a secure Web site where you can start an online meeting and collaborate on any design project across platforms and programs. You can share and annotate your computer screen or take control of an attendee's computer. During the meeting, you can communicate by sending chat messages, using live audio, or broadcasting live video. In addition, you can take meeting notes, and share files.

Share My Screen

1. Click the **File** menu, and then click **Share My Screen**.

2. Enter your Adobe ID and password.

   ◆ If you don't have an Adobe ID and password, click the Create a Free Adobe ID link, and then follow the online instructions.

3. Click **Sign In**.

   ◆ If prompted, sign in to ConnectNow.

4. To share your computer screen, click the **Share My Computer Screen** button.

5. Use the ConnectNow toolbar to do any of the following:

   ◆ **Meeting.** Use to invite participants, share your computer screen, upload a file, share your webcam, set preferences, end a meeting, and exit Adobe ConnectNow.

   ◆ **PODS.** Use to show and hide pod panels.

   ◆ **Help.** Use to get help, troubleshoot problems, and set account and Flash Player settings.

6. Click the participant buttons at the bottom to specify roles, remove a user, or request control of a user's computer.

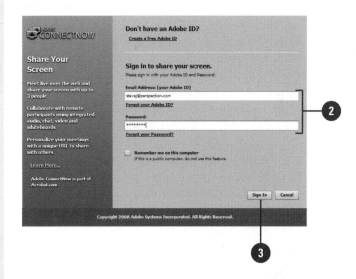

Managing Files Using Adobe Version Cue

With Adobe Drive CS4, you can access Adobe Version Cue CS4, a file versioning program you can use to keep track of changes to a file as you work on it and create projects to keep all your related files together. Version Cue allows you to access and manage Version Cue files and projects. You can use the Inspector panel and buttons in the Content panel to view, navigate, and access information, projects, and files on the Version Cue servers. You can check files in and out to make sure you're the only one making changes and then synchronize the changes.

Before you can start using Version Cue, you need to install and configure the Version Cue Server, create a project to store master copies of files and related information, and assign users to it. The Version Cue Server gets automatically installed on your computer with Adobe Creative Suite 4 Design, Web, or Master Collection. Even though it's installed, you still need to turn it on. Click My Server in the Adobe dialog box or in Adobe Bridge, and then follow the onscreen instructions to complete the initial server administration settings. If you're sharing files and other assets in a workgroup, you should reinstall Version Cue on a dedicated network computer.

Version Cue file management provides access to projects and files. To use file management, you need to enable it. Version Cue is enabled by default in all Adobe Creative Suite programs (except Flash and Acrobat). To turn it on in an Adobe program, open the Preferences dialog box using the Edit (Win) or program name (Mac) menu, and select the Enable Version Cue check box in one of the categories. If you disable Version Cue file management in one Adobe Creative Suite program, you disable it in all others, except Acrobat, Flash, and Bridge.

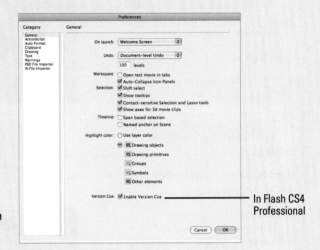

In Flash CS4 Professional

Working with Adobe Drive

Adobe Drive (**New!**) allows you to connect to and use Version Cue servers as if they were a local hard drive or mapped network drive. After you set up a connection, you can work with Version Cue files by using the Open, Import, Export, Place, Save, or Save As dialog boxes, and Explorer (Win) or Finder (Mac). After you start Adobe Drive, you can establish a connection to a Version Cue server, and then work with files on the server like a local or mapped drive. To change Adobe Drive preferences, click Preferences, specify caching and error logging settings, and then click Save.

Click to establish a connection

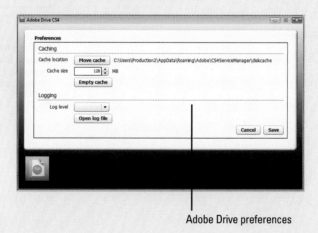

Adobe Drive preferences

Exploring Adobe Device Central

Device Profiles tab
Displays detailed information about devices, including support details for Flash, bitmap, video, and Web.

Emulator tab
Displays a simulation of how content appears on specific mobile devices.

Device Sets panel
Displays sets of devices for testing; availability depends on the content type.

Online Library panel
Downloads specific mobile device specifications.

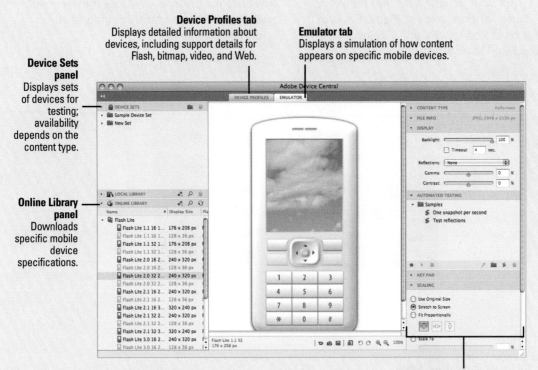

Testing panels
Displays a number of panels for testing content based on the selected options.

Checking Content Using Adobe Device Central

Testing your content on as many different devices as possible allows you to reach a wider audience. Adobe Device Central makes it easy to test your content on a wide variety of different mobile devices in one place. Device Central provides a library of devices from which to choose, and each device includes a profile with information about the device, including media and content support types. Device Central uses an emulator to simulate the way your content will look on a selected device. An emulator is not the same as the real device. However, it allows you to quickly test devices to get initial results.

Check Content Using Adobe Device Central

1. Start Adobe Device Central from the Start menu (Win) or the Applications folder (Mac) or from the File menu in Photoshop and choose Device Central.

   ◆ In Bridge, right-click a file, and then click **Test in Device Central**.

2. From the Welcome screen or the File menu, select the option you want:

   ◆ **Open for Testing.** Opens a file for testing with the Emulator tab. Use the buttons on the mobile device to test your content.

   ◆ **Device Profiles.** Displays mobile device profiles. In the Available Devices panel, expand a folder with devices. On the Device Profiles tab, click links to display profile information.

   ◆ **Create New Mobile.** Creates a new mobile document for Flash, Photoshop, or Illustrator; select a mobile device, and then click **Create**.

3. Select the Online Library panel where you can download specific mobile device specifications.

4. If you're testing, select the options you want in the Testing panels.

5. When you're done, click the **Close** button in the Device Central window.

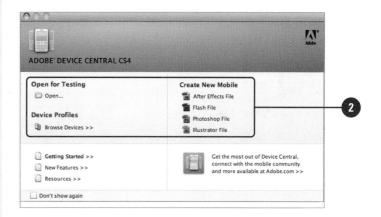

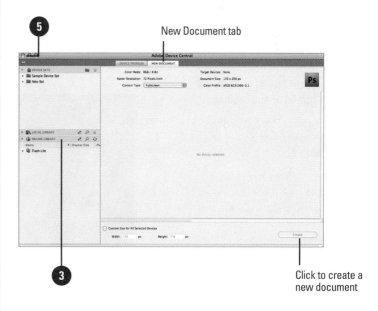

New Document tab

Click to create a new document

Using Adobe Extension Manager

The Adobe Extension Manager CS4 is a program you can use to install and delete added program functionality, known as extensions, to many Adobe programs. The Extension Manager is automatically installed when you install Flash, Dreamweaver, or Fireworks. You can use the Extension Manager to access the Adobe Exchange site, where you can locate, research, and download many different types of extensions. Some are free and some are not. After you download an extension, you can use Extension Manager to install it. Extension Manager only displays extensions installed using the Extension Manager; other extensions installed using a third-party installer might not appear. After you install an extension, you can find and display information about it.

Download and Install an Extension

1. Start Adobe Extension Manager CS4 from the Start menu (Win) or the Applications folder (Mac).

    TIMESAVER *In Flash, Dreamweaver, or Fireworks, click the Help menu, and then click Manage Extensions.*

2. Click the **Exchange** button on the toolbar.

3. Select the extension you want to download, and then save it to your computer.

4. In Extension Manager, click the **Install** button on the toolbar.

5. Locate and select the extension (.mxp) you want to install, and then click **Install**.

6. You can perform any of the following:

    ◆ Sort. Click a column heading.

    ◆ Enable or Disable. Select or clear the check in the Enabled check box next to the extension.

    ◆ Remove. Select the extension, and then click **Remove.**

7. Click the **Close** button.

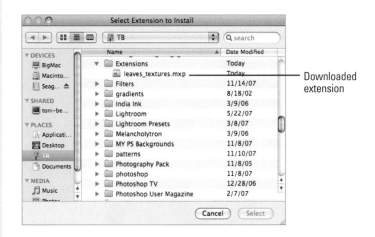

Downloaded extension

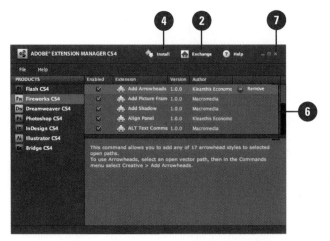

Workshops

Introduction

The Workshop is all about being creative and thinking outside of the box. These workshops will help your right-brain soar, while making your left-brain happy; by explaining why things work the way they do. Exploring InDesign's possibilities is great fun; however, always stay grounded with knowledge of how things work. Knowledge is power.

Getting and Using the Project Files

Each project in the Workshop includes a start file to help you get started with the project, and a final file to provide you with the results of the project so you can see how well you accomplished the task.

Before you can use the project files, you need to download them from the Web. You can access the files at *www.perspection.com* in the software downloads area. After you download the files from the Web, uncompress the files into a folder on your hard drive to which you have easy access from InDesign.

Project 1: Creating a Master Page

Skills and Tools: Master pages

A master page holds and displays all the elements that you want to appear on every page in a document, such as headers, logos, page numbers, and footers. The master is like a background layer to a page. Everything on the background layer appears on the page above it. Master elements appear on document pages surrounded by a dotted border to make them easy to identify. When you create a new document, you also create a master page. You will take a document with facing pages and set up a master page to add auto page numbers on all page numbers except the title and last page. Next, you will create a master page that is built upon the first master page and add an extra element to it, then apply that master to the internal left-facing pages of the booklet.

The Project

In this project, you'll take a 12 page document and create two master pages, apply them to pages within the document, and override selections on selected pages to change some of the master page elements.

The Process

1 Open InDesign CS4, open the document master_pages_start.indd, and then save it as **my_master_pages.indd**.

This document has a title page, copyright page, and five spreads with placeholder text on the left-facing pages and graphics frames on the right-facing pages.

2 Select the **Pages** panel.

Right above the icons for the individual pages and spreads, you will see the master page icons. Every document has a master page called None and A-Master. The None master page can be applied to any pages you don't want to have any recurring elements on.

Decide what elements of the design that you want to be repeated on multiple pages. For this project, we will be adding auto page numbers to all of the pages after the title page and before the copyright page. We will also be adding a colored header rectangle above the placeholder text. First, let's use the A-Master to add in the auto page numbers.

3 Double-click the **A-Master** page on the top part of the Pages panel to make it active.

4 Select the **Type** tool, and then drag out a text frame anywhere on the page where you want the page number to appear on every page.

5 With your cursor blinking inside the text frame, click the **Type** menu, point to **Insert Special Character**, point to **Markers**, and then click **Current Page Number**.

The current page number special character appears as "A."

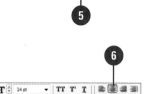

6 Select the text ("A"), and then center it within the text frame. Click the **Center** button on the Control panel.

Next, let's rename your new master page.

7 Select the **A-Master** page in the Pages panel (if necessary), click **Options** menu, and then click **Master Options for A-Master**.

The Master Options dialog box appears. For this project, let's call this page A-PageNumbers.

8 Enter the name PageNumbers, and then click **OK**.

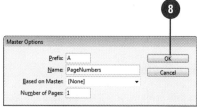

9 Select pages 2-11 in the Pages panel to make them active.

10 Click the **Options** menu, and then click **Apply Masters to Pages**.

11 Click the **Apply Master** list arrow, click **A-PageNumbers**, enter **1** for the Number of Pages, and then confirm that 2-11 is specified in the To Pages box of the Apply Master dialog box.

Next, let's create a new master page to add in a colored rectangle as a header on top of the placeholder text on left-facing pages. We're still going to want page numbers on these pages so let's build the new master page from the A-PageNumbers master page so our page numbers will already be included on the new master page.

12 Click the **Options** menu, and then click **New Master**.

The New Master Options dialog box appears. For this project, let's use the A-PageNumbers master page as the base for the new master and call this page B-HeaderPageNumbers.

13 Click the **Based on Master** list arrow, and then click **A-PageNumbers**.

14 Enter the name *HeaderPageNumbers*, and then click **OK**.

15 Select the new master page named **B-HeaderPageNumbers** in the Pages panel.

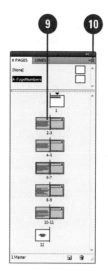

We're going to add a colored rectangle to serve as a header for each text page.

16 Select the **Rectangle Frame** tool on the Tools panel, and then click the master page.

17 In the resulting dialog box, enter *4.75* (in inches) for the width and *.8056* (in inches) for the height, and then click **OK**.

18 Select the **Selection** tool on the Tools panel, and then move the rectangle to fit inside the frame at the top.

19 Click the **Fill** box on the Color panel, and then choose a color for the rectangle.

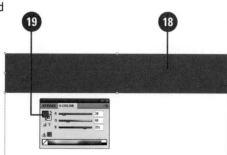

We only want the colored header boxes to appear on left-facing pages, so we need to select only those pages, and then apply the B-HeaderPageNumbers master page to them.

20 In the Pages panel, select pages 2, 4, 6, 8, and 10, click the **Options** menu, and then click **Apply Masters to Pages**. Click the **Apply Master** list arrow, click **B-HeaderPageNumbers**, and then click **OK**.

Now, let's select and modify master objects on document pages. For this project, we'll change the color of the rectangular box for each of the four left-facing pages after page 2 to indicate different sections of the booklet.

21 Double-click on page 4 from the Pages panel, press Ctrl+Shift (Win) or ⌘+Shift (Mac), and then click to select the rectangle.

22 Click the **Options** menu, and then click **Detach Selection from Master**. Objects can only be selected and detached if Allow Master Item Overrides on Selection is active on the Options menu.

23 Click the **Fill** box on the Color panel, and then choose a different color for the header. Follow the same process to detach the header rectangle on pages 6, 8, and 10 and fill with different colors.

At this point, your document should have a beginning title page with no page numbers or header boxes, and a final copyright page with no page numbers or header boxes. No master pages should be associated with these two pages. Even-numbered pages should have the B-HeaderPageNumbers master page associated with them and odd-numbered pages should have the A-PageNumbers master page associated with them.

The Results

Finish: Compare your completed project file with the document master_pages_fnl.indd. ☞

Project 2: Creating Layouts with a Table

Skills and Tools: Tables

A table organizes your information into rows and columns. The intersection of a row and column is called a cell. You can create a blank table, and then enter text, or make a table from existing text separated by paragraphs, tabs, or commas. The first row in the table is good for column headings, whereas the leftmost column is good for row labels.

The Project

In this project, you'll take a list of new book titles for your client, a book publisher, and create a price list in the form of a table. This table can then be inserted into the publisher's current book catalog. You will insert a table into a new InDesign document and make changes to the table structure. Then you will add graphics and text data, formatting the data with different sizes and colors. After you create your first table, you will duplicate the table to create two more instances of the same table for two more book titles.

The Process

1 Open InDesign CS4, and create a new document. Click the **File** menu, point to **New**, and then click **Document**. Choose **Letter** for the page size, 8 ½ x 11 inches for width and height, one column, ½" margins all around, and then click **OK**.

2 Save the new document as **my_layout_tables.indd**.

3 Click the **Type** tool on the Tools panel, drag a frame that is the size of your document, and then click to place the insertion point in the text frame.

④ Click the **Table** menu, and then click **Insert Table**. Change the number of Body Rows to **5** and number of Columns to **6**, and then click **OK**.

Now you'll need to customize the design of your table to accommodate your data.

⑤ With the **Type** tool, drag to select all six columns on the first row.

⑥ Click the **Table** menu, and then click **Merge Cells**.

This merges the top row into one long cell. Next, you'll need to create a cell that can fit a small graphic of each book.

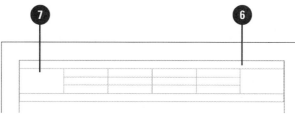

⑦ With the **Type** tool, click in the second cell in the first column, and then drag to select cells 2, 3, and 4 in the first column. Click the **Table** menu, and then click **Merge Cells**. Now do the same thing for cells 2, 3, and 4 in the last column and merge them as well. This last cell will hold the price for each book. Now select all the cells in the last row and merge them as well.

This completes the design of the table structure. Next, you'll begin adding in the data for the first book. You'll use the top row for the company name.

⑧ With the **Type** tool, click to place the insertion point in the long cell in the first row, and then type in the book publisher name: Better Books Publishers.

⑨ Highlight the text, and then format it. Click the **Justify** button on the Control panel and then use the **Font Style** list arrow on the Control panel to make the text bold.

Next, add the graphic for the cover by drawing out a graphics frame in the cell.

⑩ Click the **Rectangle Frame** tool on the Tools panel, and then draw a graphics frame in the first large cell in the second row.

Now, let's add a graphic to the graphics frame in the table.

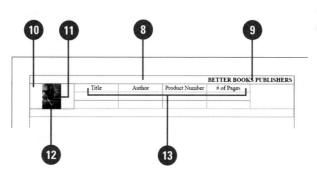

⑪ Click the **File** menu, click **Place**, and then double-click the file GoatsGoWild.psd.

⑫ Center the image in the frame. Click the **Object** menu, point to **Fitting**, and then click **Fit Content Proportionally**. Click the **Object** menu, point to **Fitting**, and then click **Center Content**.

Next, type in header titles in the second row for title, author, product number, and number of pages. The final, larger cell in the final column will be for the book price.

⑬ Select all the headers and center them. Use the **Align Center** button on the Control panel.

⑭ Now, type in the text data in the cells underneath the headers as follows: Goats Go Wild, Trudy Milkmaid, BK-01, 177 pp. Type $14.95 at 24 pt font size in the cell for the book price and center the text.

15 With the price still selected, select the **Character** panel, and then change the **Baseline Shift** to -10 pt.

Now, let's add some color to the cells and text.

16 Change the text color of the first row to white. Select the **Type** tool, and then select the text in the first row. Select the **Color** panel, click the **Text** icon, and click on white. Now, fill the first row with black. With the **Type** tool, point just to the left of the top row (cursor turns into a right-facing arrow), and then click to select the row. With the Fill box selected, click on black on the Color panel to fill the row.

17 Change the fill color of the header cells. With the **Type** tool, drag to select the header row. Choose a fill color on the Color or Swatches panel. Color the blank row underneath the data with the same color to separate it visually from the other data.

Now you're ready to duplicate this one section that gives data about one book so that you can fill more rows with other books.

18 Click the **Selection** tool on the Tools panel. Click the whole table to select it, then hold the Alt (Win) or Option (Mac) key as you drag downwards to create a duplicate of the table. Repeat this to duplicate one more time.

19 Use the **Place** command on the **File** menu to replace the current table graphics with the files ShelterFromStorm.psd and WeddingShoesBlues.psd, and then replace the rest of the data for each of the other two books. Delete the company name from the duplicated tables and fill the last row with black.

The Results

Finish: Compare your completed project file with the document in layout_tables_fnl.indd. 👈

	Title	Author	Product Number	# of Pages	
					BETTER BOOKS PUBLISHERS
	Goats Go Wild	Trudy Milkmaid	BK-01	177 pp	14.95
	Title	Author	Product Number	# of Pages	
	Shelter from the Storm	Ron Weatherman	BK-02	244 pp	16.95
	Title	Author	Product Number	# of Pages	
	Wedding Shoes Blues	Monica Bridetobe	BK-03	300 pp	17.95

Project 3: Using Conditional Text

Skills and Tools: Conditional Text

Conditional text (**New!**) allows you to create different versions of the same document. If you want to create two versions of the same document without having to create two separate files, you can create conditions for different text, and then show and hide conditions to create multiple versions. You can apply conditions to text in a frame or table. A condition includes formatting indicators to make it easy to see in a document. To display different versions quickly, you can create condition sets. A condition set saves the visibility settings for all conditions.

The Project

In this project, you'll produce different versions of a book order form using conditional text. One version will be for "early-bird" buyers of a new book in the US or UK; the other version will list the regular price for people in the US or UK who buy the book after the initial sale prices have expired.

The Process

1 Open InDesign CS4, open the document conditional_text_start.indd, and then save it as **my_conditional_text.indd**.

This file has the sale price for US customers and shipping prices to US customers.

2 Create a new condition. Select the **Conditional Text** panel (click the Window menu, point to Type & Tables, and then click Conditional Text).

3 Click the **New Condition** button on the panel. Name it US Currency, leave the defaults for indicator appearance, and then click **OK**.

4 Create four more new conditions named US Shipping Prices, US Addresses, US Sale Price, and US Regular Price for the US. Now create five more new conditions named UK Addresses, UK Currency, UK Regular Price, UK Sale Price, and UK Shipping Prices for the UK.

It's time to associate specific text with specific conditions.

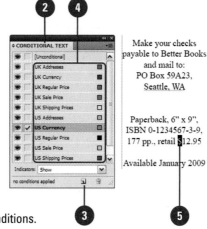

Make your checks payable to Better Books and mail to:
PO Box 59A23,
Seattle, WA

Paperback, 6" x 9",
ISBN 0-1234567-3-9,
177 pp., retail $12.95

Available January 2009

5 First, highlight all the dollar signs in the document individually and select the check box for *US Currency* to apply the condition to that text. Now, highlight the dollar amount for shipping and associate that text with the condition *US Shipping Prices*. Next, highlight the book price (in both places in the document) and associate the text with *US Sale Price*. Now change the price to $14.95, highlight, and associate with *US Regular Price*. Finally, highlight the words *Seattle*, *WA*, *State*, and *Zip* and associate that text with the condition *US Addresses*.

Now we need to create text that we can use for our UK customers.

6 First, change the dollar signs to Euro signs. Select the **Glyphs** panel (click the Type menu, and then click Glyphs), and in the **Show** list arrow, select **Currency**, and then the **Euro** symbol. Double-click to replace the highlighted dollar sign with the Euro sign. Replace all the dollar signs with Euros and then associate them with *UK Currency*. Make sure *US Currency* is not checked.

Associate with UK Currency condition

7 Change the rest of the four UK variables: sale price, regular price, shipping prices, and addresses. For *UK Addresses*, add *US* to *Seattle*, *WA* and change *State* to *Region*, *Zip* to *Code*. Then associate that new text with the appropriate conditions.

Since we have several different possible scenarios for our order form, it will make it easier to create Conditional Text Sets to group conditions together so we can choose them all at once.

8. Before you can create sets, you need to display the **Set** list arrow. Click the **Options** menu, and then click **Show Options**.

9. In the Conditional Text panel, click the **Eye** icon for only those text variables that apply to a specific order form. We'll start with an order form going out to US customers with the sale price of the book. Deselect all the **Eye** icons dealing with UK conditions and deselect the *US Regular Price* condition.

10. Now click the **Set** list arrow, click **Create New Set**, and then name it SaleUS. Next, deselect *US Sale Price* and select *US Regular Price* with all the other US conditions selected. Save a new set named RegPriceUS.

11. To make two UK sets, one with the sale price and one with the regular price, follow the same steps we did to make the two US sets. Turn off all US conditions and activate only the sale price or only the regular price for the UK. Then create two new sets, SaleUK and RegPriceUK.

12. Now choose different sets from your **Set** list arrow and you will see the order form change to reflect the different scenarios (US/UK, Sale Price/Regular Price).

The Results

Finish: Compare your completed project file with the document in conditional_text_fnl.

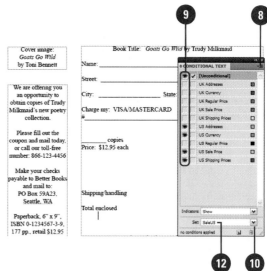

Want More Projects

You can access and download more workshop projects and related files at *www.perspection.com* in the software downloads area. After you download the files from the Web, uncompress the files into a folder on your hard drive to which you have easy access from InDesign.

Get Everything on DVD

Instead of downloading everything from the Web, which can take a while depending on your Internet connection speed, you can get all the files used in this book and much more on an InDesign CS4 On Demand DVD. The DVD contains task and workshop files, tips and tricks, keyboard shortcuts, and other goodies from the author.

To get the InDesign CS4 On Demand DVD, go to *www.perspection.com*.

New! Features

Adobe InDesign CS4

Adobe InDesign CS4 means superior results faster, with new features and enhancements that help you create and manage your images more easily and efficiently. The indispensable new and improved features help graphic web designers, photographers, and video professionals create the highest quality images, with the control, flexibility, and capabilities that you expect from the professional standards in desktop digital imaging.

Each new release of InDesign brings with it new features, improvements, and added sophistication. This edition is aimed at the Web designer, interactive media professional, or subject matter expert developing multimedia content, and the application developer.

Only New Features

If you're already familiar with InDesign CS3, you can access and download all the tasks in this book with Adobe InDesign CS4 New Features to help make your transition to the new version simple and smooth. The InDesign CS4 New Features as well as other InDesign CS3 to InDesign CS4 transition helpers are available on the Web at *www.perspection.com.*

What's New

If you're searching for what's new in InDesign CS4, just look for the icon: New!. The new icon appears in the table of contents and throughout this book, so you can quickly and easily identify a new or improved feature in InDesign CS4. The following is a brief description of each new feature and its location in this book.

InDesign CS4

◆ **Tabbed Document Window (p. 6, 18-19, 26)** Display multiple documents in a tabbed view or open them side by side so you can easily compare or drag items from one document to another. Simply click a document's tab to open it, or click Close (x) on a tab to close it.

◆ **Application Bar and Workspaces Menu (p. 6, 41, 43, 46, 48, 52-53)** From the Application bar at the top of each Creative Suite application, provides menus and options in one easy to access place. Use the workspace switcher to quickly jump to different workspace configurations to meet your specific needs. Also along this bar, you can access Adobe Bridge and the document arrangement panel

◆ **Arrange Document Window (p. 18-19)** Use the intuitive Arrange Documents window to quickly arrange your open documents in a variety of configurations.

◆ **Community Help (p. 22-23)** InDesign Help uses a Community Help site on the web at *adobe.com* (which is updated regularly) to help you find the information you need. When you start InDesign Help, your browser opens, displaying a web site with InDesign help categories and topics. Along with help text, some help topics include links to text and video tutorials. In addition, comments and ratings from users are available to help guide you to an answer.

◆ **Adobe Product Improvement Program (p. 23)** This is an opt-in program that allows you to test Adobe products and make suggestions for future products. This program enables Adobe to collect product usage data from customers while maintaining their privacy.

◆ **New Pages Sizes (p. 28-29)** New common monitor resolution sizes are available in the Page Size menu in the New Document dialog box. These options make it easier to design a document to a specific monitor size for interactive Flash and PDF workflows.

◆ **Spread View Rotation (p. 37, 65)** Temporarily rotate the spread view without physically turning your monitor. Enjoy full editing capability at 90 and 180 degree angles so that you can work on non-horizontal design elements, such as rotated calendar spreads and tables.

◆ **Ruler Origin on Spine (p. 41)** Correctly place the ruler's zero position of X at the spine of your document so that the X values are positive for right sided pages and negative for left sided pages when Facing Pages is enabled.

◆ **Quick Guide Deletion (p. 43)** Instantly clear all selectable guides on your current spread or master page by right-clicking (Windows) or Ctrl-clicking (Mac OS) a ruler and choosing Delete All Guides.

◆ **Smart Guides (p. 46-47)** Align, space, rotate, and resize multiple objects in one step. Align to the horizontal, vertical, or center of page edges. The guides, object dimensions, rotation, and X,Y coordinates appear dynamically so you can snap objects in relation to other objects in the layout.

◆ **Smart Dimensions (p. 46-47)** When you create, resize, or rotate one object, Smart Dimensions shows the width, height, or rotation of your object, highlighting when the dimensions or rotation matches nearby objects.

◆ **Smart Spacing (p. 46-47)** Evenly space multiple items on your page by snapping objects into position without having to use the Align panel.

◆ **Leading-based Baseline Grid Increments (p. 48)** If you specify a different measurement system, such as millimeters or inches, baseline grid values still use points to match text size and leading.

◆ **Undo Improvements (p. 54)** Viewing actions such as Set Preview and Show Guides are no longer included as Undo items.

- **Visual Pages Panel (p. 56-57)** See thumbnails of your pages in the Pages panel for easy navigation and page arrangement. If transparency, page transitions, or spread rotation have been applied to pages, you can turn off their associated icons for a cleaner Pages panel.

- **Slug area Enhancements (p. 62-63)** Move pages and see that your objects in the slug and bleed area also move. Page numbers in the slug area display a number rather than the pasteboard index entry (PB).

- **Links Panel (p. 137, 424-425)** Find, sort, and organize placed content with the redesigned Links panel. Scan link attributes and click to view details such as scale, rotation, and resolution. Customize the Links panel to suit your working preferences. Quickly replace low-resolution images used as placeholders with high-resolution images based on filename. Filename extensions are ignored. Simply relink to a new folder.

- **Kuler (p. 208-209)** Kuler is an extension that provides access to the Kuler online community. The Kuler application is added as a panel in InDesign. You can add the Kuler color theme to the Swatches panel.

- **Data Merge Output to PDF (p. 354-355)** Run a data merge operation and output directly to PDF in a single pass, thanks to the Export to PDF command now included in the Data Merge panel. An intermediate InDesign document is no longer created. The PDF file takes advantage of PDF XObjects for static parts of the page, resulting in a reduced-size PDF.

- **Live Preflight (p. 400-401)** Preflight while you design for better results, greater time savings, and lower production costs. Continuous preflighting alerts you to potential production problems in real time. The new Preflight panel lets you navigate to and select the objects that are triggering the preflight error. View contextual tips to help you correct errors directly in layout.

- **Smart Cursors (p. 409)** When transforming objects, the cursor displays X and Y position, width and height, or rotation information. The Show Transformation Values option in Interface preferences lets you turn smart cursors on and off.

- **Adobe ConnectNow (p. 442, 453)** The Share My Screen command on the File menu allows you to connect to Adobe ConnectNow, which is a secure Web site where you can start an online meeting and collaborate on any design project across platforms and programs.

- **Adobe Drive (p. 442)** Adobe Drive is an AIR program that allows you to connect to hosted services, such as Version Cue CS4 servers.

Text Improvements

- **Style Group Management (p. 78-79)** Move styles in or out of style groups when synchronizing a book without creating duplicate styles.

- **Smart Text Reflow (p. 96-97, 410-411)** Treat InDesign as a word processor. Let InDesign add or remove pages automatically when you type text, hide conditions, or change or your text flow.

- **Autocorrect Editing (p. 100)** Edit entries on your Autocorrect misspelling list without having to delete and add entries.

- **Table Enhancements (p. 258-259, 268-269, 313, 316)**   Tables in the Story Editor display text in sequential columns and rows for easy editing. Apply changes to cell and table borders without reselecting the stroke proxy borders. Add inline notes in tables to collaborate more effectively. Store alternate text, designer communications, and other annotations in notes linked to specific text in a table.

- **GREP Styles (p. 282)**   Apply character styles to any text in a paragraph that matches the GREP expression you specify.

- **Style Creation in Context (p. 282, 306)**   In dialog boxes where you can select a character or paragraph style, you can create a style without having to exit the dialog box. This ability is especially useful when you're generating a table of contents, creating nested styles or GREP styles, or using Find/Change to change text formatting to a style.

- **Nested Line Styles (p. 288-289)**   Use nested line styles to apply complex character formatting through the end of a line. Formatting remains unchanged when text is edited.

- **All Language User Dictionary (p. 300)**   Add a custom word, name, or phrase to a user dictionary and all languages treat the term as correctly spelled.

- **Conditional Text (p. 350-351)**   Use conditional text deliver multiple versions of a document for different users and channels. Create conditions and apply them to text for audience customization. If you hide conditions, the remaining text and anchored objects reflows automatically in your layout.

Graphics and Drawing Improvements

- **Graphics Placement (p. 128)**   A frame drawn while an image is in the loaded cursor constrains to the proportions of the graphic. The graphic then fits to the frame proportionally and is centered unless frame fitting options have been applied to the frame. While dragging out a frame with the loaded cursor, the scale is displayed as part of the cursor. Hold down Shift to drag a non-constrained frame.

- **Multiple Artboard Placement (p. 129)**   Cycle through multiple artboards created in Adobe Illustrator CS4 for quick placement in your InDesign document.

- **Placing Multiple Graphics as a Contact Sheet (p. 132-133)**   Quickly create a contact sheet by placing multiple images in a grid arrangement. When placing multiple images, hold down Ctrl+Shift (Windows) or ⌘+Shift (Mac OS) to drag a grid of images. Use the arrow keys to control the number of rows and columns in the grid.

- **Edit Original Graphic (p. 140)**   Use the Edit With command to choose which application to use to edit a placed item instead of relying on the operating system to default to the appropriate program.

- **Free Transform Tool Improvements (p. 170)**   Resize an object more easily using the Free Transform tool, thanks to larger hit zones around object handles and the ability to resize along object edges.

- **Text Stroke Control (p. 216-217)**   Adjust stroke cap, end join, miter limit, and stroke alignment on text without having to convert characters to outlines. These stroke options are also available in styles.

- **Convert Point Menu Commands (p. 237-238)**   Convert corner points to smooth or line end points using the Convert Point commands that are now accessible through the menus.

- **Pathfinder Panel Buttons (p. 240-242)**   Use one step to join paths, open paths, or reverse paths by clicking a button in the new Paths row in the Pathfinder panel.

- **Keyboard Shortcuts for Scaling and Sizing (p. 427)**   Use new options in the keyboard shortcut editor to easily create shortcuts for increasing and decreasing size. Separate keyboard shortcuts are included for scaling and sizing objects.

Interactivity Improvements

- **Hyperlinks Panel (p. 324-325)**   Use the redesigned Hyperlinks panel to easily create hyperlinks that navigate to external URLs, link to files with supplemental information, launch an e-mail client, or jump to a page or section of a page within the same or even a different document. Verify your hyperlinks directly in InDesign CS4 with no need to export the document to a PDF or SWF file for testing.

- **Cross-References (p. 326-327)**   Insert and edit cross-references. Choose among different formats, or create your own. Cross-references are easily updated when pagination changes.

- **Page Transitions in PDF and SWF files (p. 332)**   Apply page transitions directly in InDesign to individual pages or all spreads at once with a single click. See previews of available transition types, and control the direction and speed of your transitions for output to Flash (SWF file) and PDF.

- **Enhanced Buttons (p. 334-338)**   Build interactive buttons using the updated Button panel. Design custom buttons or select a button from the integrated button library. Create buttons that let you navigate within a dynamic document, launch a movie, or play a sound.

Integration Improvements

- **Interactive PDF Enhancements (p. 324-338, 364)**   Author interactive PDF documents by adding SWF files, Quicktime movies, and sound clips to your page layouts. Create interactive buttons, apply page transitions, and embed hyperlinks, cross-references, and bookmarks to create an immersive reading experience.

- **InDesign Markup Language (IDML) (p. 358)**   InDesign Markup Language, an XML- based file format, allows developers to assemble and disassemble InDesign documents using standard XML tools and without having to open INDD files. As a result of the new markup language, many filename extensions have changed in the InCopy workflow.

File Type	CS3 extension	CS4 extension
Assignment files	.inca	.icma
Content files	.incx	.icml
Exported files	.incx	.icml
Package files for InCopy	.incp	.icap
Package files for InDesign	.indp	.idap
InCopy template files	.inct	.icmt

◆ **Export to Flash (SWF) (p. 360, 374-375)** Create dynamic content without having to work in the authoring environment of Adobe Flash. Export SWF files directly from within InDesign, complete with page transitions, interactive buttons, rollovers, and hyperlinks. Automatically launch the Adobe Flash Player and preview a SWF file simply by exporting your InDesign layout.

◆ **Export to Flash (XFL) (p. 360, 376-377)** Export your InDesign document in the new XFL file format for opening in Adobe Flash CS4 Professional. Use the Flash authoring environment to add video, audio, animation, and complex interactivity. InDesign text exported as XFL remains fully editable when the XFL file is opened in Adobe Flash CS4 Professional. InDesign automatically converts high-resolution print assets (CMYK) to low-resolution web assets (RGB) upon export as an XFL file. An image placed multiple times in your InDesign document is saved as a single image asset with shared locations when exported as an XFL file.

◆ **Assignments Improvements (p. 435-436)** New Assignment operations in InCopy workflows are now enabled for unsaved InDesign documents. You care now prompted to save the document. The Assignments panel also included different options to update assignments. These options include Selected, Out-of-Date, and All. The All option updates all assignments, including those that aren't out of date, thereby letting you view design changes that don't affect the compositions of assignment text.

◆ **Integration with Adobe Version Cue CS4 (p. 442, 455)** Connect to Version Cue Server projects using Adobe Drive. The connected server appears like a hard drive or mapped network drive in Windows Explorer, Mac OS Finder, and dialog boxes such as Open and Save As.

◆ **Integration with Adobe Bridge CS4 (p. 443, 445-447, 451)** Browse, organize, label, and preview graphics and InDesign documents, templates, and snippets in Adobe Bridge. Drag and drop assets from Bridge into layouts easily and efficiently. Search for files using metadata that specifies keywords, fonts, colors, and more.

Adobe Certified Expert

About the Adobe Certified Expert (ACE) Program

The Adobe Certified Expert (ACE) program is for graphic designers, Web designers, systems integrators, value-added resellers, developers, and business professionals seeking official recognition of their expertise on Adobe products.

What Is an ACE?

An Adobe Certified Expert is an individual who has passed an Adobe Product Proficiency Exam for a specific Adobe software product. Adobe Certified Experts are eligible to promote themselves to clients or employers as highly skilled, expert-level users of Adobe software. ACE certification is a recognized worldwide standard for excellence in Adobe software knowledge. There are three levels of ACE certification: Single product certification, Specialist certification, and Master certification. To become an ACE, you must pass one or more product-specific proficiency exams and sign the ACE program agreement. When you become an ACE, you enjoy these special benefits:

- ◆ Professional recognition
- ◆ An ACE program certificate
- ◆ Use of the Adobe Certified Expert program logo

What Does This Logo Mean?

It means this book will prepare you fully for the Adobe Certified Expert exam for Adobe InDesign CS4. The certification exam has a set of objectives, which are organized into broader skill sets. The Adobe Certified Expert objectives and the specific pages throughout this book that cover the objectives are available on the Web at *www.perspection.com*.

 ID 3.1

InDesign CS4 ACE Exam Objectives

Objective	Skill	Page
1.0	**Laying out a document**	
1.1	Given a scenario, work with master pages (scenarios include: locking master page items; loading, creating, and applying master pages; based-on master pages; overriding master page items; text wrap).	66-67, 68-69
1.2	Use Quick Apply to assign styles and choose menu commands.	294-295
1.3	Use Layers to organize the structure of a document.	178-184
1.4	Explain the process of using Data Merge to build a template and import data into a final InDesign or PDF document.	354-355
1.5	Create and use a snippet file.	348-349
1.6	Modify and transform objects by using the transformation tools and the Control panel (including scaling, rotating, and resizing).	160, 170-173
1.7	Use the Info panel to find hidden or non-obvious information about your document.	51
1.8	Create, apply, and modify an object style.	290-291
1.9	Create, edit, and manipulate text on a path.	84, 88-89
1.10	Describe the use of Smart Guides (including their preferences).	46-47
1.11	Arrange multiple document windows (options include tabbed, floating, N-up views).	18-19
2.0	**Working with text**	
2.1	Insert special characters by using the Type menu, Glyph panel, or context menu.	70-71, 117-118
2.2	Given an option, edit text (options include: Story Editor, Drag and Drop text, Autocorrect).	98-101, 313
2.3	Adjust the look of text inside a text frame by using Text Frame Options (including columns, inset spacing, first baseline offset, and vertical justification).	120-121
2.4	Manipulate text flow by using text threading, smart text reflow, resizing, and text wrap (including ignore text wrap).	92-97, 120-121
2.5	Given a scenario, create and apply styles in an automated fashion (scenarios include next paragraph, nested styles, grep styles).	278-282, 286-289
2.6	Create a basic GREP expression for find/change or GREP styles without having to write code.	282, 306
2.7	Create a user dictionary and populate it with custom words.	300
2.8	Import an RTF or Word file and map style names to styles in the current document.	90-93
2.9	Assign and format automatic bullets or numbering to paragraphs including numbering across multiple non-threaded frames).	114-115

C

Objective	Skill	Page
2.10	Given a scenario, set up a document or frame-based baseline grid.	48-49
2.11	Make a dynamically changing running head (options include: text variables, section marker).	66-71, 74-75
2.12	Given a feature, avoid widows, orphans, and other typographic problems (using features such as Keep Options, Justification, Hyphenation).	309-311
3.0	**Working with tables**	
3.1	Modify tables (options include: adding or removing columns/rows; merging cells; splitting cells; selecting cells).	258-264
3.2	Edit and format a table (options include: formatting text, editing tables in the Story Editor, adding Notes, strokes and fills; text alignment).	258-259, 265, 268-273, 316-317
3.3	Create, apply, import, modify, and organize cell and table styles.	254-257, 292-293
3.4	Update the information in a table when the original data has changed (via linking or copy/paste).	256-257
4.0	**Managing graphics**	
4.1	Given a scenario, determine the best settings for choosing and placing an image (options include import options, Illustrator artboards, choice of file format, resolution, ICC color profiles, layers, and transparency).	128-131
4.2	Locate the XMP metadata for an image placed in InDesign.	141
4.3	Determine the current resolution for a placed image.	137
4.4	Hide or show layers in placed PSD, AI, INDD, and PDF files, and discuss how image transparency is handled.	129-131
4.5	Manage placed files by using the Links panel (including revealing metadata and attributes in Link Info, editing the original, relinking to new files, and updating modified files).	137-140
5.0	**Understanding color and transparency**	
5.1	Explain the use of named swatches versus unnamed colors.	200-201
5.2	Given a scenario, create, modify, and apply gradients to objects or text using the appropriate panels and tools.	204-205, 220-223
5.3	Describe how and why to create mixed inks.	206-207
5.4	Assign transparency effects to stroke, fill, and image/text individually (options include such as opacity, blending modes, drop shadows, feathering, and other effects).	214-217, 223-229
5.5	Given a scenario, choose the best course of action to manage color (options include Transparency Blend Space, Color Settings, Overprint Preview, ICC profiles, mixed RGB and CMYK).	188-191, 206-207, 210-211, 224-225

Objective	Skill	Page
6.0	**Creating and working with long documents**	
6.1	Insert and format footnotes in a document.	314-315
6.2	Create a book in a book panel and paginate the documents.	74-79
6.3	Create a table of contents across one or more documents.	80-81
6.4	Synchronize master pages, styles, and swatches in a book.	68-69
6.5	Define and insert text variables.	72-75
6.6	Create and apply text conditions and condition sets.	350-351
6.7	Create and apply cross-references, edit cross-reference format.	326-327
7.0	**Importing, exporting, and working with cross-media**	
7.1	Select the appropriate options for exporting to XFL for use in Flash CS4.	376-377
7.2	Create interactivity for an InDesign document that will be exported as a PDF document (including adding movie, sounds, and buttons).	330-331, 334-338
7.3	Create functional hyperlinks in exported PDF documents or SWF files (options include Hyperlinks panel, Table of Contents, Cross-References, and Buttons).	320-327, 334-338, 362-363, 374-375
7.4	Apply and customize page transitions for exported PDF documents or SWF files.	80, 332
7.5	Select the appropriate options for exporting to XHTML for use on a Web site.	378-379
7.6	Define and assign XML tags, and export an XML file.	356-357
7.7	Map styles to tags and XML tags to styles using the Tags panel and the Structure view.	356-357
8.0	**Managing prepress and printing**	
8.1	Troubleshoot common printing issues by using Live Preflight (options include using Basic profile to locate and correct errors, create custom profile, create a Preflight report, share profiles).	400-401
8.2	Troubleshoot common printing issues by using the Separations Preview panel (options include process inks, spot colors, ink density, and the Ink Manager).	368, 389, 390-391
8.3	Troubleshoot common transparency printing issues by using the Flattener Preview panel.	394-395
8.4	Given a scenario, choose the appropriate Print dialog box options (options include Printers Marks, Bleeds, Output Space, PPD fonts).	382, 384-388, 390-391, 394-395
8.5	Given a scenario, choose the appropriate PDF Preset or PDF Export settings.	362-371

Choosing a Certification Level

There are three levels of certification to become an Adobe Certified Expert.

◆ **Single product certification.** Recognizes your proficiency in a single Adobe product. To qualify as an ACE, you must pass one product-specific exam.

◆ **Specialist certification.** Recognizes your proficiency in multiple Adobe products with a specific medium: print, Web, or video. To become certified as a Specialist, you must pass the exams on the required products. To review the requirements, go online to *http://www.adobe.com/support/certification/ace_certify.html*.

◆ **Master certification.** Recognizes your skills in terms of how they align with the Adobe product suites. To become certified as a Master, you must pass the exam for each of the products in the suite.

Preparing for an Adobe Certified Expert Exam

Every Adobe Certified Expert Exam is developed from a list of objectives, which are based on studies of how an Adobe program is actually used in the workplace. The list of objectives determine the scope of each exam, so they provide you with the information you need to prepare for ACE certification. Follow these steps to complete the ACE Exam requirement:

1 Review and perform each task identified with a Adobe Certified Expert objective to confirm that you can meet the requirements for the exam.

2 Identify the topic areas and objectives you need to study, and then prepare for the exam.

3 Review the Adobe Certified Expert Program Agreement. To review it, go online to *http://www.adobe.com/support/certification/ace_certify.html*.

You will be required to accept the ACE agreement when you take the Adobe Certified Exam at an authorized testing center.

4 Register for the Adobe Certified Expert Exam.

ACE testing is offered at more than a thousand authorized Pearson VUE and Thomson Prometric testing centers in many countries. To find the testing center nearest you, go online to *www.pearsonvue.com/adobe* (for Pearson VUE) or *www.2test.com* (for Prometric). The ACE exam fee is US$150 worldwide. When contacting an authorized training center, provide them with the Adobe Product Proficiency exam name and number you want to take, which is available online in the Exam Bulletin at *http://www.adobe.com/support/certification/ ace_certify.html*.

5 Take the ACE exam.

Getting Recertified

For those with an ACE certification for a specific Adobe product, recertification is required of each ACE within 90 days of a designated ACE Exam release date. There are no restrictions on the number of times you may take the exam within a given period.

To get recertified, call Pearson VUE or Thomson Prometric. You will need to verify your previous certification for that product. If you are getting recertified, check with the authorized testing center for discounts.

Taking an Adobe Certified Expert Exam

The Adobe Certified Expert exams are computer-delivered, closed-book tests consisting of 60 to 90 multiple-choice questions. Each exam is approximately one to two hours long. A 15-minute tutorial will precede the test to familiarize you with the function of the Windows-based driver. The exams are currently available worldwide in English only. They are administered by Pearson VUE and Thomson Prometric, independent third-party testing companies.

Exam Results

At the end of the exam, a score report appears indicating whether you passed or failed the exam. Diagnostic information is included in your exam report. When you pass the exam, your score is electronically reported to Adobe. You will then be sent an ACE Welcome Kit and access to the ACE program logo in four to six weeks. You are also placed on the Adobe certification mailing list to receive special Adobe announcements and information about promotions and events that take place throughout the year.

When you pass the exam, you can get program information, check and update your profile, or download ACE program logos for your promotional materials online at:

http://www.adobe.com/support/certification/community.html

Getting More Information

To learn more about the Adobe Certified Expert program, read a list of frequently asked questions, and locate the nearest testing center, go online to:

http://www.adobe.com/support/certification/ace.html

To learn more about other Adobe certification programs, go online to:

http://www.adobe.com/support/certification

Index

N

naming/renaming. *See also* Adobe Bridge; layers
  assignments, 436
  bookmarks, 328–329
  master page, 67
  plug-ins, 429
  styles, 284
navigating pages, 60–61
nesting
  creating nested styles, 288–289
  graphics in frames, 148
  paragraph styles, setting, 279
  tables, creating nested, 254
New Character Styles dialog box, 280
New Document dialog box, 32
new documents
  presets, creating with, 32
  template, creating from, 30
New Features, Welcome screen links to, 4
New Hyperlink From URL command, 322–323
New Paragraph Styles dialog box, 278
Newsletters template, 30
New Workspace dialog box, 52
next page, navigating to, 61
next spread, navigating to, 61
Nikon NEF format, 447
90-degree angles, drawing lines at, 156
Noise effect
  with feather effects, 229
  with glow, 227
  with shadows, 226
nonbreaking space, inserting, 118
non-Latin text, setting preferences for, 412
non-printing content
  Adobe PDF option, 365
  in package files, 405
  printing options for objects, 384
Normal view, 36
North American,
  Prepress 2 color settings, 188
  Purpose 2 color settings, 188
  Web/Internet color settings, 188
notes. *See also* footnotes
  to Adobe InCopy managed files, 433
  creating, 316

Notes panel, working in, 317
  preferences, setting, 420
  tables, adding to, 316
  text to notes, converting, 316, 317
Notes panel, 317
No Wrap option, 122
Numbering and Section Options dialog box
  chapter numbers, adding, 72–73
  master pages, page and section numbers for, 70–71
number of pages
  changing, 34
  master spread, specifying for, 67
  new documents, selecting for, 28
numbers. *See also* bullets and numbering; chapter numbers; number of pages; page numbers
  footnotes, numbering, 315

O

objects. *See also* anchor points; gradients; graphics; layers
  aligning, 166
  anchored objects, creating, 177
  blend effect, creating, 224–225
  buttons, converting object to, 334–335
  colors
    applying, 193, 214
    Eyedropper tool, using, 194–195
    overprinting colors, 210
  copying, 162–163
    layers, copying objects between, 184
    scaling and copying objects, 172
  defaults, setting, 232
  deleting, 157
  deleting combined object, 165
  Direct Selection tool
    grouped objects, working with, 164–165
    inline object, creating, 176
    selecting with, 157, 159
  distances and angles, measuring, 185
  duplicating, 162–163
  Find/Change command, using, 302–303, 308
  flipping objects, 171
  Free Transform tool, transforming objects with, 170